WTF

HAPPENED

#WakingTheFeminists and the Movement That Changed Irish Theatre

WTF

HAPPENED

#WakingTheFeminists and the Movement That Changed Irish Theatre

Sarah Durcan *with* **Lian Bell**

UCD
DUBLIN

UNIVERSITY COLLEGE DUBLIN PRESS
PREAS CHOLÁISTE OLLSCOILE BHAILE ÁTHA CLIATH
2025

First published 2025
by University College Dublin Press
UCD Humanities Institute, Room H103,
Belfield,
Dublin 4

www.ucdpress.ie

ISBN 978-1-7390863-9-8

CIP data available from the British Library

Typeset in Merriweather by Gough Typesetting Limited
Cover design by Fiachra McCarthy
Printed in Scotland on acid-free paper by
Bell & Bain Ltd, Burnfield Road,
Thornliebank, Glasgow, G46 7UQ, UK

We saw a vision of Ireland, free, pure, happy.
We did not realise this vision. But we saw it.

Helena Molony, Irish actor and revolutionary, on the 1916 Rising

Contents

Foreword by Mary McAuliffe   ix
How This Book Was Written   xiii
Who's Who   xv
Timeline of the Year   xviii
Introduction   xxi

PART ONE

1	Social Media Storm	3
2	Gathering and Planning	40
3	Public Meeting at the Abbey Theatre	53
4	Speeches from the Public Meeting	69

PART TWO

5	Preparing for a Year of Campaigning	121
6	Seeking Advice and Meeting the Arts Council and Government Ministers	137
7	Meetings with Theatre Companies, and the Advance Programme (*Ardú*)	146
8	Other Events and Power Plays	162
9	Winning Awards	173
10	*Spring Forward*: International Women's Day Public Meeting and Speeches	181
11	The Things We May Not Say in Case We Get in Trouble	223
12	Research, Statistics, and Data Analysis	228
13	*One Thing More*: Final Public Event	239
14	Speeches from *One Thing More*	251

PART THREE

15	After the End: Legacy and Impact	315
16	What Now? Looking to the Future	333

Waking Patriarchy by Moynagh Sullivan   338

Afterword by Catriona Crowe   353

Notes   359

Acknowledgements   381

Select Bibliography and Further Reading   383

Index   389

Foreword

Mary McAuliffe *is a historian and lecturer in gender studies at University College Dublin. She specialises in Irish women's/gender history, trauma histories of gendered and sexual violence of Ireland's revolutionary period and histories of sexualities. She completed her BA (Hons), MA, and PhD at the School of History and Humanities, Trinity College Dublin (TCD). Her most recent publications include* The Diaries of Kathleen Lynn *co-written with Harriet Wheelock (UCD Press, 2023), and a biography of the feminist, trade union activist, and revolutionary woman,* Margaret Skinnider *(UCD Press, 2020). She is co-editor, with Emilie Pine (UCD) and Miriam Haughton (NUIG) of 'Commemoration, Gender and the Postcolonial Carceral State', published in November 2021.*

The inclusion of women's stories in Ireland's Decade of Centenaries (2012–2023) did not have the most auspicious of beginnings. In 2011 an Expert Advisory Group on Centenary Commemorations was set up by the Taoiseach to 'advise Government on historical matters [and] to ensure that significant events are commemorated accurately, proportionately and appropriately in tone'.[1] However, the commemoration of women in the list of planned commemorations would not be until 2018, with the commemoration of the 1918 'General Election with new franchise including women'.[2] The activities of suffrage, trade union and nationalist women prior to 1918 were overlooked, and the 'multiple identities' referred to here were not especially inclusive of women's histories and experiences. Where were the commemorations of women and militant suffrage, women of the 1913 Lockout, the foundation of Cumann na mBan in 1914, women's involvement in World War I, women's participation in the Easter Rising of 1916, women's central role in reorganising the revolutionary groups in 1917/1918? Where indeed? It would seem from this commemorative list that women's achievement of a limited franchise in

1918 happened out of nowhere. This is often the case with women's histories: no back story, no historical context, just a brief footnote and back to the important male-centric narratives!

However, a cascade of voices began to grumble, and complain and agitate about this very slight inclusion of women in the Decade programme. In 2013 a group of young activists took the opportunity of the construction of a new Luas bridge which would connect Dublin's Marlborough Street with Hawkins Street to campaign for it to be named after a woman. The public process of naming the bridge was very popular. After Dublin City Council invited nominations over 18,000 people participated. Eventually, 'ten nominations of the eighty-five names put forward were referred to the council's naming committee.'[3] While there were campaigns for the other nominees, the Rosie Hackett Bridge Campaign was by far the most visible, and the most innovative. With its use of traditional methods of lobbying (councillors and politicians), public meetings, radio interviews, articles in print media, and its inventive use of social media, setting up both a Twitter and Facebook account, and an online petition, it created widespread engagement with the public.[4] The campaign served to raise awareness of Hackett's life story as well as to demonstrate the lack of female representation in civic and public spaces in the capital city. It was a successful campaign. On September 2, 2013, Dublin City Council voted on the name: the Rosie Hackett Bridge won. It came just over 100 years after she and her co-workers had been locked out of Jacob's Factory for trade union activities.

If this was a corrective to official neglect of the participation of women in the revolutionary period, it soon became evident that the government had no plans to commemorate the centenary of the foundation of Cumann na mBan in 2014. Founded in Wynn's Hotel, around the corner from the Abbey Theatre, Cumann na mBan would become the largest women's organisation in Ireland, espousing feminism, separatism and, indeed, cultural nationalism. In 1914 the cultural nationalist, feminist, and separatist organisation Inghinidhe na hÉireann (founded in 1900) became a branch of Cumann na mBan. Inghinidhe had been one of the most influential cultural nationalist women's organisations. It was founded by Maud Gonne as women were frustrated at being excluded as women from membership of cultural and political organisations in Dublin. Inghinidhe provided a platform for women and men in Irish literature, theatre and politics, and were particularly well known for producing *tableau vivant* of legendary Irish figures from history, including Queen Maeve of Connacht, Granuaile, Brigid (whom they adopted as their patron), as well as female figures from European history, such as Joan of Arc. The *tableaux* were effective in demonstrating that women had a part to play in Irish history and politics and particularly in Irish nationalism.

They also helped to radicalise a generation of Irish women; many members of Cumann na mBan in Dublin recall their journey to militant nationalism through cultural nationalism, and the particular influence of the women of Inghinidhe.

In 2014 the importance of both Inghinidhe na hEireann and Cumann na mBan were not high on the State's commemorative agenda. It was left to the Women's History Association of Ireland (WHAI) to organise three days of commemorative events in April of that year. The success of these events encouraged more focus on the role of women during this period of Irish history. One of the major commemorative projects for 2016, and the centenary of the Rising, was the Richmond Barracks renovation project. The Barracks was where all the 1916 rebels were taken after their surrender at the end of Easter week, 1916, among whom were 77 women. When the Barracks project was announced in 2014, the role of women was not mentioned, but as noted by Laura McAtackney, by 2016 and the opening of the Barracks 'The women of 1916 and the Irish Revolution' was one of the core themes.[5] 'Clearly', she writes, 'there were changes in both personnel and the public discourse between 2014 and 2016 to refocus ... Richmond Barracks from a normative history to a site that explicitly engages with the previously marginalised roles of women.'[6]

This engagement by feminist academics and activists had impacted, in a central way, on the inclusion of women's histories in the Decade of Centenaries. Events in 2015, however, were to prove there was still a lot of work to be done. As we see from this important publication, when, in 2015, the Irish National Theatre, the Abbey Theatre announced their *Waking the Nation* season for 2016, which focused on the centenary of the 1916 Easter Rising. While the programme included many plays and events of interest, it had '18 men on the programme in terms of writers and directors and just two women – and all the plays were written by men, apart from one play referred to as a "monologue for children".'[7] In response to the privileging of the male voice and the exclusion of women's voices, a meeting of women producers, artists, writers, activists and academics, was held at the Abbey Theatre on 12 November 2015, where #WakingTheFeminists was launched. #WakingTheFeminists was set up as a 'one-year grassroots campaign ... November 2015 to November 2016 and had huge success in advancing equality for women in Irish theatre'.[8] Its impact was global with major Hollywood actors such as Meryl Streep tweeting support. In response to the exclusion of women's voices the Arts Council of Ireland funded #WakingTheFeminists to commission a research document into gender balance in Irish theatre.

The journey over the course of that year is detailed in this book. In many ways #WakingTheFeminists reads like the awakening of so many women, in various historical contexts, to activism in 20th and 21st century Ireland. In the early 1970s the young women of the Irish Women's Liberation Movement (IWLM) and its successor Irishwomen United were aware of the impact of grassroots activism; we can see this from their famous campaigns, such as the Contraceptive Train and the invasion of the Forty Foot, as well as the pub campaigns, and their campaigns for gender equality, equal pay, equal access to the workplace and full reproductive rights. In the 21st century it was #RepealThe8th and the campaign to undo the 1983 insertion of the eighth amendment, which forbade all access to full reproductive rights, into the Irish constitution. This was successful in 2018, ironically on the centenary of Irish women achieving limited suffrage. All of these campaigns included grassroots activism, women meeting in rooms and having conversations with each other, women writing documents, creating posters, women insisting that their voices be heard. In this way #WakingTheFeminists can take its place among the many famous campaigns of modern Irish feminism. It was a focused campaign on a particular issue, it mobilised many women and organisations around that issue and it was a successful campaign. It brought conversations out into the open, not just of inclusion of women in the Decade of Centenaries commemorations but of inclusion of women in Irish theatre spaces, including women playwrights, women directors, women producers, women actors, and all those women who participate in, and are the backbone of, Irish and international theatre spaces.

Often we wait a decade or two to have an insight into what happened during these activist campaigns, so it is very important that we have this book, from those who were part of #WakingTheFeminists, and who detail its campaign, its use of traditional activism, of meetings, of focus groups, of the creation of posters, of the iconic photograph taken outside of the Abbey Theatre, which is so similar to the iconic photograph of the 1970s IWLM women returning on the Contraceptive Train from Belfast with their condoms and their pills. It outlines for us how a successful grassroots campaign can be run, even by those who had no experience of campaigning prior to that, of learning on the fly, of the mistakes that were made and of the successes that were gained. It also helped ensure that after 2016 women would be equally included in any decade of centenaries commemorations, in any research, in any books published, and it added to the work of academics and historians and feminists who had been campaigning for so long for full inclusion of women's lived experiences and voices in all areas, from culture to politics to literature to society. #WakingTheFeminists takes its place, proudly, among the feminist stories of Ireland.

How This Book Was Written

WTF Happened was made possible with the support of Irish Theatre Institute. The source material from the #WakingTheFeminists digital collection used throughout this publication is reproduced courtesy of the National Library of Ireland.

WTF HAPPENED was written by #WakingTheFeminists core group member Sarah Durcan with editorial support from Campaign Director Lian Bell. This book allows us to tell the story 'from the inside' in our own voices in a way that we hope is inspiring and helpful to future generations of activists, academics, theatre makers, audiences, and those with an interest in systemic feminist change in any field.

From the start of the campaign, it was an ambition of the organisers to retain archival records of what was happening for posterity. We amassed a huge amount of material: social media posts, photographs, letters, minutes of meetings, emails, recordings of the public meetings, press coverage, scripts of speeches, samples of merchandise, the #WakingTheFeminists website and social media accounts, and our internal communications on Slack, an online messaging platform. This material was invaluable in researching and writing this book. A digital archive of the campaign is now preserved for future generations in the National Library of Ireland, with a physical archive housed in the National Museum of Ireland.

In 2021 and 2022 Sarah interviewed a number of people who were involved with the campaign. Quotes from their interviews are included throughout this book. The interviewees were: Anne Clarke, Caroline Williams, Kate Ferris, Loughlin Deegan, Noelle Brown, Maria Fleming, and Tanya Dean. Each of Sarah's and Lian's recollections reproduced here were written by themselves.

It was always imperative that we include and record as many voices as possible in order to show the plurality and collective nature of the #WakingTheFeminists movement. This book includes speeches from all our public events, interwoven with a narrative of how the movement and campaign unfolded.[1] We have tried to ensure people are properly credited for their role in the movement – we apologise for any oversights, which are unintentional.

However, in a publication that is about breaking silence and amplifying the voices and stories of women underrepresented in the arts, there are infuriatingly still Some Things We May Not Say in Case We Get in Trouble. There are gaps in this account that we would have liked to say more about but have been advised not to. It is an infuriating situation, but a reality nonetheless; we specially thank Noelle Moran and UCD Press for their support and guidance. We hope that in time and with the 'development and adoption of more feminist jurisprudence',[2] these gaps can be more freely and fairly discussed.[3]

Throughout this book we have chosen to refer to everyone by their first names as a feminist refusal of patronymic referencing practices. Also, as this campaign was born and thrived on social media, to ensure greatest searchability we (Anne Clarke) insisted on always using the hashtag. So while other writers often describe us as Waking The Feminists, we are and always will be #WakingTheFeminists.

Sarah and Lian
Dublin, August 2025

Who's Who

The campaign involved the work of a great many people volunteering their time and expertise. All worked in or adjacent to the performing arts in Ireland. In order to provide some context and to highlight the collective nature of the movement, it is useful to describe several of the key people and some of their contributions to theatre prior to 2015. This list echoes what was published on the website early in the campaign.

Aisling O'Brien – FRINGE LAB Coordinator, Dublin Fringe Festival

Anne Clarke – Producer of Landmark Productions, former Deputy Director at the Gate Theatre, and former Chairperson of Theatre Forum Ireland

Aoife Spillane-Hinks – freelance director

Brenda Donohue PhD – Research Assistant at Educational Research Centre, St. Patrick's College (became Lead Researcher on *Gender Counts*)

Caroline Williams – freelance producer, Producer with Rough Magic, former General Manager of Dublin Dance Festival, researcher with Irish Theatre Institute, and founder of Glasshouse Productions

Christine Monk – freelance PR and Press manager

Cian O'Brien – Director of Project Arts Centre

Dairne O'Sullivan – freelance PR and Press manager

Gavin Kostick – dramaturg and playwright, Literary Manager of Fishamble: The New Play Company

Gina Moxley – freelance playwright and actor

Grace Dyas – director, writer, producer and member of THEATREclub

Irma McLoughlin – Manager of Theatre Forum Ireland

Jane Daly – Co-Director of Irish Theatre Institute and theatre producer

Jen Coppinger – freelance producer

Jo Mangan – Artistic Director of The Performance Corporation

Kate Ferris – freelance producer and teacher at The Lir National Academy of Dramatic Art; stage manager

Lian Bell – freelance set designer and arts manager (became Campaign Director)

Lisa Tierney Keogh – freelance playwright (based in New York)

Loughlin Deegan – Director of The Lir Academy, Trinity College Dublin, former Director of Dublin Theatre Festival, and former General Manager/Producer with Rough Magic

Lynne Parker – Artistic Director of Rough Magic Theatre Company

Maria Fleming – Theatre Programmer at The Ark Cultural Centre for Children, producer, and former General Manager with Barabbas Theatre Company

Niamh Ní Chonchubhair – Programme Manager and Producer at Axis Ballymun

Noelia Ruiz – freelance digital marketer and dramaturg

Olwen Fouéré – actor and theatre maker, former Abbey board member

Oonagh Murphy – freelance director

Róise Goan – freelance producer, previously Director of Dublin Fringe Festival, former Abbey board member

Sarah Durcan – General Manager of Science Gallery International, previously theatre producer and festival manager, former board member Theatre Forum Ireland

Siobhán Bourke – Co-Director of Irish Theatre Institute and film producer

Tanya Dean PhD – freelance dramaturg and theatre academic at National University of Ireland, Galway, former Editor of *Irish Theatre Magazine*

Tríona Ní Dhuibhir – General Manager of Dublin Theatre Festival

UCD Press

Preas Choláiste Ollscoile Bhaile Átha Cliat.

H103

Humanities Institute

Belfield

Dublin 4

T +353 1 716 4680

E: ucdpress@ucd.ie

W: www.ucdpress.ie

WTF Happened
#WakingTheFeminists and the Movement
That Changed Irish Theatre

Written by Sarah Durcan with Lian Bell

A copy of *WTF Happened* is enclosed for review

FORMAT: Soft Jacket
PRICE: €30 £25
ISBN: 9781739086398
SIZE W x H: 246 x 180 mm
Page extent: 432 pp
EDITION: 1st
CATEGORY: Social Justice/ Gender Studies
PUBLICATION DATE: September 2025

A copy of your review would be much appreciated. We would appreciate it if you mentioned www.ucdpress.ie in your review.

UCD Press books are distributed in **Ireland** by **Gill Distribution,** Hume Avenue, Park West, Dublin, D12 YV96, Ireland, E: sales@gill.ie, T: +353 (1) 500 9500

in the **UK and rest of Europe** by **Central Books**, 50 Freshwater Road, Chadwell Heath, London RM8 1RX, England
T: 0044 20 8986 4854 E: orders@centralbooks.com

in **North America** by **The University of Chicago Press,** Chicago Distribution Center, 11030 South Langley, Chicago, IL 60628, USA, E: orders@press.uchicago.edu, T: (773) 702-7000 (Rest of world)

in **Australia and New Zealand** by **Wiley Global**, C/WeWork, 310 Edward Street, Brisbane City QLD 4000, E: custservice@wiley.com T: 1800 777 474

For further publicity information contact Yvonne Reddin, publicist for UCD Press

Ph: +353 (0) 863910229 E: yvonne@yvonnereddin.com

For Immediate Release WTF Happened: The Untold Story of #WakingTheFeminists

A new book captures the passion, power and legacy of the grassroots movement that reshaped Irish theatre and reverberated far beyond. Great theatre changes how we see our lives. Great campaigning changes how we see our future. When the Abbey Theatre's 2016 centenary programme announced just a handful of women artists, it triggered something extraordinary: a nationwide movement for gender equality in Irish theatre.

What began as outrage on social media rapidly evolved into #WakingTheFeminists - an award-winning, year-long campaign that transformed the Irish theatre landscape, made global headlines and left a legacy still felt today.

> *"#WakingTheFeminists made me realise that...there was no point asking any more, because the people who thought they were listening, really were not listening. And besides, what is that posture? The one where you ask, and are accepted or turned down? I realised we had to come at it from outside the system because the system was incapable of regulating or fixing itself. In 2016 I learned the power of counting, because numbers are factual, and the facts don't lie, or feel sorry for themselves, or quote Yeats back at you, or wish you were more like their mother, or less like their mother. In 2016 I realised that men find it hard to change when it is not in their interests to change so, sadly, sometimes you have to run them over with a truck. Or with a crowd. In 2016 I did something I find difficult, as an individual artist, to do: I joined a benevolent and righteous crowd. I have not looked back. "* – Anne Enright.

WTF Happened goes behind the scenes of this groundbreaking movement, revealing its untold story. Written by Sarah Durcan, one of the core organisers alongside Campaign Director Lian Bell and leading activists, academics, historians and arts professionals, the book brings the campaign to life in vivid detail. This is more than a book about theatre. It's about the power of collective action and how voices joined together can change an entire landscape.

Drawing on photographs, speeches, social media interactions and memorabilia - now archived in the National Library of Ireland and the National Museum of Ireland - this book is both a historical document and an activist manual. It captures the urgency, exhilaration and tensions of #WakingTheFeminists while reflecting on its lasting impact and lessons for future campaigns. Relevant to readers interested in gender studies, women's history, arts and theatre, cultural policy, social justice and contemporary Irish history, WTF Happened situates the campaign within a wider tradition of Irish activism - connecting it to the movements that came before and those still unfolding today.

About the Editors

Sarah Durcan, Executive Director of Science Gallery International and lead organiser of #WakingTheFeminists, writes on gender, theatre and culture.

Lian Bell, Campaign Director of #WakingTheFeminists, is an artist whose 25-year practice spans scenography, visual art, and social activism with leading Irish arts organisations and performance makers.

For more information, to request an extract, or to arrange an interview with the author, contact Yvonne Reddin at yvonne@yvonnereddin.com or call 0863910229

ENDS

Researchers for *Gender Counts*

Brenda Donohue PhD – Research Assistant at Educational Research Centre, St. Patrick's College (became Lead Researcher on *Gender Counts*)

Ciara O'Dowd PhD – theatre assessor for the Arts Council

Tanya Dean PhD – freelance dramaturg and theatre academic at National University of Ireland, Galway, former Editor of *Irish Theatre Magazine*

Ciara L. Murphy – PhD candidate and Regional Editor for Ireland for The Reviews Hub

Kathleen Cawley – independent producer and dramaturg

Kate Harris – drama facilitator and theatre maker

Timeline of the Year

(Distributed as part of a handout at *One Thing More*, the final public event in November 2016)

October 2015

Announcement of Abbey Theatre's 2016 Waking the Nation programme.

Lian Bell, Belinda McKeon, and Gavin Kostick start a conversation on social media.

November 2015

#WakingTheFeminists goes viral internationally, with support from major public figures.

The Abbey Theatre Board acknowledges that the 2016 programme doesn't represent gender equality.

First public meeting of #WakingTheFeminists at the Abbey. 30 women take to the stage.

The Abbey Theatre Board forms a gender equality subcommittee.

December 2015

#WakingTheFeminists begins to meet with major Irish theatre organisations.

January 2016

Supporters hold #WakingTheFeminists events across Ireland and in New York for Nollaig na mBan/ Women's Christmas.

March 2016

Lian Bell and #WakingTheFeminists win an *Irish Times* Irish Theatre Award.

#WakingTheFeminists presents to a plenary meeting of the Arts Council.

Second public meeting held on International Women's Day at Liberty Hall. Eight key theatre companies publicly commit to gender equality.

May 2016

#WakingTheFeminists wins first ever international Lilly Award in New York.

June 2016

Ground-breaking research commences into gender breakdown of ten top Arts Council-funded theatre organisations.

Supporters hold #WakingTheFeminists events across Ireland for Feminist Midsummer.

July 2016

Abbey Theatre publishes eight guiding principles on gender equality which have been adopted by the Board.

Sarah Durcan of #WakingTheFeminists appointed to the Board of the Abbey Theatre.

Abbey Theatre announces the remainder of its programme for 2016 including significantly more female artists.

Oct 2016

Announcement of Selina Cartmell as first female artistic director of the Gate Theatre.

Graham McLaren and Neil Murray take up their roles as Directors of the Abbey Theatre.

Nov 2016

Anniversary public meeting of #WakingTheFeminists at the Abbey Theatre, and end of the campaign.

NOW IT'S YOUR TURN

Introduction

Great theatre changes the atmosphere in the room
and reshapes how we see our lives.

Great campaigning changes our vision of society and reshapes our future.

This is a history of #WakingTheFeminists, a seismic movement that brought about radical change in Irish theatre by exposing the underrepresentation of women artists in Ireland. Its shockwaves reverberated in sectors of Irish society far beyond the arts, and even beyond Ireland. #WakingTheFeminists combined a spontaneous grassroots movement active across the country, and an organised, focused campaign across multiple platforms, resulting in profound transformation.

WTF HAPPENED: #WakingTheFeminists and the Movement That Changed Irish Theatre documents and analyses how this historically unprecedented and unique movement began and developed; it provides an important account of those involved, how individual and collective power was used to bring about steep cultural change, and records the changes brought about by #WakingTheFeminists.

This book takes you through the early days of chaos and gathering,[1] the planning and execution of events and campaign strategy, the motivations and manoeuvres, the backroom meetings, fraught conversations, support from major Hollywood stars, internal and external transformations, and the fun and allyship that networked across industries and continents, through a range of documentation and analysis that reflects how we worked.

#WakingTheFeminists ignited on social media, primarily Facebook and Twitter, at a time where what is now called the 'manosphere'[2] increasingly made virtual space unsafe for women and other marginalised people. So, although trolling and vicious commentary was not uncommon in 2015, it was a very different time where the backlash was nowhere near as toxic, violent, or orchestrated as it is now. This campaign was of its context and time. It's doubtful that it would play out the same way in 2025.

There is no single story of how #WakingTheFeminists mushroomed in those first brimming weeks from the end of October 2015. No single account could encompass all that unfolded. WTF HAPPENED attempts to show the complex fabric of what went into making this happen, and includes the reflections of several of the accidental activists involved in organising the key public events and what became a year-long campaign targeted at changing the larger theatre organisations and funders. #WakingTheFeminists was inherently open source, and intentionally encompassed everyone who wanted to call themselves a part of the movement. There was never any one person or one group of people that was #WakingTheFeminists and this book seeks to mirror this.

#WakingTheFeminists remains important as an example of collective action that grew out of a sudden online Twitterstorm. It entirely reframed what matters in Irish theatre and who gets to be represented. While achieving full gender equality in Irish theatre remains an imperfect, open-ended and ongoing process, the short, sharp year-long campaign was enormously impactful in setting the groundwork for deep and lasting change. This impromptu, targeted campaign delivered extraordinary results, and is still referenced as a touchstone by artists, politicians, academics and the media.

A campaign that began as a protest against the Abbey Theatre/Amharclann na Mainistreach, the National Theatre of Ireland (the Abbey), has ironically and importantly become a part of the official national story, and is now archived in both the National Library of Ireland and the National Museum of Ireland's collections. It even featured in the official, government-commissioned book about the 2016 commemoration year;[3] published while the campaign itself was still running.

#WakingTheFeminists may now be embraced by the establishment (it seems), but its origins were deeply anti-establishment. That said, it changed national policy in relation to equality in the arts, and drove and informed other national policy more broadly in relation to gender equality. It influenced several other equality movements in Ireland and internationally, across the artforms of music, dance, literature, poetry, and film, and in many other communities and workplaces. It was part of a period of social agitation and activist movements internationally that energised and fed off each other, including #MeToo,[4] #BlackLivesMatter,[5] and #LoveWins[6]; this was a brief period of time where social media operated as a positive platform to bring people together around social movements.

#WakingTheFeminists was also part of a period of rapid and momentous social shifts in Irish society that came to a head between 2015 and 2018; these shifts were ushered in by effective campaigns that were often decades in the making and represented years of grassroots activism. The Yes Equality[7] campaign drove the positive result of the Marriage Equality Referendum in May 2015, while the Together for Yes[8] campaign powered the positive outcome of the Referendum to repeal the 8th Amendment to the Irish Constitution. These campaigns won the constitutional right to same sex marriage and the right to abortion care – two of the most socially and politically contentious issues in Ireland for decades. Suddenly, Ireland's long-held reputation for being conservative and traditionally Catholic was upended. Ireland was beginning to look positively liberal, inclusive, and progressive.

Those of us involved in #WakingTheFeminists were, for the most part, very inexperienced activists. While the campaign sought to appear highly professional and media-savvy, it was completely made up on-the-hoof. We weren't lobbyists, or policy experts; indeed many of us had only a passing familiarity with feminism. We hadn't yet heard of unconscious bias or diversity, equity, and inclusion initiatives. They simply did not appear to exist in the arts in Ireland in any substantial way that we were aware of, and systemic patriarchal bias was a term that was not a part of our discourse. Previous campaigns in the arts had been more focused on increasing public funding and audience attendance than interrogating our internal biases or questioning representation. We didn't even know the depth or impact of the problem until we started talking more openly that October/November in 2015.

This small campaign from a niche corner of Irish society, that is the world of theatre, achieved far more than any of us involved might have dreamed at its start. We hoped that if we made a significant, and public, change to our corner, it might have knock-on effects elsewhere. While theatre, amateur or professional, may not be everyone's cup of tea, it is still seen as deeply important to Irish identity and is linked to both the origins and continuing evolution of our national story. It's a big aspect of our soft power internationally. Even as one of Ireland's most internationally renowned art forms, theatre is often perceived as elitist, but for those of us who work in and attend theatre, we understand that it has a deep relevance to how we live as humans. The stories we tell ourselves about ourselves are powerful and shape our collective sense of who does and doesn't matter, on and off the stage.

Despite the challenges we faced and our initial lack of expert knowledge in activism and feminism, <u>we did an amazing job</u>. We managed to run an internationally successful campaign, effect measurable change at the heart of Irish theatre practice, and sparked wider discourses on women and equality in Irish society and culture.

One of our advantages which made the campaign seem so professional and headline-grabbing from its inception is that we are theatre folk with skill-sets totally tailor-made for this: we know how to put on a great show. As organisers, performers, promoters, directors, producers, writers, designers, and technicians, we are used to working fast, being deeply collaborative, and being ready for opening night. We are also good networkers and negotiators, and know the impact of featuring names and faces that the public recognise and admire: star power. Drawing people into a story they didn't know existed and making them feel something different is our bread and butter.

We didn't spend a year 'debating' the existence of the gender equality issue in theatre. Thanks to the extensive sharing of stories of exclusion and marginalisation, we got that out of the way irrefutably in the first couple of weeks, which in turn allowed us to move rapidly into 'fix-it' mode. We held public events, commissioned ground-breaking research, made representations to leaders of all the major Irish theatre companies, met with ministers and government departments, pressed for policy change and measurable action plans to be implemented, not only by theatre companies, but across the arts. We were loud, we commanded serious attention, and we won many awards in Ireland and internationally. The attention and approval the campaign generated meant that those in power simply had to at least appear to listen.

External factors also contributed to and interlinked with our success. We were able to capitalise on the warm glow of 'love wins' after the successful campaign to introduce same-sex marriage into Ireland (the first country in the world to do so by public vote) when the public seemed much more receptive to equality-based principles. If one form of equality matters, then so too do all other forms of equality. We were informed by and learned from Yes Equality (they helpfully published a book on their campaign methods in December 2015[9]), and our experiences fed into the Repeal campaign, especially in making a different kind of space for women to own and speak up about their own stories. Many of us involved in #WakingTheFeminists were also involved in one or both of those campaigns too. The campaign also ran with the backdrop of Brexit in summer 2016 and the US presidential election that failed to elect their first female president. It was an extraordinary time to be awake and involved in social agitation; especially to be part of a campaign that was sending out ripples that were felt internationally.

#WakingTheFeminists also contributed significantly to #MeToo in the Irish context, which is explored more in the chapter on legacy and impact. When that hashtag reignited in 2017, stories of bullying and harassment, including sexual harassment, were shared with an immediacy and authority that we couldn't have imagined in October 2015.

There is still no country in the world where a woman has the full lived experience of being equal. There have been great advances in legislation, hard won by previous generations of feminists; but equality in principle does not always translate to equality in practice. Exclusion and marginalisation are traumatising, with long-term consequences. The problem of exclusion of women is not unique to Irish theatre, but for a concentrated, exhilarating period of time in late 2015 and throughout 2016, the Irish theatre scene was a perfect tinderbox: small, locally and internationally connected, vocal, and full of furious and talented can-do women who knew how to organise and put on a sell-out show.

Setting the Scene

Waking the Nation was the 2016 programme of Ireland's National Theatre, the Abbey,[10] and part of the Government of Ireland's public programme to mark the centenary of the Easter Rising, the violent rebellion that led to Irish independence from the United Kingdom. Since its foundation in 1904 by Lady Augusta Gregory and William Butler Yeats, the Abbey and its artists were deeply involved in creating the imaginative conditions for a new national identity to distinguish Ireland from Britain; a key part of the Celtic Revival. Several members of the Abbey Acting Company and staff were also directly involved in the Rising including Helena Molony, Ellen Bushell, Seán Connolly, Peadar Kearney, Edward Keegan, Barney Murphy, Máire Nic Shiubhlaigh, and Arthur Shields.[11]

The Proclamation of the Republic drafted by the insurrectionists was uniquely progressive for its time in addressing the men and women of Ireland. Women were prominent and active in the Rising itself,[12] and many of the male leaders were supportive of the causes of women. However, in the years between achieving independence and the foundation of the Irish State, the recognition of women's public role was largely erased as the country became increasingly patriarchal and controlled by a conservative Catholic Church that greatly influenced the drafting of the 1937 Constitution.[13]

'Waking' in an Irish context is a play on words with a double meaning: to be awake, but also to 'wake', to gather together in order to mourn and celebrate the recently deceased. The Abbey's programme was a clever campaign meant to interrogate and complicate the previous century of Ireland's story. The programme launch on 28 October 2015 was marketed with a rousing video and the words of Helena Molony,[14] the Abbey actor, feminist, labour activist, and republican who was actively involved in the 1916 rebellion: 'We saw a vision of Ireland, free, pure, happy. We did not realise this vision. But we saw it.'

Sara Keating wrote about Helena Molony in the *Irish Times* on 6 November 2015:

> In an interview with RTÉ recorded just before her death, in 1967, Molony spoke about the shared root of her attraction to nationalism and feminism as one of equality, 'the abolition of the domination of nation over nation, class over class, and sex over sex'. Molony would likely be disillusioned by how her words are being used to prop up the programme for Waking the Nation, which privileges the patriarchal narrative of Irish history.[15]

The promotional video featured only women actors (Kate Stanley Brennan, Hilda Fay, and Nyree Yergainharsian) replicating a well-worn masculinist trope in Irish culture long noted by feminist scholars, where the realities, creative work, and voices of women are obscured by the use of women as symbols of the Irish nation, or Irish culture, which creates an optic of inclusion.[16] But as for women artists in the programme? Well, that's why you're reading this book.

Waking the Nation was launched by the Tánaiste (Ireland's deputy prime minister), Minister for Social Protection and leader of the Labour party, Joan Burton, and the Minister for Arts, Heritage and the Gaeltacht, Heather Humphreys.[17] The Minister of State for Equality Aodhán Ó Ríordán was also in attendance, as well as some of the programmed artists. Bridie Murphy, whose father Barney worked at the Abbey and was a 1916 volunteer, was photographed with Abbey Director Fiach Mac Conghail during the launch.[18] Fiach himself was also at the time a Senator in Seanad Éireann, the upper house of Irish legislature.

The initial press and online reactions were generally positive as indicated in the *Irish Independent* on 29 October 2015:

> Arts Minister Heather Humphreys said that the arts will be centre stage next year during the centenary celebrations. She said she was confident that the 'fantastic programme' of both old and new will leave theatregoers 'very excited' and added there was no better way to showcase the best of Irish culture at home and abroad than through the Abbey Theatre.

For many years, women in Irish theatre had known that opportunities for them were scarcer than for men. If this was acknowledged or spoken about at all, it was in whispered private conversations, not on public stages or media platforms. In these conversations women would talk about how they were racked with personal doubts, inadequacies, and imposter syndrome; it is clear now that this was internalised misogyny and the result of millennia of systemic inequality and of bias that has profoundly warped our own sense of our abilities. This forced many talented and ambitious women out of theatre. They eventually chose not to compete in this skewed system or left the country to find flourishing careers elsewhere. The theatre industry masqueraded as meritocratic, while privileging men over women season after season, year after year. If you didn't 'make it', it was a personal fault.

To be a theatre-maker was to be in the margins, placing one on the peripheries of wider and mainstream culture. While the theatre world forms a broad community, in some ways more inclusive than other sectors (for example, for many years theatre and the arts had been perceived as places where LGBTQI+ people could thrive and be seen), Irish theatre remains largely white, middle class, and ableist. Gender inequality was not the only area that needed to be addressed. But with women making up over 50 per cent of the population, it was the biggest area, intersecting with almost all other areas of marginalisation and exclusion.

As women working in theatre we were in denial too, subscribing to the common notion that theatre and the arts in general are inclusive, equitable, welcoming of difference, questioning of authority, reflecting difficult truths to society, and always on the side of the excluded. It felt right-on and worthy, and for a long time most of us were much too nice and responsible to kick up a fuss about the issue of women's representation in theatre. Making theatre was already difficult enough in these times of austerity. We didn't want to pitch stones at ourselves. In our industry, many subscribed to the notion that everyone got the same opportunities and started from the same point. We were more concerned with keeping the show on the road.

Besides, theatre *seemed* very female: the overall majority of both arts workers and audiences were women. The independent and festival sector was full of internationally successful and highly regarded female artists. But men held the most powerful decision-making roles with the big money in the big institutions. Many of us didn't know how to articulate the impacts of gender inequality in any meaningful way that would change anything. We were completely unaware that we had the power within ourselves to change it.

There are some commercial theatres in Ireland, but by and large when scholars, critics, reviewers, and theatre goers talk about Irish theatre we're talking about publicly funded institutions in receipt of competitively awarded grants from the Arts Council, the independent Irish state agency that funds the arts. The majority of these are not-for-profit organisations with charitable status, governed by voluntary boards. Public funding is crucial to how the campaign of #WakingTheFeminists played out, as we were able to link theatre policy to broader policies for equality at national level.[19] The Abbey, as one of a small number of officially recognised national cultural institutions (NCI), is unique in being funded through the arm's length approach of the Arts Council; all the other NCIs are funded directly by the government department responsible for Culture and the Arts. Because of this, of all the artforms supported by the Arts Council, theatre had long been the biggest recipient of funding by a significant margin.

The Abbey, the Gate Theatre, Druid, Rough Magic Theatre Company and Dublin Theatre Festival were the informal 'big five' in terms of Arts Council funding, with by far the highest percentage going to the Abbey, as the single biggest recipient of funding. In 2012, according to Theatre Forum[20] analysis, the Abbey received 17 per cent (€7.1m) of total AC funding that year, the rest of the theatre sector received 11 per cent, and venues 14 per cent. (Other artforms such as dance, literature, film, opera and literature all received between three per cent and nine per cent.)

For the preceding 30 years leading up to 2015 both the Abbey and the Gate had been led by men; in the Gate's case just one man. Dublin Theatre Festival had been led by men since its foundation in 1957. Two women had led the Abbey in its 110 year history: Garry Hynes had a brief tenure in the early 90s (1991–1994), and 20 years before her, Lelia Doolan also had a brief tenure (1971–1973). Each of their periods of leadership was notably shorter in comparison to the male artistic directors who preceded and succeeded them. Independent production companies Druid and Rough Magic were led by women since their establishment in the 1980s, Garry Hynes and Lynne Parker respectively.

Dublin Fringe Festival is notable for its more equitable gender balance in its leadership over its 20 years of operation. Between them Ali Curran (1997–2000) and Róise Goan (2008–2013) had led Dublin Fringe Festival for half its existence. To be feminist in theatre *was* to be fringe. Most of the individual women artists and independent women-led companies from the 1990s through to 2015 started out or were showcased in fringe festivals, including Annie Ryan's The Corn Exchange (est. 1995), Jo Mangan's The Performance Corporation (est. 2002), Máiréad and Ionia Ní Chrónín's Moonfish Theatre (est. 2006), Sarah Jane Scaife's Company SJ (est. 2009), Louise White Performance (est. 2009), Amy Conroy's HotForTheatre (est. 2010), and Sophie Motley's and Sarah Jane Shiels's WillFredd (est. 2011). Companies with women co-directors such as Aedín Cosgrove with Pan Pan (est. 1993), Grace Dyas with THEATREclub (est. 2008), Louise Lowe with ANU (est. 2009) can also be considered in this category.

Women set up independent companies due to the difficulties they faced in trying to advance through the bigger, building-based institutions.[21] Independent companies are significantly more precarious than venue-based organisations, and they also have to rely more on touring and being programmed in festivals. On the positive side, they get to decide for themselves what work to make. These women-led companies were successful on the fringe and often worked internationally, being invited to present work in festivals and theatres around the world.

#WakingTheFeminists gave us all the opportunity to look at our industry with fresh eyes. By gathering together online and in person, sharing our stories, and bringing our fragmented experiences together in one place, we could see in the glaring light the shape of the whole range of the patriarchy working insidiously in our industry. Once we developed a sharply focused understanding that patriarchal privilege for men and exclusion for women was systemic, we could start to figure out how to dismantle it. We were determined that this particular problem – the underrepresentation of women in Irish theatre – would never become invisible again to future generations of theatre workers and audiences.

The arts can be insular: we talk amongst ourselves, and often look only to the Arts Council, to the power structure directly above us rather than taking a more contextual view of the wider communities and structures within which we operate. The problem of under-programming women artists in Irish theatre was not unique to the Abbey, and we wanted to take a holistic and interdisciplinary view of this entire ecosystem.

The financial crash of 2008–2009, and the subsequent cuts in public arts funding, had a disproportionate effect on smaller independent companies – mostly run by women – compared to the bigger institutions, which were protected from the worst of the cuts in funding and were mostly run by men. From 2010 this led to a consolidation and a concentration of both power and money in the bigger male-led organisations, and not only male-led but male-focused in their choice of work.

The thing about systemic inequality is that it is not always so easy to spot from the inside. It's so insidious that it becomes familiar, and what's familiar is considered normal, in the same way that privilege can be invisible to those who have it.[22] The idea that publicly funded theatre in Ireland should actually reflect the public who pay for it was a fairly radical notion in 2015. Women are not a minority at over 50 per cent of the population, but they are marginalised and underrepresented across our country's power structures, including in the arts.

On 28 October 2015, in the hours after the Abbey's Waking the Nation programme was announced, a few initial posts on Facebook and Twitter – most notably from set designer and arts manager Lian Bell – broke the silence around the inequalities in Irish theatre, specifically but not exclusively those affecting women. A subsequent torrent of posts, letters, and speeches from multiple women blew us out of our complacency. Suddenly we were awake and no longer prepared to accept this so-called normality as an inevitable continuum.

Lian's first Facebook post questioning the lack of women in the Abbey's programme unknowingly touched a deep nerve of trauma and created a space for women to share their stories of exclusion and exile. It took courage to share testimonies and call for accountability and action in those early hours and days. There was a real sense of jeopardy and a fear of consequences and backlash for speaking out. However, the volume of stories, taken together, created an uncomfortable counter-narrative to the received notion of Irish theatre as meritocratic, diverse, liberal, and inclusive.

Speaking truth to power in public has consequences, all too often negative. One or two voices are easy to dismiss – but hundreds of voices calling out for the same change are not so easy to brush off. The backlash we were expecting was nothing like we feared. Pushback was there, in the background, slow-rolling, because creating equality necessarily means withdrawing some privilege from those who benefit from imbalances. The patriarchy is a persistent, tricky fecker, always seeking to undo and upend any advancements. But through #WakingTheFeminists we found public support we were not necessarily expecting and made some glorious progress.

Silence turned inward becomes depression. Silence broken turns into action. Action gives agency. Agency brings power, and power effects change.

PART ONE

ONE

Social Media Storm

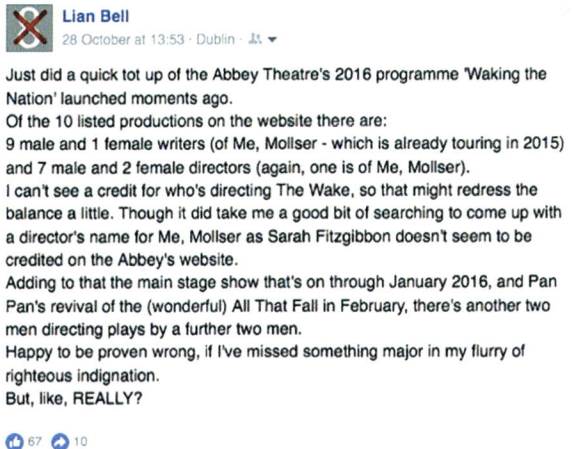

Lian Bell
28 October at 13:53 · Dublin · 🏢 ▾

Just did a quick tot up of the Abbey Theatre's 2016 programme 'Waking the Nation' launched moments ago.
Of the 10 listed productions on the website there are:
9 male and 1 female writers (of Me, Mollser - which is already touring in 2015) and 7 male and 2 female directors (again, one is of Me, Mollser).
I can't see a credit for who's directing The Wake, so that might redress the balance a little. Though it did take me a good bit of searching to come up with a director's name for Me, Mollser as Sarah Fitzgibbon doesn't seem to be credited on the Abbey's website.
Adding to that the main stage show that's on through January 2016, and Pan Pan's revival of the (wonderful) All That Fall in February, there's another two men directing plays by a further two men.
Happy to be proven wrong, if I've missed something major in my flurry of righteous indignation.
But, like, REALLY?

👍 67 ↪ 10

Screen capture of Lian Bell's first post about Waking the Nation.

On Wednesday, 28 October 2015, freelance set designer and arts manager Lian Bell was sitting at her makeshift desk in a cold artist studio she rented in a converted sausage factory on Cork Street in Dublin. Checking Facebook, she noticed the announcement of Waking the Nation, the Abbey's 2016 programme.[1] There were not many names of female directors mentioned in the announced programme. Looking again there were even fewer female writers mentioned.

Lian was tired. She had just finished participating in Dublin Theatre Festival's Next Stage programme: a marathon two and a half weeks of attending shows, workshops, and talks. On top of that, she had had a rough few months with work and was at a point of wondering whether she wanted to continue working in theatre at all. Disappearing and going to work in a bar in the south of France had become a recurring fantasy. She was past the point of caring what folks in the theatre community might think about her or her thoughts. During her lunch break, she posted indignantly about the Abbey's programme on Facebook. If her post went down like a lead balloon, so what? Safe to say, it didn't.

> **Lian Bell** [*Twitter, 28 Oct 2015*]
> Just did a quick tot up of the Abbey Theatre's 2016 programme 'Waking the Nation' launched moments ago. Of the 10 listed productions on the website there are:
> 9 male and 1 female writers (of Me, Mollser – which is already touring in 2015) and 7 male and 2 female directors (again, one is of Me, Mollser).
> I can't see a credit for who's directing The Wake, so that might redress the balance a little. Though it did take me a good bit of searching to come up with a director's name for Me, Mollser as Sarah Fitzgibbon doesn't seem to be credited on the Abbey's website.
> Adding to that the main stage show that's on through January 2016 and Pan Pan's revival of the (wonderful) All That Fall in February, there's another two men directing plays by a further two men.
> Happy to be proven wrong, if I've missed something major in my flurry of righteous indignation.
> But, like, REALLY?

Lian by her own account would acknowledge that at this point she knew as little about feminism as about the Easter Rising and the foundation of the Irish State. She was neither an activist, nor a spokesperson, nor was she an expert on arts strategy, policy, or organisational governance. For her, as for all of us involved in #WakingTheFeminists, the following months were to be a gigantic learning curve.

Thankfully, Lian wasn't the only person to begin posting online on 28 October 2015 about the Abbey programme and its lack of women writers and directors. Actor Brían F. O'Byrne tweeted about it from the United States, and Gavin Kostick, Literary Manager with Fishamble: The New Play Company, also posted on Facebook.

Brían F. O'Byrne *[Twitter, 28 Oct 2015]*
So the @AbbeyTheatre launches #WakingtheNation.
Seems you can only wake #Ireland if you're male.
#NoFemalePlaywrights #disgrace

Gavin Kostick *[Facebook, 29 Oct 2015]*
The defence given on RTE is that (a) they picked the best
and most relevant, and (b) this is only up to September.
(a) is another form of insult and (b) is pretty weak but
does give some form of wriggle room.
More to come on this I think.

Over the next 24 hours Lian and Gavin were hosting long threads of conversations under their Facebook posts. Others chimed in. Women and men who worked in theatre echoed Lian's frustration. They also began to outline a wider context for the current situation. Some posts mention that a programme of female playwrights was put together by the Abbey in 2009 called The Fairer Sex, and spoke to the palpable frustration of the writers involved in that initiative. More and more posts unleashed many years of pent-up frustration that so many women experienced in their relationship with our national theatre.

Due to the rising online clamour, the following day, Thursday, 29 October, Fiach Mac Conghail, Director of the Abbey and independent Senator, decided to hold a 30-minute tweet-conversation on the bus on his way to the airport to go on holiday. The setup was not ideal and felt like the issue was not going to get the attention it deserved. Lian missed this exchange as she was working, having just started working with choreographer Fearghus Ó Conchúir and Project Arts Centre on a giant endeavour called *The Casement Project*. However many others tuned into the conversation, including the writer Belinda McKeon, then based in New York where she was a professor in creative writing at Rutgers University. She was also at that time under commission at the Abbey.

Fiach Mac Conghail *[Twitter, 29 October, 2015]* All my
new play choices are based on the quality of the play,
form and theme. It's my call and I'm pleased with the
plays I picked for #wtn

> **Fiach Mac Conghail** I'm sorry that I have no female playwrights next season. But I'm not going to produce a play that is not ready and undermine the writer #wtn

> **Fiach Mac Conghail** I don't and haven't programmed plays or productions on a gender basis. I took decisions based on who I admired and wanted to work with.

Fiach's series of tweets appeared to lack awareness of the magnitude of the growing discontent, particularly in an exchange with Belinda where he taunted her to 'write your play', this one stood out:

> **Fiach Mac Conghail** Also, sometimes plays and ideas that we have commissioned by and about women just don't work out. That has happened. Them the breaks.

'Them the breaks.' The steam whistled out of the ears of women across the country. This tweet in particular galvanised many of those who had been silently observing to actively engage in the conversation, start commenting online, and contact Lian. Fiach's Twitter feed went silent as he departed on holiday. A perfect storm: he had thrown petrol on a fire and was not on hand to make a public statement, so the staff of the Abbey had to stay silent for several days while the winds around them rose. Any director of the Abbey is in such a disproportionately powerful position that being publicly critical of the leadership of the Abbey was perceived as seriously detrimental to one's career in theatre. However, Fiach had in recent months announced he would be stepping down from the role, and the Board had already announced his successors. So he was on the way out, not just on holidays.[2]

Lian realised that keeping the flow of stories, opinions, and rage circulating could encourage more people to add their own. Lian asked everyone's permission to post screengrabs of what they were saying on Twitter, with the hope that it would make the conversation more public and connect with more people. Director Maeve Stone mocked the Waking The Nation programme title by tweeting 'Waking The Feminists'. Scrabbling around for a hashtag that might work to anchor this rush of posts that kept coming, Lian grabbed the phrase and started using it in all her subsequent social media posts.

Lian recalled, 'Only later, when someone congratulates me on how clever a hashtag is, I realise it's also WTF, What The Fuck. That said, other people say to me that they don't feel comfortable with the use of the word Feminist. Late 2015 hasn't yet seen the full-blown reclamation of that word, and it still has a mildly embarrassing hectoring fustiness about it. I feel it myself, but pretend not to.'

In the last couple of days of October, messages of support started to pour into Lian's inbox, alongside stories and testimonies that the writers didn't yet want to make public. People got bolder as the hours and days ticked on, and emboldened each other. Lian realised that if more people were seen to talk publicly, then more people would feel able to join in, so she encouraged people to say what they wanted to say on a public forum. As the stories and voices multiplied, it was blatantly obvious that this was not a problem that stopped at the door of the Abbey. It was everywhere. Our society is simply riddled with sexism; it is built on it.

Lian recalled:

> [t]he more I can see it, the more of it I see. I wonder how I've managed to live so long with this right before my eyes, and not see it. I know that others around me are feeling exactly the same, and my hastily chosen hashtag of #WakingTheFeminists grows more and more appropriate.
>
> It feels a little strange that people are turning to me, but it's exciting to see the fire beginning to build. I give people options, –, to post them attributed or unattributed with identifying features redacted. It's not easy. There's a real sense of danger, putting your strongly voiced opinion out in critique of the national theatre. I've never much cared to work there, so I personally feel like I don't have much to lose, but there are many others who don't want to risk their reputations. People fear repercussions in this precarious industry. I get it.
>
> I remember the feeling of nerves I had on behalf of some of the women sending me stories to post for them. *Do you really want to say this?* I check with them. *Are you sure?* The stories are cracking something open. They're brave, and they're raw, and they feel dangerous. I'm hoping that no one says something they come to regret. A year later I re-read some of those stories and think – *oh, is that all they said?* In a new world order, with people speaking their minds more freely and more confidently, what felt dangerous a year before is now part of our day-to-day conversations.
>
> No one was in control of all this – no one could be. It was absolutely brilliant. Exhilarating and out of control and scary and necessary. A tiny glimpse emerges of what it must be like to be part of a revolution

– the surge, the people pushing forward with no clear goal or clear leader, but with a power and urgency that is overwhelming.

From Friday, 30 October, advice and suggestions about what to do next started to pile into Lian's phone and inbox. Lots of suggestions for action were being shared on Facebook, many building on earlier inputs with just a few contradictory ideas. Nonetheless there was a shared sense that it was imperative to do *something*, as the following exchange posted on 30 October in the 169 comments under Lian's Facebook post shows:

> **Caroline Williams** How about a public meeting? There was one following the 'oversight' of only including a meagre handful of women writers in the 3-volume *Field Day* anthology–where the editors interrogated their choices and omissions. Let's really 'interrogate' this–I'm happy to coordinate/co-coordinate.
>
>> **Sarah Durcan** I believe a meeting is in order, and that meeting should take place in the Abbey. The aim of which should be the development of a clear and time bound plan of action, and the development of an official policy by the Abbey at Board level, to address sexism in its programming, and all related departments.
>>
>> **Tanya Dean** I think a forum would be a brilliant idea. And particularly one where we can talk about active choices that we as individuals and as an industry can undertake to change this wearily endless status quo.

Lian had recently broken her mobile and was working off a €20 phone with buttons and no internet. By Monday, 2 November, she was spending 12 hours a day glued to her laptop, feverishly shuttling screen grabs of messages from Facebook to Twitter, and vice versa, answering emails, texts, phone calls from colleagues and friends. Her partner left her in the morning and returned in the evening to find her still sitting in the same position, still wearing pyjamas, and with a half-finished bowl of muesli beside her from breakfast.

Producer and arts manager Sarah Durcan suggested writing a letter directly to the Chairperson of the Abbey board to seek an official statement. Lian was coached in drafting this letter by Sarah, Anne Clarke (Producer of Landmark Productions), Loughlin Deegan (Director of The Lir Academy), and Lynne Parker (Artistic Director of Rough Magic). None of them had worked directly with Lian before but were among those who contacted her to help in the early days. The friends and work colleagues who Lian would have automatically called on first – producers Jen Coppinger, Róise Goan, and Caroline Williams – were coincidentally all out of the country in these first days, although they jumped in as soon as they returned. All quickly recognised the seriousness and peril of what Lian was attempting to do, and how fast she was becoming a lightning rod and a (reluctant) spokesperson for the emerging conversation.

3 November 2015

Dear Fiach and members of the Board,

I am writing to you to officially ask for a public statement from the Abbey in response to the outcry about gender-bias in the 2016 programme, and in the theatre's artistic programming more generally.

As you know, the calls have been for the National Theatre to address the lack of equality of representation in such a symbolically important year, but more crucially to address the systems in place leading to the bias around the programming of work written and directed by women, in a way that will be practical, significant and long-lasting.

Since I have been the person channelling the conversations via social media, I am aware of many calls for a public meeting or forum. A group of us are currently working to make this happen, and would like for the meeting to take place on the main stage of the theatre.

Can you let me know if and when this would be possible? If it is not possible for the Abbey to host the meeting, we will of course be inviting you to take part once the details have been clarified.

Regards,

Lian Bell

In the early days of November, the leaders of several leading theatre companies and venues posted their support for #WakingTheFeminists online: Siobhán Bourke and Jane Daly (Co-Directors Irish Theatre Institute), Cian O'Brien (Director of Project Arts Centre), Kris Nelson (Artistic Director Dublin Fringe Festival), Willie White (Director Dublin Theatre Festival), Mark O'Brien (Director of Axis Ballymun), Loughlin Deegan (Director The Lir Academy), Lynne Parker (Artistic Director of Rough Magic Theatre Company), and Jimmy Fay (Executive Producer of The Lyric, Belfast).

Kris Nelson [*Artistic Director Dublin Fringe Festival, Facebook, 4 November 2015*]
Very inspired by what's happening in the #WakingTheFeminists conversation. The dialogue advocating for gender equality is asking all of us to question, act and change.

Cian O'Brien [*Artistic Director Project Arts Centre, Facebook, 4 November 2015*]
I have been following #wakingthefeminists with great interest in the last few days, and I'm glad to see so many people contributing to the conversation. It's a discussion that desperately needed to happen and it's something that has never been far from my mind when programming for Project Arts Centre over the last 4 years. It is time, as a community, that we talk about this openly and I am happy to offer Project as a space for this vital discussion.
I fully support the #wakingthefeminists conversation and I look forward to where it might take us.

There was complete silence from the Abbey. This online upsurge of indignant dissatisfaction could possibly have been rapidly shut down with an early communications response, to mollify and brush us off, but that did not happen. The continuing silence created a vacuum in which people slowly began to feel safer to speak up without such fear of consequence. More and more writers, directors, designers, managers, technicians, and actors began to speak out in the first week of November. There was a sense of safety in numbers. Maybe this insurrection could work. We were articulate and networked around the world. Maybe this time we would be listened to. We *were* the theatre community after all.

It was important to determine and articulate what needed to change and who needed to do the work of change. The urgency of this was expressed by theatre director Grace Dyas on 1 November when she asked Lian on Facebook, 'What would be your ideal outcome from all of this?' Lian responded:

Lian Bell [*Facebook, 1 November 2015*]
Good question—though I'm very conscious that I'm not (and don't want to be) a spokesperson. I really just want to help gather all this energy together and see if

the momentum will get people moving. I think, at the most basic level, an acknowledgment of the bias that exists in the Abbey programming. Then a clear effort by them to change that bias in a meaningful way–by programming more plays written by women and hiring more women directors. I think they need to look at their internal structures to make sure that everyone's getting a fair deal, but I don't know much about those structures so can't be much more specific than that. I think the timing is potentially good for this, seeing that the new directors are coming in and I think it will be useful for them and for us if we are able to articulate our issues clearly. I also think that simply airing all these conversations encourages other people/organisations to look at themselves and ask questions. And for us to talk as a community about how this kind of bias really does happen, and that if we talk about it we can start to change that. Ideally.
What would be your ideal outcome?

Sarah Durcan

A sustained policy of inclusion and active positive support of female artists throughout the organisation. Resulting in a year-on-year increase in the representation and employment of female artists, with measurable targets, with progress reported on at every board meeting. And training for all key staff on gender bias and unconscious biases of all kinds. Policy, action, training, measurement, accountability, results.

Especially on the main stage. And not just at the Abbey. It's a good place to start though, especially as it gets the bulk of funding, and is, you know, the National Theatre.

Meanwhile the conversation was spreading from social media to traditional media outlets. Una Mullally's opinion piece in the *Irish Times* on 2 November highlighted what was fast becoming a debacle:

If the Abbey Theatre announced that 90 per cent of its 2016 programme was made up of plays written by women it would be viewed as extraordinary.

It would be a 'statement'. Yet when the national theatre announced its programme celebrating the 1916 centenary, 90 per cent of the plays programmed are by men. That is not a 'statement', it's just the norm.

I am tired of having to bang this drum, but every music festival line-up that disproportionately features male musicians, every theatre disproportionately programming male playwrights, every film festival screening mostly films by men, every literature prize shortlist being mostly male, shows that we are not beyond this most basic of conversations.

People who deny that there is exclusion are rarely the ones who are excluded. We are often told that women don't put themselves forward enough, but this magical thinking ignores the discriminatory environment within which women are making art. And so the cycle goes: male-made art gets seen, therefore is perceived as better, therefore more men make art when they continuously see their perspective reflected and have male role-models to aspire to, therefore more male-made art gets made, therefore more male-made art succeeds, and so on.

Conversations about women in the context of 1916, and the fierce battles for their republic and their suffrage that they so bravely fought for, are gaining traction. One of the reasons why it's so important to shine a spotlight on the female aspect of the birth of our republic is because of how extensively it was erased, not least by our subsequent Constitution. 100 years later, much has changed for the better, yet the conversation about gender equality is just as relevant and perhaps even more heated. What an opportunity the Abbey has missed – not alone to represent the artistic output of women in Ireland, but also to acknowledge that conversation. Naturally, The Plough and the Stars features in the programme. Maybe it's time for another riot.[3]

A letter by playwright Erica Murray was published in the *Irish Times* on Monday, 2 November,[4] highlighting the outrage felt by many (see her speech in chapter four, Speeches from the Public Meeting). This was joined by another powerful letter on Wednesday, 4 November, from the researcher in the arts and education Dr Brenda Donohue, also published in the *Irish Times*, which outlined the results of her academic research:

> Some of my latest research … has focused on the number of plays written by women and presented on the Abbey stages from 1995 to 2014. It found that of 320 plays staged in this period, just 36 plays were written by a woman, 24 of which were new plays, while 12 were revivals.
>
> On average, over the period studied, just 11 per cent of the plays staged by the National Theatre were written by a woman.

A stage that presents 11 per cent of writing by women does not accurately represent the wealth of Irish people's experiences. We are only getting half the story.[5]

Alongside Brenda's letter in the *Irish Times* that day, playwright Jimmy Murphy wrote:

The Abbey Theatre is under no obligation to foist poorly written plays on a paying audience just to fulfil a programme and address balance. Anyone who thinks otherwise is deluded.[6]

Jimmy Murphy's letter received a swift response in the paper the next day, Thursday 5 November from theatre educator John Delaney:

Jimmy Murphy is right (November 4th). The Abbey Theatre is under no obligation to foist poorly written plays upon a paying audience to fulfil a programme and address balance. But anyone who thinks the Abbey has not already foisted hundreds of poorly written plays by men upon its beleaguered paying audience is clearly deluded.[7]

On Thursday, 5 November, the *Irish Times* also published a letter from Garry Hynes, director of Druid Theatre Company:

While the conversation (November 3rd) on gender inequality in the arts has been triggered by the announcement of the Abbey's Centenary Programme, the questions and issues involved are for all of us who work in the performing arts in Ireland. We need to hear further from the Abbey's director and, given the theatre's role as a national theatre, and the imminent change of leadership there, we also need to hear from the Abbey board.

But we are all at fault here. We must have the conversation internally within our own organisations and more broadly between us as an industry and we must do this as a matter of priority.

This is a significant moment and what Irish theatre looks like a hundred years from now will in large part be determined by how we respond to it.[8]

The conversation was also live among the Irish diaspora, as many women theatre makers had had to leave to work elsewhere. On 5 November, New York–based playwright Lisa Tierney Keogh quickly ran some figures from the information available on the Abbey's website, and found there was a stark

SINCE 2006, IRELAND'S NATIONAL THEATRE HAS PRODUCED OR PRESENTED 111 PLAYS WITH 7 OR MORE PERFORMANCES ON THE ABBEY AND PEACOCK STAGES.

12.6% WERE WRITTEN BY WOMEN.

HOMELAND by Paul Mercier Abbey, 2006
EURIPIDES' THE BACCHAE OF BAGHDAD a new version by Conall Morrison Abbey, 2006
TURGENEV'S A MONTH IN THE COUNTRY a new version by Brian Friel Abbey, 2006
THE IMPORTANCE OF BEING EARNEST by Oscar Wilde Abbey, 2006
DOUBT by John Patrick Shanley Abbey, 2006
THE SCHOOL FOR SCANDAL by Richard Brinsley Sheridan Abbey, 2006
JULIUS CAESAR by Shakespeare Abbey, 2007
THE CAVALCADERS by Billy Michael Roche Abbey, 2007
THE CRUCIBLE by Arthur Miller Abbey, 2007
THE BIG HOUSE by Lennox Robinson Abbey, 2007
KICKING A DEAD HORSE by Sam Shepard Abbey, 2007
THE PLAYBOY OF THE WESTERN WORLD a new version by Bisi Adigun and Roddy Doyle Abbey, 2007
THE RECRUITING OFFICER by George Farquhar Abbey, 2007
ROMEO AND JULIET by Shakespeare Abbey, 2008
THE SEAFARER by Conor McPherson Abbey, 2008
THREE SISTERS by Anton Chekhov in a version by Brian Friel Abbey, 2008
AN IDEAL HUSBAND by Oscar Wilde Abbey, 2008
HAPPY DAYS by Samuel Beckett Abbey, 2008
THE RESISTIBLE RISE OF ARTURO UI by Bertolt Brecht Abbey, 2008
THE PLAYBOY OF THE WESTERN WORLD a new version by Bisi Adigun and Roddy Doyle Abbey, 2008
THE COMEDY OF ERRORS by Shakespeare Abbey, 2009
LAST DAYS OF A RELUCTANT TYRANT by Tom Murphy Abbey, 2009
THE RIVALS by Richard Brinsley Sheridan Abbey, 2009
TALES OF BALLYCUMBER by Sebastian Barry Abbey, 2009
AGES OF THE MOON by Sam Shepard Abbey, 2009
THE SEAFARER by Conor McPherson Abbey, 2009
CHRIST DELIVER US! by Thomas Kilroy Abbey, 2010
MACBETH by Shakespeare Abbey, 2010
BOOKWORMS by Bernard Farrell Abbey, 2010
THE PLOUGH AND THE STARS by Sean O'Casey Abbey, 2010
JOHN GABRIEL BORKMAN by Henrik Ibsen in a new version by Frank McGuinness Abbey, 2010
FREEFALL by Michael West Abbey, 2010
ARRAH-NA-POGUE - THE WICKLOW WEDDING by Dion Boucicault Abbey, 2010
RAOUL by James Thierce Abbey, 2011
THE PASSING by Paul Mercier Abbey, 2011
THE EAST PIER by Paul Mercier Abbey, 2011
PYGMALION by George Bernard Shaw Abbey, 2011
TRANSLATIONS by Brian Friel Abbey, 2011
CURSE OF THE STARVING CLASS by Sam Shepard Abbey, 2011
JUNO AND THE PAYCOCK by Sean O'Casey Abbey, 2011
THE GOVERNMENT INSPECTOR by Nikolai Gogol in a new version by Roddy Doyle Abbey, 2011
BOOKWORMS by Bernard Farrell Abbey, 2012
ALICE IN FUNDERLAND by Philip McMahon and Raymond Scannell Abbey, 2012
THE HOUSE by Tom Murphy Abbey, 2012
THE PLOUGH AND THE STARS by Sean O'Casey O'Reilly Theatre, 2012
PICTURE OF DORIAN GRAY by Oscar Wilde in an adaptation by Neil Bartlett Abbey, 2012
THE DEAD by James Joyce in a dramatisation by Frank McGuinness Abbey, 2012
KING LEAR by Shakespeare Abbey, 2013
DRUM BELLY by Richard Dormer Abbey, 2013
MAJOR BARBARA by George Bernard Shaw Abbey, 2013
THE HANGING GARDENS by Frank McGuinness Abbey, 2013
THE RISEN PEOPLE by James Plunkett Abbey, 2013
SIVE by John B. Keane Abbey, 2014
TWELFTH NIGHT by Shakespeare Abbey, 2014
ARISTOCRATS by Brian Friel Abbey, 2014
HEARTBREAK HOUSE by George Bernard Shaw Abbey, 2014
OUR FEW AND EVIL DAYS by Mark O'Rowe Abbey, 2014
SHE STOOPS TO CONQUER by Oliver Goldsmith Abbey, 2014
A MIDSUMMER NIGHT'S DREAM by Shakespeare Abbey, 2015
HEDDA GABBLER by Henrik Ibsen in a new version by Mark O'Rowe Abbey, 2015
THE SHADOW OF A GUNMAN by Sean O'Casey Abbey, 2015
OEDIPUS by Sophocles in a new version by Wayne Jordan Abbey, 2015
YOU NEVER CAN TELL by Bernard Shaw Abbey, 2015
THE GROWN UPS by Nicholas Kelly Peacock, 2006
TRUE WEST by Sam Shepard Peacock, 2006
HOWIE THE ROOKIE by Mark O'Rowe Peacock, 2006
BLUE ORANGE by Joe Penhall Peacock, 2006
ALICE TRILOGY by Tom Murphy Peacock, 2006
KICKING A DEAD HORSE by Sam Shepard Peacock, 2007
SAVED by Edward Bond Peacock, 2007
TERMINUS by Mark O'Rowe Peacock, 2007
FOOL FOR LOVE by Sam Shepard Peacock, 2008
BURIAL AT THEBES by Seamus Heaney Peacock, 2008
THE BROTHERS SIZE by Terrell Alvin McCraney Peacock, 2008
BIG LOVE by Charles L. Mee Peacock, 2008
DELIRIUM by Enda Walsh, Based on Dostoevsky's The Brothers Karamazov Peacock, 2008
LAY ME DOWN SOFTLY by Billy Roche Peacock, 2008
LA DISPUTE by Pierre Marivaux Peacock, 2009
AGES OF THE MOON by Sam Shepard Peacock, 2009
ONLY AN APPLE by Tom MacIntyre Peacock, 2009
THE NEW ELECTRIC BALLROOM by Enda Walsh Peacock, 2008
TERMINUS by Mark O'Rowe Peacock, 2009
OUTSIDERS by David McWilliams Peacock, 2010
THE GIRL WHO FORGOT TO SING BADLY Peacock, 2011
SILENT by Pat Kinevane Peacock, 2011
SHIBARI by Garry Duggan Peacock, 2012
QUIETLY by Owen McCafferty Peacock, 2012
I, MALVOLIO AND I, PEASEBLOSSOM by Tim Crouch Peacock, 2013
RICHARD II by Shakespeare Peacock, 2013
ALL DOLLED UP RESTITCHED by Panti (Rory O'Neill) Peacock, 2013
MAEVE'S HOUSE by Eamon Morrissey Peacock, 2013
SILENT by Pat Kinevane Peacock, 2013
CONSERVATORY by Michael West Peacock, 2014
QUIETLY by Owen McCafferty Peacock, 2014
MAEVE'S HOUSE by Eamon Morrissey Peacock, 2014
THE WASTE GROUND PARTY by Shaun Dunne Peacock, 2014
DEATH OF A COMEDIAN by Owen McCafferty Peacock, 2015

MARBLE by Marina Carr Abbey, 2009
SHUSH by Elaine Murphy Abbey, 2013
BY THE BOG OF CATS by Marina Carr Abbey, 2015
A NUMBER by Carol Churchill Peacock, 2007
WOMAN AND SCARECROW by Marina Carr Peacock, 2007
LITTLE GEM by Elaine Murphy Peacock, 2010
NO ESCAPE compiled and edited by Mary Raftery Peacock, 2010
B FOR BABY by Carmel Winters Peacock, 2010
NO ROMANCE by Nancy Harris Peacock, 2011
PERVE by Stacey Gregg Peacock, 2011
16 POSSIBLE GLIMPSES by Marina Carr Peacock, 2011
B FOR BABY by Carmel Winters Peacock, 2011
I (HEART) ALICE (HEART) I by Amy Conroy Peacock, 2012
SHIBBOLETH by Stacey Gregg Peacock, 2015

97

14

#WAKINGTHEFEMINISTS

WHY 7 OR MORE PERFORMANCES? A public reading, limited run, literary event, or talk is not a production.
SOURCES: Abbey Theatre Three-Year Reviews 2006-2008 and 2009-2011, Abbey Theatre Annual Reports 2012-2014, the Abbey Theatre Performance Database, and the Abbey Theatre website
NOTE: A previous version of this document incorrectly listed 100 plays written by men. This version has been revised for accuracy. Thank you to Twitter for the fact-checking.

SINCE 2006, IRELAND'S NATIONAL THEATRE HAS PRODUCED OR PRESENTED 112 PLAYS WITH 7 OR MORE PERFORMANCES ON THE ABBEY AND PEACOCK STAGES.

19.6% WERE DIRECTED BY WOMEN.

HOMELAND directed by Paul Mercier Abbey, 2006
EURIPIDES' THE BACCHAE OF BAGHDAD directed by Conall Morrison Abbey, 2006
TURGENEV'S A MONTH IN THE COUNTRY directed by Jason Byrne Abbey, 2006
THE IMPORTANCE OF BEING EARNEST directed Conall Morrison Abbey, 2006
DOUBT directed by Gerard Stembridge Abbey, 2006
THE SCHOOL FOR SCANDAL by directed by Jimmy Fay Abbey, 2006
JULIUS CAESAR directed by Jason Byrne Abbey, 2007
THE CAVALCADERS directed by Robin Lefevre Abbey, 2007
THE CRUCIBLE directed by Patrick Mason Abbey, 2007
THE BIG HOUSE directed by Conall Morrison Abbey, 2007
KICKING A DEAD HORSE directed by Sam Shepard Abbey, 2007
THE PLAYBOY OF THE WESTERN WORLD directed by Jimmy Fay Abbey, 2007
ROMEO AND JULIET directed by Jason Byrne Abbey, 2008
THE SEAFARER directed by Jimmy Fay Abbey, 2008
THREE SISTERS directed by Jason Leveaux Abbey, 2008
AN IDEAL HUSBAND directed by Neil Bartlett Abbey, 2008
THE RESISTIBLE RISE OF ARTURO UI directed by Jimmy Fay Abbey, 2008
THE PLAYBOY OF THE WESTERN WORLD directed by Jimmy Fay Abbey, 2008
MARBLE directed by Jeremy Herrin Abbey, 2009
THE COMEDY OF ERRORS directed by Jason Byrne Abbey, 2009
LAST DAYS OF A RELUCTANT TYRANT directed by Conall Morrison Abbey, 2009
THE RIVALS directed by Patrick Mason Abbey, 2009
TALES OF BALLYCUMBER directed by David Leveaux Abbey, 2009
AGES OF THE MOON directed by Jimmy Fay Abbey, 2009
THE SEAFARER directed by Conor McPherson Abbey, 2009
CHRIST DELIVER US! directed by Wayne Jordan Abbey, 2010
MACBETH directed by Jimmy Fay Abbey, 2010
BOOKWORMS directed by Jim Culleton Abbey, 2010
THE PLOUGH AND THE STARS directed by Wayne Jordan Abbey, 2010
JOHN GABRIEL BORKMAN directed by James MacDonald Abbey, 2010
ARRAH-NA-POGUE - THE WICKLOW WEDDING directed by Mikel Murphy Abbey, 2010
RAOUL directed by James Thiérrée Abbey, 2011 (James Thiérrée)
THE PASSING directed by Paul Mercier Abbey, 2011
THE EAST PIER directed by Paul Mercier Abbey, 2011
TRANSLATIONS directed by Conall Morrison Abbey, 2011
CURSE OF THE STARVING CLASS directed by Jimmy Fay Abbey, 2011
JUNO AND THE PAYCOCK directed by Howard Davies Abbey, 2011
THE GOVERNMENT INSPECTOR directed by Jimmy Fay Abbey, 2011
BOOKWORMS directed by Jim Culleton Abbey, 2012
ALICE IN FUNDERLAND directed by Wayne Jordan Abbey, 2012
THE PLOUGH AND THE STARS directed by Wayne Jordan O'Reilly Theatre, 2012
PICTURE OF DORIAN GRAY directed by Neil Bartlett Abbey, 2012
THE DEAD directed by Joe Dowling Abbey, 2012
DRUM BELLY directed by Sean Holmes Abbey, 2013
SHUSH directed by Jim Culleton Abbey, 2013
THE HANGING GARDENS directed by Patrick Mason Abbey, 2013
THE RISEN PEOPLE directed by Jimmy Fay Abbey, 2013
SIVE directed by Conall Morrison Abbey, 2014
TWELFTH NIGHT directed by Wayne Jordan Abbey, 2014
ARISTOCRATS directed by Patrick Mason Abbey, 2014
OUR FEW AND EVIL DAYS directed by Mark O'Rowe Abbey, 2014
SHE STOOPS TO CONQUER directed by Conall Morrison Abbey, 2014
A MIDSUMMER NIGHT'S DREAM directed by Gavin Quinn Abbey, 2015
THE SHADOW OF A GUNMAN directed by Wayne Jordan Abbey, 2015
OEDIPUS directed by Wayne Jordan Abbey, 2015
YOU NEVER CAN TELL directed by Conall Morrison Abbey, 2015
THE GROWN UPS directed by Gerard Stembridge Peacock, 2006
TRUE WEST directed by Jimmy Fay Peacock, 2006
HOWIE THE ROOKIE directed by Jimmy Fay Peacock, 2006
ALICE TRILOGY directed by Tom Murphy Peacock, 2006
KICKING A DEAD HORSE directed by Sam Shepard Peacock, 2007
SAVED directed by Jimmy Fay Peacock, 2007
TERMINUS directed by Mark O'Rowe Peacock, 2007
THE BURIAL AT THEBES directed by Patrick Mason Peacock, 2008
DELIRIUM directed by Joseph Alford Peacock, 2008 (Theatre O)
LAY ME DOWN SOFTLY directed by Wilson Milam Peacock, 2008
LA DISPUTE directed by Wayne Jordan Peacock, 2009
AGES OF THE MOON directed by Jimmy Fay Peacock, 2009
THE NEW ELECTRIC BALLROOM directed by Enda Walsh Peacock, 2009 (Druid)
TERMINUS directed by Mark O'Rowe Peacock, 2009
LITTLE GEM directed by Paul Meade Peacock, 2010 (Guna Nua/Civic Theatre)
OUTSIDERS directed by Conall Morrison Peacock, 2010
B FOR BABY directed by Mikel Murfi Peacock, 2010
NO ROMANCE directed by Wayne Jordan Peacock, 2011
16 POSSIBLE GLIMPSES directed by Wayne Jordan Peacock, 2011
B FOR BABY directed by Mikel Murfi Peacock, 2011
SILENT directed by Jim Culleton Peacock, 2012 (Fishamble)
SHIBARI directed by Tom Creed Peacock, 2012
QUIETLY directed by Jimmy Fay Peacock, 2012
I, MALVOLIO AND I, PEASEBLOSSOM directed by Karl James and A Smith Peacock, 2013 (Tim Crouch Theatre)
RICHARD II directed by Michael Barker-Caven Peacock, 2013 (Ouroboros/Everyman)
ALL DOLLED UP RESTITCHED directed by Phillip McMahon Peacock, 2013 (THISISPOPBABY)
MAEVE'S HOUSE directed by Gerard Stembridge Peacock, 2013
SILENT directed by Jim Culleton Peacock, 2013 (Fishamble)
CONSERVATORY directed by Michael Barker-Caven Peacock, 2014
QUIETLY directed by Jimmy Fay Peacock, 2014
MAEVE'S HOUSE by Éamon Morrissey Peacock, 2014
THE WASTE GROUND PARTY directed by Gerard Stembridge Peacock, 2014
DEATH OF A COMEDIAN directed by Steve Marmion Peacock, 2015
SHIBBOLETH directed by Hamish Pirie Peacock, 2015

THE RECRUITING OFFICER directed by Lynne Parker Abbey, 2007
HAPPY DAYS directed by Deborah Warner Abbey, 2008 (National Theatre of Great Britain)
FREEFALL directed by Annie Ryan Abbey, 2010 (Corn Exchange)
PYGMALION directed by Annabelle Comyn Abbey, 2011
THE HOUSE directed by Annabelle Comyn Abbey, 2012
KING LEAR directed by Selina Cartmell Abbey, 2013
MAJOR BARBARA directed by Annabelle Comyn Abbey, 2013
HEARTBREAK HOUSE directed by Roisin McBrinn Abbey, 2014
HEDDA GABBLER directed by Annabelle Comyn Abbey, 2015
BY THE BOG OF CATS directed by Selina Cartmell Abbey, 2015
BLUE ORANGE directed by Annabelle Comyn Peacock, 2006
A NUMBER by Annabelle Comyn Peacock, 2007
WOMAN AND SCARECROW directed by Selina Cartmell Peacock, 2007
FOOL FOR LOVE directed by Annie Ryan Peacock, 2008
THE BROTHERS SIZE directed by Tea Alagic Peacock, 2008 (Foundry Theatre/Public Theater NY)
BIG LOVE directed by Selina Cartmell Peacock, 2008
ONLY AN APPLE directed by Selina Cartmell Peacock, 2009
NO ESCAPE directed by Roisin McBrinn Peacock, 2010
THE GIRL WHO FORGOT TO SING BADLY directed by Lynne Parker Peacock, 2011 (Theatre Lovett/The Ark)
PERVE directed by Roisin McBrinn Peacock, 2011
I (HEART) ALICE (HEART) I directed by Amy Conroy Peacock, 2012 (HotForTheatre)
FOLLOW directed by Sophie Motley Peacock, 2014 (WillFredd Theatre)

90

22

#WAKINGTHEFEMINISTS

WHY 7 OR MORE PERFORMANCES? A public reading, limited run, literary event, or talk is not a production.
SOURCES: Abbey Theatre Three-Year Reviews 2006-2008 and 2009-2011, Abbey Theatre Annual Reports 2012-2014, Abbey Theatre Performance Database, and the Abbey Theatre website
NOTE: A previous version of this document incorrectly listed 21 productions directed by women. This version has been revised for accuracy. Thank you to all who contributed fact-checking.

difference between the number of programmed male artists and female artists since 2006. Lisa and her husband Charlie Veprek hastily cobbled together the first infographics demonstrating visually the deep disparity between male and female playwrights at the Abbey: 100 vs 14 since 2006 or only 12.3% by women. It was our first foray into data visualisation, and we began to realise the power of statistics and the story they told. Lisa and Charlie made a similar one for directors (only 19.6% women) in which the disparity was just as stark.

On 4 November 2015 Anne Clarke, Belinda McKeon, and publicist Christine Monk started a Twitter campaign, #IStandWithYouWomenInIrishTheatre, to gain celebrity support. In just a few days it spread rapidly from Dublin to New York to Los Angeles, London, Addis Ababa, Melbourne, Sydney, and Paris. Debra Messing,[9] star of NBC's *Will and Grace*, gave us our first celebrity endorsement. #WakingTheFeminists was now trending on Twitter. Tweets appeared from Irish and international stars of stage and screen including Nicole Kidman, Saoirse Ronan, Simone Kirby, Denise Gough, Fionnula Flanagan, Olwen Fouéré, Martha Plimpton, Christine Baranski, Cherry Jones, Dana Delany, Amy Ryan, Rose Byrne, Elizabeth Rodriguez, Alemtsehay Wodajo, Gabriel Byrne, Simon Callow, Brían F. O'Byrne; from writers Emma Donoghue, Anne Enright, Marina Carr, and Enda Walsh; directors John Tiffany and Wim Wenders; the Belarus Free Theatre Company, the all-female cast of the Donmar Warehouse's production of *Henry IV* including Harriet Walter; and Dr Alula Pankhurst, grandson of Sylvia Pankhurst, among others.

This public support from such internationally recognised names was hugely significant in building wider awareness and made it much more difficult for the establishment to dismiss us and our concerns. As the volume of tweets surged, the media began to really take notice, and coverage of #WakingTheFeminists went beyond the arts and culture sections to news, opinion and even editorial.[10] With each post and article the pressure was mounting on the Abbey to respond.

Having called for a public event, the movement urgently needed to get even more organised. One week on from the original posts, a group of us were in a room discussing what this event should be. We still weren't even sure where or when it would happen.

Rose Byrne

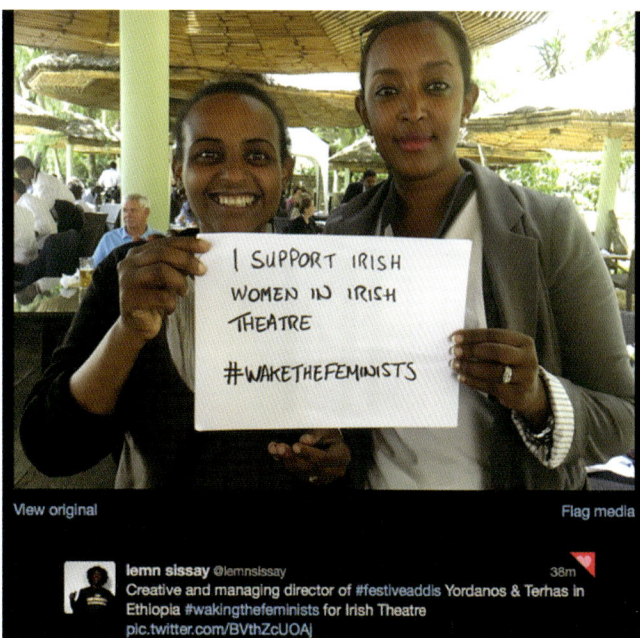

Terhas Lagasse and Yordanos Haile

Unlike   Comment

Tag photo

Colm O'Callaghan

A feminist shout out to Waking The Feminists friends in Ireland from the Women In Theatre and Screen, Australia - WITS forum convened in Sydney last night. Ping Lizzie Schebesta, Lian Bell, Anne Clarke, Sarah Durcan. #WITS #WakingTheFeminists

Album: Timeline Photos

Shared with: 👥 Friends (+)

🏷 Tag this Photo

Women in Theatre and Screen Australia

Martha Plimpton

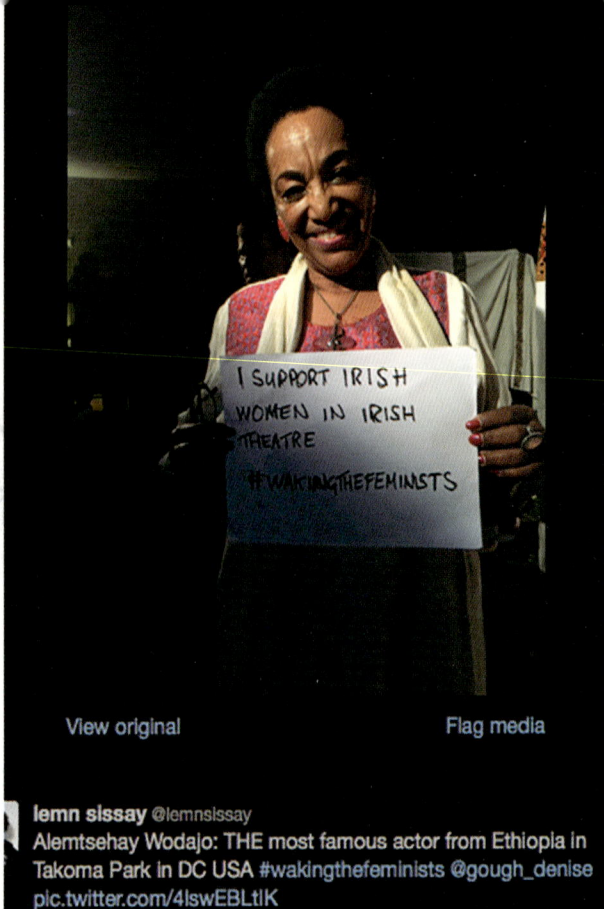

View original   Flag media

lemn sissay @lemnsissay
Alemtsehay Wodajo: THE most famous actor from Ethiopia in
Takoma Park in DC USA #wakingthefeminists @gough_denise
pic.twitter.com/4IswEBLtlK

Alemtsehay Wodajo

Abbie Spallen shared a photo to your timeline.
43 mins · 👥

The fantastic Women's Project Theatre Lab in New York with the wonderful
AD Lisa McNultystand with #wakingthefeminists. 'Well some of us stand,
others of us sprawl on the floor with drink'. x

Lisa McNulty and Women's Project
Theatre Lab, New York

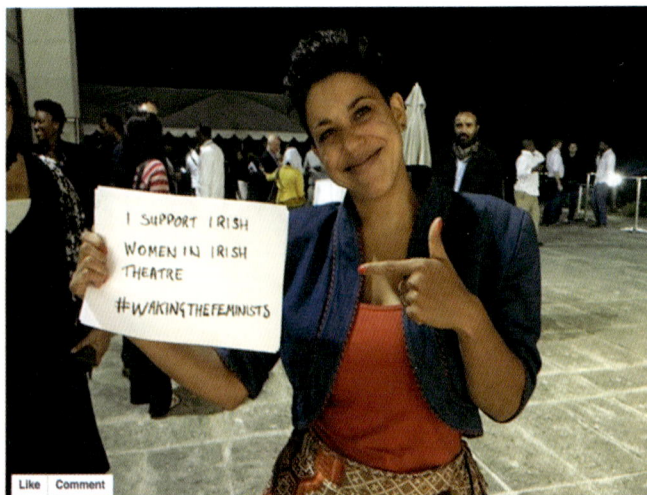

Like   Comment

Lemn Sissay
Jess majekodunmi @ipicnic worked with Angie Gough & works in Addis Ababa for The
Girl Project #wakingthefeminists

Album Timeline Photos
Shared with Public

Jess Majekodunmi, Girl Effect Ethiopia

Enda Walsh

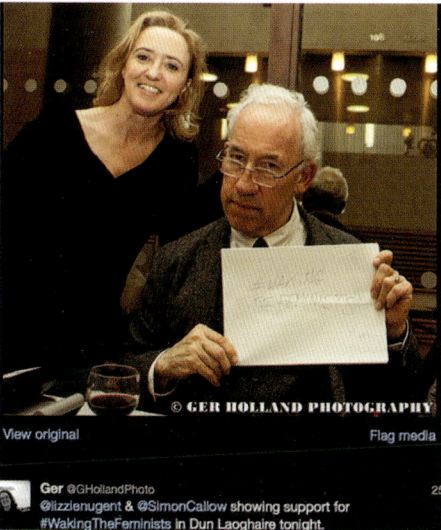

Liz Nugent and Simon Callow

Elizabeth Rodriguez

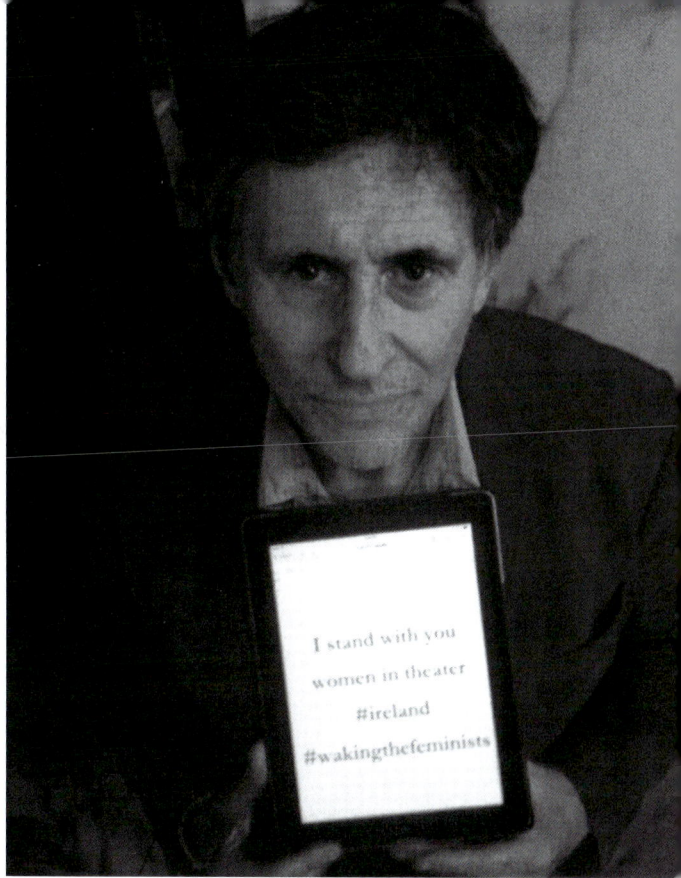

(above) *Gabriel Byrne*
(below) *Emma Donoghue*

The cast of Henry IV, Donmar Warehouse Production at St Ann's Warehouse Brooklyn, directed by Phyllida Lloyd. Cast includes: Harriet Walter, Jade Anouka, Clare Dunne, Jenny Jules, Susan Wokoma, Jackie Clune, Shiloh Coke, Karen Dunbar, Zainab Hasan, Sharon Rooney, Sophie Stanton and Carolina Valdés.

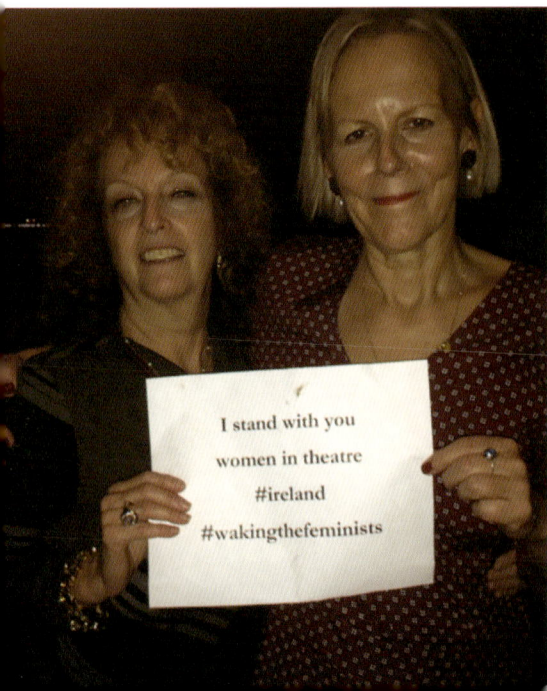

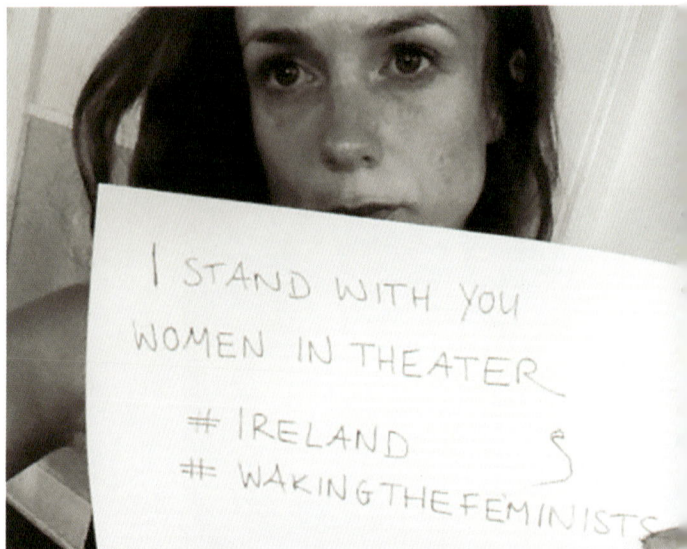

(left) Susan Feldman, Director St Ann's Warehouse Brooklyn and director Phyllida Lloyd
(above) Kerry Condon

Cherry Jones

Wim Wenders

Saoirse Ronan

(above) Dana Delany
(below) Amy Ryan

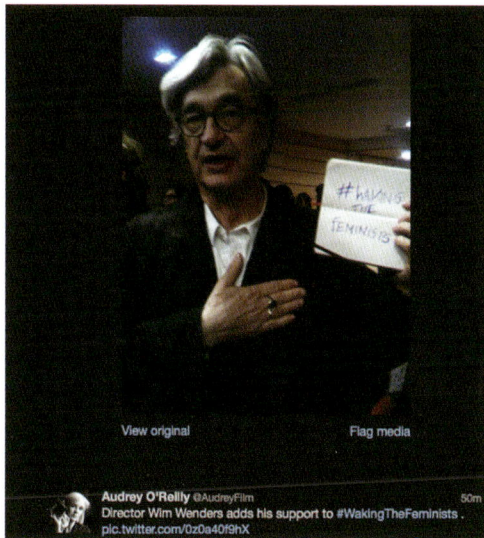

(left) Denise Gough

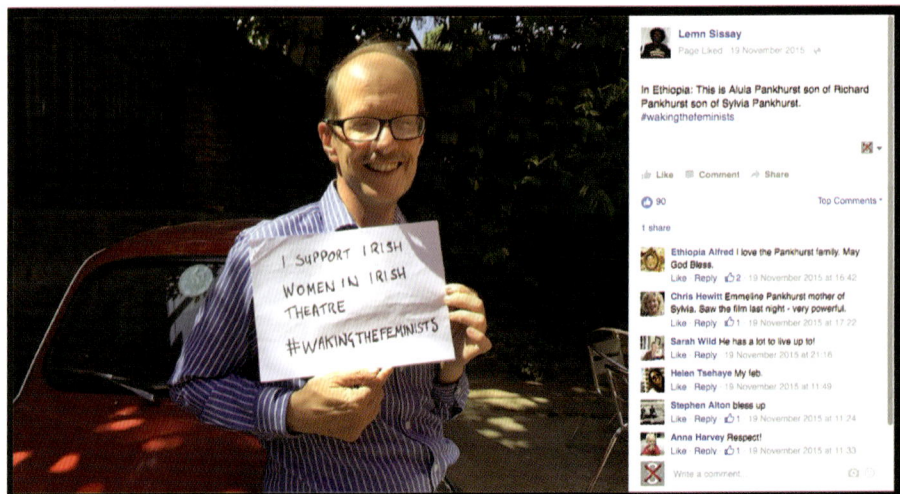

(right) Alula Pankhurst

Early Social Media Posts

Lian Bell *[Facebook, 30 October 2015]*
Still mulling over what the conversations on FB and twitter about the Abbey Theatre's male-dominated programme for 2016 have brought up for me.

Found myself seething, wrote a giant list of questions, and then read the excellent conversations being had below Gavin [Kostick]'s post from yesterday (go read).

So here is a barrage of thoughts & questions, if only to get them off my chest. Answers or more questions welcome. Deathly silence welcome too.

– is the decision to have only 1 in 10 female writers and 3 in 10 female directors in the big symbolic 2016 programme (for whatever reasons that that happened) not a big enough deal for the National Theatre to talk about as part of announcing the programme? Could they have done something in the programme that as some kind of redress to the balance by other means? In an institution whose mission statement's central tenets include reflecting Irish society and placing the artist at the centre of the work, how can this go so wrong in relation to women (tip of the iceberg) and not be addressed in a more open and robust way by them?

– the 'I chose the best plays available' reason is so infuriating. Is there really such an imbalance in the quality of m/f writing? Is it down to a male-centric taste of the programmer and (at the least) that could be acknowledged? If the systems in place to generate and produce work to support the theatre's mission statement are failing, don't the systems need to change?

– what has the Abbey been doing to foster the kind of work from women writers that will 'fit' in their programme, and why isn't that working? Do women not write the kind of work that is seen as 'fitting' (in both the physical and content sense) for the Abbey stage? If not, why not? (I really don't know–comments from playwrights and programmers welcome.) Should the Abbey change the programming to fit the kind of work that women writers/directors are interested in making? Wouldn't that be presenting their work in a truer sense? (Is that a very naive question?)

I suppose the main question lies in what the national theatre is for, and what we want it to do for us. Maybe that's the next can of worms.

Belinda McKeon Dylan Tighe Aoife Courtney Sinéad O'Loughlin Annie Ryan Sarah Durcan Lisa Tierney-Keogh– would love to hear from you. Though would love to hear from other people who haven't said anything yet too.

Emma O'Grady *[actor and writer, Facebook, 30 October 2015]*

The director of the Abbey came to talk to us when I did my MA (2007) and told the class 'there are no female Irish writers ready to write for the big stage and no female Irish directors ready for the big stage'. I said 'OK so how do we get them ready?' and the reply was a shrug. I stopped paying much attention to our national theatre that day.

Ursula Rani Sarma *[writer, Facebook comment 31 October 2015]*

Emma O'Grady's comment above I think tells us all we need to know about how this has happened. This is the genuine belief. The work we female Irish playwrights are producing isn't good enough. So basically all of the other Irish companies and international ones staging our work have got it wrong then? Is this the implication? That they just are not as discerning as the Abbey? How patronising is that? How dismissive of those of us with productions occurring nationally and internationally every year? What angers me the most is not just the programme itself, but the implicit attitude that these choices and statements are entirely acceptable. I was part of the Fairer Sex, I cringed at the title and I cringed at the fact that all the playwrights faces were plastered on the poster to advertise the event like a lovely girl competition. They just keep getting it wrong and then more wrong and perhaps the only error we are making is to expect different behaviour when each opportunity presents itself.

Abbie Spallen *[writer]*

The play I'm writing for the National is for the Olivier stage and has a cast of over 25. My last performed play had a cast of twelve. I'm also writing a musical. I feel a bit ready. Anyone else feel a bit ready?

Dylan Tighe [*writer, director, actor, musician, Facebook, 30 October 2015*]

While I fully support the need for gender equality as an absolute, immutable minimum, my feeling is that all inequality in terms of representation needs to be taken together – whether its gender-based, on account of being an ethnic minority, disabled etc (the programme fails on all these counts) rather than fought as separate issues, as they are all deeply linked to wider questions of structural inequality, discrimination, sexism, racism, exclusion. All of these demographics can be incredibly powerful together as an allied force. 2016 is a perfect time for everyone to come together to finally bury the patriarchal bias (on all levels) and demand that the vision of the proclamation of guaranteeing "equal opportunities to all its citizens' and of "cherishing all children of the nation equally" be structurally embedded at the heart of funding and cultural policy.

> **Olwen Fouéré** [*actor, director, writer*]
> So true, Dylan. It's not only about gender, that is only one of the threads.

> **Abbie Spallen** [*writer*]
> Dylan Tighe This is a tricky one. The exclusion of minorities is a disgrace. Women, however, are not a minority. We make up half the population. I believe that the presentation of women as a minority actually feeds the problem. It reinforces the idea that men are 'the norm' and women are 'the other'. I don't know if I've articulated that properly. I hear where you're coming from but it's tricky.

Tanya Dean [*dramaturg and academic, Facebook, 31 October 2015*]

Below are the two cents I offered on this issue.

There's been a lot of debate recently (and always) about the lack of representation of female artists in theatre programming. It is a very difficult challenge, both for female artists and the industry. I have my own thoughts on it, below. But I'll open by saying what I'm actually going to DO:

For the next year, I pledge to buy 1 ticket per month for a production by a female playwright. Each time I do, I'm going to tag it with #fairplayforwomen

If anyone would like to join me on this, then simply buy a ticket or two to productions by female playwrights or with female directors and post about it under #fairplayforwomen

It's simple; but it's also using our economic force to drive the conversation of equality in the arts, and it's actively supporting women artists.

So, here's the thoughts part:

I think there are three parts to this issue; programming is one of them, certainly. There has to be a will at the highest echelons of artistic influence to consider diversity and representation as integral to artistic integrity. To be fair, I don't think there's any theatre or company in Ireland which consciously programmes only male playwrights or directors. These institutions are also in an incredibly tricky balancing act between economic factors, artistic factors, and ethical factors when it comes to programming.

Do they programme the best play available to them? Do they programme the best play from within a certain demographic that's historically underrepresented? How to find the balance between the two? Will audiences attend? How to address the fact that the majority of extant plays considered classics (and therefore worthy, marketable, programmable, etc.) are written by men due to cultural inheritance?

Annie Ryan *[director, performer and Artistic Director of The Corn Exchange Theatre Company, Facebook, 31 October 2015]*

It is a bit humiliating when people ask me why I've never been asked to direct on the Abbey stage or the Gate. I have continually expressed a desire to engage. (Well, not so much at the Gate.) I don't really believe it's because of the work. I have had moments when I thought, oh, it's because I'm a woman, it's because I freak them out, I'm too demanding, I have strong opinions, I'm not from here, etc, etc … And, God knows, those might be the reasons. The trouble is if you internalise these notions and some part of you believes it, and it can discourage you into silence and apathy. I realised a few years ago that my yearly meetings on the top corridor, which I always enjoyed, were all instigated by me. So I stopped inviting myself and moved on to other conversations. When the big job came up, I considered applying because I feel so strongly that the only way to create anything good is to empower the artist to manifest their vision and to actually nurture them along the way, but the truth is, as pathetic as this sounds, that I didn't believe I would be listened to. I didn't feel welcome. Some part of myself let all those thoughts dampen my fire. Don't get me wrong, I really wouldn't want to run the place, but I didn't let myself engage in the conversation because I wasn't invited and I didn't feel it would be worth the effort. That's awful to admit. It makes me cringe – what am I, in high school? The point I'm trying to make reminds me of Panti's famous speech. It's about recognising the misogynistic tendencies in ourselves – the forces which hold us back from realising fully what we want for ourselves, in our lives, in our work. When you are not being invited to participate or when your ideas are being rejected (or indeed being used but transformed by other people!), it's important to reconnect with what you truly value and persevere to reignite your inner fire and get back to work.

Belinda McKeon [*writer, response to Annie Ryan, 31 October 2015*]
Annie, thanks for what you shared. My own experience as a writer under commission to the Abbey has not been the most cheering either. I mostly blame myself, but I have wondered a lot why it is that I can, e.g. write novels and feel absolutely driven to do that, whereas this commission has been a bit of a nightmare for me, not because I can't write the plays (they are plural – I workshopped and abandoned one, & am now on another), but because it has always felt pointless, because at a deep level that I don't quite understand I've never truly believed that anything is going to happen with it. I'm aware of the irrationality in that feeling, and it's not based on anything

the literary department have ever said to me, but it's been remarkably powerful for me. This is also humiliating for me to admit, and I can imagine it'll solicit scorn and cop-yourself-on from some quarters. I'm just sharing what's been a really paralysing, weird reality for me, usually a focused, fairly prolific writer, for going on six years now. (And maybe I've just shot myself in the foot by saying that, but if Annie Ryan, who's a hero of mine, can be so honest, then so I bloody can too.)

Caitríona McLaughlin [*theatre director, response to Lian Bell, 1 November 2015*]
In support of Lian and her wise words!
Until now I have delayed weighing in on the issue of the Abbey's Waking The Nation programming for 2016. I have hesitated because I have a vested interest, having directed my Abbey debut, Monsters Dinosaurs Ghosts, at the Peacock earlier this year, and hope to direct there again; it is my National Theatre. However, being female, in the first instance (there are other omissions that are equally relevant but whose inclusion here would dissipate from the thrust of Lian's original post), I am so disappointed by this programming that I feel compelled to say something. So my own personal homage to the women who fought for equality in 1916 is to stand up for what I believe in and vocalise my belief that we are still regularly in the background and that has to end here. The weight of the argument thus far has been around writers and there have been comments that things are not finished/ready etc. If we accept, and I don't, that there aren't any plays that are production ready by brilliant contemporary female writers, then what of the canonical work of great female dramatists of the past? Are they not ready? Firstly, this is not an excuse in my book: there are any number of great finished scripts by female writers (Irish and other) relevant to this time in our history; their exclusion on that score doesn't really hold water. And aside from all of that, for a moment, consider what is the excuse regarding directors; are we not as good or not as ready as our male colleagues?

Lian Bell

As you said, I don't for a moment think these imbalanced decisions are made maliciously–but the carelessness of the decision making is terrifying. From the programming to begin with, to making a promo video for the programme that features women speaking women's words, to failing to invite the only women writer in the programme to the launch, to the Abbey director having a casual half hour tweetback to address the issues. All these things pile up.

I have only ever been treated with respect and support by the Abbey Theatre staff when I've engaged with them professionally, and there is zero maliciousness in my own (passionate) call for change.

However, there is something deep seated within the institution that I cannot take anymore without saying something.

I just can't have these conversations again. I can't keep watching fantastic, talented women artists being overlooked. I can't allow my national theatre to be so skewed in its reflection of the nation. I can't believe that I have this much anger and frustration about it, but I do.

It is my deep respect for the institution that makes me feel so strongly that it has to be challenged. It's SO important for us all to hear each other's voices saying these things. It's SO important for them to listen to us (as I hope and believe they will).

Oonagh Murphy [*theatre director, Facebook, 1 November 2015*]

Very very late to this thread, but have been reading and really enjoying the discourse, and kudos to everyone who has stuck their head above the parapet. Although there are many brilliant women ahead of me who deserve the gig, from my perspective as a former resident assistant director at the Abbey, I too have banged my head quite a lot on that glass ceiling of the top corridor.

Notably, there were six consecutive female (resident/staff) assistant directors in a row over the past seven years (gender quotas look good in funding applications). Yet, the last AD to graduate to the main stage was male. After my time as AD, I was lucky enough to be given a small Peacock show, but after that, followed countless meetings where the offer for me to direct another show was pushed back again and again, until I too stopped sending emails to arrange meetings, and the meetings stopped. ADing is hugely rewarding but is ultimately an apprenticeship. It involves no real commitment to the ability of the individual. In the same way, the statistic offered forth that a huge majority of the participants of the New Playwrights Programme were female, smacks of the same tokenism.

The lack of critical self-reflection on the part of someone who largely engages with/employs women in these ways (paternalistic at best, patronising at worst) to see the gendered pattern therein, has long been something I've found amusing (because if I didn't laugh etc.). It's the same lack of self-reflection that allows him to make 'thems the breaks' type comments, and write female-authored work off without considering a personal taste.

Anne Clarke [*Producer of Landmark Productions, Facebook, 2 November 2015*]

As a woman who has been working in the theatre for over three decades now, I've seen a fair amount of discrimination – both overt and covert – in every area of the business. When I set up Landmark, I was told by a very senior – male! – writer that I would never make a producer. It took a long time before it wasn't simply assumed that, by virtue of being a woman, I would take the minutes at meetings. And, in truth, it took a long time for me to suppress the instinct to volunteer to do that. We internalise patterns of discrimination, and it's a hard thing to shake.

Having said that, I've also seen a huge number of ferociously talented women leading companies and making theatre on their own terms. Maybe it's because they haven't been able to tear down the doors to the big stages, but I'm thinking of Annie Ryan, Olwen Fouéré,

Lynne Parker, Deirdre Kinahan, Jo Mangan, Annabelle Comyn, Louise Lowe and Grace Dyas for example (in addition to Garry Hynes, who obviously did).

I think we need to empower female producers as well as female writers and other artists. We need to build their capacity, their confidence, their belief that their judgement is just as valid as that of their male counterparts. And that will help to get us further down the road.

A fire has been lit!

Ali White [*actor and writer, Facebook, 2 November 2015*]
The great Una Mullally[11]… says she's tired of banging this drum. (I know we're all looking forward to the day when we can put our big combined boots through it, throw petrol on it, and bung it on the bonfire.) But I'm glad she did. And I'm very glad all the mighty supporters of gender equality in the theatre have been speaking out so articulately, and often so movingly too: Lian Bell, Annie Ryan, Belinda McKeon, Noelle Brown, Olwen Fouéré, Abbie Spallen, Sarah Fitzgibbon, Gavin Kostick, Raymond Keane and many more. My own position in the whole thing is strange. My name is cited in these memos and the publicity fanfares—but I'm not really there. (In my own 'checking myself' way, I feel I don't deserve to be anyway, seeing as I've only ever written this one piece for the stage. But that's beside the point here isn't it..) Fiach tweets that he's sorry he hasn't any female playwrights in the next season. So.....I'm not a playwright then? And my play has become 'a specially commissioned monologue for children.' So......it's not a play? I'm just glad that the piece itself, isn't particularly about a female character. She happens to be female, but Mollser is very definitely an individual. I'm glad she's getting out there again. And until the TB gets her—she'll be kicking. We'll keep going.

Tríona Ní Dhuibhir [*General Manager of Dublin Theatre Festival, Facebook, 2 November 2015*]
I undertook a study of almost 200 Irish arts organisations in receipt of recurring funding from the Arts Council. I counted staff listed on websites and counted the number of women and men. If staff lists were not available online I

contacted organisations and asked them for staff gender breakdowns directly.

197 organisations across all art-forms are staffed by 1225 individuals – 430 are men and 795 are women – or 35% men and 65% women.

I then looked at the male/female ratio at CEO level. I found that 41% CEOs were men and 59% were women. I concluded that coming from an Ireland where many of our mothers had to leave their jobs on the day they got married – the arts sector wasn't doing too badly.

With a staff to leadership relationship – 65% women staff to 59% women CEOs – the situation seemed almost balanced.

I had a niggling feeling however. The figures were correct but the picture did not seem right. Something told me to follow the money.

I analysed the level of Arts Council funding of these arts organisations – looking at the percentages of public money controlled by CEOs who are men and by CEOs who are women. Therein lies the rub. My study showed that the 41% male CEOs are charged with 61% of funding and the 59% female CEOs are charged with 39% funding. At funding level, arguably power level, the relationship flips.

To put this more simply – for each €1 of public funding a woman CEO is charged with, her male counterpart is charged with €3.

When the issue of gender imbalance is tackled at power level – in the theatre sector this translates to programming level, there is a chance that the gender imbalance in programming can be addressed.

Brian Singleton *[Samuel Beckett Professor of Drama & Theatre at Trinity College Dublin, Twitter, 2 November 2015]*

@lianbell patriarchy does not see the masculine as a gender but as 'natural' and thus does not recognize gender as something that matters.

Lynne Parker [*Artistic Director of Rough Magic Theatre Company, Facebook, 3 November 2015*]

For as long as I can remember the most dynamic and interesting work in Irish theatre has been produced by independent companies, most of them led by women. Charabanc changed the nature of theatre in Northern Ireland, largely by shifting the perspective from which the story is told. Druid, The Corn Exchange, ANU, Prime Cut, HotForTheatre, TheEmergencyRoom, Landmark, WillFredd, THEATREclub, Pan Pan, Performance Corporation, Theatre Lovett, Then This, Rough Magic... The list goes on.

But sometimes we forget, because we create our own ground-rules, what the establishment looks like. And the establishment is still fundamentally male, to the detriment of everyone.

That powerful, female, subversive, creative energy – so evident now in the independent companies and artists – is the raw material of theatre. The Abbey ignores it at its peril.

Jimmy Fay [*Executive Producer of the Lyric Theatre, Belfast, Facebook, 3 November 2015*]

When this started a week ago, I thought I'm not getting involved in this. This I thought, is throwing bricks in glass houses. I don't programme the Abbey I don't need to defend or attack it. I've got my own programme(s) to launch soon enough. And I'm learning continuously how hard it is to program. The plays chosen by the Abbey I'm pretty certain were on merit. I'd read one of them David Ireland's Cyprus Avenue and it's excellent.

But it's 2016. It's a time of reflection and frankly interrogation. Those of us who feel we're cool, we're equal, we voted for marriage equality, we're down with the rights of men, of women, of children, of gender discrimination, of balance, of choice, of refugees, of travellers, of forgiveness, of self determination, of progressiveness, of hope, well, we may need to stand back and, in the words of one famous recent speech from the Abbey stage, we may need to "check" ourselves. Those of us who, unhesitatingly, call ourselves feminists may need to spend some time exploring how that words in action and what it means in deeds.

For example, costume designers, despite working continually long hours with casts & directors throughout the production process, get roughly 3/4 quarters down to a half or less of what set designers get. Is this, simple question, because costume design has historically more female creatives than men? Or is that rubbish? I don't think so. This debate is about exclusion and equality. And it's about addressing balance in pay, in visibility, and, in accountability.

It's been incredibly edifying and stimulating to see and read honest appraisals on the Facebook/Twitter feed from friends, colleagues and strangers and I hope this momentum grows and remains positive and progressive. #wakingthefeminists.

Willie White [*Director of Dublin Theatre Festival, Facebook, 3 November 2015*]
Equality concerns all of us as theatre makers and citizens and diversity is about more than just gender. #WakingTheFeminists

> **Ciaran O'Melia** [*designer*]
> For some reason this reads as a little 'Yeah, but... ' to me

> **Willie White**
> Not at all. I think the debate about representation should be widened. Theatre shouldn't be a special case where inequality is tolerable as it wouldn't be for citizens. Why stop at gender equality when looking at how equal our arts are?

> **Sarah Baxter** [*theatre and opera director*]
> Thanks for clarifying—also thought similar to Ciaran. It has to start somewhere though. Starting the conversation (and hopefully action on) gender equality and continuing on until equality and for all.

Vicky Featherstone [*Artistic Director of the Royal Court in London, and one of the three women directors in the Abbey's 2016 programme, Twitter, response to being tagged in the conversation, 5 November 2015*]:
Long overdue conversation. Only 1 play out of 6 by a man in the current @royalcourt season. It's not hard.

Oonagh Kearney [*writer and director, Facebook, 8 November 2015*]
Marian Larragy just sent me an email saying: 'I see that Waking the Feminist is planning a meeting on 12th Nov 2015. I am struck by the fact that the launch of the Contraception Action Programme was 12th November 1975 at Liberty Hall. For weeks beforehand, some of us who were in Irishwomen United screenprinted posters by Bernadette McAleevey, a single line outline of a pregnant woman – on butcherpaper/newspaper and then roamed around pasting them where we could. My proudest effort was on to the base of the Daniel O'Connell monument at the bottom of O'Connell Street. The meeting was oversubscribed and lots of people could not get in.'

Tara Furlong [*Company Stage Manager at the Abbey Theatre, Facebook, 9 November 2015*]
I love the Abbey. I'm deeply proud of it and of the role that I play there now. It feel[s] like [its] always been a part of my life. I'm deeply proud of the fact that though a bit of skill and a lot of luck I got a job there. I'm excited to see the changes that are ahead of all of us in theatre. I've been in the Abbey for almost 10 years and before that I was freelance for about the same length of time. Call me gullible but it's only in the past few years that I have recognised sexism for what it is. I can smell it a mile off now and have learnt for the most part to brush it off or at least try not to take it personally.
I try to tell my daughters … so that they can hone their sexist bullshit radars for later life. For years I was told that female directors were the worst to work with. That they were so demanding, so bitchy. I'm still waiting to meet this woman director that's so much more needy than the male directors I work with. For years the 'pushy' women I

worked with were labelled mad bitches and you'd stay in your box for fear of being tarred with the same brush. I'm sure that suited some people very well. I'm happy that my daughters won't face half of the same amount of this bullshit. It's depressing to think of how much harder half the population has to work. Let this signal an end to all of it and fairplay indeed to #wakingthefeminists #ilovetheabbey #itsahardauldstation

Aaron Monaghan [*actor and director, Facebook, 10 November 2015*]
I've been in London for the past while but I've been intently watching the remarkable events happening within the artistic community back home. I'm not particularly good on social media and I have to admit that both the Abbey's programme launch and the initial reaction to it entirely passed me by, and I came to the entire event typically late.
The first thing I noticed was the lovely and brilliant Charlotte McCurry talking about 'career math' over a week ago. So I quietly set about doing a little bit of career maths in my own head, dwelled on the curious conclusions of those calculations, then put it aside for the time being not quite knowing what to do with it. I silently and privately resolved to do what Tanya Dean decided to do, to buy a ticket to a play by a female playwright once a month, then quietly go about my business. Then I watched the flood of posts and updates populate my feed, beautifully passionate, incredibly articulate statements, sentiments that provoked anger and shame in me, that genuinely and sincerely opened my eyes just a little bit, but ultimately sentiments I have neither the insight nor the articulation to construct myself. So I said nothing.
Instead I made a quiet resolve, inspired by a speech made on the Abbey stage not so very long ago. I resolved to 'check myself'. I don't think I've ever been a victim of sexism or inequality, how can you be in such a tolerant and beautifully inclusive environment as the Irish theatrical community? But isn't that the way it works? You don't realise you're on an uneven playing field if you're not suffering the consequences of it. So I read post after

incredible post, fact after beleaguering fact, dwelled on each one, and opened my mind and my eyes a little bit more. Still I resolved to 'check myself', and said nothing.

I wanted to say something. But in truth I found I couldn't find anything worthwhile to say. I only had questions, or reactions, and once or twice I almost posted something, but would see a comment about men weighing in on the debate or not, whether we had a right to or not, and so I would retreat half in fear of causing some kind of offence to someone. So still I said nothing, and silently and privately echoed the comments of those posts which I agreed with. I cheered on Garry Hynes' brilliant and succinct letter to the Irish Times, and silently applauded two brilliant and personal posts by Brían F. O'Byrne and Donal O'Kelly, because they summed up more personally, from a male perspective, all the things I was feeling myself. But still, I didn't say anything.

But I keep reading all these incredible posts and facts and statements. These are posted by my colleagues. My mates. And they're hurting. And I never realised how badly they're hurting before. And when your mates are hurting, it kind of hurts. So I'm not sure it's not good enough just to quietly resolve to do things and say nothing. Saying nothing makes you complicit, and I don't want to be complicit in something that hurts people I love and admire and respect. The thing is, I still don't know what to do. But I do want my colleagues and my dear friends to know I stand fully and supportively behind them in midst of this extraordinary revolution.

Michael West [*writer, excerpts from Facebook, 10 November 2015*]

In these exciting times where everything seems possible, I've been reflecting on my own experience of sexism and marginalisation in the Arts. I understand that as the possessor of genes and chromosomes that confer dominant gender, ethnicity and sexual orientation, not to mention education, class and physical good fortune, the only thing I could do to enhance my chances of a production on the main stage of the Abbey would be to be dead.

...

In the last 25 years I have been commissioned (sometimes more than once) by 10 institutions – 9 run by men, as it happens, and two of which have had 7 different men running them over this time and no women. (By institutions I mean buildings in which performances occur, or Festivals which commandeer the use of buildings.) I have also written for 4 independent companies – by which I mean companies without buildings – 3 of which were run by men.

Of the 30 or so works commissioned by these bodies, four have not made it to the stage. Thems the breaks.

But I am still staggered to find that only one – ONE – company or institution run by a woman has ever produced my work in 25 years and I have only worked with one – ONE – female director on an original production in all that time.

I am of course immensely fortunate that this company is The Corn Exchange ... and that the director is Annie Ryan who is among the finest working anywhere in the world today. (I am as objectively certain of that as I am aware that I am objectively biased: Annie Ryan was also present when my mother married us and is one of the few people who can say the priest turned into her mother-in-law in the middle of the ceremony.)

I have also realised that all of the dozen or so shows I have done with The Corn Exchange were produced by women (including my sister, Kerry West, Jenny Huston, Jenny Jennings, Áine Beamish, Rachel Murray, Sarah Durcan and currently Lucy Ryan).

But if there's any truth in the idea that the work of a company led by women, produced by women and directed by women is treated even marginally less seriously or has its chances of touring and further life compromised in the smallest degree then even I, from my privileged position – of birth, but most of all of having worked with these remarkable colleagues – will have suffered.

And that is the simple truth of this matter:

Inequality hurts us all.[12]

Dee Roycroft *[actor and theatre-maker, Facebook, 11 November 2015]*

I have been glued to Facebook since Lian's original post at 13.53 on Oct 28. I quietly watched the twitter exchange with Fiach. I have read every post, and comment – by people I know and people I don't know. I've clenched my teeth, and shouted at the computer, turned it off, then turned it back on. I must have written and deleted over a hundred comments. I have cried. And cheered. And then shouted a bit more. Then cried again. I have welled up reading posts on buses, darts, and in the car on the school run. I keep writing and deleting even this. Because I find it hard to catch my breath, I find it hard to articulate. Because this has tapped into something long-hidden and deep-buried, something dark and twisty that for some reason I have trained myself not to think about, not to talk about. Something maybe to do with middle-age and motherhood, and being moved on. When did that happen? When did I let that happen? I wish I could be there tomorrow. I'm gutted to not be in the thick of it. To hear some of these amazing voices speak with such clarity, and blast these crazy glass citadels apart. Tear it down my friends! Tear it all down!! We can rebuild. I am so hopeful! I can smell Change in the air, and oh, is it sweet!

TWO

Gathering and Planning

Sonya Kelly [*actor and writer, Facebook, 1 November 2015*]
It has been an inspiring week on the internet.
I wonder if on Halloween night, I could have stopped one of the souls of 1916,
Floating through the ghouls and revellers and asked,
'Excuse me Mr. Connolly, how would you like to commemorate the Rising?'
I hope he might have said,
'By starting another.'

This chapter delves into the sheer frenzy in the run-up to a public meeting at the Abbey Theatre on 12 November 2015 – just two weeks on from the original online outcry on 28 October. The following is a collection of viewpoints of that time from several of the participants.

Producer Caroline Williams was in Berlin visiting family when she saw Lian Bell's first post and saw the social media storm brewing. On her return to Dublin, she emailed Lian and a couple of others who were commenting online. The email thread, initially small, grew hour by hour.

Caroline later recalled:

> I've always had a lot of respect for Lian. I have a cynicism about social media pile-ons, which can lead to a lot of outrage, but actually very little action. As theatre makers we were all connected to one degree or another. I knew I could bring in people that would trust me personally

in the way that I had that trust in Lian. And a physical meeting would be useful.

By the evening of Thursday, 5 November, a group of us were gathered in a room above Rough Magic's offices on South Great George's Street. It was just one week on from the first social media posts. Theatre offices in Ireland are never glamorous, and this was a very typical theatre office. Rough Magic was a very buzzy building, with a lot of comings and goings over its three cramped floors. It was a good spot for revolution. Central, adaptable, it had this dishevelled quality, but it was cold; it wasn't a comfortable building. We pulled a motley array of chairs together, and were packed in after work around a bockety table, two stories above the traffic and the Good World Chinese Restaurant.

Present along with Lian were: Anne Clarke, Caroline Williams, Dairne O'Sullivan, Loughlin Deegan, Lynne Parker, Maria Fleming, Gavin Kostick, Kate Ferris, Jane Daly, Jo Mangan, Siobhán Bourke, Sarah Durcan, and Tríona Ní Dhuibhir. Each one of us had got in touch with Lian over the past week to offer help and support. Anne, Lynne, Jane, Siobhán, and Loughlin had the most experience in dealing with official power structures, boards, and the politics of theatre, and their insights and guidance were hugely valuable.

We came from various personal and professional backgrounds. Each of us was taking a risk with our careers, and we each possessed particular and valuable skills. We were a mix of venue and festival managers, producers, stage managers, artistic directors, publicists, literary managers, designers, venue programmers; all at different stages of our careers, some working in organisations, some freelancers, and each of us was at this meeting in a personal capacity. Many of us had never worked together before this, and some had never even met. This unconventional gathering disrupted typical and traditional hierarchy in Irish theatre, merging artists and managers, and those central in the establishment with those more often on the periphery. As a set designer and independent arts manager, Lian straddled the worlds between freelance artists and organisations, which greatly helped build trust. She was widely recognised as an open and honest broker.

Producer Anne Clarke recalled:

> I didn't know Lian, but I saw her post. It chimed with me, and I posted about my experience of starting my own production company – Landmark – and being told by a renowned Irish male playwright that I wasn't up to it. It knocked my confidence and I carried that with me for a long time. I was concerned for Lian and what she'd unleashed

with all of this. She looked so slight, and this was a lot to carry on her shoulders.

Sarah Durcan chaired the meeting at Caroline Williams' suggestion, as they had recently worked together at Science Gallery International. Caroline reckoned that Sarah had what she called the 'radical but not conservative cool-headedness' for the situation. Sarah herself was not so sure.

Sarah recalled:

> The possibility of real change was tantalising, but equalled by the terror of the huge effort required to shift years of misogynist conditioning. I was also conscious that every feminist movement and progress splinters and backslides at some point. But right at that moment, we had strong intergenerational support and experience to draw on. I put aside my usual producer's caution – imagining everything that could go wrong and preparing to fix problem after problem – and I allowed myself to imagine *what if this works?*
>
> I opened the meeting: 'You know what we decide here around this table, if we get it right can have long term implications, so let's not fuck it up. But also be kind with ourselves – we're going to make mistakes, and that's ok. It's important that each one of us is free to say whatever we think, and to speak out in public. However this group has a collective responsibility to manage the message – our tone should be strong but respectful. How we do whatever we're going to do is just as important as what we do. These are our friends and colleagues so we should be careful. I also think that the form of the public meeting has to be something that no-one has ever seen before. We have to fully occupy the theatre, the stage, the story.'

Publicist Dairne O'Sullivan recalled:

> I got involved because I abhor boys' clubs, or any kind of club. I just thought the Abbey's programme was desperately unrepresentative, and it didn't reflect the Irish theatre that I loved. I looked around the room, there were a lot of people. I saw Anne Clarke there, I saw Sarah. It was a long time since I'd worked with Lian, and so I couldn't quite remember how she worked. But I just got a sense that there were people in this room who were going to be clear headed and productive. Seeing Anne there – it kind of galvanised me as well. Anne in particular had a lot to lose. I thought, well, if she feels strongly enough about it and is prepared to step up then I can too.

It would have been so easy to continue to personalise the whole thing and make it about Fiach, and it was very much leadership from Lian, Anne and Sarah that the initial protagonists were soon forgotten. We quickly moved past personalising our grievances and concerns and it became about the system, what was wrong with it, and how it all needs to change. I think that on the outside a lot of people would have said, 'oh, there's just a whole bunch of women sitting around bitching about men', and we didn't do that. It was very stringent.

Kate Ferris, lecturer in stage management and producer, recalled:

I'm a card-carrying feminist. Probably when my father told me at the age of seven that I couldn't be an altar girl, because I was born a girl and not a boy and the Pope said the girls don't belong on the altar. I think from that moment I was a feminist.

Lian is a good friend of mine. Caroline asked me to come to the meeting – Caroline and Allie [Caroline's partner] and I are also good friends – we all go sea-swimming. Caroline was such a linchpin. I'd been working in and around Rough Magic as I was starting out as a producer. One of Caroline's most brilliant things is to bring people together, and she is so smart, she knows the right people to be in the room. And because she always has such integrity, she was absolutely clear on the core message and the fundamental idea of what it was we were trying to do.

I'm such a practical thinking person – I'm a stage manager, I train stage managers – I can look at a problem and understand systems and what it is we need to do, and get it done. I lent my hand in the campaign, I just did what I knew I could do, which was to get stuck in and help with the organisational side of things.

At the meeting we discussed how the public was going to respond to all this? What was our relationship with the Abbey now? Is this about Fiach or is this about the broader sector? What were the board of the Abbey actually responsible for? For me, it was so new to listen to these conversations, but I knew that I could organise a gang of stage managers in about two hours and help with the technical and practical side. The first thing I did was take minutes for the meeting.

We all agreed at this initial meeting that structural systemic change was required. This change needed to start at the very top. It had to be about more than just one artistic director's programme choices for one year. This was about all of us, in all areas of theatre, across the country.

Lian remembers:

> A magical thing begins in that room that first evening: everyone quietly packs their ego away. It's something I've never seen before, and I don't imagine I'll see again. There's a pure selflessness of action that takes over for the following week; a collective understanding that this is more important than any single one of us, and that we have a responsibility to take the opportunity and do our best with it. And it's not just in this room. Everyone is working out what they can offer and simply getting on with it, even if it is nothing to do with what their 'real' job is (such as the theatre director Oonagh Murphy putting together the first #WakingTheFeminists website, which goes live the next day [6 November]). It's magical, potent, empowering. Everyone feels the responsibility, takes ownership, and does an incredible job.

After days of silence, Fiach Mac Conghail, Director of the Abbey, returned from his holidays on Friday, 6 November, and was interviewed by Sara Keating for the *Irish Times*:

> I deeply regret my intemperate reaction on Twitter. I said some incendiary things. This is the first opportunity since then that I have had to respond again. I regret my exclusions [in the programme] but I am eager to support and be part of the conversation. The reaction has made me question my own filters and the factors that influence my decisions. Is it time for gender blind reading? Is it time for quotas to be introduced, like in the political system?[1]

Also on Friday, 6 November, an open letter from Fiach appeared on the Abbey's website: 'To everyone taking part in the debate on #WakingtheNation #WakingTheFeminists':

> I regret the gender imbalance in our WAKING THE NATION programme for the significant year ahead. The fact that I haven't programmed a new play by a female playwright is not something I can defend.
>
> This experience has presented a professional challenge to me as a programmer and has made me question the filters and factors that influence my decision-making.
>
> I believe we have made improvements in advocating for and promoting female artists of all disciplines at the Abbey Theatre since 2005 but there is still a long way to go.
>
> I welcome the vigorous debate that has ensued since the announcement

of the WAKING THE NATION programme. I look forward to participating in an open and frank dialogue and offer the Abbey Theatre as a venue for this discussion. Our challenge now is how to address this imbalance both here at the Abbey Theatre and nationally in the arts community and beyond.

Preparations for a public meeting began at a pace. Organising an event of this scale, with this level of anticipation and visibility, in less than a week was absurd on every level. Producers ordinarily wouldn't even agree to organise a simple post-show discussion in that timeframe. Fortunately, as theatre professionals we were well used to making the improbable possible, often at short notice. It was a good thing we didn't quite know what we were getting ourselves into. But we love a challenge, and only this group of people with our particular skillsets could have pulled it off in these circumstances. It was the ultimate opening night deadline. Rage, solidarity, and determination drove us to put together a very public meeting that could turn out to be the most significant event of all our professional lives.

It happened to be the one time of the year (after the Dublin Theatre Festival and before the Christmas show rush) when there is a brief lull in the theatre calendar. Although most of us were still working solidly, we had just that little bit more capacity and time to get involved. Anything that could be shelved temporarily was shelved. We juggled our professional and personal obligations with spending every other minute working on the public meeting. Fear and adrenaline coursed through us, keeping us sharply focused. We didn't have time to think, we just had time to do. We had to rely on our instincts and professional experience, trust each other, move decisively, and at speed. We knew intuitively that this was serious and no one wanted to mess it up. The adage that constraints are good for creativity was about to be tested to its limits.

There was a lot involved in putting together an event like this. We had to decide on the form and content: who will speak, how many, how long the event will run, whether or not to have a questions and answers section at the end, who will run the ticketing of the event, will we pre-allocate tickets to certain people, or leave it wide open? We required a technical team to run the sound, lighting, and stage-manage the production so everyone would know where they needed to be. We needed a director and editor for the content as well as someone who would contact and confirm the speakers. Photographers, videographers, someone on social media to live tweet, sign language interpreters, childcare, some kind of visual identity, an event MC; the list grew as we talked things through. By our second group meeting on Saturday, 7 November, several individuals and theatre companies had each pledged €100 towards the cost of the event and Theatre Forum,[2] the members' resource organisation representing the performing arts, had agreed to cash flow and manage the finances.

After this Saturday planning meeting, Lynne had arranged for a quiet pint with the incoming directors of the Abbey, Graham McLaren and Neil Murray, who were in town for an Abbey board meeting. Lynne knew Neil, as did Kate Ferris, and they both invited Lian along. They met in a quiet pub on Capel Street, chosen because they were not likely to be spotted there as it was not a typical theatre pub. No one wanted to make it appear like the two men had some hand in what was being planned.

Lian recalled:

> It's my first pint in weeks, and I'm so tired I'm only just about able to sit on the bar stool. As we chat, over the shoulder of Neil, I see the door of the bar open and Fiach walks in with a friend. It's the first time I've seen him since this all blew up. He spots us, ignores us, and goes to the bar. There are a few awkward minutes, and then Graham gets up to invite him over. Apparently, Fiach jokingly tells him 'This town is too small for a conspiracy'. Fiach joins us, stays a few minutes, and was polite and diplomatic with his chats. But he doesn't look at me or address me once.

This particular story quickly grew legs, and became vastly exaggerated in its retelling amongst the gossipy parts of the theatre community, turning into a story about a fight breaking out between the outgoing and incoming directors. The women involved (Lian, Lynne, and Kate) were written out of even this story.

By Sunday, 8 November, we have a confirmed date for the meeting: Thursday, 12 November, just four days away. Caroline Williams quickly organised an online petition on Change.org calling on the board of the Abbey to lead the way in establishing equality for all women artists, and furthermore calling on all other theatre companies and festivals in receipt of public funding to follow suit.[3] It garnered 5,500 signatures in ten days. Articles appeared in both *The Sunday Times*[4] and *Sunday Business Post* on the 8 November. #WakingTheFeminists Gmail, Twitter, and Instagram accounts were set up.

On Monday, 9 November, the Abbey Board and Director released a statement on social media and on their website:

The Board and Director of the Abbey Theatre acknowledge that the 2016 programme does not represent gender equality.

The Board commits to work with the Director and new incoming Directors to develop a comprehensive policy and detailed plan to help address gender equality with the cooperation and input of the wider Irish theatre community.

The Board and Director of the Abbey Theatre have acknowledged and approved requests received for the Abbey auditorium to host a #WakingTheFeminists debate on Thursday, 12 November at 1pm.

Lynne Parker and Lian were invited onto one of the first episodes of the *Irish Times Women's Podcast*, which had recently been started by journalists Róisín Ingle and Kathy Sheridan. A few days of back and forth followed as the producers wanted to change the line up to include Fiach. This would be the first conversation between Fiach and anyone behind the #WakingTheFeminists movement, and Lian in particular was extremely uncomfortable with the idea:

> Fiach left messages on my phone when it was off and I was at work, asking to talk. I had no intention of talking to him because I was petrified of his powers of argument (he was a Senator after all) and I barely had a handle on what was going on. There would be no contest.
>
> I had a late evening ultra-condensed media coaching session over the phone with publicist Kerryann Conway, who I didn't know. Sarah had called her and handed her mobile to me. She gave me some practical tips and a general sense that I could feel more in control when dealing with the media than I had been so far. She told me that if I didn't want to do the podcast I could say no. This filled me with relief, and I did say no.

The final participants were Belinda McKeon, Dr Brenda Donohue, and journalist Fintan O'Toole; episode nine of the *Women's Podcast* was released on Monday, 9 November.[5]

Also on 9 November, more articles appeared in *The Guardian*,[6] *Irish Independent*, and online at *RTE.ie*, *The Journal*, *entertainment.ie*, and *US-Ireland Alliance*. Several preparation meetings were held that week, all in Rough Magic. The group split into smaller working groups spaced throughout the building: box office and ticketing, production, press, campaign objectives, and messaging. It was a frenzy of rapid-fire decision making.

Caroline Williams was laughing gleefully at it all. A feminist activist in Irish theatre since the 1990s, she had produced the festival 'There Are No Irish Women Playwrights', and had helped compile the contemporary theatre part of the 'women in the annex', volumes IV and V of the *Field Day Anthology of Irish Writing*.[7] After one of our late night meetings in Rough Magic, Kate Ferris commented to Caroline, 'I'm sure you've been waiting a while for this moment.' Caroline responded, 'Kate, I've been waiting 30 years for this stuff.'

Kate recalled:

> It's such a moment for me, because I respect Caroline as a theatre elder, and I realise that I'm slightly new to this world. But this was something that Caroline and a lot of women before us have been battling for decades. And I hadn't even heard about *Field Day* or any of the other previous things that have happened, because I'm quite new to Ireland, as I grew up and studied stage management in Australia.

Lian asked journalist and *Yes Equality* activist Una Mullally to meet with us and she joined a meeting on the evening of 9 November. Realising there were others like her who were vastly more experienced at running activist campaigns, having Una's counsel was enormously useful. It was a 20-minute download of golden advice. Una spoke to us about the 'feminist split' and the danger of in-fighting tearing any feminist group apart before it could achieve anything worthwhile. She warned us that all campaigns have peaks and troughs, times of high activity and public attention, and lulls where not much was happening and energy dissipates. She also warned us not to feed the trolls online. Then she introduced us to the glory of Slack, a free online messaging tool that stopped us from being overwhelmed by constant monster email threads. Although it took effort for us all to learn yet another technology platform quickly, moving communications to Slack turned out to be a sanity saver.

We survived that week on take-away and meals in Yamamori restaurant across the road from the Rough Magic offices. Caroline sometimes brought in big bowls of salads to feed us. There were a lot of typing cat memes doing the rounds. At this point we hadn't yet made the move to Slack, so we were using every method of communication going. Emails, texts, and posts flooded Lian's inbox. She continued to be amazing at being able to channel all of this in a respectful, compassionate, and completely non-egotistical way.

Sarah recounted:

> By Sunday my brain was in overdrive. I took myself to an early morning screening of *Suffragette* for a break. I couldn't switch off entirely – so I checked my phone and saw a message asking if we could provide childcare for the public meeting. I was upset that anyone felt they had

to ask permission to bring their child in the absence of alternative childcare. #WakingTheFeminists then put out a notice saying that parents are welcome to bring their children with them to the meeting.

I went home and wrote my closing speech. I had been thinking about my grandmother Kathleen Cameron who had died at 96 just a few months before – of what she had lost in never seeing herself or her life experiences reflected on stage or screen. I was thinking of what our granddaughters would inherit, and what bit of the struggle could we ease for them by taking action now. I was thinking of our place now in between these generations.

A Facebook post Lian made on the evening of Sunday, 9 November, four days before the public meeting, gives some indication of the furious pace of work:

Today we:
- finalised & published a mission statement
- distributed minutes from last night's meeting
- fancified and updated our website
- collated women's statement texts on the site (men pending)
- wrote press releases & a media strategy
- launched an online petition
- got our first 322 signatures
- started designing visual quotes for an instagram account
- got a gmail address & a twitter [sic] handle (@ WTFeminists)
- worked out how to use tweetdeck
- sent and read around 36,000 emails
- sorry, got our first 346 signatures
- got our first celeb endorsement (thanks Debra Messing!)
- did a phone interview for the Guardian
- had, what, 3 articles in the Sunday papers?
- got a production team & action plan together for Thursday
- made yet more FB & twitter friends
- tweeted & posted more great texts from theatre makers
- sorry, got our first 386 signatures
- got an indian takeaway (well, I did)
Take a bow: Sarah Durcan, Kate Ferris, Anne Clarke, Dairne O'Sullivan, Noelia Ruiz, Oonagh Murphy, Caroline Williams, Niamh Ní Chonchubhair & Lynne Parker
Anything/one else I'm missing out, ladies of the revolution?

Playwright and sometimes-graphic designer Kate Heffernan designed a series of badges to be handed out at the event, including one featuring Lady Gregory, the co-founder of the Abbey. One design quickly became our logo, and greatly added to the visual impact and subsequent reach of the campaign.

#WakingTheFeminists – Gregory & WTF   / / / / / / KATE HEFFERNAN

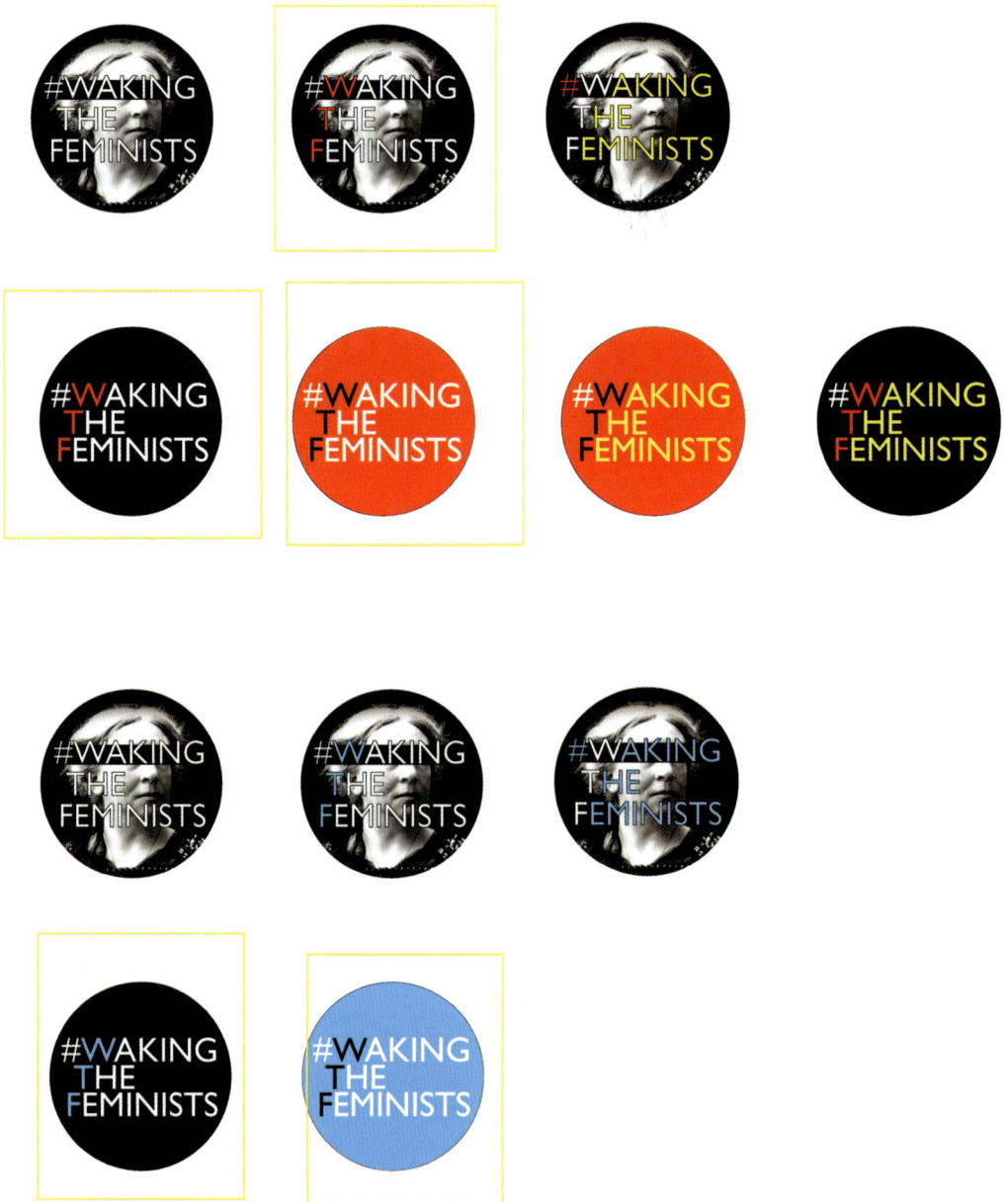

Image of badge designs by Kate Heffernan

Early on the morning of Tuesday, 10 November, two days before the public meeting, six of us met with Fiach for the first time in the café at the Westin Hotel on Westmoreland Street to brief him on our plans. We sat around him at a starched white linen-covered table drinking teas and coffees, while he ate his morning porridge. He congratulated us on the campaign, and offered to do all he could to make the public meeting run smoothly. There wasn't a lot to discuss as our production team and the Abbey's in-house staff were ironing out the practical details; it was more a terse courtesy chat. He offered, but we insisted on paying the bill.

Back in Rough Magic, Caroline and Lynne were busy editing the texts from the speakers. We decided there would be 30 speakers giving testimony on stage, all women, each speaking for about 90 seconds. This was pragmatically as many as we felt we could fit on the stage and within the running time constraints. Selecting the bulk of the speakers was straightforward enough; there had been a wealth of testimony posted on Facebook and Twitter over the previous week. Caroline edited several of the speeches for time and repetition, and Lynne tested them for cumulative running time. Maria Fleming and Tanya Dean helped recruit additional speakers, where they felt there were gaps in representation, background, and experience. They worked out a running order. Some women were not available to give testimony in person, so female actors were asked to speak their words for them.

We had put together a list of ticket 'holds' for key industry people at the event. This was an exceptionally short and strict list, as we wanted to release as many as possible to the public. We had announced online that there would be no charge for tickets, and that booking would open at 11am on Wednesday, 11 November, the day before the event. At 10.50am Lian tried frantically to get hold of Oonagh Murphy, who was due to make the ticket booking system live, but nobody had her phone number. Oonagh was stuck on a bus without internet. We were beginning to panic. We knew there was going to be significant demand, with people standing by their computers to book. Oonagh finally got a signal and was able to press go on the ticket release, only a minute late. Moments later we were booked out: over 400 tickets were snapped up within a record seven minutes. Now we had to think about a live relay of the event into the foyer of the Abbey where those who couldn't get a ticket could also congregate, and a live stream on Periscope so that people around the world could access it too.

At our final planning meeting the day before the event Anne Clarke said, 'I think we need a banner.'

Sarah: 'You're right, we need a banner.'

Who's going to do a banner at this short notice? Sarah remembered a design student, Molly O'Cathain, who would probably have access to necessary supplies. She called her straight away, and thankfully she was able to do it.

'How big should it be?' Molly asked.

'As big as you can manage!'

Molly hightailed it to Ikea to buy canvas and with the help of two friends and fellow designers, Liadain Kaminska and John Gunning, gaffer taped the letters, and rolled over it all with black paint, the kind you use to paint theatre floors. They worked late into the night and then the next morning she got two broom handles, sewed pockets for them, and the banner was ready to go. It was brilliantly DIY. The banner became one of the most iconic artefacts of #WakingTheFeminists, and is now preserved in the collection of the National Museum.

At 11.30pm the night before the event we were still in the Rough Magic offices. Stickers were being printed for the organisers and speakers to wear so everyone would be easily identifiable. The event running order had just been finalised. It had taken an epic effort, but we were ready.

Lisa Tierney Keogh, Meryl Streep, Christine Baranski, and Laoisa Sexton

THREE

Public Meeting at the Abbey Theatre

This chapter takes you through the day of the public meeting in the Abbey on Thursday, 12 November 2015. This was an unprecedented meeting in the history of the Abbey: the building, the heart of the state's cultural identity, was taken over by people protesting the Abbey's own programming, critiquing its work and the wider theatre community from its own main stage.

Overnight, media interest in #WakingTheFeminists had hit the stratosphere when Lisa Tierney Keogh posted a photograph on Twitter with Meryl Streep and Christine Baranksi holding a message of support written on a napkin. What had seemed like a little theatre tiff exploded out of the arts pages and into the main news, and within hours every news outlet in town was clamouring for interviews and comment from the #WakingTheFeminists organisers. The producer rang from RTÉ's *Morning Ireland*, and the national broadcaster's biggest morning news radio show. They wanted a spokesperson live in studio first thing that morning before the public meeting. Everyone was exhausted and no one jumped at doing it. At best, any media experience most of us had in the past was arranging for someone else to go and speak to an arts programme about a forthcoming show, or the odd local radio interview. Sarah Durcan volunteered, and Dairne O'Sullivan insisted on accompanying her out to RTÉ for moral support. Sarah and Dairne sat in the green room just outside the studio, Sarah holding a page of notes to help her respond to any questions. She was running through them with Dairne when Leo Varadkar, Minister for Health (later Taoiseach, the Irish Prime Minister) arrived with an assistant. Sarah took out her phone and showed him the Meryl Streep 'I support women in Irish theatre' tweet and explained why we were there, the issue with the gender imbalance in theatre, and asked him for his support. He responded that 'surely it's a matter of picking the best plays on merit'. He didn't think he should get involved.

Sarah:

> In my body I feel as if I'm constantly on the verge of a heart attack, I can feel my pulse thundering in my ears 24/7. I hadn't slept. Dairne is so kind and helps keep me calm.
>
> Áine Lawlor grills me on air. I do not rise to the bait of criticising Fiach. Catching my breath afterwards, I spot a detailed thread on Reddit accusing me of not being able to have the numbers or name a long list of female writers. Who has time to write long critical threads on Reddit at this hour of the morning, I wonder. I think we're going to need some research here to back this up. I pre-record a quick spot for the One O'Clock News, and hop in a taxi with Dairne to the Abbey.
>
> The organising team started arriving at the Abbey when it opened at 10am. Along with Kate Heffernan's badges, we wore simple printed labels to identify us as #WakingTheFeminists.

Maria Fleming recalled:

> I'm one of the first to arrive at the Abbey and I bump into Fiach going up the stairs where we're gathering pre-meeting and he says, 'Oh, good luck today'. And I say, 'Thanks very much and the same to you. Best wishes for today, I hope for all of us it goes well.'
>
> The staff at the Abbey have been brilliant all week – super helpful in accommodating what we need.

The influential writer Anne Devlin travelled on the train from Belfast to Dublin. She didn't have a ticket to the event but came anyway. As photographers gathered outside the Abbey, one of them, Fiona Morgan, was testing a group shot of the organisers and accidentally caught the moment when Anne was greeted by stage manager Margarita Corscadden as we beamed down from the window above. Photojournalist and press photographer wrangler for the day, Kate Horgan, recognised Anne and her importance and luckily stopped Fiona from deleting the image. A few days previously Anne had sent Lian a note: 'Thank you for doing this. I always thought it was my fault', demonstrating yet again a woman taking on responsibility for a perceived failure that was systemic, not personal.

Fiona Morgan took a photograph of most of the organisers upstairs in the Abbey, standing in front of the only two portraits of women in the foyer:

Playright Anne Devlin approaches the entrance to the Abbey as #WakingTheFeminists organisers look on. Photo: Fiona Morgan

Many of those who put together the first public meeting in record time. Front row from left: Aisling O'Brien, Niamh Ní Chonchubair, Noelia Ruiz, Róise Goan, Gina Moxley, Lian Bell, Maria Fleming, Anne Clarke, Lynne Parker, Siobhán Bourke. Second row from left: Aoife White, Amy O'Hanlon, Yvonne O'Reilly, Tanya Dean, Sarah Durcan, Jen Coppinger, Irma McLoughlin, Claire O'Neill, Kate Ferris, Oonagh Murphy, Tríona Ní Dhuibhir. Back row: Jane Daly, Cian O'Brien, Caroline Williams, Dairne O'Sullivan, Christine Monk, Fiona Keller, Anna Walsh. Photo: Fiona Morgan

Annie Horniman,[1] the founding patron of the Abbey, and actor and activist Máire nic Shiubhlaigh.[2]

The #WakingTheFeminists team hit the ground running: sorting tickets, setting up backstage, organising lighting cues, checking sound, and gathering speakers in the green room. We had to be super strict on timing. The meeting could not start late or run over as there was another show due on stage (titled *The Forgotten,* ironically) that evening. Thankfully that show did not have a set, so the stage was empty, which worked well with our bare-bones aesthetic. The production team had just 15 minutes to get into and set up the auditorium and stage – an unheard of time limitation in theatre. The simplest of get-ins can take at least a day, and a long day at that. While Kate Ferris, production manager Rob Furey, and the stage managers were working some kind of magic to sort the production side of things out in record time, Aisling O'Brien, FRINGE LAB Coordinator at Dublin Fringe Festival, and freelance producer Jen Coppinger were preparing front of house. Technical support on the day for the Abbey was provided by Tara Furlong, Lisa Farrelly, Anne Kyle, Kevin McFadden, and Andy Keogh. Assistant stage manager (ASM) volunteers on the day were Aaron Kennedy, Margarita Corscadden, Fiona Keller, Clive Welsh, Lisa Kearns, Lisa Krugel, Fodhla O'Brien, and Sarah Purcell, with Lisa Mahony and Caroline O'Leary as crew. It was like a military operation. Free badges, sign language interpreters, petition, childcare, live relay into the foyer from the stage, disability access, photographers, videographers, online livestream, and as diverse a range of female voices as we could muster – we'd tried to think of it all. By noon the entrance and foyer areas were jammed. First up was the photoshoot and press call outside the front of the building.

Dairne:

> It was sort of divide and conquer between myself and Christine Monk. She managed the crowd, walking around with a megaphone we'd got from Waltons music shop, shouting at everyone to get in line. And I managed the photographers. Everyone was there: there was the *Indo* [*Irish Independent*], the *Irish Times*, the Press Association – I just couldn't get over the level of interest. The Abbey asked Ros Kavanagh to take photographs on the day, and Lian's sister Kate Horgan was also wrangling press photographers for us. Sinéad Crowley from *RTÉ News* arrived with a camera crew to interview folks in the foyer before the meeting, as did a crew from the *Irish Times*. Paula Geraghty[3] and Jamie Tanner videoed the meeting for #WakingTheFeminists – there were a lot of cameras everywhere.

Kate Ferris, Christine Monk, and photographers. Photo: Ros Kavanagh

(above) Dairne O'Sullivan helps wrangle the crowd. Kate O'Toole holds an 'Eastrogen Rising' sign. Photo Ros Kavanagh

(below) Getting in place for the photo call, Maeve Stone, Mary Duffin, Janet Moran, baby Ben, Dr Tanya Dean. Photo: Ros Kavanagh

Kate Ferris:

> Janet Moran had suggested the photographer Fiona Morgan, and as I also know her, I'd asked her to be our official photographer on the day. I reckon that there won't be time for the speakers to do the photograph at 12.15pm and also make it backstage in time for the start of the event at 1pm, and I tell this to Anne Clarke. Anne relays this to Christine Monk, and Christine comes over to me, gives me one long stare, and with that, all the speakers make it into the photograph, and also get backstage in time.

Fiona Morgan was up an a-frame ladder on the street across from the Abbey to take photographs. The guards were struggling with the traffic control on Marlborough Street as there was such a huge turnout. Cars started beeping their horns. Anne Clarke was annoyed that, despite our best plans and requests, there were still bikes chained out front in our way, but in the end there was such a massive turnout, the crowd hid them.

Sarah:

> The place is giddy – the vast energy released when long silence is broken.
> As I'm coming out the stage door and heading towards the front of the building, I'm confronted with a large crowd of chatting, laughing, hugging women, milling about. We're waiting for the banner to arrive and Molly O'Cathain is running late. She cycles up with a banner way bigger than anything I had imagined – pretty much the entire width of the Abbey portico, and brilliantly stark and homemade in black and white – we are ready for the photograph.
> I encourage two well meaning male actors to get out of the photo. While we appreciate their support – there's an important political point of visibility and representation to be made in this photo.

Maria:

> [Writer] Rosaleen McDonagh had said she wasn't confident of her voice, so I put myself forward to liaise with Rosaleen and be her voice. Then there was the awful realisation that on top of everything else that was wrong in the Abbey, in order to get Rosaleen on stage she was going to have to go through the loading bay. The crew at the Abbey have purpose-built a ramp up to the scene dock, where normally trucks would load-in theatre sets. She won't be able to sit in the green room where we were arranging everybody because there was no access. So

Smiling women, hands in the air. Photo: Ros Kavanagh

I was kind of isolated from the larger group on the day. I've arranged to meet Rosaleen outside. It still upsets me slightly because I'm not in the photograph, and Rosaleen is because I'm over waiting for her by her ramp, getting worried that she won't be able to get through the hordes of people! And there she is hopping in the photograph!

Alongside Aisling O'Brien and Jen Coppinger, Cian O'Brien and Loughlin Deegan distributed the tickets. As heads of their respective organisations, Cian and Loughlin would not normally be on the ticket desk for events. Kate Heffernan's #WakingTheFeminists badges were handed out to all the audience in the foyer, and abortion rights campaigners were also handing out free badges. Of course lots of people, like Anne Devlin, turned up without tickets hoping to get in. A few lucky people did, including Anne. It was a total scramble to get everyone with tickets seated. Dairne also managed to get a few extra press people seated. Everyone else had to watch the live relay in the foyer. Project Arts Centre also had a livestream going so any overflow of people without tickets could gather there. In London, film director Oonagh Kearney and actor Kathy Rose O'Brien had a livestream event organised at the Unicorn Theatre.

At 1pm it was time to start. 30 empty chairs filled the stage.

Sarah recalls calming herself before going on stage:

'Breathe. Chin down. Plant your feet, and square off your hips.'
I repeated this over and over to calm myself as I paced the upstairs

Photocall at the Abbey, with Pom Boyd holding a WTF? poster. Photo: Ros Kavanagh

foyer, drumming my closing speech into my body, and trying to control the adrenaline coursing through me. As a strictly behind-the-scenes person, my memory grasped at any fragment of advice from my previous theatre producing days, recalling Annie Ryan of The Corn Exchange's constant refrain in workshops: 'plant your feet and square off your hips', as she brought actors into their physical bodies to explore emotion, expression, story. I'd no time for consultation or rehearsal beforehand, so this mantra was all I had. Minutes later, as I'm standing in the wings beside Lian with a stopwatch and my speech in my hand, she turned and said, 'This is the biggest thing we will ever do.' I nod back, it's not doing my nerves much good.

The stage manager Margarita Corscadden practically pushed us onto the stage. As we entered from stage left, Senator Ivana Bacik, who co-chaired with me, entered from stage right. Between us on the stage are 30 empty chairs, with two podiums on either side flanked by #WakingTheFeminists pull-up banners. As Lian began her speech, I took a quick photo behind her looking out into the auditorium, as a wall of women and men rose to cheer her in an instantaneous standing ovation.

Lian read her opening speech, which started:

'Hello. Welcome to *our* national theatre.
    Two weeks ago I started posting my thoughts online about gender

Derbhle Crotty, Cathy Belton, and Sarah Jane Scaife onstage during the public meeting. Photo: Fiona Morgan

equality because I was tired of quiet conversations in corners. I wanted the conversation to be louder, and centre stage. I didn't realise I had this much anger and frustration about the situation, but apparently I do. Apparently we all do.

For the past two weeks I've been listening to everything you've been saying. While passing on your extraordinary posts, your comments and testimonies via social media, I've been deeply moved and deeply angry. We can't keep watching talented women artists being overlooked. We can't allow audiences to be given only half of what is, after all, their story.

This is what has been happening. This is what we have let slide. Two weeks ago I sat alone at my laptop feeling angry and thought – Fuck it. Press send.

I didn't expect much to happen. But here we are.'

Later, Lian recalled the moment:

After reading this speech and the campaign objectives, I sat down to overwhelming applause. Throughout the next two hours I gripped the edges of my seat, willing myself not to fall off or cry with emotion and exhaustion. I hadn't had a chance to eat anything all morning.

Actor and writer Amy Conroy opened the testimonies. One by one the speakers followed her, entering from alternate sides of the stage, reading their text, and then taking a seat beside the previous speaker, until the stage was full. Amanda Coogan and Caroline O'Leary alternated as Irish Sign Language interpreters. This was the biggest number of women, as well as the first wheelchair user, gathered on the stage of the Abbey in its history; a visual and political statement in itself. They included actors, producers, designers, directors, dramaturgs, and writers.

For those of us used to only working behind the scenes or sitting in the audience, it was terrifying being out front, and while the performers in the group may have been well used to being on stage, they usually inhabit a role performing someone else's words, not their own. Most performers dislike speaking as themselves in public. It's a risk to say what we really think. The testimonies read that day were of course about the Abbey and Irish theatre as a whole, but they were also designed to encapsulate a wide spectrum of women's experience and marginalisation in Irish society including bodily autonomy, gender–based violence, disability, Traveller and LGBTQI+ rights, class discrimination, and racism. We hoped there would be power in numbers, in this chorus of righteous criticism, but we didn't know how it would be received or interpreted. There were no rehearsals or previews for this opening night. Everyone was nervous. We willed each other on, digging our nails into our palms. It was imperative that nobody started to cry; if one person broke down it could lead to a cascade of emotion, and we felt we had to keep it together. Despite our exhortations not to clap until everyone had spoken, so as to not overrun our time limit, there was rapturous applause and shouts after each speaker. The audience was with us, and we felt their enthusiastic support rolling over us. We wanted to occupy that stage so fully, for our words to scorch into the building's fabric, so that this day would leave a permanent mark. All that had gone before in terms of this desperate inequity would no longer be acceptable or tolerated.

After the testimonies concluded, Ivana Bacik moderated statements from the audience. We were determined for this not to turn into a question and answer session, and each speaker was told to keep it very short so we could have as many statements as possible. Many important statements and additions to what had been said on the stage were heard from the floor. Fiach Mac Conghail was given an opportunity to respond on behalf of the Abbey; his speech in full can be found in the next chapter of this book.

Sarah recalled her reaction to Fiach's words:

> As I was listening to Fiach, he made a comment that instead of thinking about female representation, 'I was thinking about war stories, about poverty, about housing, about disenfranchisement, I was thinking about the Middle East, I was thinking about Northern Ireland.' I

The audience at the first public meeting. Photo: Fiona Morgan

couldn't help but think that women too are affected by all of these things, and have something important to say about them. They are not inherently male narratives.

After thanking the Abbey, Rough Magic for their support over the past weeks, and all those who spoke, I continued:

> How can we in the arts interrogate and reflect society with integrity, if we do not hold our own leaders to account and interrogate our own practices?
>
> This is also just the start of discussion on the solutions. We all have more work to do to achieve full equality, inclusion and diversity in theatre. We will continue that work, together, with respect and honesty.
>
> In this national theatre, funded by a woman,[4] co-founded by a woman, and with a mighty Queen charging forth on its logo, this call goes out from this stage, to every stage, to the leadership of all theatres and arts organisations. We must look at our programming practices, and beyond that look at our commissioning and our marketing and our pay and contracting and employment structures, look at everything we do and root out this blight of inequality.
>
> Those three women are not spinning in their graves – their wake is over – today they are rising with us. Listen up: we are all ready for you. Get ready for us. *Now*. It's just time for some *Respect*.

Speakers celebrating at the end of the first public meeting. Photo: Fiona Morgan

Cue the music. Aretha Franklin's voice singing 'Respect' began to fill the auditorium as the audience erupted into applause and jumped to their feet. Then the dancing began and it was joyous.

Thanks to our exceptional organising, the meeting ran bang on time. Afterwards, Noelia Ruiz, who had organised the live stream, found that we had 1.8k live viewers from across Europe and around the world, as far as Sydney, Washington, and Bangkok. Many of these would have been groups, so the viewer numbers were likely much higher. We also found out afterwards that, mid-way through the event, due to such an unusually high volume of engagement, Twitter had suspended our account. One of our live tweeters, Niamh Ní Conchubhair, thankfully knew someone who knew someone. She moved like lightning and the suspension was lifted.

We got a glimpse of the enormity of what we had all just pulled off; the depth of feeling, emotion, and demand for change was far bigger than we even realised in the run-up. After the meeting concluded a wave of euphoria and exhaustion hit us. Backstage in the green room we ate cake and jelly shots made by Gavin Kostick to keep our energy up. It was just after 3pm.

Sarah recalled:

> Speaking to some other high-powered male colleagues afterwards in the foyer, I saw something different in their eyes, a puzzlement, a faltering in their usual super-assured stance. It's the look of someone

66

who has seen their power in the world turn upside down. The game that was usually theirs, the rules in their favour – all suddenly unrecognisable. For one brief moment they don't know the rules, they don't even know the game. They were now in our game, our rules, our story.

In the Abbey foyer, Sinéad Crowley, Arts and Media Correspondent for RTÉ News, asked Dairne to find a woman to interview for television. Dairne asked Lian whether she would go on the *Six One*. Lian didn't own a television and didn't know what 'the Six One' was. Dairne had to explain: *Six One News* was the main evening news programme of our national broadcaster. Neither Lian nor anyone else wanted to do it. Those of us who were familiar with the *Six One* felt daunted and unprepared for an impromptu live news appearance. It was highly unusual, if not unprecedented, that someone from the arts would be interviewed live in–studio like this. When Dairne told Sinéad this, Sinéad, in friendly exasperation said: 'You know, if I asked a room of men did they want to be on the *Six One News*, every hand would go up!' She was right of course; we were all media shy, and not used to the arts being a leading story on the national news. In the end Deirdre Kinahan, playwright and member of the board of the Abbey, volunteered to be interviewed by Bryan Dobson on the *Six One*. Dairne went with her, going to RTÉ for the second time that day.

Dairne recalled:

> Deirdre and I were to get a taxi back from RTÉ. Bryan Dobson offered us a lift, it was really sweet actually. I was just so tired I couldn't talk. I sat in the backseat and Deirdre and Bryan sat up front. They're sitting there and chatting away, and I felt like a tired little girl being out late with her parents, while they're having this very grown up conversation in the front.

It took Lian almost an hour to get from the stage to the front door of the Abbey with so many people wanting to talk to her. Almost at the point of collapse, she went straight home and slept for 12 hours with a fever. Meanwhile, many of the speakers and organisers had decamped to Wynn's Hotel[5] on Abbey Street for chats, tea, sandwiches, and drinks. Much of the fun and impact of theatre is in dissecting it post–show with friends; it's a social activity, not just consumption of art. In Wynn's we watched Deirdre on the big TV in the lounge, still giddy with the events of the day. We discussed bias training, reading groups, how to bring men on board, and how to go about uncovering and reevaluating existing overlooked plays; the invisible canon. So many ideas bubbled up over tea and pints. The high energy of the day shifted into a desire to do more, and the seeds of a campaign began to form. Most of us were wrung out by 7pm and went home; we were not done with our meetings, but right at that moment all we needed was sleep.

(above) Lian Bell in the foyer of the Abbey just before speaking at the first public meeting. In the background are portraits of playwrights Sebastian Barry, Thomas Kilroy, and Tom MacIntyre, painted by Mick O'Dea and Colin Davidson. Photo: Kate Ferris

(below) Supporters without tickets listen to live audio of the public meeting being relayed into the foyer of the Abbey. Photo: Kate Ferris

FOUR

Speeches from the Public Meeting

The speeches are reproduced here in running order.

Ivana Bacik, *Senator for Trinity College Dublin*

It gives me great pleasure to welcome you all here today for this hugely important and timely event, #WakingTheFeminists. I'm very honoured to have been invited to Chair the event along with Sarah Durcan. I want to thank the organisers for all the hard work they've done in putting this event together so quickly and to thank the Abbey Theatre for hosting us, and thanks, of course, to all of you for coming.

It's a very fitting venue – the auditorium of our National Theatre where so many historic events have taken place. And of course it was the launch of the Abbey programme that has served as the catalyst for this discussion. It has sparked off this discussion, this debate and this highlighting of the lack of gender balance in the arts, and more generally, in women's invisibility in the public sphere and in public life. I know that today's event is going to be a very positive and a very constructive contribution to the debate and the need to ensure that we will address the issue of women's invisibility in our public life, women's exclusion from so much of our public life, from politics and so many other areas. We will be talking more about that later.

But first, I just want to give you the running order for today.

After the opening statements from Lian Bell and Sarah Durcan, we will hear a number of contributions from women across the spectrum of theatre in Ireland. Some of these were written for today. Some are based on statements that have already appeared in social and other media.

After this, we will invite people from the audience to make contributions. This isn't a Q&A, but we want to hear your thoughts and we want your input into today's important event. I will be moderating the contributions and just so you know we will have a strict time limit of 90 seconds each so that the maximum number of people can be heard.

We have wonderful signers here who will be doing some sign interpretation. I'm going to try and speak more slowly and clearly as I know all of you will too. After the contributions from the floor, the Abbey will then make a statement on behalf of the Board and management, and I'm really glad we have that input. Then we will have our guest speaker Lucy Kerbel who will tell us about her experience in the advancement of gender equality in the theatre in Britain, after which Sarah and I will give a short summing up.

We'll be finished by three o'clock and I look forward to what promises to be a hugely positive, important and lively discussion.

Lian Bell, *set designer and arts manager*

Hello. Welcome to our national theatre. My name is Lian Bell.

Two weeks ago I started posting my thoughts online about gender equality because I was tired of quiet conversations in corners. I wanted the conversation to be louder, and centre stage. I didn't realise I had this much anger and frustration about the situation, but apparently I do. Apparently we all do.

For the past two weeks I've been listening to everything you've been saying. While passing on your extraordinary posts, your comments and testimonies via social media, I've been deeply moved and deeply angry. We can't keep watching talented women artists being overlooked. We can't allow audiences to be given only half of what is, after all, their story.

This is what has been happening.

This is what we have let slide.

Two weeks ago I sat alone at my laptop feeling angry and thought – Fuck it. Press send.

I didn't expect much to happen. But here we are.

I've been asked to read out our mission statement, which is also at the heart of an online petition – launched on Sunday night and currently with 3,600 signatures and counting.

We call on the Abbey as our national theatre to lead the way in establishing equality for women artists. Our three campaign objectives are:

- A sustained policy for inclusion with action plan and measurable results
- Championing and equal advancement of women artists
- Economic parity for all working in the theatre

Thank you.

Amy Conroy, *actor and writer*

This may sound a little preposterous, a little outrageous but bear with me, it's all true.

'No', you'll gasp, 'it can't be', 'but it's 2015.'

Earlier this year I was bombarded with images, advertising campaigns, politicians, columnists, taxi drivers, bus drivers, priests, strangers, and acquaintances ... sorry ex-acquaintances, all telling me in no uncertain terms, that I am not equal. That I am not worth what they are worth. That my humanity, my dignity, my rights are not as important as theirs.

I mean they had no problem with me personally, they mentioned that I had great taste in hoodies and sneakers – they seemed to have a problem with me theoretically. A problem buried deep in their marrow, something they didn't know was there until they had to think about it.

'I mean I'm not homophobic but ... But.'

There are no 'buts'. You either are or you are not. You believe in equality or you do not. It's very simple.

During the marriage equality campaign, I attended a most moving and powerful afternoon in this very building, on this very stage. Fuelled solely by the desire to do something, to do anything to help. To do, and to be seen to do what is right, to cherish all our children equally.

This room filled to capacity, this our national theatre consolidating yet again its place and its importance as the voice of the people.

Our national theatre, recognising its weight and placing it on the right side of history.

It moved me to tears and it filled me with pride, as an artist, as a human being.

It was an imploring, an advocating, and a very noble call[1], shouting 'we will not accept anything less than equality. No ifs. No ands. No buts.

It is 2015.

I want to hear that same call reverberate through this building and cherish all our artists equally.

No ifs. No ands. No buts.

Sarah Jane Scaife, *director*

The issue at the Abbey at the moment is far bigger than a badly thought-out programme for 2016. It is reflective of women's socio-historical placing within the Constitution itself. This side-lining of women within the family and the home needs to be interrogated and addressed through our art and of course through a changing institutional and governmental culture. The old boy's club has operated in the theatre and in politics for years in Ireland; as women, we have come to recognise it very well. Many of us who couldn't compromise or keep our mouths shut went outside the institutions and made theatre wherever we could.

I can think of many female artists at the moment, working outside of the institutions and architectural frameworks of what has hitherto been accepted as the domain of 'theatre'. Whilst I don't condone the exclusion, the current expression of it should be seen as a good thing in many ways; we need to shake up the whole notion of what is understood by 'theatre': who makes it and for whom?

We need to think of the National Theatre as being more than the architecture of its present expression or even location. It should be seen as the national expression of its people, inside or outside the building itself. Maybe being on the main stage is not the goal, but to be commissioned and acknowledged as artists worthy of interrogating our nation's past, to speak to the people of Ireland, not just those who come in the door of the building is and should be our right.

It is not too late to bring these voices into the conversation, pragmatically and theoretically. Some very exciting theatre could be created through this very vital discussion. That is why we create theatre in the first place, to interrogate our place in the world, our relationship with those we live with and hopefully find a new sympathetic system that we can live by.

Caitríona McLaughlin. Photo: Fiona Morgan

Caitríona McLaughlin, *director*

As a director, I often say to actors I've worked with, 'drop me a line just to say hello, and remind me you are here', because seeing so many actors, in different places, sometimes I forget about people, even if they're perfect for a part. In fact, it's happened so often that I started to keep a list of actors' names; it seems only fair I take on that responsibility and of course ultimately it makes my work better. And really that's my point today: being fair takes work. It takes an active engagement in looking around to notice who is missing and doing something about it. We have all been careless for too long, in fact forever. We have all let this happen, and we all need to end it, here, now, today.

I believed I could work in theatre because I saw myself in the work of Frank McGuinness and Brian Friel. Because of them I knew I had a voice and a place in theatre and for that I'm eternally grateful. But they only tell half of the story. It's no longer enough to be 'given' a voice anymore. I cannot continue to let them speak for me.

I am here today to use my own voice, and to say it's now time to hear all those other stories; from the streets, from the pubs, from the workplace, from our living rooms; voices that are tender, questioning, quizzical, full of wonder; voices that are dark, probing, bitter; voices that are bright, curious, sceptical. They are joyous, proud, defiant voices; they are sensual, and they are raging. They are the voices of half of this nation, and most of this audience, and they can not be muted or ventriloquised anymore.

It's time to hear them, unmediated and unqualified; it's time to hear them in all their righteous fury and their terrible beauty. Lads, it's time to listen. Ladies, it's time to speak up.

Belinda McKeon, *writer*
read by Cathy Belton, *actor*

Is this our moment? Yes and no. Yes because it's undeniably a moment – look around you. I can feel the atmosphere from 3,000 miles away. I am so proud of you all and I am so inspired – and grateful. For what it's worth, I am WRITING MY PLAY![2]

But no: *not* a moment … because this is so much more than a moment. This is a sea change. This has to be. From this point on, we think differently, we act differently – all of us. We do this together. A rising tide lifts all boats.

Rosaleen McDonagh, *writer*
read by Maria Fleming, *producer*

As a playwright from a minority ethnic group that lives and works in a country that has yet to recognise my ethnic status as a Traveller woman officially, the issue at hand, and the lack of women playwrights in the Abbey, is secondary.[3]

Nonetheless, my solidarity lies with all women whom the Abbey and other artistic institutions and arts organisations overlook. There is a belief that including issues of equality and diversity in the context of women artists somehow detracts from or dilutes the overall message of sexism and misogyny.

The absence of women in theatre reflects the lack of diverse women. These women include deaf actors, writers, and performers. They are also Black and ethnic minority artists who choreograph, perform, and sing. Additionally, these women include disabled curators, writers, administrators, and front-of-house staff. All these women aspire for our work to be recognised, critiqued, and respected in terms of what constitutes 'merit'. Do not ignore or negate our gender. We are a footnote in someone else's revolution.

Many of us have paid the price for our gender. Intersectional women are messy and dangerous. The edge keeps shifting. Clinging on or remaining marginal within the arts is an oversight. The rich texture of our lives offers a valuable source of knowledge and cultural artistic capital.

As feminists in the arts, let's not replicate male behaviour by excluding specific categories of women. Relegating us to the corner labelled 'special artists' is archaic. My ethnicity, gender, and impairment, along with many other experiences, inform my writing. They are not interruptions to the story – they are the story. We want to collaborate as women, artists, peers, and equals.[4]

Derbhle Crotty, *actor*

A fortnight ago, at the Theatre Upstairs[5] Halloween party, a young woman introduced herself as a recent graduate of The Lir;[6] a bright and beautiful girl. In no time another young woman joined us. She was ablaze with a passion for the theatre, eager to tell me about the parts she had played, and morphing from one character to another in quicksilver time. I later met another Lir girl, an irrepressible character, both confident and self deprecating, and another, fiercely intelligent and very impressive. All ardent theatre lovers, all true believers.

Those four young women have played on my mind in these last ten days. What chances will they get to set the stage on fire? Will they be employed to populate a world in which the men are more complex and interesting than themselves? And will they be employed at all? Will they, like almost all the young women who graduated from Trinity in my year, fall away from the profession, because the paltry portion of young women's roles are not enough to sustain all this talent?

I was blessed to begin my career in a series of roles written by women, which gave scope to my own contrary, turbulent, and passionate nature. Characters who you wanted to kiss one minute, and kill the next. I was directed in these roles by women who didn't blanch at violent emotion, who understood struggle themselves, and who weren't afraid of a bit of female mess. I want all this for these four, and for any young woman who takes the theatre into her soul. I want more women's scripts staged, more women putting them on the stage, and more women *on* the stage. Many more. *Nunc tempus est*. The time is now.

Ursula Rani Sarma, *writer*
read by Clare Barrett, *actor*

This is not a new conversation. Some of us have been having it for years. Every time I saw another article headlined 'Where are all the Female Irish Playwrights' I would want to scream, 'we are right here, being produced, published, and academically studied throughout the world.' Is there some sort of giant firewall surrounding Ireland that means our success is invisible to many within? Does it mean nothing because it hasn't taken place on home ground? I've spoken out about this in the past, publicly and privately and often have been met with 'you would want to be careful what you say, your work may not be programmed' or 'people might think you are bitter'. And I guess I was bitter, that this was the attitude to my questioning of the gender imbalance within the programming of new Irish plays.

So many of the voices speaking out over the past week have echoed these sentiments, so many felt too afraid to speak out, afraid that people would think they were embittered as their own work had been rejected in the past. How incredible for these voices to now be in chorus. I have felt so moved by this solidarity and the fierce conviction of the women who have made today happen.

I keep thinking that theatre is in its essence collaborative and how dialogue is at its heart. Today's vital gathering is the beginning of a much needed and long overdue dialogue: an opportunity for those denied a voice thus far to talk back and to ask how this has been allowed to happen.

And this is an extremely exciting time to be an Irish female playwright. More of us are being produced throughout the world than ever before. As I write this from Washington DC, where the Women's Voices Festival has recently showcased the work of three Irish female playwrights, my prevailing feeling is excitement and anticipation. Because we are no longer waiting for change to happen, we are demanding it.

Oonagh Murphy, *director*

I worked as resident assistant director here at the Abbey at the beginning of my career. I was proud to work here, in that it's my national theatre, and it wears its history of incendiary activism like a badge of honour.

But there's a brutality to working on a stage for nearly two years and in that time never working with a female director, and never on a play written by a woman. It seems to endorse the insidious, yet powerful voice telling Irish women:

'You are less important.'

It's that same message that caps women's careers across all industries.

It's that same message that means those who do make it to positions of power are attacked for their hair, their clothes, their lack of humour, the tone of their voice.

It's the same message that means the girls will do the washing up.

It's that same message that snidely positions a world-class women's rugby team as amateurs and sex objects.

It's the same message that blocks access to affordable childcare for all.

It's the same message that means the lad gets called a legend and the girl gets called a slut.

It's the same message that still sends 12 women every day overseas for clandestine abortions.[7]

As a queer woman standing on this stage, my eyes have been opened so that I check my own privilege and look around to see who is there on the margins, entirely voiceless, without any way in.

On this stage the work is always branded important, but the work that feels important to me is happening elsewhere, in smaller rooms, in arts centres, in derelict buildings and sheds, and in communities away from here.

But now, in this moment, we can right a wrong, and begin to listen to the voices of Ireland in 2016; ethnically diverse voices, queer voices, voices of different classes, ages, bodies, and abilities. So that we can talk back to that insidious voice.

And say – we are important.

What we have to say is important.

It is undeniable. It is relevant. It is revolutionary.

Oonagh Murphy. Photo: Fiona Morgan

Gina Moxley, *actor and writer*

This is about power and respect. We live in a country where women do not have autonomy over their own bodies therefore being patronised and under-represented is endemic. On a fundamental level we are not trusted. Women with opinions or ambition are regarded as trouble – awkward cunts, crazy bitches – and are sidelined or blacklisted. Far too many talented women, particularly writers, directors, and actors, have left Ireland or retrained out of utter frustration with the lack of opportunity and support here. The theatre we produce is the poorer for it.

The structures that need to be 'interrogated' in the current debate are the Abbey Theatre, the Arts Council, and the Department of the Arts, Heritage and the Gaeltacht. What is important is that we see the women artists who are excluded due to whims of taste and favour. While I am not in favour of quotas, we are in the insidious position of fighting for visibility. Fighting for a fair and equal go of it. Fighting for a livelihood. A fair share. Today's extraordinary turn out will make it very difficult to un-see us. We've picked the lock of the closed door. We're not asking, we are coming in. We're here.

Kate Gilmore, *actor*

My name is Kate and these views are my own.

I believe the role of a national theatre is to reflect society back at us. Well, females make up half of society, so I believe that our national theatre hasn't been doing its job. I believe we, the arts community, have always expected this to change – particularly looking to the launch of the centenary programme as a springboard for this much sought after change. I believe we were wrong.

Earlier this year, I performed in a musical about the Contraceptive Train which departed Connolly station for Belfast in May, 1971.[8] The women on this train were members of the Irish Women's Liberation Movement. I was lucky enough to meet some of those women during the run and their passion has motivated me to stand up for what I believe in and not be silenced by fear.

The Irish Women's Liberation Movement didn't ask for change or expect change. They demanded it. They made it happen. They made it impossible for them to be overlooked and now, over 40 years later, their courage continues to inspire. We not only have a right, but an obligation to these women, among others, to be brave and make it impossible for us to be unseen or unheard.

Be the change you wish to see in the world.

Thank you to those who have ignited the flame. May it rage like an inferno.

Olwen Fouéré, *actor, director, writer*
read by **Aoife Duffin,** *actor*

Greetings to all who are gathered here in support of the new insurrection! What a great moment this is, what a powerful catalyst for change. And what a shameful moment. Yet again we have to confront GENDER INEQUALITY as a humiliating CULTURAL REALITY. To admit how deeply it is embedded in our lives and in our work. And how clearly this inequality intersects so many other discriminatory practices, not only in the Abbey, not only in the theatre, and not only in Ireland. It is way past time for an act of rebellion against the hierarchies and the autocracies we have almost always accepted as insurmountable barriers. It is way past time for many great artists, who also happen to be women, to reclaim their rightful place in the artistic canon of this country.

It is entirely appropriate that the Abbey stands as the initial site of our dissent today. The Abbey Theatre is our theatre. It belongs to all of us and to no one. The principles of any National Theatre have to be founded on equality and inclusiveness, particularly one as symbolically important as the Abbey, and especially in a programme which sets out to interrogate the insurrection of a hundred years ago. And here we are at a great moment! Today, here and now, wherever we are, is the opportunity to examine our practice, to reclaim our theatre, beginning with our National Theatre, by transforming it into a site that can lead by example – by listening, by inclusiveness, by non-autocratic artistic leadership – and real interrogation. It will take a while, time is running out and we must not stop for a second. Huge thanks to Lian Bell who started the fire. Long may it burn!

Maeve Stone, *director*

To quote Marina Carr:

> The rage in women is terrifying ... it doesn't come out of nowhere. The rage comes out of being said no to just one time too many, where you should have been said yes to, if the world was fair. If society is always saying no to you, that rejection has to go somewhere. It turns dark, and it erupts then ... Women's rage turns inward most of the time. How wonderful to be able to burn down the whole world. Even if it is only a stage.[9]

I've been working in Dublin for six years and I know exactly what Marina is describing in that quote. I have seen countless talented women lose heart, get angry, turn away, and begin again in a new life somewhere else. Or, even worse, silence their voice as artists. For many, it's too much to feel like you are the only one who believes in your ability. It is the difference between personal failure and systemic failure. These women have not failed themselves, the system has failed them. We have failed them. I've learned that even those directors and writers, who I look up to as successful women, have also been kept at arm's length. Kept off the big stages, kept out of programming positions, kept quiet.

I do believe that conscious and unconscious prejudice have inhibited the development of myriad female voices in all aspects of theatre in Ireland. I believe this is an old narrative that has been learned and reinforced by the certainty of male authority and also through the female internalisation of these limitations. As Margaret Atwood says, 'We still think of a powerful man as a born leader and a powerful woman as an anomaly.' We have all learned the wrong way. I want that to change. I want it to be the last promise of the centenary year.

Ali White. Photo: Fiona Morgan

Ali White, *actor and writer*

For the last 15 days, I've found myself caught up in a riddle.

Some say I'm the one woman playwright in the next Abbey season – others say there <u>are</u> no female playwrights in it, and my play is not a play.[10]

Figure that one out.

But whatever the answer is – it's not good enough.

And we all know, the imbalance is everywhere. It runs frighteningly deep. It seeps into us through osmosis. It makes me doubt and check myself; it trips up my confidence, and silences me.

And I can't help thinking there is something very fitting about the fact that my play – that – steady – might not be a play – depending how you look at it – is about Mollser in *The Plough and the Stars* – that bullet-riddled pillar of a play.

Mollser has no more than a dozen lines. She's a little half-life. A shadow. But I found out she has loads to say. She rails against poverty, war, and yes – injustice. Inequality. If she was here, there would be no stopping her.

And I am happy, and proud, to be here today with all of you who believe in equality. And who love the crazy, practical, human alchemy of theatre. This has to be the start of something better. If we have a tither of sense, we'll start from here.

Jen Coppinger, *producer*

For many years now I have told myself to cop on.

I've learned that it's best to keep my disquiet to myself, to do things on my own, to work on shows that are presented in many venues across Ireland and further afield but to never expect to produce a show in my National Theatre. That won't happen. Cop on.

I have learned that relationships with other venues and festivals are vital for survival and these organisations have helped me and the female artists I work with to produce work that is high quality, that has won awards, critical success, standing ovations. Work that has toured internationally and all over Ireland and yet when I have tried to get this work produced by my National Theatre, I realised that's not going to happen. Cop on.

I am ambitious. I am honoured to work with incredibly talented and ambitious artists like Amy Conroy, Olwen Fouéré, Kellie Hughes, Emma Martin, Gina Moxley, who make their own work, their own way.

They do not bend their vision, they make work that they, and I, believe is important – politically, emotionally, and socially. These artists have proven themselves to be successful and yet they have not been produced by their National Theatre. None of their work has originated here. Cop on.

So with all this ambition and the experience of working with these brilliant inspirational artists, I've learned to accept that somehow we weren't good enough for the National Theatre.

The time for copping on is now... Let's go!

Emma Jordan, *director*
read by **Andrea Irvine,** *actor*

I have been avidly following the amazing galvanization of energy that is #WakingTheFeminists – and I am so sorry not to be able to be with you today, but proud that that's because I am directing a one-woman play by Stacey Gregg.

I've been watching from afar because that's how it feels from the Northern perspective of theatre, always on the edge of things, peering through the window – never mind smashing the glass ceiling. My experience of growing up in the North and my work in Bosnia eradicated any sense of romantic attachment to the idea of nationhood. I find the concept of nationalism and therefore a national theatre difficult. I cannot relate to it either in regard to the Abbey or the Lyric.[11]

But I do know that to direct in either building would feel like a seismic shift in my career trajectory; which has been varied and circuitous and like many before me only possible through the support and mentoring of brilliant women who believed in me when I didn't believe in myself.

This dialogue is challenging on so many fronts and goes far beyond the Abbey 2016 programme – if the experience and under-representation of women playwrights is a disgrace, where would we even begin to address the daily humiliating scenarios and grinding sacrifices made by our women actors?

The prejudice is deep and internalised. This past week I have looked at myself and my company Prime Cut, and when I look back at the 23-year catalogue of our work I find us wanting – it is not just the major institutions that are holding their heads in shame.

I *can say* that we are deeply committed to empowering the next generation of women theatre artists. We are putting our money where our mouth is, our company is female led, empowered and empowering – maybe we have had one eye open and one eye shut – maybe we are all wide awake now.

Mary Duffin, *actor and writer*

I'm a 46-year-old Irish woman.

I'm a writer … now. I tried acting but, 'Well you'll never play Snow White! Maybe Cleopatra' said my famous-on-the-telly-at-the-time acting teacher. I was confused because Sr Bosco had cast me, aged nine, as a boy in the Tony-worthy *Ag Goid Ull* (*Stealing Apples*) so I *knew* I could play anything! But I took it.

I'll write them myself, I thought. So off I went to do an MA. 'Why are all the characters always white?' I asked. 'You have to write in the vernacular of the country you're living in.' So I'm not in the vernacular of my own country I thought. But I took it.

So, MA done and I've a *great* idea for a character. I'm running it by a very successful male writer friend of mine. (For the record, *The Walking Dead* was only mid Season 2.) 'She's black, with dreadlocks, and carries a samurai sword.' 'You can't just stick yourself in it.' he laughed. I argued, 'but aren't *all* the characters me?' But I took it. (Then Michonne appeared, armless Zombies in tow, and wielding that samurai sword like a boss! RAGE!)

And now? I have a dark human story to tell. Written, directed and performed by me, *except*, it won't be performed by me. Because in order for this dark woman's story to be received as the valid story that it is, I shall have to cast a white woman, otherwise it'll be relegated to the 'black' story pile, and seen as a 'black' issue.

So Dear Abbey,

To paraphrase the wonderful Chimamanda Ngozi Adichie's TED talk 'The Danger of a Single Story':

You, dear Abbey, are propagating a single story; a single story of Ireland, a single story of Irishness, a single story where I simply don't exist.

But guess what? Now? 'I'm mad as hell and I'm not gonna take it anymore.'

Zia Holly, *lighting designer*

I grew up in a house of boys. I have four brothers. And I have always wanted to be one of the boys. I remember being told encouragingly that I could do anything the boys could do. This was a powerful message but *why* did I *have* to be told this? The boys never got told they 'can do anything girls can do'.

Conscious or unconscious, there is a perception that women cannot necessarily do what men can do and that perception pervades our society. I have factored that into my life. So from a very young age I have inherently known that I would have to prove myself equal.

When I started in college I remember working on a show for the first time and, when it came to do the get out, some of the guys started de-rigging the lights. I remember thinking I'd like to do that so I asked if I could help. I was told it would be *really* great if I could tidy the dressing rooms.

The next time there was a get out I didn't ask if I could help. I just grabbed a free ladder and started taking down the lights. I remember someone saying 'oh cool, Zia's technical'. Instantly their *perception* of me had changed. My foot was in the door and that's all it took. Suddenly my work and my ability could speak for itself. The hardest thing is to get your foot in the door and it seems that it is harder again for women, and the Abbey feels like a fortress. Women's work speaks for itself. We just have to let it have a voice.

This industry is brimming with talent. Writers, directors, producers, designers, composers, actors, stage managers; men and women alike. This movement is powerful. There is a force behind it. I've realised I don't feel like I need to be one of the boys anymore. I'm proud to be one of the girls.

Noelle Brown, *actor, activist, and writer*

I have spent 30 years working in Irish theatre as an actress, sometimes director, and now a theatre maker. I have experienced sexism in all shapes and forms. If you are assertive as a female actor you can be called a diva, aggressive, bitch, difficult to work with, high maintenance, ball breaker. I have never heard men spoken about in that way for voicing their opinions. If you question the imbalance in theatre in terms of gender you can be called a man hater. So you stop speaking out because you are frightened of not getting work from the men who mostly have the power to give you work.

I thought when I became a theatre maker it would be different. While I have had incredible support over the last two and a half years from men and women in theatre who aren't afraid to support middle-aged female voices, it's still a struggle to be heard. Sexism is not confined to theatre. A friend of mine is a novelist and she says she faces the same random sexism in the literary world. A friend of mine who works in the corporate world says she faces similar acceptable sexism every day. This struggle goes beyond the Abbey, beyond the arts in Ireland, and is deeply rooted in Irish society and therefore there is a lot of work to be done.

It's not a malicious imbalance. I don't think the men in theatre who make the decisions sit in rooms plotting ways to further inequality towards us. In fairness, I think they would have more sense than to deliberately take on any of the women who raised their voices over the past couple of weeks. Instead this acceptable prejudice is so ingrained in society that it is the norm.

Women have a huge role to play in changing things. It's not all down to men. We need to support each other more and acknowledge sexist situations together when they occur. Things can't go back to the way they were now because awareness has been raised and our voices cannot be ignored. The fire has been lit and any fear I had about speaking out is well and truly gone. I don't want special treatment as a female actor or as a theatre maker. I want equality.

Nancy Harris, *writer*

As a playwright, my instinct is usually to let my writing do the talking, because I think that anything that needs to be said should be said in the work. Unfortunately, however, when that work can't find an outlet, I can't let the writing do the talking, and so I have to do it myself. Playwrights, all playwrights, are in an unusual position, unlike other writers, our work cannot exist solely on the page. Plays live and breathe in performance. So plays which are not produced essentially do not exist. It is therefore simply not enough to commission a playwright, the real test is to produce that playwright's work.

I've worked at the Abbey before, and I believe there's no lack of goodwill here towards commissioning female writers. Yet what we're not seeing is the work of those writers make its way onto this stage. Is it that the plays we're writing are not seen as big enough, relevant enough, or national enough? It has traditionally been asserted that men write plays that are 'big': historical, social, political; while women write plays which are 'small': domestic, relationship driven, personal. Aside from the fact these are gross generalisations in every way, the truth is we don't really know what women are writing about, because we're not hearing from them enough.

Yet women are being commissioned by this theatre. The implication, therefore, is that whatever it is we are writing, it does not accord to the concept of National Theatre. It seems obvious then, that we need to change our concept of National Theatre to include women and what women want to write about. Rather than asking female playwrights to conform to tired templates of what a National Play should be, we need our national theatre to risk making a commitment to that which it has commissioned. That way our work could speak for us and we wouldn't need to stand here speaking for it.

Joan O'Clery, *costume designer*

The view from my side of the curtain.

I have been lucky enough to work in theatre for 25 years. Through that time I have seen all theatre companies suffer financial crises, with cut after cut, and a questioning of the very value of the art form.

None of us, actor, director, or designer, working in this sector, consider ourselves to be particularly well paid. But some are more equal than others.

I come from the relatively unthreatening security of the Costume department. My craft is seen as essentially feminine and indeed 69 per cent of practitioners in costume are female.

But, still I look at my pay cheque at the end of the production, having spent on average, three months of dedicated and skilled work, and I ask, 'Is there an unconscious gender bias to the value placed on one design discipline over another? Does this stem from a perception of traditional roles?'

I ask for an examination of the status quo in relation to rates of pay. I ask for the norm to be called into question in the light of fresh thinking on old conventions.

Let us look again.

Let us unlearn what we think we know.

Laura Bowler, *student director*

They're giving up. Giving in, to things that seem inevitable
throwing what took years to cultivate in the bin and why not?
Stability sounds ideal after a few years of real.
Real closed doors, real no work, and real friends far away on a whim
because here, there's no way in.
I'm back to educating, for the sake of making sense of the time it's
taking.
Nothing tangible is yours or mine.
We rent, but we might always rent.
Or live with parents we don't want to resent but do.
There's a queue of women with ink-stained fingers and pages full
of life on Abbey St,
and we're ploughing through the stars one more time,
and murdering Desdemona post prayer.
We're there.
100 years after and 400 years since, and dead men still taking
precedent over living women, nothing new, no new stories told, not
for the sake of not hearing the old.
Hundreds of students who may never work.
Why educate if we can't translate these words that live in us to
stage?
These words live in us,
and we're giving up and going away and getting jobs we never
wanted
to support lives we hate.
I will always rent if I get to live on a stage. I will not own if I get to
tell you my story how I think it should be told, I will stay if you will
have me.
But I won't wait.
For every 1 in 9 decision you make, 8 will leave, or give up or think
'I wasn't good enough' well tough.
The pool will get smaller, when you only listen to half of us you can
only ever get half the story.
We shouldn't need to hashtag wake the feminist we've been awake
for so long it's you that is
sleeping, and when you wake, we'll be gone.

Eleanor Methven, *actress*

My name is Eleanor Methven, and I am a chronic insomniac. I've been awake since about 1976.

I was co-founder and joint artistic director of Charabanc Theatre Company, Ireland's first women's theatre company – yeah, I know, we've been inundated ever since – and no theatre company has ever been called a man's theatre company – semantics is majorly important in feminism. I'm very proud of what Charabanc achieved, ten new plays created and toured internationally between '83 and '95, written by and about women, and several women practitioners have been kind enough to cite the company as an influence and an inspiration.

But here's a quote from me speaking in 1983:

> We were frustrated by the lack of good roles for women and decided we'd have to write them ourselves. We were tired of playing somebody's wife, somebody's girlfriend, somebody's sister. We wanted to be the Somebody.

Last week I read Jo Cummins of Moonfish Theatre Company:

> Frustrated by the lack of good roles out there for women, we knew we'd have to set up our own company and write the material ourselves. Roles where we could play more than merely the female appendage for the male protagonist.

32 years in between. Any wonder I'm desperate for some sleep? To the younger women who told me this week they'd always felt unsure about saying they were feminists because they didn't know the theory: you are the living breathing epitome and essence of it, the all singing all dancing hard-working fact of it. Make 2016, not just in theatre, but in all other sectors, the year of The Eastrogen Rising.[12]

Erica Murray, *writer*

This is an extract from a letter I wrote to the *Irish Times* last Wednesday when the programme was announced because I felt disheartened and frustrated at the lack of female writers. If only I had known I would be reading it on the main stage a week later.

I know so many gifted female playwrights. The newly founded Lir Academy has had a majority of female playwrights enrolled in its MFA programme. So that is the last three years of graduates. Why is this not reflected on our national stage? Or why not look to the Fringe or Theatre Festival, where there are new and established female writers making amazing work. These are not obscure places to look if the Abbey was serious about fostering and developing a diverse range of voices. And if these female writers aren't given the opportunity to make the leap, how will things ever change?

Historically, there has been a shameful track record of gender inequality on this stage and this should be made an urgent priority when programming. We are, after all, half the audience, and we were also around during 1916. You would think they would have had the foresight to have anticipated this and would have been looking for the past few years to commission. They wouldn't have had to look very far.

It begs the question, why should I go and support my national theatre when I cannot see the female voice being represented or respected?

Lisa Tierney Keogh, *writer*
read by Mags McAullife, *actor*

I wrote my first play 14 years ago. I've watched conversations about the lack of women playwrights surface again and again, and every time I'd think to myself, '*no there isn't!*' Over the years, I learned to suppress the pain of being overlooked and ignored, the pain of being constantly pushed back. I watched my male contemporaries being produced and celebrated, as I kept plugging away, trying to hush that quiet voice inside me that kept saying '*this is wrong*'.

I was a member of the Abbey Theatre's inaugural New Playwrights Programme. I was under commission here from 2010 to 2012. I'm one of those women playwrights for whom it just didn't 'work out'.

Except that's not the truth, is it?

The truth is the odds were stacked against me. Because I was born a girl, I had a less than 15 per cent chance of actually getting my play on stage in my own country's national theatre.

I'll let that sit there for a moment.

The hurricane inside all of us will change this. There's no going back now. There can be no more quiet. There can be no more hush. There can be no more shoving us into a corner labelled 'reading series' or 'short plays', the programming equivalent of a *snug*. That's your place, ladies. Off you go and sit in it.

I want a future where Irish women are equal, included, and not just tacked on, as an afterthought, to their national theatre. I want to know that if I pour my heart and soul into writing a play, I at least stand a chance of being at the table. I implore all of us to remember, and honour, the bravery and courage of the women who fought for our independence. They fought for *us*. So that we would be free, so that we would be *equal*.

Let no man tell me I'm not ready. *I* decide when I'm ready. *You* decide when you're ready. And let me tell you, we are *all* ready.

Ionia Ní Chróinín, *actor and theatre maker*

Is mise Ionia Ní Chróinín agus is comhstiúirteoir ar Moonfish Theatre mé. Is mar aisteoir a rinne mé mo thraenáil ar dtús, insan RCS i nGlasgú, ach nuair a d'fhill mé ar Éirinn ba léir dom nach raibh sé so-dhéanta oibriú ann mar bhan-aisteoir phroifisiúnta, de bharr nach raibh ach méid beag páirteanna ar fáil do mhná.

Bhí orm comhlacht do mo chuid fhéin a bhunú, in éindí le mo dheirfiúir Máiréad, le go mbeadh an deis againn amharclannaíocht dhá-theangach a chruthú a thug an saoirse agus cumhacht dúinn páirt lárnach a ghlacadh sa phróiséas chruthaitheach, agus a chur páirteanna ar fáil dúinn a bhí duthlánach agus uiltaobhach.

Tá ag éirigh linn mar chomhlacht amharclannaíochta, ach is é sin in ainneoin, seachas buíochas le, institiúidí cosúil le Amharclann na Mainistreach. Níor bhraitheamar gur fháiltigh nó gur mhol Amharclann na Mainistreach muid ariamh. Dá bharr sin rinneamar an cinne gan iarracht a dhéanamh caidreamh a bheith againn leo – gan leannacht orainn ag cnagadh ar dhoras a bhí dúnta inár n-aghaidh. Ina áit sin táimíd théis ár bhfuinneamh a dhiriú ar amharclannaíocht a chruthú ar ár mbealach féin. Amharclannaíocht gan bacanna inscne, bacanna teanga, nó bacanna i dtaobh cá gcruthaítear í.

Tá Amharclann na Mainistreach théis a bheith mar fhórsa díchumachtú dúinne agus do ealaíontóirí eile cosúil linne. Ach creidim go hiomlán go bhféadfach sé bheith mar fhórsa láidir cumhachtú dúinn. Bhí tréithe inár léiriú deirneach go mbíonn dearcadh dúiltach orthú go minic: ba mná is mó a bhí sa chlaor agus sa chriú; bhí Gaeilge ann, agus cruthaíodh taobh amuigh de Bhaile Átha Cliath é. Chuaigh sé ar camchuairt ag deich ionad náisiúnta i mbliana agus díoladh amach é. Más féidir linn é sin a bhaint amach gan tacaíocht ónár n-amharclann náisiúnta, samhlaigh cad a bhféadfadh muide agus ealaíontóirí eile cosúil linne a bhaint amach lena chuid tacaíochta.

My name is Ionia Ní Chróinín and I am co-director of Moonfish Theatre.

I originally trained as an actor at the RCS in Glasgow and when I returned to Ireland I found the lack of roles for women in Irish theatre made it practically impossible to live as a female professional actor.

It took the setting up of my own company, with my sister Máiréad, to eventually be able to devise theatre bilingually that offered us and the women in our ensemble fulfilling roles in the creation process and challenging and multi-layered characters to play.

We have been successful, but this has been despite, not because of, our relationship with theatrical institutions such as the Abbey. We have never felt welcomed or encouraged by the Abbey. Our reaction to this was to choose not to engage, not to beat against a door that stayed steadfastly shut. Instead we have put our energies into creating theatre on our own terms. Theatre that provides roles that are not gender-defined, theatre that is not defined by the language in which it is performed, or by where it is created.

The Abbey has been a force of disempowerment for us and for other artists like us. But I sincerely believe that it could be a force of empowerment. Our last production had everything that supposedly is a disadvantage: a predominantly female cast and crew; a mixture of Irish and English, and it was made outside of Dublin. We toured it to ten venues nationally this year and it sold out. If this is what we can achieve without the support of our national theatre, imagine what we and all the other artists like us could achieve with it.

Garry Hynes, *director* and Marie Mullen, *actor* read by Marie Mullen

Because Garry and I founded our own company (and by the way Mick Lally[13] said, 'Good on ye, girleens'), we were able to make our own weather. It was only in later years, as we came more and more into contact with the professional theatre, that we realised with a shock that women's voices had to fight to be heard. Both of us have long acknowledged to the other that if we had tried to become an actor and director by the established route, neither of us would be making theatre today. We are speaking today to make sure that that never happens for any of the young women coming up behind us. Buíochas.[14]

Róise Goan, *producer*

So, what happens next? How can the Abbey begin to make reparations for the years of exclusion it has, if unconsciously, committed? Commissioning new work by women playwrights is an immediate imperative, but it will take time for these commissions to reach fruition and it's likely that they won't reach the stage within the tenure of the current director. So, what can the Abbey do now?

Ensuring that women directors and designers are represented in the remaining part of the 2016 programme is an absolute necessity. This will not be difficult. The independent theatre sector in Ireland is led by women whose work tours nationally and internationally to wide acclaim.

So too is looking at the body of work, not commissioned by the Abbey, that Irish women playwrights have presented elsewhere in the last ten years to great acclaim, and bringing that work home so Irish audiences can enjoy them.

A lot of these writers and directors have been ignored by the Abbey for so long, and have made their own successes elsewhere, with busy schedules, so it might take some work to persuade them to take a job at the Abbey. That work should start immediately.

In thinking back on what the Abbey could or should have done differently, the canon is an area that needs to be addressed. To my shame, as a woman, a feminist, and somebody who studied Irish theatre history, my knowledge of the work of Irish women playwrights between the work of Lady Gregory and the 1990s is paltry. I don't think I'm alone.

The Abbey needs to shed light on this work, and share it with the sector. This can start immediately. For example, working with the Playography Project and the Abbey archive to start a reading group with writers, directors, designers and producers in the sector, to make a commitment to produce work from the canon of Irish women playwrights over the next five years.

Róise Goan speaking at the first public meeting 12 November 2015. Photo: Fiona Morgan

Tanya Dean, *dramaturg and lecturer*

My name is Tanya Dean, I am a professional dramaturg with Then This Theatre Company and I also lecture in the Drama, Theatre and Performance Department at NUI Galway. Recently, I instigated the #fairplayforwomen pledge on Facebook and Twitter, which is a promise to book one ticket per month for a year to see a play by a female playwright or artist. The question I want to consider today is: what is behind the systemic inequity that restricts female representation and participation in Irish theatre? And it is systemic, it is cultural.

Today I'm drawing on the work of an amazing organisation, Women for Election, which has classified the reasons for women's under-representation in Irish politics as the '5 Cs'. I think these five Cs can easily apply to theatre as well:

- Confidence
- Cash
- Candidate selection: the decision-making behind programming choices by theatres, companies, and funding bodies is often opaque and difficult to navigate for those outside the institutions
- Culture: The current cultural norm is for the arts in Ireland to be dominated by men at the higher funded levels
- Childcare

If women aren't empowered beyond these conditions to write plays, then the plays simply won't be available for theatres to programme. I think these five Cs are perhaps all the more insidious because they are often, if not invisible, then certainly unconsciously internalised by us all as theatre professionals, as men and women, and as citizens. We can arm ourselves by becoming aware.

This movement has become known as #WakingTheFeminists, and I don't think that means that we were asleep; I think it's that we need to become conscious of these factors and stay conscious in order to combat them, both within our industry and within ourselves. Thank you.

Janet Moran, *actor and writer* (with **baby Ben**)

Women are not a minority. We're half the population. And if theatre is not reflecting the experiences of *half* the population, it's not working. We're *half* the population and our experiences are not being reflected. And that matters.

If a change can be effected here, it would be radical.

Any female actor will tell you that a not insignificant part of her working life consists of playing girlfriends, wives, mothers – adjuncts to the male characters. Frequently, sexpots, waifs, victims, prostitutes, virgin saints, embittered hags. Objects of desire or derision. Playing men's ideas of women. And its pretty gross when you think about it.

Think about any little girl you know, how complex, inquisitive, and smart she is. Imagine how radical it might be for her to see herself reflected in the plays, films, TV shows she watches. Not an objectified, frequently sexualised version of herself. Not just somebody's girl. But characters who are struggling, smart, inconsistent, ambitious, doubting, venal, violent or vicious, or who are just a bit crap. Like we all are at times.

If more women's plays are put on then that might start to happen more. And that would be radical. The other thing we need to talk about is money. We literally need to talk about money. Many years ago, during the run of a play, I discovered that a male actor with less experience than me, in a smaller role, who had never worked for the company before (I had) was being paid more than I was. I puzzled over it for weeks. By any criteria, it didn't make sense. So since then, I make it my business to talk about money, to let people know what I am earning and to ask what they are earning. So that I know what the playing field looks like.

Janet Moran with baby Ben. Photo: Fiona Morgan

After the testimonies, audience contributions were moderated by Ivana Bacik and limited to 90 seconds so that the maximum number of people could be heard. Contributions from the auditorium came from: director Annie Ryan; writer and Abbey board member Deirdre Kinahan; actor and writer Nuala Hayes; actor and writer Pom Boyd; activist writer and director Grace Dyas; PhD student Emer McHugh; dancer and choreographer Ella Clarke; community activist Kathleen O'Neill; researcher in the arts and education Dr Brenda Donohue; university lecturer Dr Susan Liddy; playwright and filmmaker Carmel Winters; novelist Evelyn Conlon; writer director and filmmaker Mary Moynihan from Smashing Times Theatre Company; writer, theatre student and critic Saoirse Anton; and performance artist and sign language interpreter Amanda Coogan.

Dr Brenda Donohue addressing the public meeting
at the Abbey. Photo: Fiona Morgan

Fiach Mac Conghail addressing the meeting. Photo: Fiona Morgan

When the audience contributions were over, Fiach Mac Conghail, Director of the Abbey, spoke from the auditorium:

> I want to express my gratitude to the voices of the #WakingTheFeminists movement for their call to action. I've always considered and used the Abbey stage as a platform for freedom of expression, and today is no different.
>
> Today was historical. Today it was extremely moving, and I'm extremely humbled. The events of the last fortnight have prompted me to ask myself some hard questions. Did I adequately explore the canon with modern eyes? Why didn't I address, redress the opportunity, or rather the predominantly male canon, by making sure my commissions list was predominantly female? Does my brilliant staff feel represented by the programme that they worked so hard to deliver? What influences my personal tastes? Why do I choose one artist from another? The absence of women from

the Waking the Nation programme is not something I can defend. I adore *Me, Mollser* and adore what Ali White did and I apologise to Ali for any slight, in terms of her craft, in terms of that beautiful play.

I was thinking in microscopic detail. I was thinking about the legacy of 1916. I was thinking about war stories, about poverty, about housing, about disenfranchisement. I was thinking about the Middle East, I was thinking about Northern Ireland. I was thinking about international touring, I was thinking about the Abbey theatre's canon, I was thinking about new commissioned plays on my desk that were at final draft stage, and I wasn't thinking about gender balance. I did not look up. I did not ensure that our 2016 programme would represent the experience for the nation as a whole, male and female.

I failed to check my privilege, and I regret that. Privilege is not just about structural social advantages of birth like being [a] man and white and middle aged. It's about who gets to talk – it's what Grace is saying – and who has to listen – it's what Gina is saying. I should have stopped to consider how my privilege affects the things I say and do. Society is overwhelmingly biased towards the male narrative, towards me. I see it in the government. I see it in the voices – or rather the absence of voices on the radio. I should have implicated myself in that issue by checking myself, and applying the same analytical eye to *my* world.

I have learned that we can't have true artistic freedom, until we have gender equality in our industry. As long as female artists continue to be underrepresented in Irish theatre, we're all missing out on important and exciting work. It's painful for me personally, but it's painful to think of the images, stories, and perspectives that have been lost to us already.

I have learned that I should use statistics as a provocation, not accept them as fact. Fewer women enter the playwriting industry than men. Why? What barriers are in place to stop them? What investment can we make to change those numbers for the better. Theatres across the UK and Ireland receive fewer unsolicited scripts from women than they do from men. Why is that? How can we change the system to motivate the many great women playwrights to send them to this theatre?

Visibility is what is essential here, and I agree with what Nancy Harris has said, seeing and producing plays by women on both the stages of the National Theatre. Commissions are vital, but productions, productions are paramount. I learned that a 50/50 gender balance in commissioning won't balance out decades of invisible women. Under the weight of centuries of male privilege and an overwhelmingly male canon, some positive affirmation intervention is required. For a time, I need to commission more women than men to redress the balance.

I can't wait to read the eight plays by female playwrights we currently have under commission. I'm excited too by the work yet to come from the 13 talented female graduates of our new playwrights' programme.

I learned to look at initiatives like Tonic Theatre's work in the UK and the Jubilee Project in the USA, which is an amazing project, for pathways to sustained gender balance. We want to achieve gender equality on our stages, not just for a season, but for the long term.

And I'm listening to what Róise said, and it's a good idea to start from scratch, to relook and re-examine through contemporary eyes – through other eyes – the canon of playwriting of the last couple hundred years.

We have to acknowledge in this theatre today, the fact that it will take time and investment for the industry to address inequality, and I won't be found wanting. We have to make an urgent commitment to gender balance, so that we don't lose out in the same way in the future. We have #WakingTheFeminists and all of you on the stage this afternoon to thank you for this wake up call.

The Board of the Abbey Theatre have made that commitment this week, and I look forward to working with them, as do the incoming directors.

Finally, and more crucially, the most important thing for me and for artistic directors of theatre companies, is to listen. Or as Caitríona McLaughlin says 'be fair, time to listen'. And after we have listened, to question: to question the systems, to question the classics, to question our choices and to do better by both artists, and audience. Go raibh maith agat.[15]

After the contributions from the floor, there was a slightly longer speech given by Lucy Kerbel, theatre director and founder of Tonic Theatre, an organisation dedicated to supporting UK theatre achieve greater gender equality in its workforces and repertoires. Tonic, and its Advance programme, had been identified by Loughlin Deegan as one possible solution to the systemic gender imbalance in Irish theatre, and #WakingTheFeminists paid for Lucy to come to Dublin to share her experiences.

Amanda Coogan and Lucy Kerbel. Photo: Fiona Morgan.

Lucy Kerbel, *theatre director and founder of Tonic Theatre*

Tonic was created with the specific aim of catalysing a culture shift in UK theatre in regards to gender equality. There was a new wave of new artistic directors coming into post in UK theatre, many of them themselves women, into important organisations, and they were demonstrably committed to shifting the balance in terms of women's voices and creativity on stage. There were a greater number of women – nowhere near an equal number of women – but a greater number of women who as artists were having their work put on the biggest, best resourced, highest profile stages in the country.

There was also a resurgence in conversations around feminism, and an acknowledgement that we still needed it a great deal. It was a moment of risk as well because as in any process of change, there was a significant risk that we would all see the green shoots of change and go 'we've done it'. I think there is a tendency when something has been as homogenous as UK theatre was, and in many ways remains, that as soon as we see a few different faces there, it's really easy to accidentally go 'oh, actually it's quite mixed or quite varied'.

If you're not working out whether there are *enough* female faces rather than just a few female faces, and also who those female faces are, and whether they are genuinely representative of the full range of women, then there is still a long way to go. When a problem is raised and pointed out, sometimes the risk is that we can mistake that for being 'Oh, we've solved it', rather than, no, we've simply named it.

Tonic is a really unusual theatre company in that we don't put on any plays. When setting the company up about four or five years ago, I thought we could do a really brilliant play written by women about women. I could direct it, but realistically it would be quite small scale. I knew that wouldn't change anything in the industry, because the problem is simply not that there are no plays written by women. The problem is not that there are no female directors, no female producers, and no female talent. The problem is not that we don't have any young women studying drama, or wanting to build a career in this world, or forming the majority of just about any youth theatre company in the country, or participating in amateur dramatics or indeed in our audiences – that is not the problem. The problem is that too rarely women's ideas, creativity, art, gets to be on stages like this one.

Tonic looks at the platform. It's about the structures. Rather than us making plays, let's work with people who already do. Let's work with the biggest, highest profile, best resourced institutions across the country, those that get the majority of public subsidy and the majority of the public's attention. If we can work with the Royal Shakespeare Company or the National Theatre – organisations that might be producing 20 productions a year, if we can change the way they think, and what they do, and they communicate, and how they assess what artistic quality is, then we will really begin to shift things.

Nobody has yet been able to give me any scientifically proven evidence that men are somehow biologically better disposed to write plays, or create lighting designs or run theatres. Therefore, if men are not biologically better engineered to write plays, then when you put together a season of work, if overwhelmingly that work is by men, the problem is not with the women, the problem must be in your structure through which you select which writers you want to commission, which old plays you want to revive and survive through reviving. The problem isn't how you build relationships with those writers, it's with how you communicate with them, with the exchanges you have, with the ambition that you do or don't set for them.

One key reason I would say that previous efforts over the past 10–15 years didn't achieve the results they should have, is that they tended to focus almost exclusively on the underrepresented group. What is it about that group of people who are not in our workforce or aren't in our audience? What is it about them? Of course, you need to understand that if someone isn't engaging with your organisation, either professionally or as an audience member, of course, you need to understand why that is. But that work never encouraged institutional gatekeepers to reflect on themselves in tandem with that, to think, 'how do we make choices? How do we work?' That is instead at the centre of what Tonic does.

Just to give you one example: our *Advance* programme was a piece of work we previously ran in 2013–2014, where we worked with a cohort of 11 leading theatres over a six month period of time.

We worked with their artistic directors, chief executive and senior artistic staff and he said to them, 'okay, just choose one question that you want to answer'. Don't try and deal with gender equality in a six month period or drive yourself mad and achieve very little, but instead just work out one thing that's important to you. One theatre asked about their commissioning process with playwrights. Does it suit men better than women? Another asked what's the trajectory for assistant directors going into directing? How can we ensure that any discrepancy between men and women is removed by us? Somebody else asked 'Why is it that we and our colleagues tend to put plays by women on in the smallest houses that are less likely to do as well as the main stages?' Over the course of six months, we really looked into that. It was a combination of them looking outwards at the people they weren't currently working with or any working with to a certain level but it was also crucially about them reflecting on themselves in a very, very structured way.

Then there were the ten other lines of inquiries of the other theatres. Over the course of the process we repeatedly brought those theatres together in a room so they could talk about what they were finding difficult. They could share ideas, they could egg each other on, they could exert very positive peer pressure on one another to do better. And collectively, it was just about dreaming up a new way of being a more productive, more successful way of making theatre.

What we said to all the organisations from the beginning is that by the end of this process you will need to have come up with an action plan of what you're going to do differently, or what you're going to start to do afresh. All of them in their own way, have made tangible changes to the way that they work, both in respect to their original line of inquiry, but because all the work they did rubbed off on one another, they also responded to the other lines of inquiry. I offer that as just one example of the kind of work that can really create a tangible shift.

Now we meet every six months. I ran one of the meetings a few months ago and we had a lot of those artistic directors in a room and one of them, who's a man, a white man – he was sort of pondering – we're having a conversation and we're talking about leadership. He said, 'So I guess what we're saying here is it's not about getting women to the top of organisations. It's about getting feminists to the top of organisations.'

Actually, I think there is something in that because this is not something for the women to do on their own. It has to involve all of us regardless of gender. If you're not a feminist, go and find out about it because I promise you, it's brilliant.

Audience at first public meeting. Photo: Fiona Morgan.

Ivana Bacik

Thank you all so much for your contributions from the stage from the floor. It's been a real wake up call for all of us, just as Panti had a noble call asking us to check ourselves for homophobia, think all of us are left today knowing that we need to check ourselves to ensure that gender is visible, to ensure that we no longer just remark when there's one woman on a panel: 'Oh, look, Isn't she great?', but to check ourselves that we note that when there's a manel, (an all-male panel) that we note that that's remarkable.

Because the problem is not that there's only 28 per cent of women's voices on peak-time current-affairs radio shows, or that there's only 16 per cent of women among our TDs. The problem is the 72 per cent of *men*'s voices on peak-time current-affairs radio, and that 84 per cent of our TDs are male. That's the problem that we're seeking to challenge through the gender quota legislation in politics. That's the problem that we're seeking to challenge here today in the arts – but the arts are only mirroring the real exclusion of women and the real invisibility of women across public life in Ireland.

That's why today's discussion is so timely. Why are we talking about #WakingTheFeminists now when, in the words of the Canadian prime minister[16] when asked why half his cabinet are women he said, 'Because it's 2015.' We're awake because it's 2015.

Sarah Durcan, *producer and arts manager*

On behalf of #WakingTheFeminists, a sincere thank you to all the Abbey Board, the Director and CEO Senator Mac Conghail, and to all the staff who accommodated us here today. Thanks to my co-chair, Senator Ivana Bacik. To our amazing colleagues who have pulled off an incredible amount of work to get us here, Rough Magic for the use of the building all this week, and the students volunteers from The Lir Academy, and to all our colleagues in the theatre and the arts, we thank you for engaging so forthrightly and passionately over the past two weeks. Thanks to Lucy Kerbel for sharing her experiences with Tonic Theatre. It shows us there are many ways forward.

How can we interrogate and reflect society with integrity, if we do not hold our own leaders to account and interrogate our own practices?

It has been a difficult, humbling and yet tremendous time. (Frankly, it's been a difficult 100 years.) I feel deep sadness and fury for what we have lost, for talent cut short, snuffed out or exiled, for the important conversations muted.

Today we have heard something about the true cost of that for us all. But it will be tragic if our daughters and granddaughters have to stand here again in 50, or a 100 years time to demand the recognition of their equality.

Equality for women matters on this stage, on every stage, and in every sphere. We do not stand here and politely request it. We stand here, in our full strength and brilliance, and demand what is our right as 50 per cent of the population – equality and economic parity.

This is also just the start of discussion on the solutions. Ultimately it's simple – commit fully to supporting and programming more women artists, putting their work centre stage. We all have more work to do to achieve full equality, inclusion and diversity in theatre. We will continue that work, together, with respect and honesty. But, alongside those conversations, there must be action, and from that action there must be results.

In this national theatre, funded by a woman, co-founded by a woman, and with a mighty Queen charging forth on its logo,[17] this call goes out from *this* stage, to every stage, to the leadership of all theatres and arts organisations. We must look at our programming practices, and beyond that look at our commissioning and our marketing and our pay and contracting and employment structures, look at everything we do and root out this blight of inequality.

Those three women are not spinning in their graves – their wake is over – today they are rising with us. Listen up: We are all ready for you. Get ready for us. *Now.* It's just time for some *Respect.*

PART TWO

FIVE

Preparing for a Year of Campaigning

The last few chapters brought you into the action as the movement unfolded. This chapter covers the immediate aftermath of the first public meeting on 12 November 2015. The next few chapters pick up the pace and describe what happened over the following year to November 2016.

Lian Bell posted on Facebook, Thursday, 19 November:

> It's a week since that incredible public meeting in the Abbey Theatre. Here's a quick update on what we've been up to in the last day or so:
> - letter sent to the Board and Director of the Gate Theatre, welcoming the Director's positive engagement on RTE Radio 1[1] last weekend with the issue of creating a more gender equal theatre sector. Also looking for a meeting with some of the #WakingTheFeminists campaign organisers, and a public statement from the Gate in response to the campaign objectives.
> - letter sent to the Board and Director of the Abbey Theatre, thanking them and the staff of the theatre for the venue last week, and for helping to make it such a success. Also asking for a public timeline for the proposed policy development and implementation process, as mentioned in the Board's statement last week.
> - a large package delivered to the Abbey Theatre stage door for the attention of the Board and Director, with a print out of the 5596 signatures from the online petition

in support of the #WakingTheFeminists campaign objectives, and the comments left by many of the signatories.
- first contact made with the Arts Council, with the intention of #WakingTheFeminists following up with a more formal engagement in the coming week.
- a great turn out of #WakingTheFeminists badge-wearers at a packed Gate Theatre this evening for the unveiling of the bronze bust of Christine Longford, playwright and theatre manager.
- development starting on a new #WakingTheFeminists website, scheduled to be online next Thursday.[2]
All in all, not a bad couple of days.
Right. Dinner.

We were not so naive as to think that just exposing the problem would solve it overnight. On Friday, 20 November, the week after the first public meeting, 20 of us were back in the front room of Rough Magic for a two-hour debrief and planning meeting entitled *WTF Happened? And WTF Happens Next?* Sat in a circle were many of those who had collectively organised the public meeting: Anna Walsh, Anne Clarke, Caroline Williams, Christine Monk, Dairne O'Sullivan, Gina Moxley, Grace Dyas, Lian Bell, Loughlin Deegan, Lynne Parker, Maria Fleming, Noelia Ruiz, Oonagh Murphy, Róise Goan, Siobhán Bourke, Tanya Dean, and Tríona Ní Dhuibhir. Others who couldn't make it in person had sent notes in advance. Of the many organising meetings we had, this one meeting turned out to be exceptionally important. It set out the big themes of the coming year and began to establish a framework for how we would organise.

Theatre people are used to reviewing and discussing what happened during a show, giving notes, and incorporating them into the next performance: it's a normal and routine part of our practice. Facilitated by Sarah Durcan (and informed by her experience with Science Gallery processes), this review meeting felt different to a creative 'notes' session, and to some in the room the structure felt more reflective of corporate culture than of arts culture. The particular style of debrief turned out to have ramifications about how some people felt about being involved in the next stages of the campaign. Some welcomed this sense of structure, while some were alienated by it. In retrospect, its tone changed the dynamic of the group in a subtle but significant way.

During the debrief, we described and discussed what we thought worked well, what didn't work, what we should stop, start, or continue doing, and what we wanted to do next. We looked at what we were trying to accomplish and if we were hitting or missing our objectives. We were inspired by the significant impact we'd already had, and it spurred our curiosity and galvanised our determination to see how much further we could go. We were adamant this movement would not recede without a lasting legacy. With a taste of our power, we were highly ambitious for what we could accomplish. Brenda Donohue contributed some questions to help frame the discussion and think about future outcomes: 'What would change look like (in one sentence)? What are the things we can measure to check if progress is being made? What are other countries doing well that we could learn from?'

We reviewed what had worked best so far, and our highlights included:

· Our use of social media allowed our message to reach a broad audience. This led to a surprising wave of demand for our meeting, and our message was amplified widely in public.

· The #IStandWithYouWomenInIrishTheatre social media campaign going viral around the English-speaking world. Posts featuring celebrities like Meryl Streep, Nicole Kidman, Saoirse Ronan, and Gabriel Byrne helped enormously. Recognisable and respected people coming out to support, which gave licence to others to speak–up.

· The level of blanket coverage was extraordinary, and #WakingTheFeminists had dominated the news cycle. The Irish Film Board coming out with a statement on gender equality on the morning of the public meeting added to the media taking this story seriously.

· We had made the level of discrimination and under–representation of women visible, and significantly raised awareness of the disparity between opportunities for men and women. Having a clear mission and objectives helped.

· Lian was seen as an independent voice. The group appreciated her leadership and ability to calmly bring many disparate voices together.

· There was deep national symbolism in the public meeting being held in the Abbey. The photograph of so many women outside the Abbey was powerful; it said 'we exist, we are many, we are together.' We could not be unseen again.

· The public meeting was inclusive with a positive, focused atmosphere. It was empowering for us all. We heard afterwards from some Abbey staff, who had had a rough few weeks, that they also found it useful and empowering.

· The public meeting allowed women to talk about their personal experience of discrimination, and allowed some of them to come to the realisation that their stalled careers were not entirely their own fault; the start of the end of self-blame. It gave women licence to speak in a way that hadn't been heard before and created a space that respected what we had to say.

- Actors, directors, designers, technicians, and producers' voices were involved, as well as playwrights. We rejected the simplified narrative that gender discrimination was a problem only for women writers.

Not everything had worked, of course. There were definitely things that could have been done better and gone smoother. For instance, we'd had to contend with some (although mercifully little) trolling on social media. We didn't yet have enough spokespeople prepared to deal with the media. We remained concerned that some vulnerable artists were potentially overexposing themselves and oversharing on social media, particularly when the conversation moved towards questions of harassment. Additionally, we were not at all happy with Marian Finucane's RTÉ radio programme on Sunday, 15 November. The level of disrespect and seemingly wilful ignorance demonstrated were galling when, despite us putting forward several women to be on the panel, the producers had chosen a man, Michael Colgan, Director of the Gate Theatre, to discuss this feminist movement, simply because he was more recognised as a 'household name'.[3] Michael's comments themselves were even more galling to us.[4]

A key objective had been to change the 2016 programme at the Abbey and this had not yet been achieved. Despite the Abbey's recent commitment to revise their policy, we were still concerned: the promises seemed vague and the whole situation appeared as though it was perceived as a mere communication breakdown, rather than a serious issue. They had to show willingness for enduring change. But all in all, the small negatives we had encountered over the previous three weeks were vastly outweighed by the positives, which gave us a pathway to address the outstanding issues.

We then discussed what we would do next with our new-found power. We wanted action in several areas and from multiple agencies and organisations. Firstly, we wanted the Department for the Arts, the Arts Council, the Abbey, and all cultural institutions to develop and implement gender equality policies. We agreed to follow up on the Abbey board's promise to develop a new policy, and to request a copy of their current affirmative action policy document. We agreed we would also seek meetings with the boards of the other leading theatre organisations. We agreed we would ask the then Minister for the Arts, Heather Humphreys, for a public statement in response to our campaign. We would write to the Arts Council to enquire about their policy and stress the role of governance; because the Arts Council comes under the Department of Arts but distributes funds at 'arm's length' from it, it was important that we worked with both institutions. But ultimately, beyond all this, we also wanted to put pressure on politicians regarding equality for women more generally.

We recognised we needed more research on the figures and facts of women's inequality in Irish theatre to back up our campaign, and knew we had to expand our networks to bring others, such as academics, into this loosely forming group. We needed expertise and academic rigour, and we wanted to avail of their knowledge to help the campaign be more visible and accessible. We agreed to look for more details of Tonic Theatre's Advance Programme in the UK[5] to see if it might be something we could adapt to the needs of the Irish theatre sector. Ultimately, we wanted a cultural shift as well as an increase in the number and visibility of women in theatre. To do this we would need to articulate a vision of the future and how the structures should change, and we would maintain the positive and dignified tone of the campaign to date.

It had been a short and intense period of learning over the two weeks from Lian's first post to the public meeting. With a couple of exceptions, most of us really did not know much about feminism, activism or campaigning, and we recognised our shortcomings and lack of expertise. Over the past few weeks, we had each embarked on unique learning journeys, regularly sharing and adding to each other's knowledge. We had shared articles such as '7 Steps for Achieving Gender Parity in the Theatre',[6] and 'Achieving Equity in Canadian Theatre: A Report with Best Practice Recommendations'.[7] We set out to learn more, and continue to share our learnings with each other.

Lian felt like she was barely one step ahead at any time. When talking at meetings, with the media, and at public events, she was regularly using information she had picked up only earlier that day about feminism, gender inequality, and how power and influence operates within the arts. It was all new to her and she was having to learn and find ways to use the knowledge well at a rate of knots. We all needed more time to absorb all this new knowledge.

As this kind of activism was new to us, we were uncertain about our own way of doing things, and instinct had only got us so far. We would need help, advice, training and tools to help us progress. We knew there were likely to be similar issues in other artforms and in wider society, and that we could learn from and stand in solidarity with this wider network. Starting at this meeting, and continuing over the subsequent days, we gathered a list of people, organisations, and existing structures we could link with or ask for advice.

Despite many important women's voices being broadcast in the traditional media on the day of the public meeting, we remained deeply concerned that powerful institutionally established male voices like Fiach Mac Conghail's and Michael Colgan's would shape the #WakingTheFeminists narrative for the public; particularly if the media were going to default to them, as had happened during Marian Finucane's show. We would have to either bring in more recognisable names to speak for the movement or get to grips with dealing with the media ourselves and get a *lot* louder. If we didn't, all we had achieved in the past few weeks could quickly evaporate. We agreed to seek media training, to empower ourselves to step forward and speak up.[8] We would do our best to ignore trolls and the below-the-line commentary.

At this debrief meeting we asked ourselves how we could sustain our activism, as we simply couldn't keep up the momentum of the previous weeks. We quickly agreed to work on the campaign for one year only, from November 2015 to November 2016. Everyone felt a year was doable, and would strike the right balance between momentum, urgency and sustainability. It would keep the appropriate level of pressure on organisations to take action as soon as possible, rather than kick the can down the road. We had confidence in ourselves that we could effect change within that time frame, and a willingness to try things and do something else if they didn't at first work. In retrospect, this was one of the most valuable decisions we made, allowing us to keep the pressure high while also being mindful of our mental health in the long term. Importantly we decided to focus on producing a couple more events throughout the following year for greater visibility.

We questioned if we should advise other organisations on their gender equality policy or should they come up with their own? We realised that if we were to advise other companies, this raised the issue of us risking being used for free consultancy; we agreed we needed clarity and boundaries around our voluntary time and the focus of the campaign.

We also discussed what kind of structures would best suit this movement, and wanted to ensure it would be inclusive and porous. We were a loose collective of individuals; we conceived of an open structure that would be the wider grassroots movement, with a core organising committee and several sub-committees.

We also had to discuss who were the 'we' we spoke of and represented. We agreed that 'we' meant people who self-defined as women in theatre and/ or supportive of women in theatre. Including and communicating with men would be important, and they would be an essential part of the change we were seeking. We were wary of the responsibility falling solely on women to advocate and act. Maintaining a wide sense of ownership of #WakingTheFeminists was paramount. Anyone who wanted to call themselves #WakingTheFeminists could. The logo and identity would be accessible and open source to those

Christine Monk, Caroline Williams, Gina Moxley, Lian Bell, and Jo Mangan at the Gate Theatre for the unveiling of a bust commemorating playwright and theatre producer Christine Longford.

who wanted to use it. We were open to the potential messiness of keeping a grassroots movement connected to a more tightly organised campaign. Our legitimacy and agency as a core group only came from the support and energy of the greater movement; both were vital, and the interplay between the two had to remain fluid and transparent.

From the earliest days, Lian had been contacted by enthusiastic people saying, 'I've this idea about what we can do, can I go ahead and do it?' She realised that all most people were really looking for was permission to do what they thought should be done to support the movement. So she simply kept saying, 'yes, go ahead'. From designing cards, to publishing texts, to organising local gatherings, it was a wonderful feeling of forward movement. People took the energy of #WakingTheFeminists, channelled it, and then their successes and actions in turn fed the energy of the greater movement. The core group knew we couldn't be (and didn't want to be) responsible for every #WakingTheFeminists event and activity, but we also knew that the fact they were happening, and being organised by people who felt invested in being a part of the campaign, only helped strengthen the overall movement.

Inevitably this review and planning session on 20 November 2015 brought up more questions than we could resolve, and would require further discussion in the weeks to come. That said, it was a vast amount to cover in just two hours and, extraordinarily, by the end of it, we had a framework for the year. While we refined our focus based on our learnings as the year progressed, we broadly stuck to what we had agreed at this first debrief meeting.

Afterwards, several of the group walked up to the Gate Theatre on Cavendish Row for the unveiling of a bust commemorating Christine Longford (1900–1980), a playwright who, alongside her husband, Edward Packenham, Earl of Longford, had given financial backing to the Gate and who had also managed productions and written plays for the Gate stage. Between 1931 and 1961 she had written more plays performed at the Gate than any other writer.[9] Until the unveiling of this bust, which was privately commissioned through the efforts of a group of her friends and supporters, her pivotal contribution had largely been written out of the history of the Gate, and it chimed with the #WakingTheFeminists campaign that she was finally getting her long-overdue, just recognition.

Weekly Meetings

Several people (14 women and two men) initially self-nominated to join a core #WakingTheFeminists group and affiliate satellite committees.[10] People could rotate informally on and off these committees. Everyone's time was voluntary, and we all had other life and work commitments. We estimated our time commitment would be two to three hours each per week; however, for many of the team the campaign ultimately took much more of our time than we initially anticipated.

The core group's role was to think strategically, get things done, and link in with other area-specific groups. We discussed the participation of men in the core group, as there were some misgivings from Cian O'Brien and Loughlin Deegan about being involved, although they had been keen co-organisers from the outset. It was agreed that it was more important to the women in the emerging committee that core group members were feminists rather than women, and so Cian and Loughlin stayed involved for the early months, although both had to step back for different reasons as 2016 progressed.[11]

We agreed to meet once a week on Friday evenings. Whoever was available to meet that week were the right people for that week; there would be no judgement for not turning up. Our first weekly meeting was held on 27 November 2015 at Irish Theatre Institute,[12] a beautifully restored Georgian building on Eustace Street in Temple Bar. After that, most of our Friday meetings were back in

Rough Magic. Lian posted a weekly public update on Facebook, Twitter, and our website every Thursday at lunchtime, to share what we were doing. We wanted our activities to be as transparent as possible, to keep a connection between the wider grassroots movement and the organising group, and also to keep the campaign in the public eye while we largely focused our activities behind the scenes. Dairne recalls of our meetings:

> A lot of people might think that we are sort of just down in a quiet little wine bar somewhere every Friday night having a few bottles of wine and going 'oh, you do this, and you do that'. And that was all there is to it. There is none of that. The meetings are quite strict, quite stringent. Not much craic, especially as the year goes on. It's lovely to spend time with everybody, and work on something as productive as this. But we're not having any laughs.

In the end this core group organised two further major public events in Dublin: one on International Women's Day, 8 March 2016, and a final public meeting to end the campaign in the Abbey on Thursday, 14 November 2016. As well as a Nollaig na mBan/Women's Christmas (6 January) filled with self-organised events around the country and further afield, throughout the year people independent of us continued to organise their own activities as part of the #WakingTheFeminists movement. Whoever wanted to organise an event under the #WakingTheFeminints banner, could.

Other issues started to come into focus. The reality of bullying and sexual harassment in the theatre industry were big concerns and we were not at all sure how to deal with the many emerging personal accounts. From the earliest days of the movement, people had contacted Lian and posted on social media about experiences of bullying and generally appalling behaviour they had endured in professional work settings, and not just in theatre. None of us were surprised that those stories were there. We felt the need to get prepared to deal with further stories that we anticipated would inevitably come out. Harassment should be called out for what it is, but this was a very contentious and emotive issue and could potentially upend all other aspects of what we were trying to achieve. At the same time, we acknowledged that true gender equality could not be achieved without addressing pervasive cultures of bullying and harassment. Dealing with such allegations was far beyond our expertise, (none of us were counsellors, HR experts, or legal advisors), and we had to be very careful about what we could share in public. We decided to put a statement on our website to ask people who may want to share such stories to ensure that they had appropriate counselling support and legal advice before doing so, and shared a list of resources.

There was significant debate and dissent about this approach in the core group, with some feeling we shouldn't touch this issue with a bargepole as it would likely derail the broader movement, while others felt that if we were not actively supporting these people who had suffered bullying and harassment, we were being complicit in silencing them. Alongside this, we were uncomfortably aware that we were also continuing to engage with some of the alleged bullies who were leaders in the sector. It was an upsetting and difficult situation, and while we dealt with preparing to support women who wanted to speak out as sensitively and honestly as we could, many of us felt it was not resolved very satisfactorily.

Ultimately, it was only after the #WakingTheFeminists campaign concluded that the floodgates opened (about multiple incidents of bullying and harassment on the part of multiple alleged perpetrators), when director Grace Dyas published allegations about Michael Colgan and essentially kicked off the Irish #MeToo movement. In November 2017, Michael offered an apology for his misjudged behaviour, though he felt it was wrong to equate his conduct to sexual crimes.

As 2015 drew to a close, the Labour Party invited several of the #WakingTheFeminists group to the Dáil for drinks as part of a wider arts community gathering. Fiach Mac Conghail was there, as was Michael Colgan. In one corner Brenda Donohue challenged Michael regarding female playwrights and the canon. Michael was pontificating that there were no 'classic' plays by women. In another corner, Leader of the Labour Party, Joan Burton (then also Tánaiste[13] and Minister for Social Protection in the Fine Gael/Labour coalition government) told Loughlin she was so serious about the arts that she had just found an extra €1m for the Arts Council and that she wanted to write a protocol to fix artists' engagement with social welfare before she left office. There was no way this group of people would have been having this conversation with each other over drinks in our national parliament building without the #WakingTheFeminists campaign.

In the lead up to Christmas 2015, Gina Moxley shared on our Slack channel, 'On a cheerier note bashed into Fiach in a shop today with a mug saying GOBSHITE in his hand. He had the grace to laugh at himself getting caught.' To which Lisa responded, 'The sale of mugs with a photo of Fiach holding that mug would probably fund a large portion of this movement.' Soon after, also on the Slack channel, Lian shared theatre critic Emer O'Kelly's latest review in the *Irish Independent*, which took a sideswipe at the campaign:

> *You Never Can Tell* was programmed as the Christmas offering at the Abbey long before the current controversy concerning feminism as a

numbers game in theatre; some of those involved in that controversy could learn from the master: everything, including feminism, is helped by a sense of humour.[14]

Lian's comment on Slack was 'For anyone who hasn't seen it yet – the end of Emer O'Kelly's review of the current Abbey panto *You Never Can Tell* by George Bernard Shaw, lets us know we lack a sense of humour. I'd like to refer her to the entire conversation above re Mug-gate.' That feminists should 'learn from the master' also provoked many eye-roll emojis on our Slack channel showing that, despite what Dairne said, sometimes we did have a laugh.

As December ended, we were still elated and full of surprise at how the media attention was keeping up. #WakingTheFeminists was covered in all the news round-ups at the end of year, and Lisa Tierney Keogh wrote a piece published 17 December for the Los Angeles-based *Women in Hollywood*.[15] Following the intense activities since October, and after a month of planning, we were looking forward to a bit of a rest over the Christmas and excited for what the new year would hold.

The New Year: 2016

Despite our open invitation for new members, in 2016 our group remained mostly unchanged. In fact, the core group who met regularly became even smaller as the year progressed, and comprised mainly Anne Clarke, Brenda Donohue, Caroline Williams, Kate Ferris, Lian Bell, and Sarah Durcan. We had concerns about the lack of diversity from the very beginning of our meetings. Most of us were producers and managers, though some weeks we were joined by artists such as Amy Conroy and Nichola MacEvilly. Some within the group articulated the question that if we were not a diverse, representative, intersectional, and democratic group, what permission did we have to represent and advocate for all the women of Irish theatre? We deliberated at meeting after meeting about what we should do to make the group more inclusive. From time to time, others came along but it was difficult for them to feel part of it, and fit in with the rapid shorthand we had developed out of necessity the first weeks and months.

We were all white. We ranged in age from 20s to 50s, so at least there was some intergenerational learning, and there were also several LGBTQI+ identified people in the group; however several of us felt we were sorely lacking diversity in other areas and should address this. Our homogeneity unfortunately closely mirrored the rest of Irish theatre. We were concerned about this, and realised that there could already be a perception that this group of people was largely an elite within an elitist sector.

There is a general presumption that those who attend and participate in theatre are middle class. While this is not wholly accurate, it is unfortunately becoming more so.[16] We were not all middle class in the core group, although to many on the outside it might have appeared so. We knew we would have to struggle with theatre's inherited elitism and wanted to address this, as Caroline outlines here:

> I found, like any movement, inclusiveness was important to all of us as a principle and difficult in practice. Consensual decision making is slow. I would have been interested in collectives, which works for a small group, but actually when you have a large group being inclusive and being a collective becomes incredibly difficult.
>
> It wasn't that we were this company that had been together for years and we had this shorthand, we had just by dint of having to deliver the first event to such a preposterously short timeline. We had found this working practice where that was fine. Had we had sheaves of paper there would be paper cuts with all the 'next next next next next', because we were all working against the clock. Even when we had flipped into our year-long campaign, we were still on the clock. Re-examining our working practice, I don't think interpersonal relationships had any bearing aside from a loyalty to the first objective, but as time went on, the interpersonal stuff started seeping in and that became a little bit more challenging.

Maria Fleming later reflected on the group dynamics:

> I am the dissenting voice lots of times when I speak up now, because I know that there are other people in the room that have the same opinion, but don't feel that they can speak. But that's a hard position to be in. There were times when I withdrew from #WakingTheFeminists because it was just too hard to be a part of, because the position I took was usually quite extreme and hardline. I tend to go for the nuclear option.
>
> Whereas the committee probably got as far as it did, because people who are on the #WakingTheFeminists committee would say 'no, let's meet them halfway' or 'we'll allow them this', for example. I recognise that I came from a campaigning and lobbying background, so I was aware that some of the organisations that I would have worked with, like Afri [Action from Ireland] they never walked the line, they never

said, 'we'll keep in with the minister by saying this' – we would have said what needed to be said.

There were times when I felt really involved in #WakingTheFeminists and really at the centre of it, and then there were times when I felt outside or not sure that I agreed with everything that went on, but I didn't know if I could speak up. I didn't want to damage the entity, but also at some point be a dissenting voice. There were other dissenting voices as well, and it's only at this distance past it that a few people have come up and spoke to me saying 'I felt really disenfranchised by that as a woman in the sector. I didn't feel represented or wanted within that'. I think there is some element of truth to that and some element of yes, you couldn't wait for the invitation you put yourself forwards and arrive in. But there were times where we, to take a short cut, probably thought 'look let's just go and do this'. Not everybody's going to love it, but we'll do this anyway.

Sometimes it felt like there was the #WakingTheFeminists movement – it was a big group of people – then there was a smaller group of people, and then there was a smaller group again, and I kind of flitted in and out between. Am I in the inner sanctum, am I in the inner inner sanctum, am I on the outer sanctum, am I persona non grata completely now? And that was upsetting and it was lonely at times.

And always, always, what I wanted first was for the movement to succeed, and so to never do anything that could in any way call us into question, and I was aware as well from previous campaigns that I worked on. It's very easy for people within the campaign to fall out and then the only thing that gets damaged is the campaign. The other side wins out then, if we're fighting amongst ourselves.

To counter this, Caroline suggested that it would be useful to do some more work on our organisational structure and sign-off processes; consensus by email and Slack was really hard. She suggested bringing in an expert: Susan Coughlan.[17] Susan, operating under Art of Change, is a consultant, coach, and facilitator and an expert in organisational development, change management, and network dynamics, with a background in arts and culture. Susan met with us a couple of times; first a briefing meeting over coffee in the faded grandeur of the Library Bar in the Central Hotel on Exchequer Street, and then she attended one of our weekly meetings in Rough Magic to observe how we worked.

We explained our concerns to Susan: the tensions between keeping up momentum and building collective consensus, working out what we have permission to do and on whose behalf, wanting to keep our decision making open and transparent, and the overall diversity of this group. Susan was horrified by the brutality of our meetings and the speed at which they were run. 'Make a decision, make it now. Next decision.' She talked to us about the dynamics of creating change, of checking in with each person at the start of each meeting about how they are feeling, and holding that space for as long as is needed and then the business of the meeting can begin. She suggested the use of a 'talking stick' to ensure people were fully heard without interruption. She reiterated the importance of looking after ourselves and each other in all of this, and the emotional toll of this activist/change work. Anne Clarke was more than dubious about any notion of sitting in a circle passing around a talking stick and doing emotional check-ins. It really wasn't her comfort zone. She looked aghast at Lian and Sarah, who were more open to entertaining these kinds of practices.

After several weeks of agonising over how we could be more inclusive and representative, we faced a choice: go together, slow down, and hold space for each other, or press on, focus on the timeframe we had set ourselves and using the strengths and expertise of the group to affect a very particular building block of change at the level of governance and policy. The pragmatic producers in us won out over the inclusive activists, for better or worse. However, our deliberations with Susan were very helpful in clarifying what we needed to do. Her message to us was that what we were doing and how we were doing it was ok. So we ran with that, and there was no more talk of talking sticks, checking in with each other, or sitting in circles.

Budgeting, Funding, and the Campaign Director Role

It became very clear by March 2016 that we would have to set up a company structure in order to responsibly facilitate our activities. To become a legal company, we needed a board and a constitution (memorandum and articles). Solicitor Linda Scales drafted the constitution and completed the company registration. Anne Clarke, Caroline Williams, Kate Ferris, Róise Goan, and Sarah Durcan signed up as the original members and directors of the company called WakingTheFeminists and we set up a bank account in this name.

The finance sub-committee (Anne, Loughlin, and Sarah) drafted a budget of what the campaign would cost. We expected we would have to raise funds, and it seemed most likely to aim for a mix of merchandise sales, individual donations, some larger philanthropic donations, and hopefully Arts Council funding and funding from the Department of Equality. We budgeted for costs associated with the management and organisation of the campaign, events, communications and publicity, merchandise and retail, and media and bias training for the group. We did not factor in research costs at this stage, nor the running of a programme like Tonic Theatre's Advance that we were beginning to envision. We budgeted for honorariums for event speakers, photography and video, production and technical costs, and travel and accommodation for three further events. In the end, we only put on two more major events (International Women's Day 8 March in Liberty Hall and a final event back in the Abbey on 14 November 2016), and ultimately the campaign cost significantly less than we first anticipated, as we relied on more voluntary work and in-kind support.

The core group agreed that, once formal research into gender equality in Irish theatre began, the researchers should be paid for their time and expertise. However, we vastly underestimated the amount of work involved, and the amount eventually paid to the researchers was a fraction of what their involvement was worth. The group also agreed that Lian should receive payments for the extraordinary level of work she was doing above and beyond the rest of us. She worked freelance, and this campaign was greatly reducing her availability for other jobs. It was clear that she was doing the majority of the campaign leadership and organisation, so it was only fair that she would be paid. We wrote a role description and the original agreement was for €4,875 for 19.5 days over 13 weeks. Ultimately, Lian was paid €10,000 for her work on the campaign. The fee was nothing close to what her contribution to the campaign was worth. Additionally, she made just over €1,500 in speaker fees in 2015 and 2016, while taking on the majority of public speaking engagements for free to help keep the campaign visible, and in some cases directing speaker fees back into the campaign fund. She suggested she be given the title of Campaign Director. She reasoned that if she was going to do vast amounts of work for little or no money, she should at least get a fancy title that reflected her commitment and labour.

For fundraising support, Anne, Lian, and Sarah met with Andrew Hetherington of Business to Arts to seek advice and brainstorm ideas. We quickly drew up a list of people to ask for assistance. Andrew connected us with the Community Foundation of Ireland,[18] and we met Sara Stokes, their Grants & Donor Services Executive in the Gresham Hotel on 17 June 2016. In July we submitted a successful application to the Community Foundation for €12,400, and helped us run the public meetings. This, alongside €20,000 from the Arts Council to support our research, and €5,000 funding from the Government's 2016 Commemoration programme for the closing event, formed the majority of the income of the campaign, alongside merchandise income and some individual donations.

As 2016 progressed we honed the focus of the core group to advocating for policy changes and engaging at a governance level. At the same time, there was still grassroots activity happening across the country – the all-important wider #WakingTheFeminists movement – that was supported and encouraged and celebrated through the official social media channels and personal contacts.

SIX

Seeking Advice and Meeting the Arts Council and Government Ministers

This chapter focuses on meetings #WakingTheFeminists had with individual advisors, other organisations, government departments and agencies, including the Arts Council, the Department of Arts, and the Department of Equality. We had an exceptionally busy schedule of important meetings throughout the year, where we gained invaluable insights which further shaped the campaign and helped us navigate the complexities of advocacy, funding, policy, and political engagement.

From the earliest days of the campaign, individuals and organisations from beyond theatre had contacted us with offers of help and advice; individual women and women's organisations predominantly. We knew it would be beneficial to connect with a broader network; we had enough humility to know what we didn't know and that we would need to rely on wider expertise. One of the loveliest things of the whole campaign was connecting with and sharing learning with significant allies. In turn, we shared what we learned with others as we went along. We experienced huge generosity and camaraderie from these women and they all encouraged us to succeed. As we gained more knowledge and information, we felt far less exposed and vulnerable. These organisations included: the National Women's Council of Ireland,[1] Abortion Rights Campaign,[2] The Artists' Campaign to Repeal the Eighth Amendment,[3] Women for Election,[4] and Women in Film and Television;[5] and internationally: the League of Professional Theatre Women (USA),[6] The Lillys,[7] and The Kilroys

(USA),[8] and Equal Representation for Actresses (ERA) in the UK.[9] We also met with representatives of Accenture and Facebook.

We wanted to learn from Women for Election how addressing the 'five Cs' which hold women back from running for election (childcare, cash, candidate selection, confidence, and culture) could be relevant to women in theatre. Within our own sector we connected with Theatre Forum on their pay scale research and policy development, as well as linking in with Equity which is part of the SIPTU union, and the Association of Irish Stage Technicians.[10]

Advice on Campaigning

Early on, Anne Clarke arranged a meeting with Margaret E. Ward (Mags), entrepreneur, journalist, and broadcaster. Mags was the founder of Women on Air in 2010, a group seeking gender equality on radio, and had been appointed to the board of RTÉ in early 2015. Anne, Lisa, and Sarah met her the morning of Monday, 7 December 2015, in the cosy, carpeted Bank of Ireland Enterprise Lounge with its plush upholstered matching chairs, overlooking the corner of Grafton Street and Nassau Street.[11] Mags' experience and advice was insightful and very practical. She advised us to have a clear strategy, clear role definitions, and to ensure that each person knew what they were doing within the group. We should have one spokesperson, but rotate the person from time to time – the press would want one point of contact. We should strategise our use of social media, as it would be our friend in this campaign. We should stay on Twitter, because it's where journalists were going for their stories, and continue to use our #WakingTheFeminists handle. She, like Una Mullally before, warned us not to feed the trolls and to ignore the naysayers and to beware of sly attacks that would come our way from the media; for example, the 'she has a personal agenda/axe to grind/previous gripe' type of narrative.

She also advised on the relative strengths and usefulness of media platforms: we would get more depth out of print media, while TV was all soundbites, so the message needed to be kept concentrated, and radio would probably be about 10% of our media campaign. If #WakingTheFeminists were asked to be on a panel, we should make sure to know in advance who else would be on it and ask to be informed of any changes.[12] She recommended we get some media training and stressed the importance of facts and data. We needed research statistics to back up the stories from personal testimony, and we should keep repeating 'the studies say' and 'the facts are'. We should have a one-page prep sheet, and drill the facts into our group, especially the spokespeople.

As well as advising us to meet with boards of theatre organisations, she also advised that we all put ourselves forward for boards, to get into positions of influence where possible, and to sign up on StateBoards.ie.[13] On managing our own people and campaign, she suggested we would need to plan for the extremes and protest wings of the movement, so they wouldn't derail or distract from the core. It was vital to direct the anger where it belonged, not let it tear us apart through in-fighting. She stressed the importance of addressing structures and not just the symptoms, something that we very much took to heart.

Later that same day (7 December 2015), in one of the dimly lit back rooms off the Library Bar at the Central Hotel on Exchequer Street, Róise Goan had arranged for us to meet Bride Rosney, former advisor to President Mary Robinson, former Director of Communications for RTÉ, and at that time a board member of Druid Theatre Company. Bride was a hugely impressive person and we were all in awe of her. A small gang of #WakingTheFeminists crowded around the table to soak up her wisdom.[14] Bride asked us about our objectives. We mumbled through them. She was not impressed as we couldn't roll them off quickly enough. She said they needed to be very clear and succinct, and prompted us to go over and over them. Within a few minutes under her stern eye, we managed to refine down our core message to 'Equality for Women in Irish Theatre', which became the tagline of the campaign.

She advised that to be practical and effective we needed a small core group to run the campaign. She echoed Mags' earlier advice to meet with boards and individual board members. She warned us to stay well clear of deliberately opening up the conversation on sexual harassment, as it could derail the whole movement. She related Desmond Tutu's advice to the Elders: 'If you want to go fast, go alone; but if you want to go far, go together.'[15]

On 21 December 2015 Caroline Williams and Maria Fleming met with Karan O'Loughlin (National Campaigns and Equality organiser for SIPTU and liaison with Irish Equity). Karan was very keen to support our proposed event on International Women's Day and offered us the use of the theatre in Liberty Hall, the union's headquarters with a symbolically powerful revolutionary history. She told us of a survey on harassment and bullying that was then underway with Irish Equity and encouraged us to share it so our followers could participate.

On Friday, 8 January 2016, Lian and Sarah met with Anne O'Dea (CEO and editor-at-large) and Aisling Hyland (Events Manager) of *Silicon Republic*, a leading online news journal for science and technology based in Dublin. The initial suggestion was that #WakingTheFeminists feature in a small way at their Inspirefest conference,[16] held in the Bord Gáis Energy Theatre in Dublin

30 June to 2 July 2016; following this meeting Lian was invited to give a presentation from the main stage.

After a positive meeting with the National Women's Council of Ireland (NWCI) on 25 January 2016 at the café in the Alliance Française on Kildare Street, #WakingTheFeminists became members of NWCI. At that meeting NWCI were represented by Orla O'Connor (Director), Alice Mary Higgins (Policy and Campaigns Officer), Sarah Clarkin (Communications and Social Media Officer), and Louise Glennon (Women in Leadership Officer); #WakingTheFeminists was represented by Caroline, Lian, and Sarah.

Meeting with the Arts Council

On Monday, 25 January 2016, barely two months after the first #WakingTheFeminists public meeting, Cian O'Brien, Lian, and Sarah met with the executive of the Arts Council, represented by Orlaith McBride (Director), Liz Meaney (Arts Director for Performing and Local Arts), and David Parnell (Head of Theatre). The overall tone of the meeting was positive, but guarded. The Arts Council executives spoke about the importance of equality of access in general. In the development of their new policy they were keen to address all areas of equality including gender, socio-economic issues, disability, and diversity, as well as attending to the living, working, and pay conditions of artists.

We wanted gender equality policies to be created by all organisations in receipt of public funding, and asked that this would be a condition of Arts Council funding. We were told that this would not be feasible in 2016 as funding decisions had already been made, but that the Arts Council would be embarking on a new investment strategy and would endeavour to develop a new internal system to measure outputs; and gender would be included alongside economics, demographic breakdown, and diversity. As the Director noted at the meeting: 'the arts cannot just be for middle-class, well-educated people.'

More significantly, on Wednesday, 23 March 2016, Anne Clarke, Caroline, Lian, Oonagh Murphy, and Sarah presented to the entire Arts Council at their plenary session, chaired by Sheila Pratschke. It was very unusual for the full Council to meet in this way with an outside organisation. As well as outlining our campaign aims we presented them with several solutions to make the theatre ecosystem more gender equitable, which included research that would form a baseline to measure progress against, and introducing a locally adapted version of Tonic Theatre's Advance programme,[17] which is described on their website:

From October 2013 to May 2014 Tonic piloted the Advance process with a cohort of 11 theatres, guiding them through a six-month period of research, reflection and activity which tasked them to take an interrogative and methodical approach to understanding the root causes behind the comparative lack of women in key creative roles. Rather than settling for quick fixes or advocating a 'sticking plaster' approach, Advance tasked the theatres to understand not only where barriers to female talent exist within their organisations but why.[18]

The #WakingTheFeminists presentation to the Arts Council covered a lot of ground: key issues that contribute to the under-representation of women working on larger stages; lack of opportunities for women to rise to top level positions; a fall-off of women from the sector after training, and again after starting families; the challenges of unconscious bias in programming; women arts workers being affected by family issues more than men due to the breakdown of roles along traditional gender lines; hostile working environments; issues of bullying and harassment; and gender disparities within traditional pay scales, particularly in design roles. We asked that the Arts Council be a leading agent of change by ensuring that:

- Gender equality policy would be put in place and demonstrably imple-mented, as a requirement of funding.
- Reporting on gender breakdown would be mandatory for all arts org-anisations.
- Publicly funded arts organisations would self-publish gender stats annually.
- The Arts Council's own gender stats on allocated funding would be reported annually.
- Bias training would be established for both the Arts Council itself and for arts organisations.
- The Arts Council would make a public statement on their position on gender equality and their intent to implement policy.

We shared our estimate that well over 2,500 hours of work had already been volunteered by those involved in #WakingTheFeminists. We requested €20,000 in funding: €10,000 for the research and €10,000 towards the groundwork and feasibility study of a training programme modelled on Advance.[19]

We stated that we believed that the issue of gender inequality could be solved within five years in Irish theatre, and this would be a defining moment for all of us in the arts. #WakingTheFeminists saw this opportunity as profoundly creative in itself. The issues were complex, but the decision before us all was simple: to choose to make equality a reality for the sake of the creative future of our country and all our artists.

Council members responded that this was laudable but wildly ambitious. However, the feeling in the room was generally very attentive, thoughtful, and quietly supportive. On 10 May 2016 we received an offer of funding of €20,000 from the Director of the Arts Council, subject to further discussion and clarification on our research methodology and our procurement process around researching a suitable training provider. On 29 June 2016, #WakingTheFeminists research lead Dr Brenda Donohue met with Liz Meaney and Monica Corcoran of the Arts Council to discuss her proposed methodology for the research. We sent further details on how we planned to scope out an Advance-type programme, with a plan to cultivate and promote the appropriate action research programme for the sector once we had done a transparent process to identify both the right provider and the interested participants across the country. We now had our first funding in place: the quantitative research could begin, and we could put serious work into planning an Advance-type programme, with the hope that we could source additional funding for it in the future.

Theatre Forum, the major membership-based resource organisation for individuals, venues, companies, and other organisations in the performing arts, had been supportive of #WakingTheFeminists from the start. They had managed cashflow for donations that came in for the first public event in the Abbey in November 2015, and Anna Walsh (Director) and Irma McLoughlin (General Manager) were involved in helping run the event itself. At a meeting on 19 January 2016 #WakingTheFeminists[20] asked Theatre Forum to:

- Research, draft, and make available gender balance policy texts and diversity policies, that can be used by all kinds of performing arts organisations who work with either/both permanent staff or contract/freelance workers – both in relation to artistic programming and in the structures and systems of the organisation itself.

- Research, draft, and make available policy text on harassment and bullying in the workplace, that can be used by all kinds of performing arts organisations who work with either/both permanent staff or contract/freelance workers. Including a set of recommended procedures to be followed by people who experience this behaviour, and by people who witness or know of this behaviour happening.

- Provide/serve as a portal for high-quality unconscious bias training for those working in the arts and sitting on arts boards.

In 2016 Theatre Forum engaged Olwen Dawe to deliver unconscious bias training,[21] and Lian and Sarah attended the first training session with the board and staff of Theatre Forum in Festival House, East Essex Street on 6 January 2017.

Meetings at Government Level

On 2 February 2016, Anne and Sarah met with Aodhán Ó Ríordáin TD, Minister of State for Community, Culture and Equality. Aodhán had been at the launch of the Abbey's 2016 programme that kicked off the furore, and had been apologetic when meeting Lian subsequently, saying that he should have been more attentive to the imbalance in the theatre's programme. After our hour with Aodhán we had 20 minutes with Tánaiste (Deputy Prime Minister) Joan Burton TD. Both were very positive about #WakingTheFeminists. After this meeting, we reported to the wider #WakingTheFeminists group that we would put in a request immediately to the Department of Justice and Equality for funding towards our events, research, and an Advance-like programme.

As it turned out, the Dáil was dissolved the day after this meeting and a general election was called. After the election, there was a change in government, and it took many more months to re-engage with the new minister and Department of Justice and Equality. There was a lot of back and forth to arrange a meeting with David Stanton TD, by then Minister of State for Justice with special responsibility for Equality, Immigration, and Integration. At one point, since it was proving difficult to get a meeting in the minister's diary, Anne arranged for Lian and Sarah to be seated beside Minister Stanton at the opening night of Landmark Productions' musical *Once* at the Olympia Theatre in July 2016. We had a quick chat with him at the interval, reminding him about the campaign, and that we were still seeking a meeting.

Although we didn't have that meeting until the autumn, our chat in the theatre helped to move things on, and on Friday, 28 October 2016, Anne, Lian, and Sarah met with officials in the Department of Equality in Bishop's Square, Redmond Hill in Dublin. We prepared beforehand in the Goose on the Loose café across the road. The two officials were very helpful, at one point sliding a copy of the National Women's Strategy 2007–2016 across the table to us. We were, embarrassingly, completely unaware of its existence, even after nearly 11 months of campaigning. The Strategy was 'the key policy document in relation to the advancement of women in Irish society, across all facets of the economy and society, adopted by the then government'.[22] Many of its provisions, especially in relation to the arts, had been quietly shelved in the wake of the financial crisis of 2009.

We were particularly gobsmacked to read Objective 15: 'To increase the number of women involved in the arts in Ireland' and its ten associated actions, most of which were the responsibility of the Arts Council:

- Offer leadership in the area of governance, through the publication of policy and resource documents.
- Establish a forum for women working in the arts which will explore common issues facing them and develop a working agenda to address these issues.
- Publish guidelines on equality specific to the arts.
- Offer leadership in the area of equality, through the publication of policy and resource documents.
- Provide advice and leadership in the area of equality and the Arts Council will undertake comprehensive survey including people's experiences of the arts in 2006 and 2007.
- Arts Council survey will include measurement of women's active participation in the arts.
- Collect data regarding the number of women currently studying to become arts practitioners or facilitators.
- Provide advice to women who participate, or would like to participate, in the arts.
- Examine the current physical infrastructure for the arts and ascertain the level of usage by women.

The officials then introduced us to the concept of 'public duty of positive care', which all organisations in receipt of government funding are bound by. All of this information was so revelatory to us, it was like a smoking gun: it turned out that just about *everything* we had been calling for should have been actioned by the Arts Council several years before and that they had done very little about it in the intervening years of austerity.

The officials also informed us of an upcoming EU funding programme on entrepreneurship. We realised quickly that this could be the answer to funding the Advance-style programme to tackle gender inequality in theatre organisations. Several weeks later, after successfully establishing with them that artists can also be entrepreneurs, we submitted an application to the Department of Justice and Equality for *Ardú*, an ambitious sectoral learning programme under the Programme for Employability, Inclusion and Learning (PEIL) 2014–2020, European Social Fund, Gender Equality (Women's entrepreneurship). It was a huge piece of work in an already busy year, and was submitted less than a week before the major final event in November 2016. After all that, the application was ultimately unsuccessful, to our great disappointment. But as Anne Clarke would often remark at tough moments: onwards.

SEVEN

Meetings with Theatre Companies, and the Advance Programme (*Ardú*)

This chapter describes our meetings with the boards and executives of several leading theatre companies, and our efforts to pilot a change programme adapted from Tonic Theatre's Advance model in the UK.

It was most unusual for any independent group to request meetings with boards and executives of theatre organisations. Boards govern the strategy and values of a company and can embed policy and longer term direction more effectively than an artistic or executive director who may move on in a year or two. We knew this longer-term view would be necessary to realise the change we wanted, therefore we focused on this ultimate power-holder structure in each organisation. Fewer than a dozen theatre organisations are responsible for the vast majority of theatre productions in Ireland, so if we could convince all of these organisations to work in concert with the Abbey we could create a strong network effect with higher probability for change to stick.

We focused in particular on the boards of Regularly Funded Organisations (RFOs), those theatre organisations with a regular annual funding relationship with the Arts Council, which formed the backbone of the theatre sector. Board members of theatre organisations are volunteers, as the companies are non-profit with charitable status for the most part. They often come from sectors beyond the arts, bringing a varied skill set and broad experience. By engaging with board members, we were also starting the work of connecting with and inspiring changes in other sectors. Thankfully, most arts boards were already gender diverse and often gender balanced. As well as the Abbey, immediately after the first public meeting we wrote letters to the boards of the Gate, Druid, Rough Magic, Dublin Theatre Festival, Project Arts Centre, and Dublin Fringe Festival. Conversely, Fishamble: The New Play Company contacted us. They had charged ahead and analysed many of their work practices and were keen to share what they were doing and what they had learned. We were thrilled they were being so proactive. They made this public statement on their social media on 4 December 2015:

> Waking the Feminists is such an impressive and thought–provoking campaign. It has sparked necessary and productive discussions, including in Fishamble, where we are very proud of our relationship with many female playwrights and theatre artists. We are committed to reviewing our commissioning and play development processes to ensure fully equal opportunities exist for both female and male playwrights, as well as other theatre artists and practitioners. This is currently under discussion at executive and board level and we look forward to engaging with Waking The Feminists as part of that review in the future.

#WakingTheFeminists did not have an official remit or authority to demand such meetings, and yet the boards largely responded positively to our requests to meet and were open – to varying degrees – to our message and aims. Before 2015 was out, we had met with the boards of the Abbey (17 December) and Druid (21 December), and then in 2016 with Rough Magic (3 February), Dublin Theatre Festival (4 February), Dublin Fringe Festival (4 February), Fishamble (9 May), and Project (14 July). #WakingTheFeminists was represented at the various meetings by a combination of Anne Clarke, Caroline Williams, Lian Bell, Lynne Parker, Maria Fleming, and Sarah Durcan. Often we met with a smaller delegation from each board. The breadth of experience and background of these boards was extensive and we met with the following board members from each organisation, in some cases alongside executive team members:

> **Abbey Theatre:** Bryan McMahon, Chairperson and former High Court judge; Loretta Dignam, marketing consultant; Niamh Lunny, Head of Costume and Abbey staff representative; Mark Ryan, former Country Managing Director for Accenture; Deirdre Kinahan, playwright. (These meetings were not attended by the executive.)

> **Druid:** Cathal Goan, Chairperson and former Director General of RTÉ; Bride Rosney, Secretary to the Board of the Mary Robinson Centre for

Climate Justice, former special advisor to President Robinson, and former Director of Communications for RTÉ; Eugene Downes, Director of Kilkenny Arts Festival, and former Director of Culture Ireland; Colm Tóibín, novelist, playwright, critic and journalist; Garry Hynes, Artistic Director, and Sarah Lynch, Executive Director.

Fishamble: The New Play Company: Andrew Parkes, Chairperson and devoted audience member and supporter of many theatre organisations and festivals; Liz Nugent, novelist; Tania Banotti, Director of the Institute of Advertising Practitioners in Ireland (IAPI), and formerly Director of Theatre Forum; Jim Culleton, Artistic Director, Gavin Kostick, Literary Manager, and Eva Scanlan, Executive Director.

Dublin Theatre Festival: Terence O'Rourke, Chairperson, Chairman of Enterprise Ireland and former Managing Director of KPMG; Eithne Harley, Marketing Director of Accenture; Willie White, Artistic Director, and Collette Farrell, General Manager.

Dublin Fringe Festival: Andrew Lowe, Chairperson and joint Managing Director of Element Pictures; Peter Daly, actor and accountant; Mary Moloney, CEO of CoderDojo and former Partner/Managing Director at Accenture; Kris Nelson, Artistic Director.

Project Arts Centre: Sarah Pierce, Chairperson and visual artist; John O'Halloran, barrister; Cian O'Brien, Artistic Director.

Rough Magic Theatre Company: Gerard Smyth, Chairperson, poet, journalist and former Managing Editor for arts with the *Irish Times*; Anne Fogarty, professor at University College Dublin; Lynne Parker, Artistic Director, and Caroline Williams, Producer.

By mid-December 2015 we remained concerned that there still hadn't been any concrete action from the Abbey to indicate their next steps, despite all our efforts. We decided to put more pressure on through the press. Lian wrote an opinion piece published in the *Irish Times*[1] on 16 December, the day before we were due to meet with the Abbey Board:

The board and director acknowledged publicly that the programme announced for the first half of next year 'does not represent gender equality'. We need a declaration by McMahon and the board that they will address this inequality for the latter part of the year.

Many may wonder why we are making such a fuss about the Abbey's terrible track record in gender equality. Apart from the issue of the fair use of public money (the Abbey gets half – €6.2 million – of all the State funding for theatre), and apart from miserably failing its own mission statement as a national theatre to engage with and reflect Irish society, it is a question of who gets to tell our stories – yours and mine.

A national theatre, at its best, is a creative space for us as artists and audience to look at the past in new ways, lay bare the present and imagine a future. If the national theatre is not allowing women's voices to be heard, then they exclude half the nation in the creative imagining of our world, doing both artists and audiences an unforgivable disservice.

The word 'commemoration' rattles dryly around the country in the lead-up to next year's centenary events. Commemoration. Remembering together. Memory itself is a creative act; everyone's memory of an event is different, as is everyone's story of the event. During the past weeks, through the voices of a multitude of women and men speaking up as feminists, this word came to life for me. I realise how important exposure to a spectrum of stories is – next year more than ever.

The director, Senator Fiach Mac Conghail, admitted at the public meeting that he 'did not ensure that our 2016 programme would reflect the experience of the nation as a whole'. He expressed his regret – not in itself an apology – and appears to have done nothing about it since. That is simply not enough.

It is the Abbey's responsibility to reflect the nation, with the use of public money, and the board's responsibility to ensure that it does so. We're not asking, we're demanding.

The following day, Thursday, 17 December, we met with representatives of the Abbey board in the boardroom at the Bank of Ireland Enterprise Centre on Grafton Street. There was definitely a tension in the air as the meeting began; Lian's opinion piece had struck a nerve again. The Chairperson of the Abbey Board opened the meeting by taking us to task about the media coverage, relaying how difficult it had been for board members. They were particularly exercised by an article in the *Irish Times* by Fintan O'Toole on Friday, 13 November:

> If we ask how we got to the point where the National Theatre didn't notice that its 'nation' was made up almost entirely of people with

penises, we must of course look at the deep roots of male privilege and female marginalisation.

...

In its properly contrite statement on Thursday the Abbey board promised to 'work with the director and new incoming directors to develop a comprehensive policy and detailed plan to help address gender equality'. That it doesn't have a 'detailed plan' for gender equality is obvious, but the statement also implicitly admits that it doesn't even have a broad statement of policy. Again, this is bad governance on the Abbey's part, but it is also unacceptable that the Arts Council has never, in all its reviews of the Abbey, got around to asking it to put on paper its recognition of its duty to uphold equality.[2]

#WakingTheFeminists had no influence over what Fintan wrote. We were not firing out press releases and calling the press; the press was calling us. Maria Fleming, who had offered to act as the extremist or 'bad cop' in the group of otherwise diplomatic voices, interjected and reminded the Abbey delegation that this whole thing escalated because of some ill-advised tweets from *their* director, so they should look at their own media policy before criticising us. The meeting then settled down to a very frank and civil exchange of views. #WakingTheFeminists outlined what we thought necessary for the Abbey to do next.

The Abbey did have a Business Code of Conduct at that time that described its commitment to fairness and integrity and non-discrimination. It did not have a specific policy in relation to gender equality or diversity in its programming. #WakingTheFeminists were keen to help the board understand that it could set and monitor a broad programming strategy which included gender equality, without overly interfering in the Artistic Director's autonomy to choose the programme.

The Abbey delegates listened carefully, and at the end of the meeting, Bryan McMahon told us, 'you will succeed in this because you have right on your side'. We mutually agreed a statement which was released to the press and on social media after the meeting:

> We are happy to report that #WakingTheFeminists had a constructive initial meeting earlier today with the Chair and the sub committee of the Abbey Board responsible for developing and implementing gender equality policy. We welcomed the opportunity for a frank and productive exchange of views. There was a considerable degree of consensus about the substantive issues and the urgency of a meaningful and enduring response from our National Theatre.

We can say that there is great willingness to engage, and to create real and enduring change. They apologised for the omission regarding gender which they hadn't previously seen. The remit of the subcommittee is:

· Address gender balance
· Develop a gender policy
· Draft an implementation plan

The Chair was very vocal in his support and about the Abbey wanting to lead change in this area, and not just for the Abbey, but for all theatre and arts sector.

A statement from the Board and Director of the Abbey went up on the Abbey's website on 22 December, in which Fiach stated:

> I am determined to programme the work of women artists in the latter half of 2016. An exciting and innovative programme of plays will be confirmed when we announce our Autumn/Winter Season. A national conversation is underway; one which I look forward to participating further in with members of the theatre community. The Abbey Theatre looks forward to leading the way in achieving a much-needed cultural shift in gender equality in the years to come.

From each of the companies #WakingTheFeminists met, we sought key actions during the year: to make a public commitment to take action on gender equality at our International Women's Day 8 March event, to participate in a group meeting around the establishment of a research and training programme for the sector, to participate in a quantitative research project, and then report on progress at the final #WakingTheFeminists public event on 14 November 2016.

#WakingTheFeminists drew up a standard agenda for each meeting, as outlined in this one example from our meeting with Rough Magic on 3 February 2016:

1. Intros and Terms of Reference

2. Key Issues

  a. Underrepresentation of women playwrights, designers, and leading actors in RM's record

b. Systemic and structural bias against women artists in programming and key programming related departments (literary, marketing etc.)

c. Equal opportunity and resources

d. Commissioning procedures, contracting and pay scales

e. Policy and measurement of equality in the RM programme and accountability at Board level, and lack of measurement, awareness and procedures at Executive level

3. Process

a. RM to take leading role, nationally and internationally. As respected individuals and a leading organisation here in Ireland and on the international stage – all championing equality throughout 2016

b. Consult staff

c. Engage professional assistance (e.g. Tonic) and consider initiatives undertaken elsewhere (international theatre and cross-sector)

d. Commit to appropriate and relevant training (eg unconscious bias) for all staff and board in the first quarter of 2016

e. Commit to introducing gender balance at Board level

f. Formulate and adopt policy and procedures at Board level that give a framework for the artistic director to programme to ensure gender equality and diversity in the artistic programme

g. Formulate sexual harassment and dignity at work policies and procedures, and ensure all staff and contractors are aware of such policies and what to do if there is an issue

h. Publish policy and annual targets on their website

i. Communicate procedures towards achieving equality internally and externally to all stakeholders

j. Report stats on equality internally on a monthly basis. Report on equality in annual review

4. Measurable Outcomes

a. Engage in research project on all key gender stats in programming for the past ten years as a baseline to measure improvement against

b. Possible measurements on ongoing basis:

    i. No. of staff who have engaged in bias training over the period – self reporting on learning and impact 1 month/3 months/1 year on

    ii. Breakdown of playwrights by gender under commission for next season/s

   iii. No of plays written by women under consideration for programming in the next season

   iv. No. of female directors, designers, actors as above

   v. Ensure measurement system is weighted towards main stage full length productions / tours e.g. a play written/directed by a woman for a 2-month run is rated higher than readings by women artists

   vi. Track marketing and production spend and income as well as percentage attendance, and compare female led productions to male productions

  c. Ensure equity of treatment in contracts and pay rates

  d. [Suggest looking for overall balance in key roles over any 18-month period]

5. Timeline

  a. Announce outline policy process towards achieving equality, and specific goals for 2016 March 8th event and publish timeline to 50/50 equality

  b. Quarterly reporting to board on progress, and public updates circulated quarterly throughout 2016

6. Responsibility

  a. Board/executive/all staff/contractors

In some cases we were meeting with companies whose staff (or former staff) were also deeply involved with #WakingTheFeminists, including Caroline Williams, who was Producer with Rough Magic, and Cian O'Brien, who was CEO of Project Arts Centre. When we extended our requests for meetings, Cian felt there could be a conflict of interest for him, particularly around the pressure to participate in an Advance-like programme, and he stepped back from the organising committee in mid-summer.

The festival and venue meetings were a bit fraught as these entities did not see themselves as theatre producers as such. Dublin Fringe Festival is a multidisciplinary festival, although theatre has always been dominant in its annual programme. Dublin Theatre Festival is primarily a presenting festival, although they do commission and premiere work in co-production most years. Project Arts Centre is also a multidisciplinary venue, a presenting/ receiving house for theatre and dance, encompassing two theatres and a visual arts space. Independent companies and festivals hire the space to present work, and Project also supports a number of small companies and individual artists. The boards appeared concerned that they were being tarred with the same brush as the Abbey, and intimated that they already had a good track record on gender inclusion and diversity; Dublin Fringe Festival and Project Arts Centre in particular saw this as always having been at the core of their work. We pointed out that while they may not be in control of the gender balance of each production in their programmes, their artistic directors make programming decisions, and they were three of the preeminent platforms for showcasing work, which often went on to be programmed by other festivals and venues, nationally and internationally. We reiterated that we saw the issue of gender equality as a systemic issue for *all* organisations involved in theatre production and presentation, not only the Abbey, and that gender intersects with all other aspects of diverse representation.

We never met the board of the Gate, despite repeated requests. We wrote several letters to the Gate board, and each time Michael Colgan, Artistic Director and CEO, communicated to us that the board had authorised him to be its representative and liaise with #WakingTheFeminists. Michael, as well as being CEO, was uniquely also a board member, despite good charitable governance having long maintained that paid company officers should not be on the board. So we only met with Michael, and any attempts to directly contact the Chairperson Mary Finan were rebuked with furious phone calls from Michael to Anne. Anne, Lian, and Sarah had a first meeting with Michael at lunchtime in the Gresham Hotel on 8 December 2015. He outlined all the difficulties he saw in addressing gender equality on stage. Anne and Lian had a follow-up meeting with him in the Dylan Hotel on 6 February 2016. After much back and forth with Lian and Anne, Michael spoke at the *Spring Forward* meeting in Liberty Hall on 8 March. In mid-2016, the Gate announced Michael would be retiring, and a recruitment process commenced. While we continued to engage with him throughout the summer to get the Gate to commit to a possible Irish Advance programme, Teerth Chungh, Head of Production, represented the Gate at subsequent meetings we called between leaders of all the companies to discuss the programme (by then titled *Ardú*) in June, and at the closing of the campaign in November.

The Abbey's Eight Guiding Principles

Monday, 13 June 2016, we were back in the Bank of Ireland Business Lounge on Grafton Street at the request of board member and chairperson of the gender equality subcommittee, Loretta Dignam. She wanted to share the preliminary findings of the Abbey's gender equality subcommittee, and get our feedback. Caroline, Lian, and Sarah met with Loretta and her fellow subcommittee members Deirdre Kinahan and Niamh Lunny.[3] They talked us through their process, who they had consulted with, what they found, and the key points they had put to the Abbey Board for adoption. Their process was fast but thorough and well considered. From #WakingTheFeminists' request to adopt policy, action plans and measurable results, they crafted eight guiding principles. It was an extraordinary moment. The principles went beyond what any of us in #WakingTheFeminists could have wished for, and it was heartening and emotional listening to the committee talk and to hear the seriousness of their intent. If implemented, these actions would make a massive impact, encourage others to take similar steps and change Irish theatre for good.

On 30 August the Abbey published its 'Eight Guiding Principles for Gender Equality':

1. Update the mission statement and other key documents within the Abbey Theatre to specifically reflect a goal of gender equality. The key documents include:
   – The Mission Statement of the Abbey Theatre
   – The Memorandum and Articles of Association

2. To put gender equality as a key Board priority and responsibility, meaning that gender equality will become a permanent board agenda item with immediate effect.

3. The Abbey Theatre commits to continued gender equality at board level.

4. To achieve gender equality in all areas of the artistic programme over the next five years by presenting more work led by female theatre practitioners. Gender equality will be measured in five year periods starting from 2017. There will be ongoing flexibility within programming for a given year but over the course of each five year period the artistic programme will achieve gender balance.

5. The Abbey Theatre commits to gender equality in the play commissioning process.

6. The Abbey Theatre undertakes to deliver a workshop programme for all employees, examining issues of gender equality in the workplace.

7. With a view to raising awareness of the career opportunities for women in theatre, the Abbey Theatre will create an annual programme for second level students within the National Theatre.

8. Progress made by our gender equality initiatives will be specifically reported in the Abbey Theatre's Annual Report. This recommendation will ensure that both the focus and progress on achieving gender equality at the national theatre will be documented and detailed

within the Annual Report thus ensuring that there is clear visibility on this journey. The 2016 Annual Report will contain the first update on gender equality.

An Irish Advance Programme: *Ardú*

We had been impressed with the approach and outputs of Tonic Theatre's Advance programme in the UK. We saw a bespoke version of Advance adapted to Irish theatre (which we named in Irish as *Ardú*, meaning raise or uplift) as a practical action research initiative to help organisations understand and address gender inequality. A key aspect of the programme was that the participants worked together, they would learn from one another, having a multiplier effect, and accelerating systemic change.

Tonic worked with key UK theatre organisations to identify why women were not rising to the top in key creative roles, and provided them with tools to help find proactive solutions. Advance was an interrogative and methodical approach with publicly shared results and proven to be effective. Two rounds of the programme had been run in recent years with leading organisations including the National Theatre in London, the Almeida, the Royal Shakespeare Company, the Young Vic, Northern Stage, Sadler's Wells, and Sheffield Theatres.[4]

Each organisation formed their own research question around equality, and then they and Tonic spent several months researching the underlying causes and solutions, as outlined on Tonic's website:

> Tonic recognises the power of bringing cohorts of organisations together to work alongside each other on shared challenges and to ensure cross-fertilisation of ideas and practice. The programme brought together the Artistic Directors, Chief Executives, and senior staff of leading performing arts organisations. They recognised that something was preventing talented women in the performing arts industries from rising to the top and wanted to understand in a nuanced and complex way why this was the case and then lead the way in addressing it.

Tonic piloted the Advance process with a cohort of 11 theatres, guiding them through a six-month period of research, reflection and activity which tasked them to take an interrogative and methodical approach to understanding the root causes behind the comparative lack of women in key creative roles. Rather than settling for quick fixes or advocating a 'sticking plaster' approach,

Advance tasked the theatres to understand not only where barriers to female talent exist within their organisations but why.

Upon concluding the programme all participating organisations were required to have in place concrete and considered plans for how they would create change. This entailed them working towards progress within their own organisations but also considering how, within their cohort and with Tonic's ongoing collaboration, they could drive for industry-wide change.[5]

Loughlin and Lian liaised with Lucy Kerbel, Director of Tonic, to establish costs of an Advance programme tailored to an Irish setting. We reckoned about six companies would be the minimum to make it feasible. We proposed it run over several months, and be funded by the Arts Council with an additional contribution from each of the participating Irish companies, festivals, and venues. We just had to convince them. We arranged for representatives of several of the organisations to meet with Lucy when she came to Dublin in mid-February 2016 so she could explain the benefits of Advance.

After a lot of groundwork, on Friday, 17 June 2016, #WakingTheFeminists gathered board and executive representatives of the organisations in a studio at Dublin Fringe Festival to discuss Advance/*Ardú* and what the sector might do together.[6] As part of our funding from the Arts Council, we had been offered €10,000 to scope this action research, but we needed further buy-in from participating organisations to get it going. It wasn't an easy meeting, but at least the discussion was forthright and courteous. The Abbey subcommittee outlined their process to date, noting they each worked approximately half a day a week for two months. Sharing their learning and demonstrating the amount of work involved was beneficial for the rest of the companies as they considered planning their own processes. Those at the meeting noted how positive it was to speak together, as it was a rare (if not unique) opportunity for this group to meet this way. If we could make this process work it could potentially also benefit other issues the community could deal with collectively.

Some organisations (Dublin Theatre Festival, Project, Gate) came out quickly against participating in Advance/*Ardú*, while Dublin Fringe Festival was on the fence. They didn't think it was the right fit for them. They thought it inappropriate that a third party (#WakingTheFeminists) was demanding that they sign up to another external consultant, and would rather do their own due diligence around finding the appropriate consultants. In the case of the Gate, they were going through a succession process for a new Director, so it wasn't the right time for them. Dublin Theatre Festival had already looked into getting unconscious bias training for their team, but they considered it cost prohibitive, and asked if this was something Tonic could provide. Dublin Fringe Festival and Project stated that they also wanted to look at diversity in a broader sense; they expressed that gender was not the most important or pressing question for them at that moment. Their view was that they had already been good at gender equality for years and would like also to look intersectionally at class and race.

There was also a concern amongst some companies that Tonic wouldn't understand specific Irish nuances, but we clarified that there would be an Irish liaison in place alongside Lucy to address precisely that. The cost was a big concern for all these companies. Without further funding from the Arts Council they were not prepared to commit, and even if funding was forthcoming they would rather design something themselves. Despite the evidence from the first two rounds of Advance in the UK, there was also a question around would it work in the end. Would it be worth the effort? They also noted the difficulty all arts organisations have of finding time for reflection and any kind of staff planning and training, due to being understaffed and under-resourced in those years of austerity.

Other companies (the Abbey, Druid, Fishamble, and Rough Magic) were more positive about Advance/*Ardú* and the principle of doing something active, and being seen to lead together. They saw it as an important governance issue for both board and executives to address. We got to a point where a number of organisations were open to sharing resources, learning and looking at joint unconscious bias training, and agreeing to do something publicly together in order to show leadership around gender equality. It was agreed that a working group was to be set up to work through the details.

Sarah, who had chaired this meeting, reported back to #WakingTheFeminists in Slack later that day that she found the negativity of some of the companies very frustrating:

> Ok, so in the end, we did get consensus that it was important and beneficial for all these orgs to do and be seen to do SOMETHING publicly together to show leadership around gender equality.
> I also clarified earlier on that we are not expecting the Advance programme to result in a joint sector policy or position on gender equality, more that each organisation's learning and research would have a network effect, while being specific to each of them themselves.
> So there was SOME progress but painfully slow.

Anne Clarke, pragmatically positive as always, responded:

> In the way you learn from everything, the one thing we hadn't prepared for was for one organisation to come out so strongly against Advance early on … you live and learn. But I think we have to keep things in

perspective. We have been pushing very hard on Advance, but it is just the means to an end. I think getting all those organisations in one room (and then not letting it degenerate into an unfocused talking shop) is a triumph actually, and we should take pride (and comfort) in that.

Loughlin Deegan later recalled:

> I was hugely disappointed by the response of my male colleagues in the industry. I was shocked and surprised at their lack of self awareness, they weren't able to appreciate that they were largely afraid of getting involved or fearful of the process, because of their own concerns about how they were personally perceived and concerns about their own ego, or driven by their own ego. And it was so apparent to me. It was just a fear of 'that if I give ground, I might personally be perceived to have been somehow complicit in all of this, whereas if I continue to argue that there isn't a problem, then I personally won't be undermined in any way'. I thought that was extraordinary.

We kept pushing, right up to the last day of the campaign when we arranged a broad sectoral meeting that was our last gasp attempt to get the Advance/ *Ardú* programme going. Ultimately, since we hadn't been able to get enough organisational buy-in to do the action research part of what we had proposed to the Arts Council (which was how we'd framed *Ardú*), we didn't draw down the full funding. When we were ultimately unsuccessful in a major EU funding application that might have swayed opinions,[7] it was clear that Advance/*Ardú* was dead in the water, which was very disappointing to #WakingTheFeminists and the companies who would have liked the initiative to proceed.

Gatherings on Nollaig na mBan/Women's Christmas, 6 January 2016, in Galway (top, Photo: John Rogers) and Belfast (bottom, Photo: Amanda Coogan).

Supporters gathering in Los Angeles (top) and Limerick (bottom).

EIGHT

Other Events and Power Plays

Alongside the extensive work behind the scenes that the core team was putting in, there were a number of self-organised events across the island, the UK, and the US over the course of 2016. These were not organised directly by the #WakingTheFeminists core team, but by people who were supporters and part of the wider movement and we supported them through promotion on social media where possible.

Nollaig na mBan

Lian, Oonagh Murphy and Noelia Ruiz cooked up an idea to start the year on 6th January for Nollaig na mBan.[1] Lian sent out a message to the wider movement on all channels:

> **Kickstart 2016 with a feminist vision – make the year ahead one of community, activism and change**
> We thought it would be the perfect time for all feminists, women and men, who have been following and supporting the #WakingTheFeminists campaign to get together locally over a drink or a cup of tea. It's a chance to kick start the year by meeting each other, discussing the issues, telling their stories and having a bit of craic.
> We call for people who are passionate about equality to gather and have the chats. We call for arts centres everywhere to consider hosting an informal #WakingTheFeminists Nollaig na mBan get together for lovers of the arts. We call for members of local drama groups, sports clubs, knitting circles, book clubs, college

societies, active retirement groups, parent and toddler groups, what have you, to contact each other and see who wants to meet up. We call for anyone who is keen to host their own #WakingTheFeminists Nollaig na mBan gathering to contact a local café or bar to book some space, to tell their friends, colleagues and neighbours and get them to tell THEIR friends, colleagues and neighbours. Everyone is welcome.

Your #WakingTheFeminists Nollaig na mBan get together can be in whatever form you'd like it to take. Two hundred people in a theatre. Two people at a café table. The only requirement is that you have the chats and enjoy yourselves.

The three things we ask of you:

- plan your get together to be open and inclusive– think about what time of day will be most suitable, think about how to facilitate parents with children, think about making sure the venue you pick is accessible for someone with mobility issues, think about inviting people you wouldn't normally invite, and think about who might be in your local area that you'd like to get to know, or might like to get to know you. Once you have a plan, a time and venue, let us at #WakingTheFeminists know and we'll help spread the word for you.
- take a few photos of your gathering on the day, ideally with a sign saying #WakingTheFeminists and your location, and tweet them or send them to wakingthefeminists@gmail.com so we can share them on social media.
- talk about what you'd like to change. **We believe that feminism means examining the world around us, reimagining what it could be like if the systems in place were built to be inclusive of everyone, and working to make those changes reality.** With that in mind, take a moment to discuss with your fellow feminists what changes you'd like to see in the systems around you, big or small, and what practical steps could be taken. Choose someone to make a note of what was discussed, and send us your best ideas so we can share them publicly. Things only change when we talk about them!

Most of all: have fun, feminists.

Fourteen #WakingTheFeminists events were self-organised all over the country on Nollaig na mBan, and two took place in New York. In Dublin, we gathered in SS Michael and John (later Smock Alley Theatre and now Dublin Municipal

Olwen Fouéré speaking at the Yer Only mBan event. Photo: Emilia Krysztofiak Rua Photography.

Theatre) for an evening entitled *Yer Only mBan* organised by directors Maeve Stone and Dan Colley. Greenery, tealights, and doily decorations were strung across the room. There were long wooden tables with photos of renowned Irish women including former president Mary Robinson and writer Maeve Binchy, and platters of homemade cakes brought by the audience. It was a gorgeous relaxed evening of song, spoken word, music, and cake.

On 16 January 2016, Garry Hynes, Artistic Director of Druid Theatre, was interviewed by Marian Finucane on RTÉ Radio One. Marian asked her about #WakingTheFeminists, and Garry recalled:

> Well, it was extraordinary. I mean, Lian Bell, who has just been nominated for an *Irish Times* [Irish Theatre] Award, for that very reason, was the extraordinary person who said, 'this can't stand' so

instead of complaining about it in pubs, she actually brought a group of people together. Her leadership and those group of people drove the issue to become the key issue that it was. I think that there was another thing involved when it happened … everybody drops the ball every time again, [but] it was a pretty big ball to drop … but then the response to it was so poor, and that I think, really, the actual response when it came was … well … wow.

About the first public meeting in the Abbey, Garry remembered:

While I was there, I was actually not going to be there. Originally, I had teaching obligations in Galway and, and then about 24 hours before I thought, you know, I can't really not be there just for myself. It was packed. There was a sense of celebration, there was a sense of a great group of people being together. And there was a sense I think from everybody that we've never quite felt something like this before. And I found myself from my own personal point of view … I mean, I'm 62, I've been in the theatre all my life. I would have sort of been aware of, and yet felt that I wasn't that affected by sexism or whatever on the position of women, and I find myself first of all just hoping that this major event this momentous event goes well, and actually sort of thinking wow, how wonderful it is the whole thing starts on time. Everything is going so well. All these women are coming out and they're speaking extraordinarily, fluently and passionately. They're all recounting very different experiences. And I was really in the middle of thinking, 'What a great event this is' when all of a sudden, I just found myself in tears, because I just realised how much it was actually about me in and of itself, not about some sort of professional kind of event and so on. And it was very special, in a way that I … hadn't expected it to be.[2]

Theatre of Change Symposium

In January Fiach invited a speaker from #WakingTheFeminists to the Abbey's Theatre of Change Symposium held over three days 21–23 January 2016. Lian suggested having three voices represent the movement, concentrating on three aspects: power, men, and money. Lian, Eleanor Methven, and Loughlin Deegan were selected by the core group as our representatives. It was important to us that there were a range of ages and perspectives in choosing those three people, and it was another opportunity to keep #WakingTheFeminists in the media and part of the ongoing discourse around the centenary year of 2016. Subsequently Loughlin's speech drew him into some unexpected hot water at his job at The Lir Academy.

The symposium was held on the Abbey stage. After playing the *Irish Times* video of the #WakingTheFeminists public meeting at the Abbey, Lian began:

> As Donna Dent says in the video, there is no debate. Women theatre-makers have not had their work platformed and championed at our National Theatre to the same extent that male theatre makers have. Ever. Those of us working as #WakingTheFeminists have committed to the campaign for one year with a look back this November on what has been achieved. On March the 8th, International Women's Day we will have a second public meeting at lunchtime in Liberty Hall. We're doing this in our spare time, and we're learning as we go. We're trying to keep the structure of the group as open and egalitarian as possible and rely on people to self-select for certain tasks. It means each of us taking personal responsibility for the things we feel passionate about and have the skills for. We're listening to each other and playing to our strengths. We're rising to the challenge with glee. I wanted to give you, today, a sense of the multiplicity of the voices that have been part of the #WakingTheFeminists discourse. For that reason both Eleanor Methven and Loughlin Deegan are with me here.

Eleanor Methven gave this presentation, recalling her part in founding Charabanc Theatre Company in Northern Ireland in the 1970s:

> This month marks 38 years of my working in the Irish theatre sector – makes a girl think! In 1978, when I began my career, workplace discrimination and equal pay were hot topics. I remember an early conversation with another female colleague wherein we agreed that as feminists, we were very lucky to be actresses, as there was at least in our line of work, no chance that a man would ever be given a job that we were qualified for in preference to us, simply because he was a man. Our job after all, was gender specific. Also in the North in the late 70s, under a British – old British – Labour government, with full union recognition in our sector, we knew the men in the company at our same level of experience were being paid exactly what we were – so that's all right then! Oh, foolish virgins.
>
> When 33 years ago, we voiced our hurt, anger, frustration, the reaction was pretty much well, 'them's the breaks'. And of course,

as artist's jobs rely on being judged on talent, it is always possible to attempt to silence us with 'maybe you're just not good enough, dear'.

33 years ago, we were told to suck it up and we spat it out. Five of us formed a theatre company [Charabanc] foregrounding roles for women, written by women giving voice to the voiceless. Working class northern women in a heavily militarised society. We framed the company and the work to suit ourselves. A non-hierarchical collective; collaborative working practice; female gaze. We defined ourselves, creatively empowered ourselves, just as the men who ran the mainstream theatres have empowered themselves, reflected themselves. Just as the traditional funding bodies then in our case, Belfast City Council and the Arts Council of Northern Ireland, were also made up of men whose gaze was reflected in traditional theatre models and subject matter. But we didn't fit the male funders idea of a play, our manner of writing and the choices we made were alien to them. The subject matter, the perspective different to theirs, therefore, not to be valued, rewarded financially in the same way as, for example, Field Day. The very practice for which Charabanc was celebrated, which made us unique, was the area of our work, which they wouldn't recognise with funding. For years, only when we were in immediate pre-production and actual performance were we able to pay ourselves. That's exhausting.

I can't think of a better illustration to this problem of the power perspective than that given by playwright Ioanna Anderson on the #WakingTheFeminists website about a review she received. And whilst the reviewer didn't fault the writing they, 'just didn't want to sit through another story about a middle-aged woman and her problems.' As Ioanna says, no one says this about plays about middle-aged men. In fact, no one calls them plays about middle-aged men. They are about 'the human condition. I know what you mean, Ioanna. The *Gigli Concert* or *Quietly* or *The Weir* – middle-aged men and their problems! I am beyond exhaustion, to have to stand here reiterating things I said over 30 years ago. I do not want Lian to be in my position in another 30, and #WakingTheFeminists have made a great start. Ireland has always been a cold house for its daughters on all fronts.

Men in the arts in positions of power (and that means follow the money) have been getting away – for years – with lip service to feminism. They have had the luxury of living in the continuous past, whereas women have been asked to put up with the continual. And that seems like a good place to hand over to Loughlin.

Loughlin Deegan then presented:

I'm almost nervous. It was another actress committed to gender equality, Patricia Arquette, who reminded us recently that when men support change, it usually comes 10 times faster. As a young gay man, I became personally aware of the endemic inequalities that are hardwired into Irish society. For me, feminism was always a no-brainer. Besides, one of the reasons I was so attracted to working professionally in the theatre was because it is an industry that prides itself on being liberal and progressive and that believes that on a good day, we can actually change the world.

In the early 1990s, at the start of my career, Irish theatre, as it remains today, was largely run by women. Until I became the boss myself, all of my bosses were women. Women who made space for many voices, including that of a naive and passionate young man who had lots of opinions on what theatre we should be producing and how we should be producing it. Those women encouraged me, they mentored me and supported me all the way through my career. That is until I got to the top of my profession, when I suddenly looked around, and I wondered where all the women had gone. When you follow the money, as Eleanor said, you discover that men control the vast majority of the resources because they dominate the larger, better-funded institutions. I believe this is why we have a gender equality problem. It is all about power and money, which means it's mostly about men, or more accurately when it comes to our major theatrical institutions, usually one.

I've come to refer to it as 'the myth of the great man'. The revered one, whose taste and judgement exists at such an elevated level that he is incapable of answering his own phone. Who, like the Wizard of Oz, requires an army of young, always female, PAs and assistants to help maintain the myth. I met many classic examples from travelling for Dublin Theatre Festival. Russia probably invented the genre; there men still wear capes to work. In the UK, he is invariably an Oxbridge graduate, and in Germany, when a great man retires, all of the staff of the theatre have to go with him in order to allow the incoming great man to establish his own court. That's true. Hundreds and hundreds of people tendered their resignations. Closer to home we have always had the great man ... great men at the top of Irish theatre. The Abbey has had only two female directors in its 111-year history. Not counting Lady Gregory, of course, who always played second fiddle to Mr Yeats – surely the archetype – and of course there is a particularly fine example in situ up the road for over 30 years. Dublin Theatre Festival, which I myself ran for over five years, has shamefully never had a female director in its 59-year history.

In contrast to the independent theatre sector, patriarchal hierarchies have been embedded in our leading theatre institutions since our foundation and this must change if we are to make real progress towards gender equality in Irish theatre. Changing the culture of a large organisation takes time, but it has to start somewhere. And in the context of who leads our biggest organisations that needs to start with the composition of boards and recruitment panels. Like all of us, the captains of industry and the professions who make up the majority of our theatre boards suffer from unconscious bias. When selecting a new artistic director or chief executive, the person they want to see walking into the room looks a whole lot like them. He looks like 'a great man'.

When a brilliant female friend and colleague wrote eloquently online about the despair she felt on walking into an interview for a top job in Irish theatre, only to be greeted by a panel comprising five middle-aged white men, something shifted in me personally. Until that moment, I believed that everything I had achieved in my own career had been achieved based solely on the basis of merit. When it comes to the big jobs in Irish theatre, I no longer believe that to be true.

We have given lip service to gender balance on boards and interview panels for too long. If we are serious about fixing this, we need to catch up with other industries, acknowledge that we all suffer from unconscious bias, and think seriously about bias training. Because we all have a lot to learn.

Personally, this somewhat casual feminist has been on a very steep learning curve since my involvement with #WakingTheFeminists. One of the most important things I have learned is that feminism is not just about the belief that women should have equal rights and opportunities. That's the no-brainer bit. But crucially, in order for that to happen, we have to acknowledge that the systems themselves are patriarchal, and therefore the systems need to change.

Hierarchical systems create the conditions that allow the 'great man' or indeed the very rare 'great woman' to thrive, and in a theatrical context that means that one person, usually a man, has all the decision-making power over whose stories are told and who gets to tell them. It is our taste, and our bias, unconscious or otherwise, that determines what work is presented on this and all our main stages.

We need to broaden out the artistic leadership of our theatres beyond one person's vision. We need diversity at the more senior levels of our arts organisations. We need creative and lateral as opposed to hierarchical thinking that encourages debate and allows diverse voices to feed into programming decisions. And it's only very recently that I realised that there is nothing new about this thinking. This is feminist thinking.

And finally, what motivates me as a man to be here today is my position as director of The Lir Academy at Trinity College [Dublin]. At the Lir each year, we work hard to find the most talented students who are deserving of the training we have to offer. And as with the independent theatre sector, I'm very happy to tell you that there is no shortage of female talent presenting itself. In our first five years, women have comprised 57 per cent of the total student population rising to as high as 69 per cent of our playwriting programme. What these young women need in order for their voices to be heard on this hallowed stage and every other stage is for all of us men in positions of power and influence, all of us men who are passionate about our reach theatre, all of us men who are liberal and progressive and who control the money, to seize this opportunity to continue to check ourselves and our thinking and our work practices and our biases and commit ourselves to simply accelerating change in time for this generation of women artists. Because equality will come, and to quote my colleague Sarah Durcan, also speaking from this stage in November, only two months ago, women working in Irish theatre are not asking for change. They are demanding it.

Lian finished up the Theatre of Change Symposium presentations by saying:

Seeing my peers and colleagues changing around me, women and men, I hear a new strength in their voices when they talk about sexism that makes me think something fundamental has shifted somewhere inside them, inside us. A new space has opened up in a way that I honestly think is going to help us improve our society. Maybe that shows me up to be a little naive and earnest and optimistic. Feminism, for me, is about reimagining what our society could be. If the attitudes and systems in place were built to be inclusive of everybody equally, and working to make those changes a reality at a personal level and in the environment around us.

I'd like to make it clear that when I say equality, equality for women in theatre, I do mean equality for *all* women, not just the ones that look and sound like me. We know that there is a shameful lack of diversity in the sector.

We also know how life-enhancing theatre can be both as audience members and as theatre makers. That's why we're here. If we are smart as a sector, we will use this opportunity to ensure our theatres are more open to everyone using the battering ram of feminism to break the door down. Apart from anything else we will end up with better theatre.

The unity that has been demonstrated by the theatre sector and is resonating elsewhere. We've been contacted by women cheering us on from the visual arts business, the media, politics, medicine, academia, the tech world, the defence forces, film and television to name a few.

While our campaign is focusing on theatre, I optimistically think that 2016 can be a year of seismic change for women in our country. If we, men and women, continue to join our feminist voices together across sectors and across all areas of society. So to wrap up – it's a big job. For the next year #WakingTheFeminists are going to be focusing on change at a macro level at the level of policy, of power and of money. But if we – if you – also look at addressing inequality at a micro level, at the level of personal duty and responsibility – of self-selecting to do the things that you can do –my naive and earnest and optimistic self says it doesn't seem that hard, does it?

After the event, Michael Colgan complained to his fellow Lir Academy board members about Loughlin's inference that he was a 'great man in a cape'. Michael resigned from the Lir board. Loughlin wrote him an apology and, at Loughlin's request, his speech was removed from the #WakingTheFeminists website, although it remains on the Abbey's YouTube page. At the Lir's early-morning board meeting on the matter, Loughlin sat outside as the board discussed his fate. He was sure he was going to be fired, and was kicking himself for the intemperance of his comments. After a seemingly endless discussion, Loughlin found out that the board would back him, and he still had his job.

Loughlin:

Michael Colgan did text me on Saturday saying my speech was 'damaging, provocative, and offensive'. I responded apologising for any offence caused and explaining I was trying to facetiously implicate all of us men who run orgs, etc. All told, however, I now regret referencing him so specifically as I think it has probably damaged our cause. But I spoke to Anne on Saturday and was relieved to hear that he was still eager for the Gate to engage. Will let you know if I hear anymore from him. And please do let me know if anybody thinks there is further damage limitation I can be doing.

And with that, Michael left the last theatre board he sat on, other than his own board at the Gate. For years he had wielded power while on the Arts Council, on the Dublin Theatre Festival board, and since 2011 on the board of the Lir.

Loughlin decided to step back from publicly being involved in #WakingTheFeminists, though he continued to work with the Lir and other companies as they developed gender equality policies. In mid–2016 he was appointed as a member of the Arts Council where he became a vocal advocate for gender equality and diversity policies.

NINE

Winning Awards

What's better than an award-winning feminist movement? A multi-award-winning feminist movement. In the theatre we know awards help build reputation and secure future funding. More important than the nice feeling of being recognised by your peers, awards were very useful in keeping the work of the campaign in the public consciousness and media coverage. For #WakingTheFeminists to collect the following awards was a welcome support to confirming and driving our equality ambitions.

Irish Times Irish Theatre Awards

Nominations were published on 16 January 2016, as well as the announcement that Anne Clarke was to receive the Special Tribute Award for outstanding contribution to Irish theatre. The award ceremony took place on 6 March at the National Concert Hall, with Sonya Kelly (actor and writer) and Shane O'Reilly (actor and writer) hosting. The night opened with a video titled *LIANHEART*, adapted by Sonya, Shane,

Irish Times Irish Theatre Award for Lian Bell and #WakingTheFeminists. Photo: Lian Bell

and filmmaker Kilian Waters from the famous sequence in the film *Braveheart*, with the faces of #WakingTheFeminists supporters superimposed on the horse riders as two battle lines faced each other. It was no surprise then, when Lian won the Judge's Special Award for 'leading the Waking The Feminists movement with courage and conviction, highlighting the inequalities in Irish theatre and advocating sustainable change.'[1]

At the end of Lian's speech she asked the audience:

> All of you who are, and have been, involved in the #WakingTheFeminists organising group, could you please stand up. And all of you who have worked on or spoken at any of the #WakingTheFeminists events.
>
> All the people who were at the Abbey for our public meeting in November, all of you who are coming to our next meeting in Liberty Hall on Tuesday.
>
> And finally all of you who call yourselves feminists and who support the campaign for equality for women in theatre.

Most people proudly jumped to their feet. One or two peeled themselves up reluctantly. But whether they liked it or not, she had everyone standing in visible support of the campaign.

The Lilly Awards, New York

On 23 May 2016, #WakingTheFeminists won an award at the 7th Annual Lilly Awards[2] ceremony at the Signature Theatre, 480 W 42nd Street, New York. Caitríona Perry, RTÉ's Washington correspondent, travelled to New York with a cameraperson to film the red carpet event prior to the ceremony. She interviewed Lisa Tierney Keogh and Sarah Durcan for the Six One News. Lisa brought her husband, Charlie Veprek, who had worked with her on the initial gender statistics research and infographics.[3] Sarah's guest was the award-winning writer Belinda McKeon, whose Twitter exchange with Fiach Mac Conghail had added fuel to the spark that ignited the movement.

It was hard to control the nerves when we were seated in the front row on stage in the presence of feminist icon Gloria Steinem, who was giving the keynote address to honour actress and advocate Kathy Najimy for her activism. Other 'honorees included Tony Award winning actress and 2016 Tony Award nominee Jessie Mueller (*Waitress*), playwright Danai Gurira (*Eclipsed*; *Familiar*), Tony Award nominated actress Martha Plimpton, director Kate Whoriskey, playwright Genne Murphy, director Candis Jones, playwright Rehana Lew Mirza, actress and activist Mia Katigbak, and also recognized

Norbert Leo Butz and his organization, the Angel Band Project. As well as Gloria Steinem, presenters included Academy Award winner and 2016 Tony Award nominee Lupita Nyong'o, and Diane Paulus, Lloyd Suh, Russell G. Jones, Rachel Chavkin, and Neena Beeber.'⁴ The ceremony opened with the *Irish Times* short video of #WakingTheFeminists to gasps of horror and nods of recognition. Lisa and Sarah addressed the audience.

Lisa:

> Six months ago, I didn't know what a hashtag was. I thought Twitter was a weird foreign land where people wrote fortune cookie-length brain vomit and Facebook was a place I could post videos of cats attacking toddlers. I never in my wildest dreams imagined that Twitter could be used to mobilise an entire movement for equality.
>
> #WakingTheFeminists has awakened a force in Ireland that is spreading globally. Joining hands with the Lilly Awards and the phenomenal work you are doing has been exhilarating. To be part of the ruckus in our corner of the world is personally one of the most rewarding and inspiring experiences of my life. I would like to thank all of you here tonight for not being quiet the next time you see inequality in your theatre, in your rehearsal room, or on your set. Thank you for calling it out. Thank you for being the rising tide that is lifting the boats.

Sarah:

> The theatre community is small but its reach is wide. These two great theatrical islands of ours coexist in a global community, connected together,⁵ and we will achieve gender equality faster by working together. Everyone at every level in the theatre needs to engage with this movement. We are working with our own sector in Ireland to create policies and from those policies we must see action and from those actions we must see results. Sooner rather than later. Our deadline is five years to achieve full gender equality. Anger burns short but determination burns long, and the core group of #WakingTheFeminists, working week on week to drive the campaign, is fuelled by that determination. Women of the theatre, whether in Ballina, Baltimore, or Berlin, will no longer fade into the wings. We will no longer be told, 'wait', 'not ready', 'not good enough', 'not yet', We will not wait. Our audiences will not wait. The time for action, the time for equality, is now.

Amongst many brilliant speeches made that evening, actor, activist and writer Danai Gurira's words struck a chord and both Lisa and Sarah referenced them months later at the final event in the Abbey. Danai spoke of wanting to use her outrage and anger she felt from the #WakingTheFeminists video to fuel her writing.[6] Addressing young female playwrights she advised:

> The first thing, young female artist: have a vision; identify your outreach. The lack that is unjustifiable in what narratives are yet to be told. Embrace that burden on your heart to get that story to be told. That burden is a blessing. Then get to work. No excuses. No one in the world can do what you can do. Tell the story the way you only can tell it, so don't deprive the world of your uniqueness.
>
> This is a big one: Go where you are loved – where your voice is embraced and your vision is respected, it may not be where you expect it or where you had hoped, but it may just be where you grow and are

Sarah Durcan, Kathy Najimy, Gloria Steinem, and Lisa Tierney Keogh at the Lilly Awards in New York.

nurtured as an artist. It may just be where your breakthrough comes to pass. Don't let disappointment take hold. It is poison to your creativity. Stick to your vision and trust the right words will emerge if you keep doing your thing and putting yourself out there.

And lastly, be a finisher. Get it done. All the way. Embrace the right collaborators and *Get ... It ... Done*. It's not for you, it's for all those other young female writers who will be blessed and inspired by your product. It's for all the women you will employ. It's for those whose light will shine as a result of the excellence you pursued when you put those words on the page, and it's for the legacy you assist in building that annihilates the concept that women's concepts are weak, rare, or unprofitable.

After the ceremony, Lisa and Sarah chatted with Gloria, Kathy, and actress and fellow awardee Martha Plimpton; Lisa gave Gloria her #WakingTheFeminists necklace.

The *Irish Times* reported the next day that:

> Julia Jordan, founder of the Lilly Awards, said: '[#WakingTheFeminists] was a visceral explosion that mirrored our own struggle in the US to have women's stories told and heard.
>
> It brought home how international this movement is. We are obviously just a piece of the larger push for equality for women and girls, but we are all responsible for our own little corner of the world, and the theatre is ours to fix.'
>
> Lian Bell, one of the founders of the movement, said:
> > 'This award is a huge honour for all who continue to make their voices heard through the Waking the Feminists [sic] movement, and a testament to how far the message travels when we shout together.
> >
> > It's wonderful to have this moment to recognise the powerful solidarity that each of us feels with our feminist theatre colleagues around the world. Onwards!'[7]

In Washington DC, Sarah attended Olwen Fouéré's *riverrun*, part of a season of Irish work at the Kennedy Center. After the show, Sarah met Olwen, producer Jen Coppinger, and Her Excellency Anne Anderson, Irish Ambassador to the United States. Jen and Sarah took photographs of everyone wearing the medal; back in Dublin, it was passed around for lots of selfies.

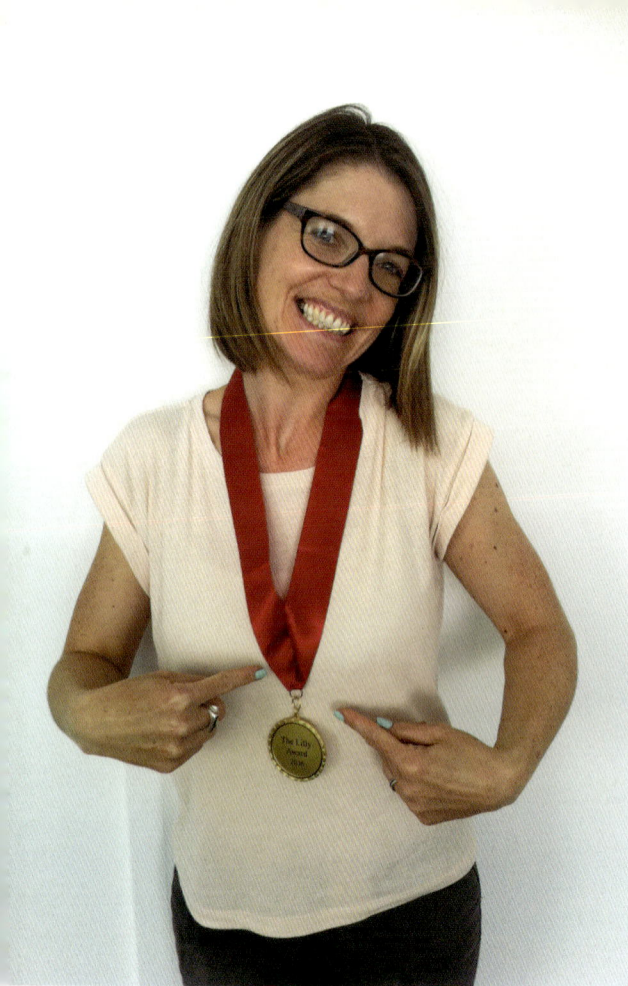

Aoife White with the Lilly Award. Photo: Lian Bell.

Lian Bell and Jen Coppinger with the Lilly Award. Photo: Lian Bell.

Tonic Awards, London

In March 2018, Lian was flown to London to receive a Tonic Award on behalf of the campaign. The awards 'celebrated the achievements of women who are changing the face of our theatre industry, and the projects, productions and organisations that are redefining the role of women in the performing arts'.[8] Lian brought Nancy Harris as her plus one, and was presented with the award by Ursula Rani Sarma, both playwrights who had left Ireland in order to be able to pursue their careers. Other awardees on the night included playwright Caryl Churchill, director Katie Mitchell, theatre critic Lyn Gardner, and UK theatre company Clean Break, at the time led by director Róisín McBrinn.

To be recognised in this way by our international peers gave us more courage for the work ahead, underlined the importance and urgency of what we were doing in Ireland, and kept the campaign visible. In this hyper-connected world, one action in one place can influence action in other places.[9] #WakingTheFeminists, the Lillys, and Tonic Theatre all strengthened each other's resolve and impact.

Playwrights Nancy Harris and Ursula Rani Sarma with Lian Bell and Róisín McBrinn at the Tonic Theatre Awards.

TEN

Spring Forward: International Women's Day Public Meeting and Speeches

Two days after the Irish Times Irish Theatre Awards we gathered in Liberty Hall for the second major #WakingTheFeminists public meeting, *Spring Forward*, on 8 March 2016, International Women's Day. We had a little longer to organise this than the seven-day sprint to the first public meeting, but it was still a full-on flurry for the final couple of weeks.[1]

The central purpose of this meeting was to get seven key organisations – the Abbey, Gate, Druid, Dublin Theatre Festival, Rough Magic, Project Arts Centre, Dublin Fringe Festival – to make a public commitment to achieving the objectives of #WakingTheFeminsts, working on gender equality policies, contributing to the research, and ideally, we hoped, to participate in an Advance-style programme. The other key purpose was to introduce the research study and explain why it mattered in achieving gender equality.

There were also a number of gaps in representation and experience from the first public meeting that needed to be filled in this event. We had a whole section on women's experiences working in technical theatre led by Kate Ferris, giving her first ever public speech. We widened the contributions beyond theatre, including voices from film (Katie Holly of Blinder Films) and journalism (Una Mullally).

There was considerable debate and disagreement within the core group whether Michael Colgan should be given a platform to speak or not. Maria Fleming felt strongly he shouldn't be included. The group decided that it was more important that all the companies be represented; if one didn't get an opportunity, it would lessen the overall peer pressure. Michael had sent us a short speech in advance, but on the day read another version. Usually a most self-assured confident speaker, Colgan appeared to be deeply uncomfortable and shook as he spoke.

The event was filmed for our YouTube channel once again by Paula Geraghty of Trade Union TV, and Kate Horgan was the official photographer. Recent graduates of Dublin City University (DCU) MA in Film & TV Programme, Sarah Barr (Producer) and Sarah Corcoran (Director) were also filming, as they intended to make a documentary about #WakingTheFeminists with the working title of *Them's The Breaks*.[2] A live recording of the meeting was featured in episode 27 of the Irish Times Women's Podcast.

Diva Voces choral group opened the proceedings with a rendition of *Battle of Jericho*.[3] Lian brought everyone up-to-date with the campaign, and introduced the spokespeople from the theatre organisations who all made commitments on their behalf. Anne Clarke then did the pass-the-basket-in-church bit to outline our fundraising requirement and fill our buckets, and we sold a selection of mugs, badges, and tote bags to support the campaign, again designed by Kate Heffernan.

The speeches from that event follow.

It was a long day for the #WakingTheFeminists organisers. Several of us were invited that morning to Accenture's International Women's Day breakfast event at the Dublin Convention Centre[4], and later that evening Lian was one of eight at a Trinity College Law Society panel event who were presented the Praeses Elit award. The discussion was moderated by journalist and broadcaster Áine Lawlor, and alongside Lian comprised academic Dr Aoibhinn Ní Shuilleabháin, journalist and activist Una Mullally, Professor and Senator Ivana Bacik, Director of Public Prosecutions Claire Loftus, writer Louise O'Neill, and joint leader of the Social Democrats Catherine Murphy.[5]

Clare Barrett collecting donations at the Spring Forward public meeting.

(right) Molly O'Cathain and Breffni Holahan selling merchandise at Spring Forward. Photo: Kate Horgan

Anne Clarke speaking at at Spring Forward. Photo: Kate Horgan

Writer Marian Keyes and journalist Róisín Ingle at Spring Forward. Photo: Kate Horgan

Kate Ferris speaking at Spring Forward. Photo: Kate Horgan

Sonya Kelly speaking at Spring Forward. Photo: Kate Horgan

Michael Colgan, Director of the Gate Theatre, speaking at Spring Forward. Photo: Kate Horgan

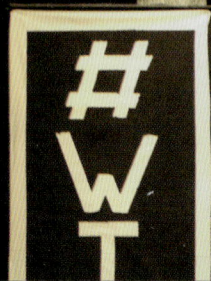

Dr Brenda Donohue presenting at Spring Forward. Photo: Kate Horgan

Speeches from the *Spring Forward* public meeting, 8 March 2016

Lian Bell, *#WakingTheFeminists Campaign Director*

Today will be a day of taking stock, of celebrating what we've achieved so far, and of setting our sights for the next part of the year. Thanks to the programming skills of the wonderful Róise Goan we have a jam-packed event for you today.

This feels like the right place to be. The *Irish Times* described the old Liberty Hall 100 years ago as 'the centre of social anarchy, the brain of every riot and disturbance'. While I think the intense planning, strategising and coordinating that's been going on since the start of #WakingTheFeminists is a far cry from anarchy, I do think that you as the supporters and activists of the campaign have managed to stage the most dignified, powerful, effective, and riotous disturbance that the theatre in Ireland has ever seen. So like I said, this feels like the right place to be.

Since we met in November, those of us who are working to advance [the campaign's] objectives have formed a loose organising group that meets weekly. We're open to hard working newcomers. I've been told to tell you that it's also sometimes fun. We've committed to working on the campaign for a year and after this meeting today, we'll be planning out a detailed strategy for the coming months.

As you may know, the campaign has resonated widely and I like to think that we've done some work in reclaiming the F word as a positive one, encouraging more women and men to identify as feminists. #WakingTheFeminists has already joined the lexicon of how we talk about culture, and how we talk about women in this country, and it's referenced in the media on an almost daily basis.

Last week saw the first official meeting of #WakingTheFeminists supporters in the Irish Art Center in New York, organised by the playwright Lisa Tierney Keogh, one day after an academic symposium titled Waking The Feminists at Fordham University also in New York. On the 6th of January, following a call from us for supporters to gather on Nollaig na mBan, there were 14 separate

#WakingTheFeminists-inspired events across Ireland from Phoenix Park to the Aran Islands, and two in New York.

We've been in touch with a number of sister organisations and campaigns in Ireland and across the world. Ones that are fighting similar fights in the arts, and in other sectors. Ones such as the Equity in Theatre campaign in Canada, the Statera Foundation and the Lilly Awards in the US, Women in Theatre and Screen in Australia, and the recently formed Equal Representation for Actresses group in the UK. Closer to home, we've become members of the National Women's Council of Ireland, and we've been in touch with Women for Election, Women on Air, Women in Film and Television, Women Aloud Northern Ireland, and Irish Equity amongst others. Irish Equity are currently conducting a survey on bullying and harassment in the theatre workplace that I really urge everybody to fill in on their website.

Our hope is to build our own obsolescence into the work that we're doing, empowering and encouraging companies and organisations to take on the responsibility of ensuring that they establish and maintain gender equality in what they do.

On a side note, we've noticed sometimes there's a bit of confusion between *equality* and *diversity*. When we talk about gender equality, we talk about ensuring everyone has equal status, equal opportunities, and equal chance to use these opportunities to their full potential. Whereas diversity is more about recognising, valuing, and including people with different backgrounds, knowledge, skills, and experiences.

Equality *and* diversity are both important, though they're different and they're not interchangeable. While #WakingTheFeminists continue to push for gender equality (and gender equality is what I'm talking about in this speech), we do urge organisations to use this opportunity to introduce both equality and diversity at a policy level.

We've started to talk to the Arts Council about gender balance policy being a requirement for funding, and Theatre Forum is looking into drafting templates. It's vital for policies like these to be put in place, but they can't just be a tick-the-box exercise. The ideology of gender equality needs to permeate the very fabric of the companies from top to bottom. This is about all areas of theatre.

But it's not just about theatre. We have an opportunity for this sector to be seen as a trailblazer – for embracing change and championing gender equality in a way that can be used as a model and as a case study for others. Other sectors are watching us to see how we get on. Now is the time for us all to step up and do it.

Representatives of #WakingTheFeminists have already met with the boards and directors of six key organisations – the Abbey, Druid, the Gate, Dublin Theatre Festival, Dublin Fringe Festival, and Rough Magic – no mean feat in itself. We discussed how gender balance issues affect each of them, and encouraged them to think about how they can take on leadership roles in the sector by examining their own structures and practices, and beginning to work to make improvements. In a few minutes they – along with Project Arts Centre – will talk to you themselves about this.

Those of you who watched the meeting at the Abbey will remember Lucy Kerbel of Tonic Theatre talking about the Advance programme she's been running with the top theatre organisations in the UK to, as she puts it, 'transform their aspirations for gender equality into reality'. The Advance programme has already yielded some extraordinary results. In 2014 Tonic Theatre worked with 11 organisations, including the RSC, the Young Vic, Sheffield Theatres, the Almeida, and the Tricycle. By the end of that programme, for example, Sheffield Theatres pledged to have equal numbers of parts for male and female actors across its in-house productions. Tonic is just starting a second Advance programme with a cohort of organisations that include the National Theatre in London, who have already pledged to have gender equality by 2021 in terms of the directors and living writers that they employ.

One of the great things about Advance is that it realises the impossibility of having a one-size-fits-all solution, which is something we feel very strongly about. Each organisation in Advance has its own idiosyncrasies; each has a different role in the ecosystem of the theatre sector, so each needs to approach the question of gender equality differently – but the learning is shared, so there's less need to reinvent the wheel. If you're interested in finding out more, they have a really great website that outlines the process and the findings of the first programme.

We've been talking with Lucy Kerbel a lot and she's ready and willing to set up an Advance programme in Ireland, starting later this year. We see this as a huge opportunity for the Irish theatre sector to avail of her knowledge, experience and expertise in this area, and an Irish Advance programme is one of the legacies we'd like to leave from this campaign.

It's still early days. We introduced the idea to the seven organisations you're going to hear from shortly and set up meetings in the last month between each of them and Lucy. The meetings were positive and the door is open. We're optimistic, though the main sticking point is funding. Each of the participating organisations will be expected to buy into the programme, but to what degree, and where any shortfall comes from, is still to be worked out. But we will do our best to make sure it is worked out. This is not an opportunity to let slip by. That gives you a very fast overview of what we've been up to and where we stand. And in the immortal words of somebody or other: a lot done, more to do.

Loretta Dignam, *Abbey Theatre Board member and chairperson of their gender equality subcommittee*

Since November the 12th last year, we've been hugely focused on the issue of gender equality. We've been engaging with a wide variety of stakeholders within the Abbey Theatre, the staff and the new incoming directors and across the wider theatre and arts community in Ireland, in the UK, and in the US. It has been a fascinating journey for all of us so far. We have learned many things. But one thing that we have learned is that this issue is complex and will require a change in many areas simultaneously, from leadership to values and culture, from structures and processes to ways of working, and from measurement to evaluation and reporting. Once we have sign-off and agreement from the Board, we will then move into implementation. And we look forward to updating you all on our progress in due course.

Róisín Stack, *theatre maker and Communications and Development Associate for Druid*[6]

Druid met with #WakingTheFeminists in December to discuss how we can better support the movement and examine our own practices in relation to gender inequality.

We can't hold our hands up as a beacon of gender balance. While we pride ourselves on having a good balance across administration staff and casting, our record on writers and directors is not so hot.

#WakingTheFeminists has reminded us that we all have a responsibility to achieve equality for women and the movement has given us extraordinary examples of how we can do this. This has been an incredibly liberating experience in and of itself, for which we at Druid are extremely grateful.

Throughout its 40 years in existence, Druid has seen a lot of societal change, and this one is long overdue.

Druid was born out of a desire to represent and express the West of Ireland. The founding members, Marie, Garry, and Mick, didn't want to have to go somewhere else or be someone else to be taken seriously as artists. They staged Synge's *The Playboy of the Western World* and established Ireland's first professional theatre company outside of Dublin.

Druid recognises a similarity between that original impulse and today's struggle to be represented, to want to make work as yourself and not feel disadvantaged because of who you are.

Referring to Synge, Yeats said 'whenever a country produces a man of genius, that man is never like the country's idea of itself.'

Our country has had a lot of ideas about itself, not all of them good.

Through this movement, we hope we produce more *women* of genius, and more importantly, to better *support* the women we already have and to finally change this country's idea of itself once and for all.

Kris Nelson, *Artistic Director of Dublin Fringe Festival*

It's good to share how invigorated we at Fringe have been since #WakingTheFeminists took fire in November. In its 21-year history Fringe has been one of the places where the country's leading women artists have made and continue to make indelible, unforgettable works. They've shaped, led, and defined the festival. In fact, I bet that many of this country's women artists can connect how they've carved out their career to the work that they've done at Fringe. While this has been true of the festival, it's not been true of the sector at large. And so giving a platform to underrepresented voices has been part of Fringe's DNA since the beginning. Equality has been part of the organisation's history – sometimes in the way of direct interventions made by the festival and sometimes as an indirect spirit of inclusion.

What's invigorating about right now is that the collective conversation inspired by #WakingTheFeminists has implored us all that even an indirect implicit kind of equality is not enough. It's important now to be explicit. So let me happily and explicitly say that for Fringe, equality is something we work on. Equality is an agenda and that agenda is wide- ranging. We are actively seeking to programme work by women, by trans artists, by artists of non-Irish backgrounds, by artists of colour, by members of the Traveller community, by artists with disabilities, by queer artists. And that goes for this year, for years past, and years in the future.

We're advocating for our sector's drive for equality to encompass a broad definition of the term. We have to look at how practitioners in our field access opportunities, and if their gender, race, class, disability, religion, language, cultural background, gives them equal opportunities or not. The move to make Irish performing arts more equal can't stop at women and men. We have to bring everyone with us.

As we programme for this year's festival we will be weighing considerations of representation and equality. And these will live alongside the other considerations on our agenda – those of excellence, readiness, rigor, potential, talent, timeliness, and singularity.

Over this next month, we will choose which ideas and voices to amplify in Fringe 2016. It's not something we take lightly. It's an aesthetic, and at times a personal process. We're guided by knowledge and instinct. We're not giving up on taste. And we're checking in on our blind spots. We are striving for a programme that is artistically rigorous and inclusive of many voices. Our agenda is to prevent a festival full of compelling works made by singular artists. What they will make is important and who they are is important.

Willie White, *Artistic Director of Dublin Theatre Festival*

I've been Artistic Director of Dublin Theatre Festival since 2011, and I've worked in Irish theatre for more than 20 years. So what can I say in two minutes? Firstly, I can say that I'm a feminist, and I believe in equality. I'm also a parent to two little boy feminists and a girl feminist for the next generation.

At Dublin Theatre Festival we have followed the #WakingTheFeminists movement since its inception. The issues raised have been the subject of lively discussion among our team, with our board, and in conversation with artists and stakeholders. Our executive and board also had a very positive meeting with #WakingTheFeminists early last month.

The past few months have been very challenging and very invigorating for our sector. Irish theatre's image is so bound up in ideas of radicalism and interrogating identity that it has been sobering to consider that we have perpetuated rather than redressed inequality.

The reasons for this are complex, but I think it's useful to try and see the problem really, really simply. As Joan Burton said at the #WakingTheFeminists event at Project Arts Centre in December, it's important to count. So we've been analysing our programme over the past decade. It offers a useful sample including as it does the work of building-based organisations, independent companies, small and large-scale projects, and Irish and international artists across a range of contemporary theatre aesthetics. Beginning with directors – to reflect the route for most projects into the festival – the decade saw a ratio of female to male directors for single director projects of 32 per cent to 68 per cent, roughly one to two. There are nuances of scale and numbers of performances, but that's the headline information. The ratio of female to male writers is lower – worse – at 20 per cent to 80 per cent.

Even allowing for a historically very masculine canon, there is clearly work to be done by all of us to increase the participation of living female writers and to create more opportunities for female directors.

We are committed to changing the numbers, and this has been embraced by the governance of our organisation. I am in dialogue with our (gender balanced) board, the Council of Dublin Theatre

Festival, about concrete measures we can undertake to advance the cause of gender equality in Irish theatre.

One of the actions that we have identified is the need to create pathways to leadership for the next generation of artistic directors, mindful of the fact that there's never been a female artistic director of our organisation, for example. We can see that planning for succession has been exacerbated by the reduction in arts funding over the past eight years, and the consequent shrinking of and structural changes to the sector. In particular, we are exploring how we can help to support the careers of independent producers and performing arts curators.

We recognise the urgent need to act, and we are eager to see change to happen soon so that the next time we count the numbers, they will manifest the equality we truly believe in.

Michael Colgan, *Director of the Gate Theatre*

Back in the late 1970s when I was running the Dublin Theatre Festival, I began counting the houses. It's what young producers do. Over time, it became increasingly apparent to me that there were more women in the audience than men. It was then that I coined the phrase 'women go to the theatre, men are brought', and when I joined the Gate I began to see that phrase as axiomatic, and when programming I began to use it as a crutch. The plays I presented were largely for women and about women, and as often as possible would have a woman's name or reference in the title. But they weren't written by women. So why was this? Given my mantra, it would have been good for me to have had more plays written by women. But I think the reason is that each theatre has a different ethos, different strengths, and we all have different poverties.

The Gate is a theatre principally devoted to the classics. And what do I mean by that? Well, by classical theatre, I mean those plays that have endured time, scrutiny, and different cultures. I'm thinking of Shakespeare, Friel, Beckett, Wilde, Miller etc. Plays that will always be performed and have been translated into many languages. The harsh reality is that there are few classic plays written by women or rather – and here's the rub – few that have been given the chance to become classics. This inequality does not occur with novels. There clearly are classical female novelists and, more than any other theatre I'm proud to say that we the Gate have given a platform to these by way of adaptations. We have adapted the work of Emily Brontë, Jane Austen, Charlotte Brontë, Daphne du Maurier, and many more. And we will continue that work. But we're hopeful that the Gate can find itself in a position where we can give a platform to female playwrights on their journey towards producing classical work or work that will be recognised as classical.

#WakingTheFeminists has been an eye opener for us. So how do we achieve this equality? How do we measure it? And for me, more importantly, in what timeline? For my own part, I would favour targets over quotas. But I would also greatly encourage financial incentives. Let's be honest, the quotas in the recent election were achieved because of the government's financial incentives, and I now believe that the Arts Council needs to play its role in incentivising theatres to achieve greater diversity and greater equality.

Let there be no mistake, the Gate Theatre has fully signed up to a policy of transparent gender equality. It is our ambition to ensure it sits easily on our stage, off our stage, in our offices, and in our boardroom. We have our problems. We have our restrictions – mostly financial. But we are now on a path to double our efforts to ensure that there will be full equality at the Gate.

Cian O'Brien, *Artistic Director of Project Arts Centre*

I'm a feminist. I'm delighted to have the opportunity to speak for a few moments today on behalf of the staff and board of Project Arts Centre. Later this year Project Arts Centre is going to celebrate its 50th anniversary, a significant moment for the organisation, and for all the artists who've been a part of our story and our legacy over the last five decades.

Since its founding 50 years ago, Project's mission has holistically embraced an inclusive, progressive ethos of equality. However, that does not mean that unconscious bias does not exist within our structures and our programmes. Over the past few months, we've been working on a new Strategy. As part of this process, I've asked myself a lot of questions about how we work. I am keenly aware of my position as a leader and programmer and the responsibility that comes with being the head of an organisation. I am conscious of my privilege in the decisions I am making. And from the many stimulating conversations I've had with industry peers over the last four months, it has become clearer and clearer to me that this privilege is most definitely invisible to those who have it. I've been reflecting on our position as one of the country's leading cultural institutions, one which has always placed artists and freedom of creative expression at its core.

In looking back at our past, our archive, and the story of Project Arts Centre, I have seen first-hand how the role of women has been underwritten, or underrepresented, with male voices pushed to the fore. As an organisation that is constantly thinking about the new and the next, it is our duty to explore the policies which need to be in place to create equality and to challenge unconscious underlying assumptions.

I look forward to continuing to work with #WakingTheFeminists over the coming year to ensure that this does not happen to future generations of women artists and that Project Arts Centre can remain truly inclusive, progressive, and equal.

Anne Fogarty, *board member of Rough Magic Theatre Company*

Rough Magic is a company with gender balance in its DNA. Founded in 1984 by a gender balanced partnership of four women and three men – the perfect equation. It was at the very start a cooperative with diversity built into its aesthetic. In 1993 we ran a competition exclusively for women writers, and two plays were taken to full production from this initiative. Many women have been commissioned to write and have been produced since Rough Magic's beginnings, including award-winning work by Pom Boyd, Hillary Fanning, Gina Moxley, Paula Meehan, Morna Regan, Ioanna Anderson, Rosemary Jenkinson, and Elizabeth Kuti. Commissions have sprung, however, not from any conscious policy. Quite simply, we are interested in these writers and the stories they have to tell.

Are you more likely to be commissioned or employed by Rough Magic because of your gender? No. But our programme favours the stories of women in society, because we find them vital and compelling. The company has a tradition of taking an original approach to the subject matter it tackles – it isn't surprising then that the distaff side, of history and the contemporary social landscape, is our natural landscape.

Rough Magic statistics show that if anything, its balance in terms of produced plays, has recently favoured female writers. The company runs a SEEDS programme, a platform for emerging creative artists from writers to sound designers to directors. In its selection of participants for this programme, the gender balance has been good, if not quite at actual parity. Why then, is there a need for Rough Magic to engage with the Advance programme?

Because Rough Magic as a company needs to ensure that its assumptions about its ethics are borne out consistently and are independent from the particular inclination of any one individual. That means formalising what up to now has been instinctive. We need the Advance programme to help us create a systemic policy, but in such a way that the company can sustain its organic progress, and the meritocracy that leads to natural gender balance.

We feel that it is necessary to keep checking that our ethical position is as good as we suppose. It is also true that in asking questions about gender and equality, we discover many invisible barriers, including the ones in our own heads. Rough Magic has a responsibility to engage with this process, because we're not just a production company. Through our SEEDS program, we're also an incubator of new talent and the next generation. So, our principles need to be beyond reproof, because they will impact on the theatre practice of the future. In linking itself with the #WakingTheFeminist initiative, Rough Magic wants to continue to make a difference.

Anne Devlin, *playwright*

Since the meeting at the Abbey in November, I have been wearing my #WakingTheFeminists badge and everywhere I go people stop me in the most unlikely places, the hairdressers, walking through the department store, a woman wielding a powder brush, a guy with a rucksack on the train, all young people, to declare 'I'm a feminist too'. I was very lucky I started my life as a playwright at the Royal Court in London, where they had structures in place to 'serve the play', as the Artistic Director Max Stafford–Clark would have it. And they did it for very little money. It was during the first big recession of the 1980s. And because there was so little money, the control was in the hands of the company: that is, the decisions about programming and content.

Recent research shows that right now, more women enter the theatre with plays while more men arrive at the end of the process with a public production. This means that it's a process from which only the men's plays emerge. So we need to put new structures in place to find a way to work in development which favours women. We need to operate laterally across the networks rather than hierarchically, and the instinct is cooperative, not competitive. In order to get beyond gender you have to take account of gender; to treat someone equally, you have to treat them differently. When I read that sentence somewhere, in place of gender was the word race. But it could also be said about class and generation. The unfinished business of my generation – we have reached our sixties and begun to feel invisible. After the last event at the Abbey, I asked myself, who is the subject of my focus? Who else is being excluded? You see, it's subjecthood not sisterhood. It's where we begin. And yes, it is political.

Caroline Williams, *theatre producer*

I'm a theatre producer and feminist. #WakingTheFeminists has moved like lightning over the last four months, but it has also taken decades. It is clear that progress has been painfully slow, but the tipping point is tipped.

In 1990 I co-founded a company called Glasshouse Productions. We produced two compilations entitled *There Are No Irish Women Playwrights*, as there appeared to be chronic amnesia at play. Women writers need to be rediscovered, uncovered, reclaimed, republished by specialist presses, given 'readings'. We need to ask why they are lost in the first place. Washed away. Yet the work of certain male writers seems to segue into the canon – indelible. I could spend this 90 seconds listing women playwrights – but the act of naming shouldn't still be necessary, or political.

Glasshouse also produced original plays, including two written by Emma Donoghue, then in her early 20s. Following her recent hattrick of Oscar nominations, an article by Fintan O'Toole in the *Irish Times* entitled 'No Oscar for Best Supporting Environment' stated: 'Maybe if there was no Glasshouse, there would be no *Room*'.

Glasshouse can't take credit for *Room*. But it did claim some space for women writers and theatre artists, as did *numerous* other independent companies throughout the 1990s. Yet, over the last two decades, this space has contracted. The independent sector has shrunk dramatically, and it is clear that the largest stages have not made sufficient room. Having just a smaller amount of room is stifling many brilliant female artists. They are leaving, they're giving up. You can hear the screech of brakes as their opportunities to make work diminishes. Them's the actual brakes. There are so many barriers facing anyone working in theatre, we have a responsibility not to heap additional ones on someone because they happen to be female. When Lian Bell received the *Irish Times* Judges' Special Award two nights ago, she asked various groupings to stand – including all those who support feminism – and the entire room was on its feet. Best Supporting Environment – we can win this one.

Sonya Kelly, *actor and writer*

I'm an actor, and a writer, and general annoyer of people. And it's a pleasure to be here today. Róise Goan a few weeks ago asked me to put together a list of helpful dos and don'ts about how to curtail casual sexism in the theatre industry. So, with this in mind, I have identified a number of test case situations and phrases used in the professional milieu by way of example. For instance:

1. 'Is that a hammer in your pocket or are you happy to see me?' is a popular question often asked to female technicians. I would like to clarify today that on 99.99999 per cent of the occasions, it is most likely to be a hammer in her pocket. The possibility of her spontaneously growing a penis and becoming aroused because you walked up to her and said 'is that a hammer in your pocket or are you happy to see me?' is equally and oppositely unlikely. If you are unsure of the physical differences between a hammer and the male member, I have brought one to show you. [*She shows the audience a hammer.*] Clearly a number of subtle and immediate differences spring to mind.

2. While we are on the subject of misconstrued items commonly found in the workplace, the banana is a popular food item also commonly housed in pockets and eaten by theatre practitioners during rehearsals and get-ins and get-outs. Any resemblance to the male member is purely coincidental. If you see a colleague eating a banana during a rehearsal or tech, remind yourself it is 99.999 per cent unlikely that they are practising a sex act and to suggest that their boyfriend or husband is in for a treat later is an inaccurate appraisal of the activity. If you are still unclear as to the difference between a penis and banana, try eating one yourself and see how remarkably dissimilar it is in texture and flavour to a banana. This should quell any further curiosity on the matter.

3. On the subject of semiotically misconstrued items of apparel commonly worn within the theatrical milieu. Flannel shirts are not automatic indices to a person's sexual orientation (… but sometimes it helps!). The correct term for flannel shirt

is flannel shirt. Not lesbian shirt, or you there in the lesbian shirt, or dyke top, or carpet muncher's uniform. Carpet as an aside, is quite unsavoury to eat and plays havoc with your digestion. I know this because I ate some once when I was on magic mushrooms. In short, a flannel shirt is no indication of the gender of the person with whom the wearer wishes to commune with sexually. That, in the context of the workplace, is none of your business. If, however, you find yourself attracted to a flannel shirt-wearing colleague, which after all, is only human nature, I suggest that you might ask them to dinner, but not to inquire 'are you into dick or vag because it's really hard to tell?'

4. When socialising with female colleagues at opening nights and festival clubs, it is advisable not to run a hand down the centre of her back to check if she's wearing a bra. This action is not required because women will know themselves if they're wearing or not wearing a bra, and will instinctively recognise this as the sexual subterfuge for what it is. In case you are tempted to perform this action, here is the mystery debunked: sometimes women wear bras, sometimes they don't. Those are the two options available to women: on and off. If you are unclear about this, try practising on light switches. The safest place to touch someone you don't know is the elbow. However, do not touch the elbow of a woman if you want to find out if she's wearing a bra. Women don't wear bras on their elbows, (perhaps in post-dramatic theatre).

5. On the subject of costume designers, costume fitters, wardrobe personnel etc. in order to execute the particulars of their brief, i.e. to fit or change a costume, they may be required to touch you. There is however no expectation or desire on their part that you touch them back or express any desire to touch them back or suggest had you been a certain number of years younger you might throw them over that sewing machine there and give them a good seeing to just like that pottery scene in *Ghost*.

So, there you have it, a few small tips to help you negotiate the quagmire of gender politically correct social banter within the theatrical milieu. It is a wonderful world we inhabit, boiling over with creativity and passion. We are in the business of creating heightened feelings. This feverishly passionate industry has born wonderful creative relationships, families, love affairs, adversaries, heartache, babies, at its most positive. The manner in which we engage with each other has the capability to do this, to exalt, mentor, burgeon. At its most negative, it can demean, subjugate, intimidate, and paralyse. None of us are saints. And we can all recall after a night out waking up and saying 'Oh my God, what did I say?' But I would encourage everyone to remind themselves, not every hammer and banana is a dick and we don't have to be one either. [*Sonya pulls a banana out of her pocket and peels it.*]

By the way, I am happy to see you!

Una Mullally, *journalist and activist*

I am not going to talk about theatre. I'm going to use this opportunity on International Women's Day at this #WakingTheFeminists event to talk about something else that impacts all of our lives, as feminists, as women, as men too. On Saturday night around the corner from my home, my housemate was viciously attacked on Camden Street for being a woman and for being a lesbian.

A few weeks previously, I was surrounded by a group of young men on the canal because I had the audacity to go for a jog at 5 pm. I stood and I shouted while they threatened to beat me with a bicycle seat and threw me in the water. They yelled disgusting abuse at me before eventually dispersing. My housemate Vickey, now with two black eyes after being repeatedly punched in the face, wasn't so lucky. Because no matter what you're wearing, no matter what time of day it is, no matter what you look like, no matter where you are, women are open to being attacked on the street and I'm sick of it.

I'm sick of having conversations between me and my friends in a pub interrupted when a guy thinks he has the right to invade our space with some kind of shite talk that nobody asked for. I'm sick of tensing up when I have to pass a group of men on the street at night. I'm sick of deciding to say nothing back when a man shouts something at me or my friends – for my own safety. I'm sick of holding my keys in my hands so that a hypothetical punch might have more impact if needs be. I'm sick of looking over my shoulder and I'm sick of harassment deniers. I'm sick of people raising an eyebrow when they think we're 'overreacting' or 'unlucky'.

Pick up a newspaper today, or any day, or look at any news website any day of the week, and you will find a litany of rape cases in court; of attacks and assaults, and abuse and violence against women – and those are just the ones reported that we hear about, and we take that information in every day. We also take in visual information of the streets and its surroundings: the catcalling, the sexual harassment we've been victims of, the dark alleys, the dodgy blokes, the groping in clubs.

And they are #NotAllMen. But they are a *lot* of men. If nearly everyone in this room, and I'm sure you have, has had an incident of harassment on a scale from not so serious to very serious indeed at the hands of men; then if I was to stand in a room with mostly a male audience, would a lot of men there have been perpetrators at some point? This is something that men are so incredibly sensitive about to the point that the conversation shuts down. But we need to open that conversation up because no amount of street lighting or extra Gardaí or vigilance will stop street violence and street harassment against women.

The only people with the power to do that are men themselves. No perpetrator, no victim. This is a country where 26 per cent of women have been victims of physical or sexual violence by a male partner or another man. But violence is not perpetrated by one small gang of marauding men. It's much more widespread than that, and we're going to have to start to be honest with ourselves about that. I know it's hard for women to face up and call out the sexual and physical and verbal violence and harassment perpetrated against us. Perpetrators are our fathers, our brothers, our partners, our friends – and women raise men. It must be hard to unlearn misogyny and I would imagine, much easier not to be immersed in it in the first place. Men need to be included in this conversation. But I'm also sick of mollycoddling. I'm sick of apologising for not wanting to be assaulted. I'm sick of looking for approachable and innovative ways to allow men to understand that shouting, groping, or beating women is not acceptable. Get on board. And if a man you know has an objection to women asserting their right to safety, if they think or feel or act ambiguously on this subject, then call them on it. Because I'm also sick of protecting men from *their* culture of violence, a culture of exerting power, of keeping women in their place with threats from microaggressions to straightforward attacks. We're not making this up. It's real. And I'm sick of it and everybody needs to wake up.

Katie Holly, *film and television producer*

I'm here in a few different guises. Firstly, as a feminist whose heart leapt on witnessing the start of this movement; as a film and television producer who has run my own company Blinder Films for coming up on 10 years; as a founding member of the Irish branch of Women in Film and Television; and as a board member of the Irish Film Board, and I'm delighted to have been asked to come here to speak about the experiences and developments in the Irish film and TV industry.

I've always loved film. *My Cousin Vinny* made me want to be a lawyer, *All the President's Men* made me want to be a journalist, *Almost Famous* a music journalist, and *In The Name of the Father* made me want to be a lawyer again. Maybe because of my enjoyment, it actually took a pretty long time for it to dawn on me that the stories I was seeing were overwhelmingly male, or from a male perspective. When I began to think I wanted to be a film producer, one of the things I did was seek out the work and writings of producers I admired. Among them were Christine Vachon and Lynda Obst. Once I'd set upon it, I don't ever remember feeling that film wasn't something that I should pursue, (probably because at the time, I had no idea how crazy and demanding an industry it was). But I do know that reading their words, and seeing their credits, inspired and emboldened me in my own career.

I love films because they can express so beautifully aspects of human experience and all their contradictions and complexity, and unite an audience in the showing. They move us, anger us, terrify us, entertain us, provoke us, comfort us. But for so long, we haven't been getting the whole story. A few years ago, I was at South by Southwest with a film and I snuck away to see the world premiere of a new TV series by a filmmaker I was really intrigued by. It was called *Girls*. I was literally overjoyed to see characters on screen whose lives were messy and imperfect and uncertain, and familiar.

It was a couple of years later at the Galway Film Fleadh that the reality of the Irish problem became acute to me. I watched three premieres over the weekend. All good films, but none of them reflected in any way my experience. They were all male stories, male perspectives. The female characters were wives, mothers, love interests, daughters. It bothered me. And it motivated me. And it made me look at my own record and my own slate. Only three Irish women have directed three or more feature films.

When I was interviewed by the former Minister for my position on the Irish Film Board, I cited equality as one of the issues I'd seek to represent. At the end of our meeting, he said he was delighted. I agreed to join as you see, they now have these quotas for state boards of 40 per cent.

As a Board member, I want to thank #WakingTheFeminists for being the catalyst for our own public statements and subsequent plan on gender equality. We've been discussing the issue for some time and intended to include steps in our forthcoming strategic plan. But the movement put pressure on us to acknowledge the inequality in our industry and in our own records, and publicly commit to making changes. We published statistics from the last five years, which show that only around 20 per cent of projects funded had a woman writing or directing. They also showed that not enough submissions are coming from producers like me, with women attached again about 20 per cent. We set a target of 50/50 gender parity in funding over the next three years. It's an ambitious target, but Sweden under the leadership of Anna Serner has achieved this and with it has increased Swedish films presence and success at international film festivals and at their own awards.

Last Friday, there was a conference by Dr Susan Liddy from the University of Limerick, which brought together many of the stakeholders in the industry, including writers, directors, producers, broadcasters, the film board, Screen Training Ireland, and the BAI [Broadcasting Authority of Ireland]. It was reminiscent in ways of the first #WakingTheFeminists event, hearing testimonies from filmmakers like Marian Quinn, who, despite having had her first feature premiere at the Berlin Film Festival, has struggled for nine years to make her yet to be realised follow-up. Or writers who just accepted that their work wasn't good enough and stepped out of the industry. The BAI, which has €17 million a year to fund projects, for the first time gathered their statistics and revealed only 19 per cent of their funding goes towards female directors. Both RTÉ and TG4 admitted that, while they are 'equal opportunities', they have no formal gender policies in place, and no published statistics around gender. These are all publicly funded bodies, and they need to be called to account.

Since the Irish Film Board plan was announced, the Film Board just started actively engaging with stakeholders, Women in Film and Television has secured funding, which will help us achieve our own goals, and the Director and Writers Guilds have jointly established an Equality Action Committee. I can feel the momentum, and a huge appetite for change. This issue is on the agenda in so many spheres and in the film industry it's at its noisiest ever. Despite the stark statistics, I'm optimistic. Irish film is riding high right now, and I know that with that there will be resistance to breaking the mould. That we should fund 'the best' rather than according to gender. But I also know that we need to challenge what is seen as 'best' and find quality in the diverse. Because if we don't, we'll fail to discover Ireland's Lena Dunham, or Andrea Arnold, or Jane Campion. Or for that matter, our next generation's Jim Sheridan, or Neil Jordan, or Lenny Abrahamson. And then everyone would miss out.

Donna Nikolaisen, *actor*
read by **Leah Minto,** *actor*

When I first decided to become a professional actor, my sister warned me that it'd be hard to find roles in Ireland owing to my ethnicity. 'It's a visual medium,' she said, 'You don't look Irish, Donna!' I didn't believe her. After all, I was born in Holles St and brought up in Cork. Sure, how much more Irish does a girl need to be? However, in time, I grew to learn that she was, for the most part, right. Most of the roles and theatre that I've been lucky enough to play have been race related. And although it gave me great pride to play these characters who needed and deserved a voice, it also deeply frustrated me that I was somehow excluded from many roles in classic, period, and contemporary plays. Actors need roles, not just to make a living, but more importantly to develop their craft.

If I was living in the UK, I would probably have more opportunities as an actor of mixed-race. There's a progressive approach to diversity in the arts across the water, which undoubtedly reflects the UK's long history of immigration. As a child I was something of a rarity in Ireland. However, the face of Ireland today is becoming a multicultural one with African, Middle Eastern, Asian, and European people living and working here and enriching our society in so many ways. The Arts have a responsibility to reflect our society and to be an inclusive force as opposed to being an exclusive one. Writers, directors, and producers of stories should be open to re-imagining the race of characters, without being said to be subverting the canon or betraying the writer's vision. The universality of the human experience is what makes us respond to stories. Let's include everyone in that story.

Lynne Parker, *Artistic Director of Rough Magic Theatre Company*

The bad news is that this country is in political, moral, and spiritual freefall. The good news is that there is a body of people and way of working that can arrest that. I was part of the core group that began this movement in November. That cathartic day of protest was achieved by a true theatre ensemble, powerful individuals acting as a unit. Shared responsibility, remarkable generosity of spirit, comprehensive lack of ego. And an event that ran like clockwork, maximised its resources and created change. Mostly, though not exclusively, engineered by women. Feminism in practice. Very good news.

And I thought, why aren't these people running the country? The theatre sector remains a better place than most to work in and it's largely because apart from a couple of institutions in need of enlightenment, it is run by women and some very enlightened male feminists. But you look at the wider landscape and you despair.

The best news is that progress is inexorable. For example, when I started all the technicians and lighting designers and production managers were male. Nowadays, nearly all the best lighting designers are women. Female crews are becoming the norm and women are among our most exciting sound designers. They weren't exactly coaxed into the industry, but the industry discovered it needed them because they were bloody good. And they wouldn't be discouraged. Kate Ferris is going to tell you about some of the hurdles she's had to overcome. And she's accompanied by two exemplars of creative technology, Alma Kelliher and Zia Holly, and two of her own team who are changing the face of theatre just by being here. And this is excellent news for men too, because everyone knows and every study has proved that a gender–balanced environment is more productive, and a hell of a lot more fun.

#WakingTheFeminists is accelerating the sea change so that first class professionals don't have to waste their valuable time and energy jumping hurdles and are able to get on with their jobs. That's the way to make it all work better for men and women who just want to work without the tiresome, wasteful, deadly poison of misogyny, pulling them and everyone into freefall. That's the way to a genuine meritocracy, a more efficient society, and a better world.

Kate Ferris, *theatre producer and Head of Stage Management at The Lir Academy*

Today I'm standing here representing some of the women who work in the production and technical sector of Irish theatre. I have a degree in Technical Production and Stage Management from the Queensland University of Australia.

I worked as a stage manager for ten years in the UK, Australia, the Middle East, and Ireland. I'm currently the Head of Stage Management at The Lir Academy in Dublin, where I'm responsible for training stage managers. So far, I've trained 30 stage managers who now work in various roles in technical theatre. I'm also a theatre producer, and have produced five successful shows of the last two years. So you might say, I'm good at more than one thing. In fact, I'm proud to say I'm pretty good at a number of things. If this were an interview, I might say I have many transferable skills over a wide spectrum of disciplines.

[*Two designers and two technicians come on stage and begin to work. The technicians bring on a large A-frame ladder and begin to rig lamps, as theatre lights are called. The two designers work at their laptops. The sound designer, Alma, works on a subtle sound track that plays behind much of the following speech.*]

Let me introduce you to the women who are joining me here on stage. We have sound designer Alma Kelliher and lighting designer Zia Holly. Many of you I'm sure would be familiar with Zia and Alma's work, both leading in their professional fields. Also with us, we have Emma and Jane. They are archetypes of the women who are currently working in Irish theatre as crew. Emma and Jane are not their real names. If these women use their real names, I'd be concerned. Well, there could be consequences. There are women currently working in the technical sector of theatre in Ireland who don't feel like they can publicly support the #WakingTheFeminists movement, as they are worried about how it will impact on their careers. At the moment, Emma and Jane are rigging one Fresnel lamp and one profile lamp. Just in case any of you don't know, Fresnels are different to profiles. Fresnels give light that is subtle and soft. They give an overall wash of the stage. One might say the backbone of a design. Profiles, however, produce clearly defined beams of light. They can do everything a Fresnel can and more. One might even say more powerful, a spotlight.

Emma and Jane have been working in the industry for around two years. Like me, they also have many transferable skills over a wide spectrum of disciplines and have huge potential to develop into more senior positions. Emma would like to ultimately become a production manager. Jane would like to become the technical manager of a venue. So they're going to continue rigging lights, ASM-ing, supporting and actualising all the creative decisions that run down the ladder of command. From cutting gel to sourcing the correct style of furniture for a period drama, building their level of competence with every job in order to advance their careers.

Both Emma and Jane have been on the receiving end of sexist comments working in theatre. Some of it has been subtle, and some quite blatant. It hasn't happened in every venue or in every theatre – but it has happened. These remarks have not necessarily come only from other crew, but also from directors, producers and actors. Emma and Jane believe that if they want to climb the ladder, they'd better say nothing. On her first year in the industry, Jane had her ass grabbed at an event by a director. The man hosting the event apologised, 'on behalf of the event', but said nothing to the man who had done it, because 'well, you know...'. There could be consequences. On the first day of her first gig, a fellow crew member asked Emma what's the similarity between a woman and a washing machine? They both leak when they're fucked.

These professional, intelligent, creative, and highly ambitious women don't want to be patronised and referred to as 'girls', 'a good girl', or 'a plucky wee girl'. They don't want to be told that they could get anyone to do anything for them with 'those eyes'.

There are women currently working in the design sector of theatre in Ireland who speak of the 'silent sexism', the one where you have to prove yourself over and over again, of not being entirely trusted to do a job or a certain type of job or a certain level of job. Or having your opinion questioned or passed over.

Both Emma and Jane would like to have a family someday, but think that because they work in technical theatre as freelancers, having children is impossible. If they do want to have kids, they know they'll only go so far.

There is currently no structure in place in Irish theatre to support working parents who are freelancers and this I believe really needs to change. We have an opportunity here to wake the nation and lead in this field. When asked about her desire to be a production manager, Emma has been questioned in the past: 'How are you going to look after your kids if you're driving a truck through the night to get from one venue to another on some really busy tour?' And she had the simple answer in her head. 'How do you? Why is that a question for me because I'm a woman and not for you because you're a man?' Jane had this great idea last week that she could approach a female technical manager to mentor her. She couldn't find one. Very recent research proves that aside from the Abbey Theatre, there is not one female technical manager in our nation's professional theatres. Apparently, it's a man's job.

So what I'd like to say to Emma and Jane, but I won't because they're up a ladder – is to quote Josie Rourke, Artistic Director of the Donmar Warehouse:

> a huge part of the conversation is how you stick at it in your 30s and what motivates you to move from middle to senior management. For those in freelance roles, theatre is a hard place to sustain a career and children: no pension, no maternity leave, just a nomadic lifestyle with unsociable hours. It will take huge wisdom and honesty for theatre to investigate its culture.

So that's you by the way. And me. You are theatre, and so am I, and it's up to you and I to investigate our culture and to ask ourselves questions and answer them honestly. So today I'm asking everyone here in this room: Am I part of the problem? Is my apathy part of the problem? Can I help fix it? I know it's hard. Well, there could be consequences.

There's been a lot of talk since 12 November 2015 about the #WakingTheFeminists movement. Now it's time for our actions to be stronger than our words. Over the coming months as one of the core organisers of the #WakingTheFeminists committee, I will be meeting with 12 female practitioners, stage managers, crew, designers, and heads of department. We will be dissecting these issues in detail, putting our words into action.

I do not want this to be the only ladder that Emma and Jane reach the top of. I want to see them advance to senior positions in technical theatre. I want to see highly competent, organised and excellent female technicians and stage managers progressing to be production managers and technical managers where their skills are so obviously transferable. I want our industry to enable them to achieve every opportunity on the career ladder.

And finally, what I also want is for the men who want to be feminists not to be concerned about their space in feminism. I want them to take the space that they have in Irish theatre and to make it feminist.

So, just to remind you again Fresnels are different to profiles. They're soft and subtle. They give an overall wash of the stage. One might say the backbone of a design. Profiles, however, produced clearly defined beams of light. They can do everything a Fresnel can and more. One might say more powerful. LX Q 1, go.[7]

[At Kate's lighting cue call the light changes in the auditorium, the cumulation of the technical work that 'Emma', 'Jane', and lighting designer Zia have been doing while Kate was speaking.]

Louise Lowe, *Artistic Director of ANU Productions*

I'm a theatre maker and I live in Ireland. And if I'm absolutely honest, I have neither sought permission nor invitation to make the kind of work that I want to make. I make it because I want to make it, because I believe that I should make it.

Once decided, I can be tenacious and stubborn and committed. And I'll do everything in my power to realise a project. I will try and find environments and partnerships and relationships that afford me the opportunity to be commissioned outside of current models and current funding structures. I make no apology for this.

I want to make work that questions who we are and why we are. I want to make work that places the audience at the very centre of the conversation and one that recognises that their being there matters. That we matter. That the issues and questions that we have as a society matters. I want to make work that is vital and brave, work that questions my world and my position within it.

My position just happens to be that I am a 41-year-old, inner-city, working-class woman, living in a country that has a shameful way of dealing with issues facing women – be that Magdalene laundries or symphysiotomies. I'm a 41-year-old woman living in a country that denies me the right to have autonomy over my own body. This makes my work complicated and contentious and frequently provokes more questions than answers.

I have been lucky enough to be surrounded by brilliant teams of artists who give their all every day to realise these projects with me. Artists of both genders who vehemently believe that we as feminists should be telling these stories, men and women who believe that it is equally important for our society to ask these questions. Nine years ago, Owen Boss, my co-Artistic Director, walked into our rehearsal room with his newborn baby daughter in a sling. I asked him was he minding her and he informed me that he was not minding her but 'parenting her'. He was angry that I should ask that question and I was angry that I had. I never asked again. Since that day, on his insistence and example, we have opened our workspace to mums and dads who need to bring their children with them. It is not unusual to find children in our studio or workplace. This morning, I shared breakfast with a three-year-old called Belle, who was sitting in the green room in the Convention Centre in her pyjamas, eating fruit.

A lot of our work over the past number of years has been about deconstructing the manipulation of the female identity and forefronting the female body as a political site. Within all of our 17 productions, even those that seem on the surface to be explicitly about men, such as *Boys of Foley Street* or *Pals*, we've attempted to ask radical questions about the role of women. One of my astounding and favourite memories was of artist Úna Kavanagh during the symposium event that marked the closing of our *Monto Cycle*. She engaged in the performative lecture about how she had embodied the female form in each of the characters she's played over 4,000 performances. Similarly, dancer Emma O'Kane in *Vardo* in the final scene of our trilogy, performed an embodied physical score based on all the dissonant gestures of all the female characters throughout the cycle. Her piece called *the business of hope*, captured their energy and dynamism, and the demand that their stories be heard.

#WakingTheFeminists allows us all to be in the business of hope. Since 2009, all of our 17 productions have been directed by a woman or co-produced by a woman. All our senior design roles including set, lighting, sound, and costume are by female designers. We have worked with incredible female production managers, stage managers, and technicians. At 68 per cent our female actors significantly outnumber our male ones. In 2016 over 180,000 audience members will engage with our work. We will present 6,302 performances with 65 actors, 41 of whom are female, in 32 locations, with 19 co-presenters, nine productions, and three commissions.

Things will change.

Things will change because we will continue to make changes.

Things will change because together we can galvanise.

But most importantly, things will change because we will cultivate a new ecology and a new ambition to lead and not just serve this industry, embracing feminism across genders.

Shaun Dunne, *playwright*
read by **Lauren Larkin,** *actor and theatre maker*

I'm an actor, theatre maker, and more recently, a pregnant woman. I'm reading on behalf of Shaun Dunne, the playwright, who can't be here today.

When #WakingTheFeminists first happened, I was upset at the stories I was hearing, confused too, but then ultimately annoyed at myself for being so naive to think that our community was different to the rest of the world.

I thought we had a level playing field. I didn't know that female writers and directors felt so held away from the stage. I think this is because female artists, programmers, and literary managers have been such a big part of my career path. They're the ones who have always heard me. How had I not been hearing them?

I felt defensive, too. Defensive and self-conscious. A knee jerk reaction. I was worried that I was part of the problem. Or seen to be. As a working-class, gay artist, I'm not used to having privilege prescribed upon me.

But I am really privileged. #WakingTheFeminists, for me, was about realising that. The fact that I'm so out of the loop on what's going on behalf of our theatre community is frankly embarrassing, because access is a huge part of my art. It's a core theme of mine. In the beginning, I thought a lot about the staff at the Abbey – I was worried about Aideen [Howard], Lara [Hickey], Jessica [Traynor], and Fiach too. And if I'm being honest, I was worried about me. Don't get me wrong. I love this movement, and I want to remain part of it. But I'd be lying if I said I didn't take a sharp intake of breath for myself during the height of it. What does this mean for me? Will my work be staged? Will my work be delayed? What happens next?

As a male writer who has been produced in the Abbey before, a lot of people have asked me if I'm alright. That makes me uncomfortable. But I understand the consideration. Because the ripples of these conversations do of course impact us all, as they should.

At the end of the day, it boils down to what kind of theatre do I want to be part of in Ireland? When I asked myself that, how I'm affected individually doesn't feel as significant, actually. I want to work in a theatre that is inclusive, accepting, wide-reaching, and whole. That's the remit, that's the goal. Happy International Women's Day to all the feminists that I know and let's continue to keep making great art.

The Things We May Not Say in Case We Get in Trouble

See *How This Book Was Written* (pp xiii–xiv) for context.

Research, Statistics, and Data Analysis

Statistics were essential to underpin our entire campaign: quantitative evidence of the problem that couldn't be disputed in the way that individual stories could. Researching the Abbey's past programme alone wouldn't be enough to show how endemic the issue was; we needed a wider picture. Academics had been vocal since the start of #WakingTheFeminists. Dr Brenda Donohue, is a member of the International Federation for Theatre Research,[1] the Irish Society for Theatre Research, and the Sibéal Postgraduate Gender and Women's Studies Network. In a letter published in the *Irish Times* 4 November 2015, she wrote:

> Some of my latest research ... has focused on the number of plays written by women and presented on the Abbey stages from 1995 to 2014. It found that of 320 plays staged in this period, just 36 plays were written by a woman, 24 of which were new plays, while 12 were revivals.
>
> My analysis shows that women playwrights are significantly under-represented on the Abbey and Peacock stages in terms of full theatrical productions. In the selected period, the annual percentage of plays written by women produced on either the Abbey or Peacock stages varied from a low of zero per cent of the plays produced in 2008, to a high of 26.6 per cent in 2003.
>
> One new play written by a woman is produced, on average, at the Abbey every year. In addition, the revival of plays by women is rare, with on average less than one revived work written by a woman staged

per year in the selected period, accounting for a meagre seven per cent of plays revived.

When responding to criticism of the under-representation of women in the commemoration programming, Fiach Mac Conghail underlined the constraints encountered in developing new plays within short windows for specific programmes.

Given this difficulty, one has to wonder why Mr Mac Conghail did not think to include some previously produced plays by women.

The reluctance to revive plays written by women is puzzling, as studies by Melissa Sihra and Cathy Leeney, as well as Patrick Lonergan's statistical analysis of Abbey plays, have shown that a body of quality writing by women is already in existence. Why not stage these plays?

A number of initiatives, such as former literary director Aideen Howard's playwriting programme, and the Fairer Sex scheme, have sought to address the lack of productions of writing by women. However, until the presentation of work written by women becomes a stated priority in development and programming terms, the problem will not be resolved.

A stage that presents 11 per cent of writing by women does not accurately represent the wealth of Irish people's experiences. We are only getting half the story.[2]

Brenda agreed to lead the research team, alongside Dr Tanya Dean and Dr Ciara O'Dowd, and assisted by Ciara L. Murphy, Kate Harris, and Kathleen Cawley.

In the immediate wake of the first public meeting at the Abbey, the team at Irish Theatre Institute had re-crunched their numbers from their Irish Playography website,[3] which had been running for over a decade, covering all the new plays produced in Irish theatre. Quickly we had a picture of the gender breakdown in new writing over the previous ten years. We thought that ten years was the right window of time to look at, as going further back would be difficult to monitor given the lack of available documentation. We wanted a realistic benchmark for companies to work from for the next decade.

Brenda steered us all through this with patience, determination, and clarity. She brought on board a statistics advisor, and worked out the detailed methodology and an Excel template with Ciara. They piloted this template with two companies, then refined it. They further refined at the request of Dublin Fringe Festival to include other genders and Brenda sought the advice of TENI (Transgender Equality Network Ireland) in doing so.

Research Process

At the Liberty Hall public meeting on 8 March, Brenda and Sarah outlined what the research would involve:

> Hi, I'm Sarah Durcan, and I am 'moderately' biased against women. I've done a test to prove it.

> Hi, I'm Dr Brenda Donohue, and according to the same Harvard Implicit Association Test,[4] I am also moderately biased against women. I was a little disappointed by the result, I was hoping to get 'slightly biased'. But, according to the people at Project Implicit, Sarah and I are in the majority, as 76 per cent of people who take the test are biased too.

> It's unsettling for each of us to realise that we are not quite the liberal, inclusive, meritocracy we believe our sector to be. Through #WakingTheFeminists, we have found ourselves confronted with an imbalance *so* glaring it was all but invisible. Surely, this can't be us, can it?

> Increasingly, I've also become aware of how emotive this subject is. #WakingTheFeminists has provided us with a beautiful moment, requiring all of us to cease business as usual, and begin to dissect the minutiae of our decision-making processes. Asking us to examine our own values and choices can make us feel our professional and personal integrity is being called into question.

> As a sector we are as agonised by change as anyone else. So let's peel away all that emotional stuff, and look at some of the facts. If we don't at the most basic level count what's going on, we won't know what counts in our theatre culture.

> Quantitative research can side-step the intensity of these emotive positions, and present a picture of the industry as it truly is. We can see the bare bones of Irish theatre broken down in numerical terms. The numbers are clear, honest, and informative. Let's use them.

> A study carried out by Princeton economics student Emily Glassberg Sands[5] used economic measures to measure the level of gender discrimination in American theatre. Glassberg Sands sent identical scripts to artistic directors and literary managers around the country – 50 per cent were listed as written by a male author and 50 per cent by a female author. The scripts with a female name assigned received significantly worse ratings in terms of quality, economic prospects, and audience response than the male ones. Glassberg Sands refers to this as taste-based gender discrimination. In many cases, it was

women artistic directors and literary directors discriminating against other women.

This is despite another of Glassberg Sands' findings that 'plays and musicals by women [on Broadway] sold 16 per cent more tickets a week and were 18 per cent more profitable over all (105). Yet even though shows written by women earned more money, producers did not keep them running any longer than less profitable shows that were written by men.'

Biases are culturally transmitted diseases. It's ok to be infected – we all are – it's just not ok to let them affect other people's livelihoods and opportunities if they don't fit into our mental picture of what's 'good', or 'looks like us'.

A good place to start is by understanding your own unconscious bias – take the Implicit Bias Test. The test is painless, takes less than ten minutes, and the results are instantaneous. A daily dose of feminism will definitely help alleviate symptoms of unconscious bias. Apply liberally.

Pointing out a slide from Theatre Forum's recent pay scales survey results, we note:

- The majority of people working in theatre are earning less than €35,000 a year.
- There are considerably more women than men working in theatre overall, but as the payscale rises, women drop off a steep cliff.
- At the top of the scale, just a few men are earning the bigger salaries.[6]

This echoes the findings of the research that Tríona Ní Dhuibhir presented at the 2015 Theatre Forum conference. She found that in the arts in Ireland, while 59 per cent of CEOs were women and 41 per cent of CEOs were men, for each €1 of public funding a woman CEO has budget control over, her male counterpart has €3.[7]

There is very little comprehensive research on the gender landscape in quantitative terms. #WakingTheFeminists is now seeking to address this gap. This research will put down a baseline in gender terms, drawing a standardised picture of what gender in Irish theatre has looked like over the last ten years. Once this panoramic image has been drawn, anyone can use this as a foundation for further analysis.

The aims of this research are to:

1. Gather robust quantitative data

2. Create a baseline for all organisations to measure progress over the next decade

3. Establish where problems lie, and what they consist of

4. Identify areas where women are successful

5. Lay the groundwork for effective and sustainable solutions

This will be ground-breaking research – the findings our study produces will be significant not only in an Irish context, but will also impact internationally. With this data, we can start to find some answers to more complex questions such as: why aren't more women playwrights and directors making it to the stages? How has this picture changed over the decade? Have some roles changed more than others?

Most importantly, the research can be used as a yardstick for progress. The results of this movement need to be measurable. We have to be certain that the impact is real and is significant. Looking at the ten year period between 2006–2015, the research will examine the gender breakdown in the theatre productions of the ten top Arts Council-funded theatre organisations and festivals producing work over that time. It will focus on the key roles of producer, writer, director, designer, actor, and stage manager. Researchers will work with each company to collect the data, ensuring consistency within the research process. To date, companies have been very generous in opening up their archives to us. We did a pilot run with two companies to date, and will roll it out to more organisations in the coming weeks.

Irish theatre has this once-in-a-generation opportunity to be at the forefront of this momentous shift in society. We need fully engaged leaders to drive the change. Policies and research are important, but will not be enough by themselves. We know the difficult part is in day-to-day decision making. That's where it gets complex and messy again. We *all* have to reach into the centre of that chaos and make bolder choices – counterintuitive decisions to change our values, to diminish our negative biases.

We must have greater expectations of our female artists, greater confidence in women's creative ability (and box office potential). We must choose and take action to fully and consciously include women on our main stages. With a concerted focused effort, we *can* achieve equality in Irish theatre within *five* years. Together, let's change the numbers – it will be the most rewarding creative challenge of all our lives.

Five years was ambitious, but we thought it was realistic as well as a good timeframe in which to measure any significant trend of change. After all, theatre is programmed in Ireland at most a year to 18 months in advance, and we knew there were plenty of women ready to step up into these suddenly expanded opportunities. It wasn't a pipeline problem, it was a choices problem. There were more than enough women coming through the various entryways into theatre, particularly in writing, directing, and acting, but their opportunities to progress to bigger and more prestigious stages were stymied by their gender, and the programmes that went on bigger stages significantly favoured work creatively led by, and featuring, men.

The researchers faced a challenge in gathering data as some theatre companies had been better at keeping their archives than others. Some were also more enthusiastic about participating in the research, readily engaging, and opening their archives immediately. There were a minority of companies in the sample that were difficult to engage with: their chief executives questioned why they were selected, questioned the credentials of the researchers, alleged their methodology and ability to count was flawed, and kept going back and forth over the criteria. At one point, one of them wrote to Brenda alleging that she couldn't count.

As with everything else we did, developing and analysing the research necessitated a lot of meetings. Brenda and Ciara met regularly at a play centre in Kildare. Brenda had a young child, so it was handy to let her play while she discussed the research with Ciara, who drove from Dun Laoghaire to meet. It is an important, but easily missed, detail to note that none of the #WakingTheFeminists meetings took place in our homes, always in offices or public spaces like cafés, hotels, and arts venues.

The #WakingTheFeminists committee put pressure on the researchers to have headline results ready for the final event at the Abbey on 14 November 2016. As theatre folk, we were used to tight deadlines and being ready for opening night no matter what, so we had a slight culture clash with the world of slower academia. Brenda kept telling us that it would take more time, because research never is completed so quickly; they needed to be careful and thorough and it couldn't possibly be ready for November. Eventually we asked: What would it take to be ready for November? The answer was more people. So Brenda brought in more research assistants, and several of the core group also swooped in to help sift through data in Project Arts Centre's archive, held in the National Library; the last outstanding piece of the data collection. The research took many, many more hours than any of us had envisaged, but in the end they were ready with headline results for the final public event.

Joanna Crawley and Caroline Williams at the National Library of Ireland, October 2016. Photo: Sarah Durcan

At that final event, Brenda, Ciara, and Tanya sat with Sarah in the first few rows of the Abbey auditorium, listening to all of the contributions. The research presentation was scheduled as the penultimate section. A few minutes before, they slipped backstage for a quick pee, and Sarah insisted on them doing Wonder Woman power poses to settle their nerves. It was then time to go on stage. They had been so close to these figures for months now and had no idea how they would be received. An awkward hush came over the audience as Brenda, Ciara, and Tanya began to speak. Then, as they went through the statistics while at the same time projecting the graphs large on the screen behind, horrified gasps rustled through the audience, especially when they revealed the overall percentages per organisation. The gender gap was so stark and now very visible. The obvious inequalities were now indisputable.

Dr Tanya Dean, Dr Brenda Donohue, Dr Ciara O'Dowd, and Ciara L. Murphy at the launch of Gender Counts. Photo: Kate Horgan

Summary of the Research

The following is an excerpt from *Gender Counts*,[8] the full research report launched on 7 June 2017:

> We collected data on 1,155 productions and counted 9,205 individual roles from ten of the top Arts Council funding organisations producing or presenting theatre over a ten year period 2006–2015: The Abbey, Gate Theatre, Dublin Theatre Festival, Druid, Project Arts Centre, The Ark, Rough Magic Theatre Company, Dublin Fringe Festival, Barnstorm Theatre Company and Pan Pan Theatre.
>
> The key findings:
>
> - The four highest-funded organisations in our sample have the lowest female representation.
> - There is a general pattern of an inverse relationship between levels of funding and female representation. The higher the funding an organisation receives, the lower the female presence in these roles.
> - Only 28% of Authors employed are women.
> - Women are poorly represented in six of the seven roles studied; i.e., in every role except Costume Designer.
> - Sound Designer and Costume Designer are gendered male and female roles respectively.
> - Only 9% of Sound Designers employed are women.
> - Women are most represented in The Ark, Rough Magic Theatre Company and Dublin Fringe Festival.
> - Women are least represented at the Gate Theatre and the Abbey Theatre.
> - The gap to achieving gender parity ranges between 41 and 8 percentage points in the roles studied.
>
> The overall percentages of female representation in each category:
>
> Directors 37%
> Authors 28%
> Cast 42%
> Set Designers 40%
> Lighting Designers 34%
> Sound Designers 9%
> Costume Designers 79%

The four highest-funded organisations in our sample have the lowest percentage of roles occupied by women. The Abbey received 57% of the total Arts Council funding awarded to the ten organisations sampled from 2006–2015, and 33% of roles there were occupied by women. The Gate received 8% of the total funding, and 32% of their roles were filled by women.

The Abbey has the highest funding of the sampled organisations, but after the Gate Theatre (32%), it has the lowest percentage of female representation across roles (33%). In the categories of Director and Author, the Abbey registers participation rates of female presence at 20% and 17%, respectively. In both cases only two organisations showed lower percentages. In individual roles, the Abbey has the lowest percentage for female cast participation of all the organisations sampled (37%). In the Design roles, the Abbey shows relatively low percentages of representation when compared to the other sampled organisations. In the categories of Set (31%) and Costume (74%) Design, only two other studied companies recorded a lower percentage in these categories.

The Gate Theatre has the lowest overall percentage of female participation across the sample: 32%. In the Director role, the Gate Theatre has the lowest level of female participation (8%) apart from Pan Pan Theatre.[9] In the category of Author, the Gate has the lowest percentage of female representation (6%) of all the organisations studied. Female authors were recorded in only three years at the Gate Theatre (2006, 2011 and 2015). Just three women were recorded as filling the role over the period studied.

In conclusion, we believe that the numbers should continue to be recorded and studied. We are conscious at this juncture, that a year of data from 2016 has now gone unrecorded. We believe that organisations can play a part in tracking the data by counting their own company's output. We recommend that all organisations in theatre count the gender balance in their programming, and release that information at regular intervals, alongside programming announcements. The data from these publicly-funded organisations demonstrate that as the funding increases, the theatre space expands and the audience reach amplifies, the opportunities for women narrow. The equality gap has now been identified and quantified. There are a maximum of 41 percentage points needed to achieve gender parity on the Irish stage.

Gender Counts was published and launched in March 2017, and was followed by a second edition, such was the demand.[10] The research project and findings are one of the most important legacies of the #WakingTheFeminists campaign.

The research template was made available to all the theatre companies who participated, and to all those involved in the subsequent working group, and was (and still is) available to download from the #WakingTheFeminists website. Some companies stuck with it as was, others adapted it to their own requirements, despite the researchers advising against it as it would lead to inconsistency in comparing organisations. In order to be able to continue to benchmark and compare, it's important that everyone count in the same way.

Dr Brenda Donohue, Dr Ciara O'Dowd, Dr Tanya Dean, Sarah Durcan, Jen Coppinger, Lynne Parker, Maria Fleming, Kate Harris, Niamh Ní Chonchubhair, Anne Clarke, and Lian Bell at the launch of Gender Counts, 7 June 2017. They are seated in the former Dublin City Council Chambers, now Poetry Ireland, 11 Parnell Square, Dublin. Photo: Kate Horgan

THIRTEEN

One Thing More: Final Public Event

Our final event, *One Thing More*, took place at the Abbey on Thursday, 14 November 2016, almost exactly one year after the first public meeting. This event was designed to close the campaign and hand responsibility for gender equality back to the theatre community. Róise Goan was lead producer/ speaker organiser along with Sophie Motley as director and Caroline Williams as editor of the speakers' scripts.

The names on our wish-list for this event were wildly ambitious as we needed a line-up that would attract the media. We wanted to ensure a broad mix of backgrounds and ages, as well as at least one high profile international guest. Back in the summer, soon after the Lilly Awards in New York, Lisa Tierney Keogh had met with writer Eve Ensler (now known as V)[1] and director Diane Paulus. They wanted to coordinate a call-out on the same day as our November meeting for 50/50 gender equality in American theatre. Lisa continued to liaise with writer Marsha Norman and Julia Jordan, founder and the executive director of The Lillys, to see if we could get some big names involved in our event. Our wish list included Meryl Streep, Nicole Kidman, Fiona Shaw, Chimamanda Ngozi Adiche, Helen Mirren, Emma Thompson, Julie Taymor, Geena Davis, Caryl Churchill, and Ruth Negga. Through our networks we were able to get in touch with most of them, even when it didn't work out for them to appear at the meeting.

Human rights lawyer and activist Simone George had organised a conference in Dublin (the Safe Ireland Summit[2]) that clashed with our date and was likely to be of interest to a similar audience. Lian contacted her, and we worked together to amplify each other. Simone had a great slate of

One Thing More speakers on the Rosie Hackett Bridge, 14 November 2016. Photo: Kate Horgan

speakers organised, and we were able to benefit from having a few of them also speak at the #WakingTheFeminists event. Iris Bohnet, Director of Public Policy at Harvard, whose book, *What Works: Gender Equality by Design*[3] had just come out over the summer, was listed as a speaker at the Summit. We really wanted her at our event, but as she was appearing by video link, that wasn't possible. Fortunately, two other Safe Ireland Summit scheduled speakers, Mona Eltahawy and V (Eve Ensler), were able to participate in *One Thing More* in person. Mona Eltahawy is an Egyptian-American journalist, commentator and activist.[4] V is a Tony and Obie Award–winning American activist, author, feminist, performer, and playwright, best known for her play *The Vagina Monologues*.[5]

There was a lot of back and forth over the timing of the public event and the provision of childcare as MAMs (Mothers Artists Makers)[6] – a group set up after the first #WakingTheFeminists public meeting to advocate for feminist mothers in Irish theatre promoting family friendly arts practice – were concerned that the event time clashed with school pick-up for young children. While many of us in the campaign were frustrated at the way that the MAMs engaged with us, their concerns were important, and were careful to make sure the tension between us did not turn into the 'feminist split', where feminist movements can implode on themselves through infighting rather than from external pressure or attacks.[7] It was the first moment that it felt like #WakingTheFeminists was being pushed back at by our supporters, which was frustrating, particularly to the members of the core team who were also mothers. We dealt with it as diplomatically as we could to minimise any negative impact. Other than this friction with the MAMs, we held together as a group for the entire year, without drama, falling out, or major burnout. We had taken the earlier advice from Una Mullally, Bride Rosney, and Margaret E. Ward to heart about not letting ourselves get distracted by potential infighting. When any tensions arose, Anne Clarke in particular would remind us to keep our 'eyes on the prize', and to keep relentlessly moving forward towards our overall goals. Working in a collaborative art form, we were experienced in navigating tensions, creative, personal, and financial. In our work we negotiate between people and organisations with various and often conflicting viewpoints, while remaining calm and focused on building consensus. We were not shy of tension, and we didn't expect everyone to agree with all of our decisions. Anne, Caroline, and Lian especially had great stores of patience and listened respectfully to anyone who had a critical viewpoint. Listening to voices that offered criticism and dissent helped us to chart our path better, and come up with more robust solutions. We all tacitly agreed that the priority at all times had to be the achievement of our aims, which allowed egos to be left aside so we could work collectively on this common cause.

The tone of this final event was very different from the previous ones. It was more of a show than a meeting, celebrating the achievements of the year, presenting the research headlines in a dynamic way, and encouraging and challenging everyone to continue to push for change. It also provided a platform for the several major theatre organisations to update on the progress they'd made since our last public meeting on 8 March. We asked speakers to share #OneThingMore they had learned, one thing they had resolved to do, one thing they had determined to do differently, one thing that had changed, and one thing that still needed to change. We wanted to use repetition to build to a crescendo. Most speakers were live, with some sending videos of support that were played on a screen on stage. The event finished again with a song, this time performed live by singer, musician, and actress Camille O'Sullivan.[8]

We also included men's voices on stage as we knew it was important not to leave the work of gender equality to women alone; men also need to take action. We set a date after the US presidential election on the 8 November 2016, which we knew would suck up all the media attention, but the shock of Hillary Clinton not being elected president still reverberated, and added an edge of anger and urgency to the meeting. We ran at the media– and MAMs–friendly time of 11am–1pm. The event was preceded by a photoshoot on the Rosie Hackett Bridge with all the organisers and speakers.

The atmosphere was buoyant, jubilant, and determined. It was hard to believe how much we had achieved in just 12 months, and how much had already begun to change. We produced a free handout for the event, *Be Equal: See It, Say It, Count It, Change It*, which included research headlines and graphs showing the vast gender disparity over the past decade, a timeline of key events over the year, and a list of practical actions anyone could take towards creating more gender equity.

Handing Back to the Sector

The content, message, and celebration of the public event was important, but the most impactful work of the day was a private sectoral meeting later that afternoon in the opulent Venus Room of Belvedere House, Great Denmark Street, Dublin 1. The #WakingTheFeminists core group was exhausted after the year, the campaign was officially over, and it was now the responsibility of the theatre community as a whole, and the leaders of its major organisations in particular, to continue the work. This meeting was to discuss how this might happen. The breadth of attendance was extraordinary, showing a serious intention to keep the work going; this kind of meeting had never happened previously, and has not since.

Susan Coughlan facilitated this unprecedented meeting and Gráinne Pollak assisted with notes. Present were Lian Bell and Sarah Durcan for #WakingTheFeminists; Anne Clarke for #WakingTheFeminists and Producer, Landmark Theatre; Lucy Kerbel (Director, Tonic Theatre UK); Anna Walsh (Director, Theatre Forum); Rachel West (Head of Theatre, Arts Council); Loughlin Deegan (Director, Lir Academy); Cian O'Brien (Artistic Director, Project Arts Centre) and Orla Moloney (General Manager, Project Arts Centre); Teerth Chungh (Head of Production, Gate Theatre); Neil Murray and Graham McLaren (Co–Directors, Abbey Theatre); Jane Daly (Co–Director Irish Theatre Institute, and Programme Manager, Galway European Capital of Culture bid); Aideen Howard (Director, The Ark) and Avril Ryan (General Manager, The Ark); Olga Barry (Producer, Kilkenny Arts Festival); Julie Kelleher (Artistic Director, Everyman Theatre); Sean Kelly (CEO, Everyman Theatre); Lorraine May (Executive Director, Cork Midsummer Festival); Lucy Ryan (Producer, The Corn Exchange); Caroline Williams (Producer, Rough Magic); Eva Scanlon (General Manager and Producer, Fishamble); Craig Flaherty (Production Associate, Druid); Aoife White (General Manager, Pan Pan); Ruth McGowan

(Programme Manager, Dublin Fringe Festival); Amy O'Hanlon (General Manager, Dublin Fringe Festival); and Willie White (Director, Dublin Theatre Festival).

It was also a final moment to try to maintain support and gain buy-in for the Advance/*Ardú* programme. Our major application for EU funding to get it off the ground had just been submitted, and we were at the point of sending out a request for tender (on the advice of the Arts Council) for the services of setting up a pilot programme if we got the buy-in from enough theatre organisations at this meeting. We didn't. The response was still on a spectrum from enthusiastic to flat out refusal, with not enough organisations definitely pitching in. We had to face the fact that our hard work on *Ardú* was likely coming to an end.

Despite this, we were heartened that the meeting resulted (thanks largely to the insistence of Loughlin Deegan) in the formation of a cross-sectoral group whose initial aims were to: articulate a sector-wide intention for gender equality; craft gender equality policy for use as template; share the research templates; and plan training in unconscious bias. This group became the Gender Equality Policy Working Group, whose legacy is described in the next chapter.

Despite our exhaustion that day, and the disappointment around *Ardú*, we had so much to celebrate.[9] But not yet. We all needed to rest. Lian, in particular, needed time to recuperate: on top of a year of exceptionally hard work and pressure, her mother, Sara Horgan, had died suddenly in mid-September. Lian was beyond worn out. There was also a lot of campaign administrative work for us all to tie up. It wasn't until 4 January 2017 that we had a party to gather all who had contributed to #WakingTheFeminists, hosted in the Mansion House in Dublin.[10]

The List

(written by Lian with input from the wider team, and circulated at *One Thing More*)

01 Call yourself a feminist, publicly.
02 Be sure you understand it and believe in it. Feminism means equality for women and men, in every circumstance.
03 Call out sexism when you see it.
04 If something feels wrong but you can't put your finger on it, talk it over with someone to work out why.
05 Acknowledge that unconscious bias exists in all of us. It's how we were programmed.
06 Become more aware of your own unconscious biases.
07 Start to think of ways to counteract them.
08 Talk about feminism and gender equality with your colleagues at work.
09 Talk about it formally – have a staff meeting.
10 Think about gender equality in relation to ALL of the people in your workplace – from actors to cleaners to designers to technicians to administrators to board members to programmers to graphic designers to managers. Don't forget your freelance and project-based staff.
11 If someone isn't joining in the conversation, ask them why. And listen to them.
12 Be patient with the people who need time to learn.
13 Be impatient with the people who should know better.
14 Keep talking about feminism, formally and informally. Change takes time and persistence.
15 Get good quality unconscious bias training.
16 Think about how things might be better, think about practical steps, no matter how small to begin with, and start to act on them.
17 Make a commitment. Quotas and targets may work for you.
18 Make it public.
19 Stick to it.
20 Set a time frame for progress on gender equality.
21 Make it public.
22 Celebrate and mark it as it happens.
23 Hire and promote more women in key roles.
24 Hire more feminists everywhere.
25 Stand up for women in your workplace.
26 Support and encourage your women colleagues to go further than they think they can.
27 If women's voices aren't being heard as often as men's at meetings, address it.
28 Encourage women to speak first in a meeting.
29 Openly call out men who speak over women.
30 Encourage women to confidently say the phrase 'I disagree with you' if a man tells them his opinion like it's the fucking law of the land.
31 Count the women in your programme.
32 Count the women behind your programme.
33 Count the women portrayed, and notice how they are portrayed.
34 Count the women on your board.
35 Count the women on your hiring panels.
36 Count the women in your staff, see which roles they fill, how much they earn and how much power they have.
37 Make sure women are being credited properly for the work they do. Keep records. No one can count women unless archives are kept.
38 Formally commit to having a gender balanced board.

39 Ask your board to include gender equality (and ideally gender equality and diversity) as a permanent board agenda item.

40 Ask your boss what the organisation's gender equality policy is. If you are the boss, make sure you have a policy in place.

41 Ask them what the bullying and sexual harassment policy is.

42 Ask them what the policy is on paid maternity leave and paternity leave.

43 If any of these policies don't exist, ask them to put it in place for both staff jobs and freelance jobs.

44 Use the opportunity to also think about equality in general – if changes are being made to support women, make sure they include women who are also part of minorities, women of all classes and abilities and women of all ages.

45 Bullying and sexual harassment are never ok. Don't stay silent. If it's happening to you or someone you know, find someone you can trust and talk to them.

46 Talk about pay. By sharing information, you strengthen everybody's power to ask for an equal wage.

47 Ask your organisation to make its pay scales public.

48 Think about how the different jobs in your organisation intersect with parenting roles.

49 Talk about childcare. Ask your colleagues how they manage.

50 Does someone have to speak publicly for your organisation? Ask a woman to do it.

51 Give them the training and support they need to do it.

52 Talk to women, especially young women, about ways to build their confidence. Make them aware if they hold back around strongly opinionated and confident men.

53 Introduce confidence building exercises in the workplace.

54 At post-show discussions, notice who has been chosen to speak.

55 Notice who's asking the questions from the audience.

56 Ask the moderator to notice it too.

57 Ask the moderator to make a point of calling it out if it seems imbalanced.

58 When you go to the theatre, watch a film, look at an exhibition, read a book, notice who the creators were.

59 If women are represented, notice how.

60 Be vocal about your support of women artists. Tweet, post to Facebook, let the programmers know you'd like more opportunities to see their work.

61 When you look at marketing material for the creative industries, think about whether gendered choices were made, and what they are. Is the show about women marketed in pink? Why? Is the photo of the woman on the poster selling a show that has male lead actors? Why?

62 Look at your own marketing material and think about what choices were made there and what they say.

63 Talk to your audience about gender. Find out what they think. Tell them what you're thinking.

64 Describe the job, not the gender. They're a choreographer, not a female choreographer. They're a technician, not a female technician.

65 Keep talking to your colleagues about feminism, about women in your workplace, about women in our culture, about women in our society. Talking helps uncover the reality.

66 If you come up with a great idea or useful information, share it.

67 Support women: celebrate their successes, amplify their voices, show your solidarity.

68 Take responsibility for making changes.

69 Yes, you.

70 You have more power than you think.

Lian Bell, Catriona Crowe, and Anne Enright at One Thing More. Photo: Kate Horgan

Mona Eltahawy at One Thing More. Photo: Kate Horgan

Colonel Maureen O'Brien at One Thing More. Photo: Kate Horgan

(above) Loretta Dignam at One Thing More. Photo: Kate Horgan
(top left) Tara Derrington at One Thing More. Photo: Kate Horgan
(bottom left) Lisa Tierney Keogh at One Thing More. Photo: Kate Horgan

Amelie Metcalfe at One Thing More. Photo: Kate Horgan

FOURTEEN

Speeches from *One Thing More*

Anne Clarke, *Producer, Landmark Productions*

One year ago, at the end of October, I was giving a talk to a group of students at NUI Galway.[1] One of them asked whether I took gender into account when deciding what plays to produce. I answered, honestly, that I did not. I wouldn't say that now.

Two days later, Lian Bell pressed 'send' and all hell broke loose. Just two weeks after that, we were standing on this stage, raising our voices in bewilderment, and anger, and frustration. What a difference a year makes.

One thing I've learned over the past tumultuous year is that it doesn't matter how much of a right-thinking, left-leaning, liberal, card-carrying feminist you are. In a sector we like to think is open and progressive, it's a shock to realise that you were part of the problem.

But one thing I know: if you're part of the problem, you can be part of the solution.

Of course, that doesn't mean turning our back on the creative relationships we already have. But for every producer, and director, and artistic director, and programmer, and curator amongst us, for anyone who has any influence in what sort of stories make it to the stage, and who gets to tell those stories on that stage – and that goes for the funders too – it means being open to new collaborators; it means not making the usual assumptions; it means counting the numbers; it means looking up.

One thing is for sure. Irish theatre is a better, more equal place than it was a year ago. And we're only getting started.

Sinéad McKenna, *lighting designer*

One thing that lit the fire under all of us last year was shock. The shock at hearing stories of exclusion from colleagues, from respected, and deeply talented and intelligent women. Shock that I hadn't noticed that I hadn't seen them in a while. And shock at hearing first hand just how many movements for change had swelled in the past only to ebb back into obscurity. We just stopped noticing.

So now, my one thing is, I'm going to *notice*.

On a positive note – I've had a year of extraordinary women: Derbhle Crotty's Juno [in *Juno and the Paycock*] at the Gate; Aisling O'Sullivan's Vera [in *The Wake*] here at the Abbey, directed by Annabelle Comyn; *Embodied* in the GPO; Grace Jones [in the documentary *Grace Jones: Bloodlight and Bami*] with Sophie Fiennes, Zia Holly, and Katie Holly.

I worked with set designer Maree Kearns on *Invitation to a Journey*, a long overdue homage to the extraordinary Eileen Gray, who despite being one of the most innovative, multidisciplinary, inventive, and breathtakingly beautiful artists and designers of the 20th century, all but disappeared into obscurity until relatively recently. She did not stop working, she was designing right up until the end. She just failed to be noticed.

But looking at it again:

I worked with three female directors in 2016. That is one quarter of all of the directors I worked with.

I worked with four female set designers out of nine in 2016.

No chief electrician I worked with was female.

No sound designer or composer was female.

No production manager was female, except for one in a production in the UK.

Costume was overwhelmingly female, unless the designer was designing the set.

So now I notice. And when I come to balance my end of year accounts, I now have a new folder in my accounts file, entitled gender balance.

Anne Enright, *writer and Laureate for Irish Fiction*

In 2013 I started to count the women reviewed in the books pages of the newspapers and then stopped counting, three weeks in. The figures were astonishingly bad. I said nothing, or nothing in public. I noticed the male–only history of publicly funded programmes like One City, One Book and I moved swiftly on. I thought there was no point talking, even very loudly, to people who can not hear.

I was proud and delighted to be appointed Laureate for Irish Fiction in 2015, but even then – even then – I couldn't do the whole woman thing. I couldn't 'be' a woman writer: labelled, dismissed, ghettoised, sometimes shamed or derided, rendered unimportant. I couldn't be that thing. Not even for Ireland. Not even for you.

Waking The Feminists gave my politics back to me. It has opened casual or urgent conversations with literary editors and arts curators, festival managers, selection committees. Some of them are in a state of denial, some are actually 'hurt' to have the numbers pointed out to them, but more of them are not. These are not bad people. It would be nice to know what people are thinking, when they practise unwitting discrimination, the fact is, they are just not thinking at all. And that is no longer possible, thanks to you.

Catriona Crowe, *archivist and commentator*

It is a privilege for me to be invited here today to help you celebrate and reflect on an extraordinary year in the history of Irish women. When you first gathered here a year ago, you were protesting an obvious gender imbalance in the 2016 programme for the National Theatre. The testimonies given from the stage that day highlighted gender discrimination in the theatre and much further afield. Society was in the dock as much as theatre was.

That day, and what has happened since, are part of a great tradition of Irish feminism, which begins as an ideology in the 1820s with Anna Wheeler's and William Thompson's wonderfully titled 'An appeal of one half of the human race, women, against the pretensions of the other half, men, to retain them in political and hence in civil and domestic slavery'. That clarion call led to the long battle for female suffrage which eventually won us the right to that most fundamental guarantee of equality – the vote, partially in 1918 and fully in 1922.

The campaign for female suffrage took two forms: first, the peaceful struggle for reform, exemplified by the parliamentary lobbying and patient bill-writing of people like Isabella Tod,[2] a Presbyterian from Belfast, and Anna Haslam,[3] a Quaker from Youghal, both staunch unionists, who pegged away at the tedious but necessary work of research, legislation, and alliance-building. The second strand comes later and is more activist and noisy: Hanna Sheehy Skeffington's Irish Women's Franchise League, founded in 1908, produced a ground-breaking newspaper, *The Irish Citizen*, and focused on many other issues besides the franchise: women's right to education, to decent treatment in prison, to equality in their households among other things.

The IWFL engaged in some genteel window breaking, using toffee hammers, not the most effective weapon for the purpose, and were imprisoned for their efforts. Their unionist sisters in the North were far more violent, bombing, burning, destroying mail, and cutting telephone wires. They were also fond of digging up golf courses, which some might say was a service to humanity at large.

The vote was partially granted to women in 1918, and fully in the Irish Free State in 1922. Then the long backlash began, with repressive legislation forcing women off juries, preventing them from working in certain sectors, outlawing contraception and divorce, and imposing a marriage bar to employment. The 1937 Constitution privileged the concept of the woman in the home, although it did nothing to help her economically.

Many valiant women, like Hilda Tweedy[4] and Andrée Sheehy Skeffington,[5] kept the flag flying for feminism during these dark years, but many women internalised the state's vision of their limitations and supported their own oppression. And in case we think that day is gone, contemplate with dismay the large number of women who voted for a known sexist and misogynist in the US last Tuesday.

The second wave of Irish feminism comes in the late sixties, following the publication of Betty Friedan's *The Feminine Mystique*, the book which blew open the concept of the contented housewife. Again, there were two strands: the legislative, report-writing, politically astute activities of the Commission on the Status of Women, and the flamboyant activism of the Irish Women's Liberation Movement, exemplified by the Contraceptive Train to Belfast in 1971. Both sides, the restrained and the noisy, had crucial parts to play in changing a culture which at that stage was unprepared for such ideas. Both sides achieved the great leaps forward exemplified by legislation on equal pay, deserted wives' and unmarried mothers' allowances, proper widow's pensions, limited contraception, and the extraordinary number of important women's organisations set up in the 1970s, from the Rape Crisis Centre to Cherish to the Well Woman Clinics and Women's Aid.

The terrible reproductive wars of the 1980s gave us the Eighth amendment to the constitution, which has caused nothing but trouble, and eventually divorce, which has not resulted in floodgates bursting open as predicted by its opponents. There is much left to do, especially the Repeal the 8th amendment, and genuine economic empowerment for poorer women in our society.

Your movement, #WakingTheFeminists, has been like a breath of fresh air blowing through our still very patriarchal society. In your approach and methodology, you have united the noisy and restrained strands of the previous waves of feminism; while the extraordinary event last year created all the right kinds of noise, it was succeeded by quality research which will be essential for any real change to occur in theatre with regard to commissioning and employment of women. And you have created a template for the rest of the feminist movement to follow: beautiful noise and super-smart evidence-based findings. Be proud. What you started will echo into the future and take its place in the illustrious history of Irish feminism.

Lian Bell, *set designer, arts manager, and #WakingTheFeminists Campaign Director*

This time last November, a group of us took a mandate from the hurricane of energy that you unleashed, and we made the commitment to throw ourselves into this campaign for one year. We said one year because, frankly, the scale of the mountain we saw ahead of us scared the crap out of us. Because our energy was already depleted in those first whirlwind weeks, and none of us relished the idea of becoming long-term campaigners. Speaking for myself, all I really wanted to do was make art and get on with my life. My nice, quiet, behind the scenes life. Reading back over some of the social media from this time last year, I found a post from another behind the scenes woman – costume designer Joan O'Clery – which simply said, 'If not now, when? If not me, who?'

That decision to run #WakingTheFeminists for a year was, without realising it at the time, one of the smartest things we did. It felt like a realistic commitment, so we weren't overwhelmed before we even started. It put a fire under us as we pushed as hard as possible for what we believe is right. And it put the skids on those around us. Things moved fast. Never quite fast enough for my endless impatience, but to be fair to us, some very good things have happened this year.

Our national theatre announced guiding principles on gender equality that set a national and international standard, placing the Abbey, and Ireland, at the forefront of gender equality in theatre. We saw the arrival of two new directors here who, no doubt, will be working hard to turn those aspirations into reality. We'd like to thank them and all the staff of the Abbey for helping us put this event on today.

A core #WakingTheFeminists team member, Sarah Durcan, was appointed to the Abbey board, putting her extensive experience and passion at the direct service of our national theatre.

The theatre landscape itself is changing. As well as the new directors here, there's been the appointment of a woman for the first time to be Artistic Director of our second highest publicly funded theatre, the Gate.[6] That wasn't something that was on the cards last November.

The Arts Council invested money for research into gender balance in theatre, meaning that the personal testimony so many of you shared will now be backed up by hard numbers. Change from now on will be measurable. Our work has been recognised and backed by both The Community Foundation for Ireland and the Ireland 2016 Centenary Programme, who we thank for their generous support.

The campaign itself had a ripple effect into other areas of society, gained international recognition, and won a number of awards. We – and you – put on some great events, from London to Limerick, from Brooklyn to Inis Oírr. #WakingTheFeminists has become a byword for successful grassroots campaigning.

Most importantly, though, we have all felt a sea change in our community. We ourselves are not the same as we were. I think back to this time last year when speaking up, proclaiming our opinions, and telling our personal stories felt, for some of us, dangerous. That we might lose too much. This year, and particularly this week, it feels even more important. That we lose too much if we stay silent.

Before #WakingTheFeminists, I'd never really spoken in public. I was, let me say it again, very much a behind the scenes person. Now I've spoken publicly for the campaign, I think about 25 times. From the Bord Gáis Energy Theatre, to seminar rooms in universities across the country. Not counting the interviews I've done for radio, television, podcasts, and print media. As a girl who dreaded being called on to answer a question in class, I've been surprised to notice my palms don't sweat the same way they used to.

I've watched women around me gaining confidence in speaking up. I've seen them growing less afraid. I've seen, and felt, what happens when you're encouraged and supported, and what happens when you're listened to.

The one thing that stands out from this year for me is: women, speak up. Use your voice to stick up for yourself and use it to stick up for those who are silent, or silenced.

Over the coming weeks the public campaign will wind down, and the #WakingTheFeminists social media channels will fall silent. But that does not mean that we, or you, can stop shouting for the things we believe in. Each of us is responsible for embedding what we've learned this year into our hearts and into our actions, forever. Each of you. Particular responsibility lies on those of you who are in positions of power and influence, from funders, to leaders of organisations, programmers, and artists who will make wonderful new work on this stage, and stages across the country, and the world, in the years to come. Speak up. If not you, who? If not now, when?

Neil Murray and Graham McLaren, *Co-Directors, Abbey Theatre*

Hello, my name is Neil Murray and this is Graham McLaren. We are the Directors of the Abbey Theatre.

It is a great privilege for us to be given this opportunity to welcome you to your National Theatre and to congratulate #WakingTheFeminists for putting the issue of gender equality at the heart of Ireland's theatre community.

Last July we announced our appointment to the Abbey Theatre with what we hoped would be a clear message: that, regardless of your gender, your race, your accent, your physical abilities, or the money in your pocket, the Abbey is your national theatre and we are here to tell your stories.

Three months ago, the Abbey Theatre announced our 'Eight Guiding Principles for Gender Equality', and we regard this as a good start but also know that we need to do much more. Not just the Abbey but everyone in this room, everyone currently watching online, everyone reading reports of this meeting. We need to find the many different ways to translate words into action. It is with that in mind that we would like to make an explicit appeal to you all, now.

Graham:

If you are a playwright, we want to hear your ideas and no it doesn't always need to be presented as a finished draft of a well made play. But it does need to be urgent and important to you. So we widen the appeal to all theatre makers – if you are a director or a lighting designer, if you are a choreographer or a dramaturg, an actor or a musician – we want to hear your urgent ideas. We want to support your passion for your work regardless of whether you think it fits a six week run on this stage or downstairs in the Peacock. For we must remember that this theatre was created to serve artists, not the other way around.

It is together that we will transform your National Theatre.

Seána Kerslake, *actor*

I want to start by saying I have been extremely fortunate with the people I have worked with in my short career so far. The majority of work that I have done has been female driven; female writers, directors and producers.

Working on the film *A Date for Mad Mary*, surrounded by women, gave me a fire in my belly about making fun, exciting work about women whose stories we haven't seen much of before. This film was written by two brothers, Colin and Darren Thornton, which made it even better because it was a group of people, of mixed gender, telling a story about females without the male gaze, that's G A Z E.

In my theatre work I've been fortunate to work with men that write women as equals, who recognise that we are real, three-dimensional human beings.

When I first heard of #WakingTheFeminists I was like 'Eh yeah, I'm up! I've been awake for ages,' but as the movement went on, I began to ask myself, 'what difference am I making to bring about the changes I want to see?'

I realised it begins with looking at yourself.

The key thing for any creative person is to find their voice.

I have been told over the years that I'm not very good at telling stories. That I go off on too many tangents. I used to believe that because I wasn't what you'd call a 'great' storyteller – that I shouldn't even bother telling stories at all – but then I realised that this is just how I tell stories. Multiple storylines running simultaneously with multiple plotlines. Sounds like a great and complex narrative to me *and* it's my voice.

Of course, It's not a gender-specific thing, 'finding your voice'. But why, from a young age, do girls stop being equal in numbers to boys in sports, in debating, in playwriting etc.?

We need to show young people of all genders that their stories, just like mine, like everybody's, are important so that they don't have to try to find their voice. They know it and they are not afraid to speak with it. It's not that I was ever discouraged from telling my stories, but somewhere along the line I felt that they were invalid. Even writing this short piece I wonder am I saying something that's relevant, is my voice valid? The #WakingTheFeminists movement has reinforced that 'yes! It is!' not just for me, but for women working in the industry everywhere.

Karan O'Loughlin, *Campaigns & Equality Organiser, SIPTU/Irish Equity*

I want to talk to you about the requirement for active feminism today. But before I do that, I am going to repeat what I have been trying to drive home all year in relation to women at work.

In 1894 the Royal Commission on Labour published a report on the conditions of women's work in Ireland. The top three issues identified for women at work at that time were:

- Child Care
- Low Pay
- Length of day

2016 and the top three issues for women at work are:

- Child Care
- Low Pay
- Length of day

122 years later women are still struggling with these issues. So we need something different, we need a strong feminist movement in Ireland.

It is important that we understand and make others understand what feminism is. Feminism is not about women disliking men or replacing men or wanting to be treated like men or to be like men. Feminism is about equality of opportunity for women and equality of access for women.

In September I met with Gudrun Schyman, founder of the Swedish political party Feminist Initiative. This party won a seat in the European parliament in the last election and Gudrun Schyman is now travelling around Europe meeting feminists to inspire them to organise ahead of the next European parliament election in 2019 so as to win enough seats for speaking rights in the EU Parliament.

The one specific thing that I commit to – to contribute to the growth and development of equality for women on this Island – is to forge strong links with our European sisters. I commit to attending their meeting in December where they are bringing together women they have met throughout the EU so that the Feminist movement can be stronger together.

The key message here is that feminism is not just for women. Feminism is for everybody.

Marie Tierney, *production manager and designer*

We live in an unequal society. The gender inequality that we have highlighted this past year is mirrored in many other aspects of our lives. Like the wage gap between men and women. At current rates, by the time this gender pay gap has closed, I will be 228 years old.

I have spent my entire adult life fighting injustice and inequality. As a freelance production manager and designer, I have been up close and personal with a bucketload of misogyny. I spend a fair bit of time thinking about it, getting annoyed that for a live event production management award, there are 71 nominees but only six are women. Getting annoyed that women technicians I know have left the industry because they can't juggle the uncertain lifestyle, long hours, and a decent home life.

So what to do? As a production manager, a fair bit of my time is spent solving problems as they arise. So, is there anything we can do to help solve this problem? One thing is to watch our language. The words we use can reinforce preconceptions and validate discrimination.

If you hear 'Irish Rugby team defeats NZ', do you feel the same thing as Irish Women's Rugby team defeats NZ. If you don't, then that's *you*. Take the time to think about what you say and how you say it. Small wonder there are so few female sound engineers, when the generic term is 'noise boys.' Or 'big girl's blouse' used to describe a non-performing male.

In my job, I have been called bossy, hard-nosed, or my personal favourite, 'sure, you're as good as any man'. A use of words unlikely to be applied to my male counterparts.

62 million girls all over the world are denied access to an education. We are a highly-educated sector. Let's use that education to start this change. I'll say it again. Watch what you say. Let us redefine the world we live in with the language we use.

Yasmine Akram (video), *actress, writer and comedian*

What I'm committed to in terms of gender equality is that I want to create roles for women and I want to play roles myself, that show all of our idiotic ways – our disgusting ways, our deeply, deeply flawed ways as human beings. It still depresses me in this day and age that a lot of the time I see on television – and I've been in an audition for many different roles – where women have the answers, or are the mature ones, or are the ones with no personality. And it's not right, and it's not true.

I think that we all want to live in a world where we're represented truly, not just idealised versions that we can never ever hope to be. So that's what I'm going to do. Make really, really flawed women. Either play them or write them, and I know everyone will enjoy that.

Jim Culleton, *Artistic Director, Fishamble: The New Play Company*

At Fishamble, we have always considered that we develop and produce a programme of new work in an open, inclusive way, to bring a range of voices to the stage. But #WakingTheFeminists has caused us to look more closely, over the past year, at our facts and figures, particularly with regard to gender.

More women than men take part in our playwriting courses, and are supported through our New Play Clinic initiative; more women send plays to our projects which call for submissions from the public; more women have been awarded the Fishamble New Writing Award over the past 11 years at the Dublin Fringe Festival.

However, when you look at figures for the unsolicited plays submitted to Fishamble, it works out at about three-quarters from men, and one-quarter from women; and about a third of plays we have produced are by women and two-thirds by men.

So we can see that our output over time is not as balanced as we'd like it to be.

One thing we have done is put in place some small but (we think) effective measures to address this, which have already created results:

- We set up a sub-committee on our board to keep track of gender balance developments.
- We have employed a senior reader, Sarah Hoover, to give a gender blind reading of every play under consideration for advanced development and possible production.
- We assessed applications with names omitted, so gender was unknown, for our current year-long director and playwright mentoring programme in association with Belltable. 16 participants are female, eight are male.
- With our partners at Tiger Dublin Fringe and Irish Theatre Institute, we realised that our Show In A Bag initiative was attracting and supporting more male than female artists over the past eight years, so we made a commitment to a better balanced programme, actively encouraged female artists to apply, and Dublin Fringe provided a female-led workshop,

and this year the gender balance shifted, with twice as many female artists involved as male artists.

We are committed to ensuring these measures – and more – are not isolated events, but continue in the future so that Fishamble expresses the voices of a range of playwrights, including gender balance, for our audiences.

Joanna Crawley, *producer, translator, and dramaturg*

Before I started producing shows in Ireland, for nearly ten years I worked as a theatre critic in Poland, and today I would like to tell you about a very tricky discussion that has been happening there for a while. And to give you some context, Polish theatre is madly political, male dominated, and absolutely hardcore. I'm talking four to seven hours of blood, semen, sex, and existential drama on stage.

And at some point, this political, mad, male-dominated theatre found itself a new mission. Let's defend the female cause. And how do we do that? By showing graphically how brutalised and victimised the women are. And so it started: Hamlet, wiping the floor with Ophelia; Petruchio brutally raping Katherina; German soldiers torturing female resistance fighters; communist militia clubbing protesting nurses. Spotlight on misogyny, a parade of men who hate women, never ending reenactments of rapes, murders, and beatings.

Actresses in Poland became experts in being dramatically hurt. They would lie on stage covered in all kinds of fluids, broken and abused by patriarchy, church, capitalism, new media – the list is long.

And when this practice became mainstream, feminists in Poland said 'please'. 'Please stop defending us'. Repeating the gesture of abuse doesn't erase it. There's a fine line between criticising something, making it visible, and between perpetuating and normalising it. A broken woman on stage is a powerful image that can trigger discussions, but it becomes dangerous when it turns into a trend, a shortcut, a special effect. And no matter how seemingly consensual, female performers were forced to enact this abuse or be fired.

As Ireland begins to create more urgent, brave, ambitious work that interrogates misogyny and gender imbalance – mainstreaming this practice of staged violence against women is one thing that I would like to spare Irish theatre.

Lisa Dwan, *actor and director*

When I left this country 16 years ago, I never imagined that I would be invited back to perform in my national theatre, and more shockingly that I would ever feel that I had the right to call the Abbey *my* national theatre. It has taken a Welshman and a Scotsman to give exiles like me, that gift of our national theatre, not only in our vocabulary, but also in the Republic of our imaginations.

Last year, I was asked how I felt about taking a break from Beckett to do some 'normal theatre'. I said I found it hard to let go of a landscape so vast, one of the great gifts of Beckett's *Not I* is the joy of having your body removed. As a woman. This is just so damn liberating. I got to play consciousness itself. I got to tour the world with only my lips exposed, and fill theatres, which is my own honest human sound. A far cry from the constantly regurgitated roles of the bitch, the bimbo – the cycles we are all continually subjected to.

It took another exile like Beckett to get me to peer past these wounds and into my own potential, to peel away the trappings and the entrapment of a woman, of internalised misogyny, of what society does to us as women, and go beyond the limitations we set ourselves.

When the younger generation turn to the arts, to seek solace from a ranting, orange, misogynistic despot, we can offer them honest portraits of ourselves and all of our bravery, resourcefulness, power, poetry, intelligence – slices of our defiance to fire the minds and expose them to their true selves.

We cannot rewrite history or call to mind all of the women who have been written out of it. But we can expand the future and we can begin that today. Here where everything begins in the Republic of our imagination.

Emma Donoghue, *writer*
read by Nichola MacEvilly, *actor*

I'm happy to be one of a chorus of voices from around the world congratulating #WakingTheFeminists on its extraordinary year of action. I got my start in theatre in the most amazingly nourishing context: I had my first two plays put on in the mid-1990s by an Irish company, Glasshouse Productions, who were committed to theatre by and about women. I owe that launchpad to someone I first met in the Women's Group in UCD, the inexhaustible Caroline Williams, and I'm so proud that she's part of #WakingTheFeminists now.

As two decades have gone by, I've come to see how lucky I was to get that great start, given how hard it is for so many women to access the institutional and financial resources they need to bring their theatre work to the audiences who need to experience it.

#WakingTheFeminists has done so much more than it was set up to do. This well-run, effective, smart, and moving arts campaign has had an impact way beyond the Abbey Theatre, way beyond Irish theatre – and way beyond theatre. It manages to combine coolheaded research and urgent testimony, insightful analysis, and passionate solidarity. It has put gender issues in a year-long spotlight and incidentally managed to make the word 'feminist' hip again. Thank you all.

Tom Vaughan Lawlor, *actor*

I met my wife doing a play in Manchester. The cast consisted of 18 men and two women. It was a play about war, and our production featured machine-guns and explosions, and lots of men screaming and shouting at each other. It was a lot of fun.

It wasn't until many months later that my then girlfriend admitted it had not always been an easy experience. She told me, 'You have no idea how hard it is to be heard in such a masculine environment'. I laughed it off at the time and teased her for not being tough enough. But over the years it became clearer and clearer to me that acting is a different profession for women.

Beside the visible imbalances in terms of pay and available roles, the focus on ageing, and weight lost or gained, there are a myriad of subtle ways that women in rehearsal rooms and on film sets are, deliberately or otherwise, made to feel less than. Once you open your eyes to it you can see it everywhere. And when you realise it deeply, profoundly affects not only those you love the most, but also colleagues who inspire you and made you want to become an artist in the first place, it is shameful if you don't at the very least add your voice to the call for change.

The one thing I have resolved to do is to strive to be active in support rather than simply standing on the sidelines paying lip-service to an ideal. To be more educated about the intricacies of gender inequality, and to use that knowledge to play a part in making change happen.

Tara Flynn, *actor and writer*

What a privilege it is, to stand on this stage and be heard. To know you are taking part in history, to have ears ready and waiting to receive your message. To follow in the footsteps of artists, revolutionaries – sometimes one and the same. This privilege should not be gendered. It's right that we be grateful when given such a platform; what we should not be is surprised.

When tradition is challenged, the absence of truth it sometimes hides becomes exposed. Unflattering. Maybe even harsh. Once truth has been revealed, it can no longer go unseen. It is not comfortable. It is not gentle. But it is necessary. How things have been doesn't have to be how things are, not if we say they aren't.

Women aren't supposed to reveal too much. It has, traditionally, been considered indecent.

This year, we told our stories. Raised our voices. It is our revolution. And we are unstoppable.

What power we have, when we work together. What a glorious noise we make in unison. What resistance we create when we push back. Not the side dish, not the afterthought: the flesh and bones and skin of this island. We are the main event. Now let us shine.

Julie Kelleher, *Artistic Director, The Everyman*

This has been an extraordinary year of personal and professional development; I have learned so much. Learning is one of the chief reasons why I love theatre and why I work in theatre: we are always learning.

This year, I learned to look harder to better see my own bias, to recognise the conditioning that has informed my idea of what makes 'good' theatre. I learned to call out misogyny; it's still hard, I was raised to behave like a good girl. I learned that we need to make a plan if we want to effect change.

But the crucial thing I learned, the one thing (and this is with apologies to my mum who has long since been a proponent of 'the little red hen' approach, that is to say 'I shall just have to do it myself') – the one thing is that it's basically easier if we're all doing it together; if we look harder together, if we call things out together, if we make a plan together. You might get overwhelmed otherwise.

And it's not that I didn't know that before: collaboration is the root of our artform at best.

I knew already that it was possible to have some limited impact, with the will of a brilliant organisation like the Everyman; we've been committed to producing plays with a majority female cast since 2014 – a small step, but a step forward.

Last November, #WakingTheFeminists blew the winds of change through doors nationwide, and suddenly the potential for greater, longer lasting impact became possible. I feel enabled now to do things I had only hoped for before as a programmer, producer, maker. Because we took stock, redoubled our efforts, and reimagined the Irish theatre landscape. Together.

Denise Gough (video), *actor*

I wanted to say congratulations to all of us for the progress that we've made this year. In putting us in our rightful place front and centre in the arts and beyond. #WakingTheFeminists has created a tidal wave of solidarity and caused such a ruckus, one of which I am so beyond proud to be a part of.

So my one thing more than I have been struck by this year is the power of us together. When we stand shoulder to shoulder for our mutual good, when we share our experiences, find identification, and empower each other to speak up and demand change, when we get behind each other, hold each other up, and cheer each other on. That is how we progress.

We still have a ways to go but we are on the right road. Massive love to all of you.

Cian O'Brien, *Artistic Director, Project Arts Centre*

I'm glad to be here again and to be speaking at another #WakingTheFeminists event. As the leader of an organisation, the movement has had an interesting, complicated impact on me and the organisation I'm representing on this stage today. I deeply believe in the core values that #WakingTheFeminists has communicated and I am committed to advocating for change; at the same time, I recognise the challenges and complexities involved. There is a sense, and I know I'm not alone in feeling this, that the leaders of institutions have been asked to speak today, not only because we can and should be instrumental in the change process, but also because we're being called on to be accountable for our positions. It is important that the reasons we as institutions stand here are not tokenistic.

Project is a unique organisation, in that we actually have less of an issue with gender balance than others when you take into account all of the art forms we present. But that does not mean we can rest on our laurels. As we move into 2017, as Project enters its sixth decade, the one thing that will be central to our work will be to ensure that our programme embraces equality and diversity in all its forms for the organisation, the artists we support, and the audiences who come to see the work. The Board and I have committed this to paper in our new artistic strategy and I look forward to sharing it with the wider community in the coming months.

Mona Eltahawy, *columnist and international public speaker on Arab and Muslim issues and global feminism*

It's January 2051.

Three women are to be inaugurated president. They got to know each other in 2015 on Twitter after a feminist they followed posted a series of tweets about #WakingTheFeminists, a campaign in which women use direct action to fight for women's rights.

Donya Zaki is 60 and is about to become Egypt's first woman president. She is also openly bisexual and a poet, the perfect antidote to decades of hypermasculine Egyptian politics. Donya had enthusiastically joined the 2011 revolution but was frustrated with how quickly it turned into a political musical chairs between the military and the Muslim Brotherhood, and how quickly women are erased from revolution.

In 2015, she joined an underground anarcho-feminist movement called Sekhmet's Sisters. Sekhmet was an ancient Egyptian goddess of retribution and sex. As Donya described her 'First she'd kick your head in, then she'd fuck your brains out.'

Areej Mohamed, 55, is about to become Saudi Arabia's first woman Mufti. She was an atheist but had agreed to accept the post of first woman mufti because she understood the unholy alliance between men of religion and men of politics. In her 20s, she formed the radical feminist movement Khadijah's Daughters Brigades which blossomed into the first feminist revolution to overthrow a regime. Their chant *Stay out of my vagina unless I want you in there* quickly turned global. One of Areej's first fatwas was to allow women to have multiple spouses – feminism and polyamory at once – not bad.

Octavia Hernandez, 53, is about to become the third consecutive woman president of the US, having just beaten Chelsea Clinton, who at 70 was considered too old. Why so many women presidents? Because in 2016, her fellow Americans had elected a fascist, racist, misogynist, bigoted sexual predator called Donald Trump. Donya fought the Muslim Brotherhood in Egypt, Octavia fought the US white Christian Brotherhood, which considered women walking incubators. She was enraged that 53% of white women voted for Trump. Asked 'why do women fight feminism?' Octavia would quote

Octavia Butler, the science fiction/fantasy writer she was named after, 'Drowning people sometimes die fighting their rescuers.'

At their inauguration, Donya, Areej, and Octavia took an oath to do one thing: *Fuck the Patriarchy!*

Molly O'Cathain, *set and costume designer*

My name is Molly O'Cathain and I'm a theatre designer. I'm here to represent Rough Magic as one of the five artists on the SEEDs program.

First I'd like to read to you the company's commitments to further improving gender equality:

- Creating a safe space so that all artists can take artistic risks.
- Sustaining our policy of gender parity in commissioning writers.
- Achieving gender parity on the board.
- Interrogating artistic choices through systematic checks.
- Formalising our practice of gender equality in employment opportunity and remuneration for all theatre-makers.
- Placing women at the heart of the national narrative.

The first year of #WakingTheFeminists has coincided with our first year as SEEDS artists. We are changing, learning, and growing as artists, as Irish theatre is changing, learning, and growing as feminists. This means that gender equality has been a constant subject in our weekly meetings. Recently, we talked about 'safe spaces'.

A safe space is any space where you know that if you speak out you will be supported. Speaking out can be scary, but you have the opportunity to make a space safe for someone else, by standing up and making yourself heard. Because if no one knows you care, then arguably, you don't.

We realised that today we feel more confident in speaking out against gender-based discrimination in our workplaces, because the likelihood that we will be heard – and supported – is significantly greater than it was a year ago. But we also realised that there are still moments when 'not causing a fuss' or 'just getting on with it' or feeling like 'I don't have time for feminism right now, we've a get-in to do' gets the better of us.

And so, we are committed to speaking out, loudly and visibly. And to making sure that never feels like a crazy or stupid or humourless thing for the people around us to do.

So that we can all, always, have time for feminism!

Selina Cartmell, *director*[7]

'If you ask me what I came to do in this world, I, an artist, will answer you, I am here to live out loud.'

These words by the French playwright Émile Zola have been a touchstone. I have reflected and still continue to reflect on the honour of being appointed the new director of the beautiful, iconic, and the much-loved Gate Theatre.

By looking back at the past, you can understand the present or where you find yourself now and, only then, can you look to the future. Over the last few months, I have thought of all the people who have inspired, nurtured, and supported me over the years, both personally and professionally. A common thread appears – that those who have made the biggest and most lasting impact are women.

And many of these women have been pioneers – telling stories from an outsider's perspective and living their lives on the margins and peripheries. They have forged a different pathway – creating their own rules, leading by example, and through collaboration, and taken risks. These are women who have stirred things up and who have questioned and challenged, despite doors being closed and gates being bolted. As a result, things are now changing and need to continue to change.

And their example has empowered, encouraged, and inspired me to be bolder and braver. And it has made me realise that I am not alone. These inspiring role models have pushed me out of my comfort zone and made me believe it is possible to think big and live out loud. These fearless women gave me the confidence to follow in their footsteps and to be an outsider on my journey in search of a new creative home.

And One Thing More... let's be fearless in our quest for change.

Jane Deasy, *composer and theatre maker*

In May 2016 the National Concert Hall announced its centenary festival programme *Composing the Island.* Of the living composers represented there were 13 women and 37 men. Of all the pieces played written by living composers, 19 were by women, 70 by men. To put this into perspective, over the three weeks, audiences listened to a total of 870 minutes of music written by men and just 197 minutes of music written by women.

When the imbalance was first pointed out, the NCH responded 'we cannot rewrite history,' and added, 'happily, due to the huge strides being made addressing gender imbalance, a retrospective of the 21st century will look very different.' Not only is this dismissive and condescending, I feel like I need to point out – we are nearly 17 years into the 21st century.

The role of a national cultural institution has always been about setting the standard of contemporary art. It writes history by imposing the standard of what is recognised as a good piece of work and what isn't. Its programming decisions determine such. 'We can't rewrite history' is a curious comment from an institution that actively writes the narrative into its record books, of what is and what is not of standard.

The canon was established by men and that is the antiquated, patriarchal standard that we are still expected to submit to, if our work is to have an outlet here.

The landscape of contemporary Irish music is rich with the work of female artists, yet the programming predicts the future of Irish contemporary music to be predominantly male. It is time to step in and not leave our future in these hands.

Aisling O'Sullivan, *actress*
read by Rachel O'Byrne, *actor*

Thank you for giving me the opportunity to voice my support for #WakingTheFeminists. I am proud to be a part of such a mutually respectful, nourishing, inclusive, and challenging movement.

We become the stories we hear and tell ourselves. I am hungry for stories that open my heart and mind. I am hungry to be fed stories from and about my sex, told by women, that challenge the sick thought systems the world has in place.

I am in America. Donald Trump has been elected President. He speaks with vulgarity about women. He objectifies us. What does it mean that America is prepared to accept a person who demeans women and people of other backgrounds and beliefs? Who has urged us to build walls, lock her up, grab her pussy, indulge in locker room talk. What story are they telling themselves in America? What is it trying to force us to tell ourselves?

Hillary Clinton spoke of her disappointment at not shattering the highest and hardest glass ceiling. She reminded us that someday someone will and that that woman may be amongst us now. She urged younger people 'to never stop believing that fighting for what is right is worth it' and she directly addressed little girls to 'never doubt that they are valuable and powerful and deserving of every opportunity in the world to pursue and achieve their own dreams'. She stated that 'our best days are ahead of us'. This is the story I will reach towards, the story I will nourish and support. The dream I chose to follow.

Thank you to Lian Bell for having the courage to act on the wild, impulsive, and outraged wisdom that sparked #WakingTheFeminists – and this feminist's awakening.

Collette Farrell, *General Manager, Dublin Theatre Festival*

I have worked in the arts for 30 years as a producer and company, venue, and general manager. I remember when #WakingTheFeminists kicked off, I had been working in Drogheda for 13 years, but things hadn't worked out as I had expected, so I was faced with searching for a new role for the first time in a long, long time. I thought, at my age, nobody is going to hire me, but Dublin Theatre Festival did. I remember feeling so grateful at the time, and it took me a while to remember, they hired me because I am bloody good!

I was reminded of this reading Gráinne Pollak's MA thesis. There was a quote from one of the interviewees 'men walk into an interview and say they can do this … women apologise and hold back'. This sense that I did hold back, I didn't go for more jobs whilst my male contemporaries just went for it. Even when Willie asked me to speak today, my first reaction was, 'it's on the Abbey Stage, let me think'. We joked that a man would just say yes and dive in.

At Dublin Theatre Festival, #WakingTheFeminists has been on the agenda all year, at board level, and at staff level – we discuss it regularly at our company meetings. We have realised that it's not enough for our team to believe in gender equality, it has to become institutionalised. We have reviewed statements on equality and respect in our handbooks so that the values of gender equality radiate beyond the core team to everyone we engage professionally. In 2017 we will undertake unconscious bias training together as a team. Our board, which is already gender balanced, has embraced this as a policy. We are continuing to count and to reflect on how there can be more progression of women theatre practitioners and arts managers so that there will be equality of opportunity in all the roles in the performing arts in Ireland.

I want to say to those young women in the sector, we will help you, mentor you and foster and develop your talent. To all those women in the sector who are my age, or close to my age, who have fallen through the gap, come back, let us further develop the talent of our generation. Women my age make up a significant proportion of the theatre going audience, so I want to see stories on stage about me, (and no disrespect to anybody, but) not just stories about the menopause, mid–life crisis – real stories for me.

Tania Banotti, *CEO, Institute of Advertising Practitioners in Ireland (IAPI)*

Every day in advertising, the most amazing perceptions are created. Advertising people can make it seem cool to smoke. They can make it seem cool to stop smoking. They can make it seem sophisticated to drink, or to stop drinking. They can make it seem like a good idea to fly Ryanair!

The reality for women in the advertising industry is that they make up just 18 per cent of those at CEO/Managing Director level. Creative roles are generally about 70 per cent male vs 30 per cent female. When it comes to how women *see* their role in advertising, we've been working hard to change perceptions. One thing we've done is create the annual 'Doyenne Award' to shine a light on female talent. We've published the fact that there's been a 6 per cent increase in women taking up senior roles. *We must know the stats to change them.* We've also proactively promoted women to the boards of industry committees.

And yet, if you ask most women in advertising if there's equality, they will say 'no'. The perception remains poor. We need more women in senior creative roles in ad agencies to help tell the story. I hope that, with more women in creative departments, the output of our industry will change. There'll be less gender stereotyping. But I'm not sure if it will. If we reach a tipping point of more female art directors and copywriters, will this change the work itself? Will we challenge existing norms? We'll see…

Colonel Maureen O'Brien, *Irish Defence Forces*

In keeping with the celebratory tone of this morning's gathering, I want to tell you about one thing that happened for me and the Defence Forces in this very special year of 2016. On 7 July I was promoted to the rank of Colonel and thereby became the highest-ranking female and the first female Colonel in the history of the Defence Forces.

This month marks my 35th anniversary of joining the Defence Forces. I joined a Cadet class of six women and 43 men, where the training was integrated. However, at that time, females were considered non-combatant and therefore restricted in the appointments they could hold at home and overseas. However, by 1992 the non-combatant policy was withdrawn and the Defence Forces are now committed to equality of opportunity in all aspects in military life, including the appointments women and men can hold.

As a consequence I have held appointments in operations, training, and strategic planning. I have served overseas on seven different occasions; I have served in Lebanon, Western Sahara, East Timor, Bosnia and Herzegovina, and Chad. I was the first female to be appointed as an Infantry Battalion Commander, something I am extremely proud of.

One thing I have learned from my 35 years of service to Ireland and the Defence Forces is that if you work hard on a level playing field, provided by robust equality policies, you can achieve whatever you set out to achieve.

One final thing, as a result of these equality policies, I know that there is absolutely no reason why I, as a woman, cannot envisage future celebrations for further promotions in years to come.[8] Thank you.

Niamh O'Donnell, *Board Member, Dublin Fringe Festival*

We've self-assessed and spoken up. Looking hard at the representation of women in Irish performing arts is now a constant on Fringe's agenda. At the same time, we're watching representation of race, of culture, of ethnicity, of artists with disability, and of class. We've advocated for an inclusion of gender identities other than male and female in all our conversations about equality. This includes trans, questioning, intergender, non-binary, and other gender identities.

We're keeping track. We're a multidisciplinary festival. At Fringe, projects are led by artists of all disciplines. We are identifying and implementing a way of record keeping and counting gender diversity that truly and accurately reflects how we interact with creative leaders; artists, curators, impresarios, producers and directors from a range of working practices and artistic discipline across all of our work.

We've declared our intentions. We've made the implicit 'Fringe is for everyone spirit' explicit. We've stated our commitment to diversity in our call out for applications and formalised it as an important criteria for festival programming. We're advancing it in every way we can.

What is our one more thing?

A rallying call. To all radicals, visionaries, dreamers, rebels, newbies, and big mouths of all gender identities, races, class, background, training, and potential – you are welcome at Fringe. We want your outrageous, your clarion calls, your shimmering visions, your artistic excellence, your nasty, and your cold hard truths.

We will amplify your voices, we'll spotlight you on our stages, and we'll help you make your mark.

Tara Derrington, *director and founder of Mothers Artists Makers*

A year ago I stood outside this theatre holding this sign. *[Tara holds up a sign saying 'Where are the Disappeared Women of the Arts? They're at the School Gates. Now']*

People took photographs of it but no one talked. A year ago motherhood wasn't on the agenda.

Today, I'm here, representing 250 feminist female theatre practitioners across Ireland who make up MAM – Mothers Artists Makers.

MAMs surveyed average four and a half years third-level training, and 16 years paid practice each. Inspired by #WakingTheFeminists, we've united to highlight issues of domestic isolation, marginalisation, and the disproportionate impact of parenting on the salaries of mothers who work in theatre. After having children, over half our members surveyed lost *all* their income from theatre. 95 per cent of the rest suffered reduced incomes. This makes theatre unsustainable for MAMs.

The Abbey, Project, FringeLab, the Lyric, Fishamble, Rough Magic, Smock, O'Reilly Theatre, Baboró – by hosting our workshops – you make us visible again.

Is your theatre making family friendly? 54 per cent of Irish women are mothers. MAM believes the *major* cause of gender imbalance in theatre is the exodus of women when they have children. This isn't Mother Theatre ensuring survival of her fittest. It's the loss of some of our brightest and best due to the unequal care burden on women. The *one thing* that is most unresolved in feminism today? Motherhood. *[Picks up sign]*

A year ago I asked you to 'Remember Us'

[All MAMs in auditorium stand]

Tara: Today we're here.

[All MAMs in unison]: Mothers. Artists. Makers.

Brían F. O'Byrne (video), *actor*

[*Speaking to someone offscreen, as he holds the camera.*]

I'll hold it and do it myself.

Yes, I know how to do it... if I self tape for audition, I can... not that I audition – I don't audition.

Just hold the sign up.

'Hi, happy birthday to everyone at Wacking The Feminists.' [*Looks off camera.*]

Okay, okay, I know... don't judge me. [*Tries greeting again.*]

'Happy Birthday to everyone at Waking the Feminist.' [*Stops again.*]

Is one feminist or should it be feminists? Is it plural?

'Happy birthday to everyone at Waking The Feminists.'

That sounds too serious. I think it needs to be more joyful.

[*With forced joviality.*] 'Happy birthday to everyone at Waking The Feminists!'

That felt more kind of, too American for Ireland, too positive or something...

What exactly is it for again, remind me?

It's a celebration of an attempt for women to be treated the same as men?

No, seriously, is that still... is that still a thing?

Alison Spittle, *comedian*

Hi I'm Alison Spittle, I'm a stand up comedian, and the sole representation of whether my gender is funny or not.

When I first started comedy, I'd get compliments such as 'I don't like female comedians but you're funny', or 'you're funny for a girl.' I lapped it up like Crema Catalana – comedians live for compliments. But then I realised compliments are like custard and misogyny is like shite. Yes it's still custard but there's flecks of shit in it and I don't want to eat it any more.

Every interview, they ask 'is comedy sexist?' Short answer, yes. Long answer, the world is sexist and if we were worried about bumping into sexism we'd never leave the kitchen. Am I right ladies? The kitchen! Ha! It never gets old.

I love stand up comedy. With comedy you have full control of what the audience see, but it can be lonely. And to be honest with you, if a woman got a sweet support slot or TV job, sometimes I'd cheer for them. But I won't lie, sometimes I'd cry, eat toast, and pretend she gave me a dirty look the last time we met, to justify my feelings. I saw women as rivals. Sure there's only one place for a woman on that panel show, one slot on that night for a woman, one unfunny girlfriend role in that shit sketch. It's toxic and it's exhausting.

This summer, buoyed by the success of #WakingTheFeminists, us comedians held our own meeting to encourage more women in comedy. The event was called Women Who Want To Do Comedy Meet-Up (snappy name) which abbreviates as WWWTDCMU, which is not as good as WTF. But we're trying. The turnout was class. The amount of support was staggering; emotional support (women!) but also practical support like cameras, script editing, but most of all encouragement. And I realised that even though comedy is a lonely job, we are a community, and without community we are nothing.

Since then, I've seen a lot more speaking out, especially on social media. Festivals and comedy nights are now being asked outright. Where's the women? And I'll tell you where we are, we're here, we're mobilised, and we're not putting up with the same auld shite.

Loretta Dignam, *Board Member and Chair of the Gender Equality Committee, Abbey Theatre*

Happy birthday #WakingTheFeminists! And what a year it has been. Thank you very much for the opportunity to attend today and to speak on behalf of the Abbey Theatre, as we continue this very important national conversation.

The Board of the Abbey Theatre set up a Gender Equality Committee, which comprised of Deirdre Kinahan, Niamh Lunny, and Mark Ryan, and I. Our remit was to develop a comprehensive gender equality policy, following engagement with a wide variety of stakeholders. And since I spoke with you last on 8th March, I'm delighted to say that the Board of the Abbey Theatre has announced our Eight Guiding Principles for Gender Equality in August 2016. The Abbey Theatre is now into the implementation phase. And all in under a year! This has happened as a direct result of the #WakingTheFeminists movement.

The Abbey Theatre wants to play a role in the gender equality conversation and now wants to move the conversation on even further; to strive for gender equality not only amongst writers, but amongst all key roles in theatre, writers, directors, producers, performers, designers, lighting, and so on. I know that this has and continues to be a priority for us at the Abbey Theatre.

For me personally, for someone without a background in theatre or the Arts, this has been an incredible 15 months on the Board of the Abbey Theatre, and I feel privileged to be involved in driving important change that is of national importance. So thank you!

Micheline Sheehy Skeffington, *botanist and feminist activist*

My grandparents were Hanna and Francis Sheehy Skeffington.[9] They were ardent feminists, nationalists, socialists, and pacifists. They never shied away from speaking out for justice and showed no fear in the face of adversity. They didn't care if they were unpopular, but always took the side of justice. In 2016, of all years, it is important to remember their lives and what they stood for.

In 2009, inspired by them and seeking justice for women in NUI Galway,[10] I took a gender equality case to the Equality Tribunal – and won! The university promotion scheme had gone too long unchallenged and it was about a wider injustice, not just about me. The system was corrupt. Only one woman, or 6.7 per cent of the female candidates, was promoted, compared to 50 per cent of the male candidates. Five other women, along with me, were deemed suitable, but were not promoted. The only recourse now left to them to get justice is the High Court.[11]

During my case, I exposed some of the dealings in that promotion round,[12] but I know there is more that will come out. So the university indulges in prevarication, misinformation, and delaying tactics to avoid such an event. Justice must be pursued. One thing that is needed is to promote the five women – now!

Niamh Townsend, *General Manager, Dell EMC*

What a difference a year makes.

As a business leader in the technology sector, a daughter of a mother who worked throughout her career, and as a mother myself to a three-year-old girl with another baby on the way soon – I am highly attuned to the perceptions, realities, and attitudes towards women in society. Specifically, day to day, my views are informed by how women are treated in the commercial world.

The past year for me has been about an awakening of the feminists, specifically my male friends and colleagues. In this respect I am lucky to work at Dell EMC. It is a company that actively promotes and supports diversity in the workplace – of gender, of sexual orientation, of ethnicity.

We believe that men need to be involved in the discussions if we are going to see real change. It's about changing mindsets. As a result of our efforts, more women have been promoted and recruited to senior roles in Dell now than in previous years.

The MARC programme (Men Advocating Real Change) is about opening minds to every lens of diversity, including gender and a subsequent survey showed that 82 per cent of participants said they have changed the way they think and/or behave. Demonstrating increased awareness and sensitivity to unconscious biases and privilege. And even more significantly, 68 per cent have seen a change in their leader's behaviours or progress with leaders showing more sensitive behaviours and that they are more open to diverse perspectives.

We are having open discussions about unconscious bias – in recruitment practices and in team building.

It's been a great year. With a lot more to come. I am looking forward to the year ahead, including the arrival of my next feminist *[puts her hand on her pregnant belly]*, be they a girl or a boy!

Emma Rice (video), *Artistic Director, Globe Theatre London*

Hello Dublin, and all my friends at #WakingTheFeminists. I'm really sorry I'm not there with you. I tried. It nearly happened, but it just wasn't possible this time.

I'm reeling. It's the day after the US elections and months after Brexit and a short month after what's happened here at The Globe.[13] So I don't know whether I've got much wisdom to impart to you.

Except I woke up this morning thinking it's all about power. If we have no power, then we can't enforce change. And I'm not talking about the big jobs. I think you need to get involved. We need – we, not you – we need to get involved with our school boards, with the boards of theatre associations, with art centres. We need to make our presence felt at every level. And in many ways without power, all of these conversations are useless. So to use the old phrase, we need to lean in and step up and make sure that boards and governing bodies represent us and everything we believe in.

But that's all I've got today except a lot of tears, an awful lot of sadness, but there's only one way to go. And that's up.

Sinéad Burke, *activist, teacher, writer, broadcaster, fashion-admirer, and advocate for disability and design*

The 9th of November is an historic date.

In 1989, it marked the fall of the Berlin Wall. Horst Kohler, President of Germany from 2004 to 2010, stated that the 'The Wall was an edifice of fear. On November 9th … it was a place of joy'.

In 1990, Mary Robinson was inaugurated as the first female President of the Republic of Ireland. In her inauguration speech, she said that there 'was nothing rational or reasonable about the campaign which developed into a barnstorming, no holds barred, battle between my ad hoc assembly of political activists, amateurs, idealists and romantic realists against the might, money and merciless onslaught of the greatest political party on this island.' Yet, as she says herself, 'We beat them'.

In 2016, we didn't beat 'them'. The 9th of November made explicit the sexism, racism, sexualism, classism and ableism that permeates our society. I woke at 6am, wishing I could return to my earlier unconsciousness. Yet, I was awake. I am awake.

As we celebrate the anniversary of #WakingTheFeminists, I'm inspired by the importance placed on female relationships. This solidarity, supportive and sincere empathy, for other women is the one thing more I wish to explore. I want to take conversations offline, exit the echo chamber and the online performance of happiness. I want my one thing more to not be limited to women who look like me, but to be authentically welcoming to those who are of different race, religious belief, sexuality, gender, ability, and class.

On the 9th of November 1990, Mary Robinson said that she was elected by the women of Ireland, mná na hÉireann, who instead of rocking the cradle, rocked the system. I'm with her. I'm with you. I'm with them.

Jane Daly, *Co-Director, Irish Theatre Institute*

What one thing do I know that I didn't know a year ago? What one thing has impacted on me from #WakingTheFeminists? Is it, in fact, possible to whittle it down to just one thing?

Is it not the culmination of things – of voices heard, of stories told, of egos set aside, of petitions signed, awards given, surveys conducted, research presented, of widespread media coverage, of departmental ears opening, of funding agencies sitting up at last, and of the cacophony of pennies dropping in board rooms and places of decision making?

Is it not the culmination of all of these things seen, heard, and done that has led to us the one thing which is this: that it is possible to make change happen? That we actually live in a country where people do care; that, when push comes to shove, people, women and men, will do something about equality – about marriage equality, gender equality, equal opportunity for all. That we live in a country where, if we care enough we can change things and that it must be done by a movement of people, people who set aside their own differences and disagreements for the common goal of equality and fairness. And in doing so we come to learn about ourselves, who each of us is, and what we really believe and, one thing in particular, which is that to do nothing is simply not an option.

What one thing do I know now? I know myself better than I did a year ago. I know that as a self–proclaimed feminist for over 40 years, I had perhaps dozed off in middle age but now I can say that I am again absolutely awake, that I will ensure that I stay awake, and I will take responsibility to wake others at every opportunity.

Amelie Metcalfe, *actor*

My name is Amelie Metcalfe. I am eight years old. I am proud to be a girl working in Irish theatre.

Soon I will be Masha in *Anna Karenina*, here on this stage. Last week, I was Freya in *A Feast of Bones* with Theatre Lovett.

That play was *designed* by a woman and *lit* by a woman and *propped* by a woman and *costumed* by a woman and *stage managed* by a woman and *produced* by a woman and *directed* by a woman and *written* by a woman. And that's how I know women can make great theatre.

I am glad that, thanks to you, women are being listened to, here in this theatre, all over Ireland and in many other countries too.

But. There is one big but.

I am, as you see, not just female, but a child. And I'd like to ask you all the question: when is Irish theatre going to wake up to children? Young people like me need good theatre just as much as adults do.

Excite us. Inspire us. Reflect our lives. Don't we deserve our space here too?

Harriet Walter and Clare Dunne (video), *actors*

Harriet Walter:

I'm here at the King's Cross Theatre, where the *Donmar Trilogy* has been going on, a Shakespeare trilogy, all female, wonder–women or warriors of political theatre, changing the world. Actually it's happening, because theatre isn't just a reflection of society, and God knows it hasn't been reflecting female society very well over the centuries. It's a mover and a shaker that provides an example and a way forward and an inspiration, and creates an ideal that we can attain. So nobody's questioning us now.

When we first started, there was a little bit of 'why should they?' And now, four years down the line, there's 'what's the problem?' And more than 'what's the problem?' – 'aren't they doing it better?' Because we've got so much commitment and so much we don't take for granted and the pleasure of doing these plays and the pleasure of changing a little piece of the world.

The thing about change is that in the past we didn't invent women doing Shakespeare, they've been doing it since Shakespeare was – 100 years after Shakespeare – and there's often been women playing men in the theatre, and women making breakthroughs in all sorts of areas in history, but it's not recorded because males write the history books. But now the record is open to all of us on Facebook, on social media.

So everyone's getting the buzz and everyone's knowing what everyone else is doing, and seeing that it can happen and seeing that it's inspirational. The glass ceiling may not have been breached, but as Hillary Clinton said, 'you recoil only to spring further next time, you don't give up'.

But there's a gathering of a head of steam now – it's not isolated moments in history that have just been written off. We've done feminist theatre. We've had a female president – or we haven't yet, but you know, we've had a female prime minister. We're now having not just one Shakespeare play, we did two then they said 'when's the next one'? We're now doing three. Glenda Jackson doing *King Lear*... it's happening all over the place now. And that's just in the area of women playing men in Shakespeare, but it's a symbolic change that's reverberating in lots of other areas of life.

We've got to get the fact that women are half the population reflected in every area of our life – backstage, on stage, in the street. And that's going to happen because even just with a little thing like ours, we're putting up a little mirror to the world of how these jobs can be done by anyone. That shouldn't sound so strange, and it's beginning to not sound strange. So one year down the line, congratulations to you. I'm going to hand you over to Clare, who is my wife, my son – what else do you play? My enemy? Yeah – in Shakespeare's plays, so here's Clare.

Clare Dunne:

That was my idol speaking right there. Who knew that I was going to be here after working with her for four years on an all–female Shakespeare production? Right now I feel like I'm in this combination of a moment in my life and in my career, and with this project in particular, and it feels incredible because it's *done*. It's already done. I stand up in rehearsals and I play a guy who is going to be king.

I stand there and I play Price Hal and it doesn't feel unnatural. I feel like a human playing another human that suits my talents, my ability, and myself physically as an actor, and it just feels like that's my job. That's my place. I deserve that. And I think that's something that I've probably only learned from the experience of this. Four years ago, I was so scared of all of this, and now it just feels like, 'No, we just deserve it. It's just space, and just take it up'.

Because the one thing that we've learned playing men is that men take up space very easily. And women are afraid to do that. But I think you can take that on many levels. Don't be afraid to take up the space that we already own and we already deserve. We've started the journey now that's just like... have the craic and keep going. Good luck, lads. Have a good party today.

Bride Rosney, *Board Member, Druid*

The one thing which has changed most significantly for Druid since the arrival of the #WakingTheFeminists movement is awareness.

It is not about getting some quick wins; it is about ensuring that where necessary there is a change in approach and mind-set. At Druid, we now put awareness into all of our decisions, always looking at a bigger picture that strives for a more equally representative organisation. This must be apparent at all levels from script-reading to production, casting to development initiatives.

#WakingTheFeminists was a shock to the system of theatre; a very welcome and much needed shock. Any shock will impact on our sense of security and indeed our complacency. It is perhaps inevitable that we all develop a degree of complacency and it is important that it is challenged, both internally at all levels in our organisations and from external stakeholders.

We should acknowledge that any shock is likely to rock our established way of doing things – and at Druid, we welcome the opportunity that presents.

When a body suffers a shock it usually has one of two automatic or reflexive reactions: mobilisation or immobilisation. No theatre body has the luxury of being shocked into immobilisation so let's not even go there.

With mobilisation there is a choice of activities – depending on the genuine commitment to responding to the shock.

Our response is focused on ensuring a change in behaviour and mindset at all levels within the organisation, starting with the Board, whom I represent here today. It starts with awareness and it leads to action.

Druid believes that the critical measure is to ensure that this awareness leads to real and sustainable change. It will take time but it must and will happen.

Rory O'Neill aka Panti Bliss, *accidental and occasional gay rights activist*

It's *One Thing* to notice something's amiss – it's quite another *One Thing* to do something about it. I stand before you as a person who draws strength from my femininity.

Because it's in my femininity that I find the qualities I need to survive: strength and perseverance. And there's a certain exquisite irony in that, because it is often the negative reaction to my perceived femininity that I'm trying to survive in the first place!

Recently, spurred on by this movement and Hillary Clinton's campaign, I took a psychological test. Developed by Harvard researchers it aims to determine if you are biased against women leaders. It's very thorough. You answer a slew of questions and then it tests your reaction time as you categorise a myriad of words as being associated with 'leaders' or 'followers'. At the end of the test I hovered, trepidatiously, over the 'result' button. Coming from a family where the women are the organisers and doers, I wanted my result to be 'unbiased', but in a world of tie-wearing leaders, could I possibly have escaped the subconscious conditioning? I closed my eyes and thought of Angela Merkel, and pressed the button.

I had, Harvard told me, a slight bias – in favour of women leaders. But I resolved to do better. I wanted a strong bias.

The next day I was at a meeting. There were three men, a woman, and a gender discombobulist. At one point the woman started to speak, but before she had got even half a sentence out, one of the men started speaking, loudly, over her. He wasn't even aware he was doing it. A couple of minutes later she tried again, and the same thing happened. It took four attempts before she finally got to say what she had to say. But they weren't really listening – they were just waiting to speak.

But she was keenly aware. And I, fresh from my Harvard test, was keenly aware, to my shame, for the very first time. I was 'woke'. And I resolved to do *One Thing*. Stay woke.

Orlaith McBride, *Director, The Arts Council / An Chomhairle Ealaíon*

Ladies and gentlemen, a century ago, the Easter Rising sparked conflagration.

In its centenary, the gender imbalance of the artistic programme of our national theatre lit a fire, not just of agitation, but a flame to cast light and to give support for women in theatre and in the arts to make a difference. It is a perpetual flame. The fire will not go out. It is vindication of Augusta Gregory. It beckons as a beacon from this stage, across a bridge named after a once nearly forgotten woman, Rosie Hackett. Women's lives will not be hidden histories. It is not for women, to do the trudging in life, and be expected to be grateful. Irish women are writers, actors, directors, activists and leaders.

Our imagination is both epiphany and conscience for our country.

Raising the drawbridge behind them, was too often the obituary for Irish rebellion, by those who led it. Breaching the walls is not enough. Cultural change is never easy, or accomplished at once. Ireland is the cradle of conservative revolution. Opportunity for women is not the full achievement of diversity. But it is, its best hope. Gender is essential to equality, but not a simple summary. We must constantly demand equality. We must constantly interrogate ourselves and the systems around us to ensure equality in life, in the arts, in theatre.

Because there are communities across this county for whom art and theatre are unknown spaces. There are women and men who live lives bereft of the fresh spring water that art offers.

Art is sunlight. Art is catharsis. Art, in its absence, is exclusion.

#WakingTheFeminists is a beginning, not an end. *One Thing More* is the end of the beginning. Now for the great work ahead, a Republic of an audience of equals, where art is inalienable from citizenship.

Susan Feldman, *Artistic Director, St Ann's Warehouse Brooklyn*
read by Erik Wallin, *General Manager, St Ann's Warehouse*

I am honoured to read this from Susan Feldman today:

I wish I could be there with you all. But somehow I ingested something toxic the day after our election that has knocked me back. The doctor says it was something I ate. I say it was something much worse I, and countless millions around the world, had to swallow.

America has chosen a dangerous throwback to misogyny and dominance and I fear there will be great suffering. It's unthinkable after a lifetime in the women's movement, celebrating the rise of feminism and the attainment of the basic right to control *our bodies, ourselves,* that we should again be in the hands of others who would malign our dignity and deny nurturing to our people and our planet.

#WakingTheFeminists as a movement for survival and change means more than ever. Huge numbers of women elected our new president. How could that happen?

Clearly there is major work to be done as our grief turns to anger and resolve. As artists and producers we have voices and platforms with which we can unleash potent creative creativity and laser sharp activism. To do this in solidarity with you and all those who celebrate their 'woman within', I pledge my resolve.

We need to wake up and stay awake, which means propelling a worldwide movement that allows us to rest and refresh during what's sure to be a marathon and not a sprint. I love you all.

Eve Ensler / V[14], *playwright, author, activist*

I have just arrived on an aeroplane from the new Trump World. I haven't slept for days. I feel like we've been in triage. Women have been camped out at my house, crying, weeping, organising mass demonstrations for five days, which is kind of amazing. And a sign of possibly the future – against a racist bigot, earth hating sexual predator. As David LaChapelle said the other night, 'we Americans essentially elected an internet troll'.

I cannot tell you how happy I am to be in this historic theatre, occupied by women rising for equality. I really want to congratulate you on this amazing achievement over one year. It is truly astounding and I know from women in New York and women in London and women all over, you are inspiring women everywhere to rise for equality. So the deepest congratulations.

I think what you've shown us is that when women are united, anything is possible.

Now more than ever, the voices of women, the voices of the marginalised, must be platformed, honoured, and heard. Theatre is the place for transmitting ideas from the body, into the body, beyond the body, for fomenting revolution, for resisting tyranny and fascism in the face of this rising authoritarian backlash, which we're seeing all around the world, and the nativism. This time of collapsing an unsustainable neoliberal capitalism, which is an engine of hate against women, Muslims, people of colour, refugees, immigrants, and LGBTQ.

This is the time for us women to write and perform and shake up the world. Women must be speaking out on reproductive rights, on sexual violence, on gender liberation, on friendship, on protecting our Mother Earth. We must use our voices to catalyse an imaginal energy that is bringing in a desperately needed new time.

I have to say this is an extraordinary beginning for #WakingTheFeminists – but I just want to share a little bit of experience, because I've been at this a really long time. And having been a feminist for 40 years, and having just experienced what we've just gone through in America – that a blatant misogynist and sexual predator has been elected to the highest office – I can tell you that patriarchy is stubborn, and an insidious virus. Without constant attention, advocacy, educating deeply, deep discourse, reaching over class and racial and gender divides, disruption, and pushing, celebrating, it is frighteningly easy to slip back. So keep going. Keep fighting.

You've gotten the window open. Now you have got to put your whole body through so it never closes again. Make your awakening awake and inspire women in the theatre and every sector in this country and may inspire all of us around the world to wake the feminist. Thank you so much.

Colm O'Gorman, *human rights activist and Executive Director, Amnesty International, Ireland*

In a week where it might seem that hate and division has won out, as we witness a man who boasts of his misogyny and his sexual assaults of women elected President of the United States; a week where those who practise what he preaches feel emboldened to give not just voice to their hate, but violent action too, I have resolved to do this one thing. I have resolved to love more; to love passionately, relentlessly, purposefully. I have resolved not to give into an invitation to division and to deeper hate. I have resolved to work to expose the cynical manipulation of desperate social need, most manifest in gross inequality in all its forms, by its very creators and its main beneficiaries, as they seek to foster hate and division in an effort to grab and hold more and more power.

I have resolved to listen, with care and attention, to those with whom I passionately disagree, and then to make my case. I have resolved to work every day to prove that love can trump hate, that real unity is not about unifying sections of society in opposition to others, but about uniting all in the recognition that together, we are always better.

I will not give in to hate. I will love. Not a quiet or passive kind of love. But a love that is powerful, and angry when needs be. I will not be intimidated, or shamed or silenced, nor will I stand by, and witness others being shamed, intimidated, or silenced.

I will stand with women, as we work to secure true equality in this and every society. I will work to repeal the 8th with even greater passion and determination. I will stand with refugees, with Travellers, with people with disabilities, with all marginalised groups. Because any one or group of us are only marginalised when the rest of society allows us to be.

Lisa Tierney Keogh, *playwright and coordinator of #WakingTheFeminists New York*

It means the world for me to be here with you today. It's especially meaningful to be sharing the stage with my mother Marie, who started me on feminism around the same time she started me on solids. Six days ago in New York, I held a ballot in my hands with a woman's name on it as a presidential candidate. In the difficult painful days since, I've thought about the work in front of us and Maya Angelou, whose words are on repeat in my head.

> You may write me down in history
> With your bitter, twisted lies,
> You may trod me in the very dirt
> But still, like dust, I'll rise.
>
> Did you want to see me broken?
> Bowed head and lowered eyes?
> Shoulders falling down like teardrops,
> Weakened by my soulful cries?
>
> You may shoot me with your words,
> You may cut me with your eyes,
> You may kill me with your hatefulness,
> But still, like air, I'll rise.

In one year we have risen so high. Last November we gathered and gave personal testimony to the pain gender bias has caused us. We told our difficult, messy stories. Together we demanded representation in our theatres, and in our society. We became a community connected, strong, bound to the belief that inequality has no place in our world.

When Lian asked me last year if she could make public my comments about female representation in theatre, I responded, respectfully, 'sure, why not? What are they going to do? Not produce my plays?'

This holds true for me even more so now because in the past year, I have learned that it is more important that I am truthful than I am produced. I have learned that it is more important to be yourself than to change your artistry to suit industry trends. I've learned that it's more important to speak up than to listen to the social message that I should be small, wait my turn, and know my place. *This* is my place.

Go where you are loved.[15] And if you can't find that place, gather your people and make your own. And remember:

I'll rise. I'll rise. I'll rise.

Camille O'Sullivan singing at One Thing More. Photo: Kate Horgan

Sarah Durcan, *core team of #WakingTheFeminists*

One year later, 1,800 homeless women live here in Ireland.

One year later, over 1,000 women live in direct provision here.

One year later, over 3,000 women here have had to travel abroad for an abortion.

And the time to close the gender pay gap globally has widened to 170 years.

One year later, I had wanted to talk of *hope*, but the outrage remains.

Making theatre is a privilege – it's not life or death. Behind each of these numbers is a woman in a life or death situation. If we can't make room for the marginalised to share their own voice from our stages, then what the hell are we here for?

If any of you doubted the real-world consequences of permitting male characters such wide-ranging scope to do whatever they want and *still* be credible figures of power, while vastly restricting female characters' access to powerful identities: *look at what just happened*.[16] That came from our *culture*. *We* shape our culture, and *how* we shape it has consequences.

Women are central to the great events and issues of our time. Our place is not at the cultural periphery, because inequality of voice compounds the inequality of our power. Exclusion festers until it explodes.

Listening to predominantly male narratives is not only delusional, it's dangerous. In failing half our talent, we fail our art, we fail our culture, and we fail our society. Attentive listening and inclusion of other voices is a powerful restorative. Equality is not a luxury we can afford to defer. Equality is a muscle that improves with feminism and exercising feminism daily strengthens everyone of us.

Getting in touch with my own dormant feminist muscle through #WakingTheFeminists has been an immense privilege and a transformative experience. Each of us working on the campaign will carry this learning into every area of our future endeavours. It will not be lost.

To female artists, this year you have heard loud and clear – your gender does not make you less capable of creating extraordinary theatre. Your voice is vital, and we need it. The flaw is not in *your* talent or ability; it is in our perception of it. *Look at this, this is what collaborative, feminist power looks like*, and it is a joyous, playful, inclusive thing.

To male artists, thank you for listening and thank you for your support, for recognising the value of #WakingTheFeminists in all our creative lives. I hope you understand that this movement is about expanding *all* our opportunities and talents, not diminishing anyone's. We welcome hearing more from you in this conversation, because all want the same thing really – to live creative lives to our fullest potential.

Now, the point of any public campaign of protest is to get a seat at the table – to rebalance the power. All year, week after week, those of us organising #WakingTheFeminists have been pulling up chairs at all sorts of tables. We have found ourselves at tables we *never* imagined we'd be sitting at! So that when you sit down to do your artistic work, you can do so in greater confidence that you will have a fair and equal chance that it will meet the audience it deserves.

And with that opportunity comes responsibility. Women of the theatre – make your work with an urgency like never before. Take on this research as a creative challenge, not a *fait accompli*. Be more ambitious than ever – equality can only be achieved with your full participation and your creative curiosity. Find your light and step boldly into it. Be brave, be big, be rigorous, but as writer Danai Gurira says, 'Get it done'.

The research shows us where we can improve. It's not about blame. It shows none of us are immune to bias. Numbers are important, but they are not the whole story. Awareness and action need to work hand in hand. No one organisation can do this alone. Implementing widely initiatives like the Abbey's visionary Guiding Principles on Gender Equality will help.

We all have an individual responsibility, and there is additional onus on our leaders to ensure the appropriate practices to support this change are activated. It's not just the right thing to do, it's the law:

> **Section 42 of the Irish Human Rights and Equality Commission Act 2014** places a positive duty on public sector bodies to have regard to the need to eliminate discrimination,

promote equality, and protect human rights, in their daily work.

This applies to all bodies financed, even partially, with public money.

To all of you, and especially to you leaders of companies, I know, through all our conversations this year, that each of you believe passionately in equality in your hearts. Together we can figure out with our heads, how to put what's in our hearts on our stages. We are not defined by these statistics we have seen here today – use them as a springboard not a weight.

This public phase of #WakingTheFeminists is drawing to a close, it has done its job as rocket fuel for this movement. But we all know there is more to be done. What comes next is slower and more deliberative, because true change takes time and collective, careful attention to be deeply rooted.

In order to manage the legacy project, we have set up a temporary non-profit company. Its two aims are to publish the research, and to establish a learning programme in gender equality. Later today, we are coming together with our colleagues in the theatre to continue that work.

Last year we asked you to *Stand with Us*. This year we're inviting you to make equality a reality within five years. Today is our momentous opportunity for leadership. Each one of you decides how this story, this history, plays out – *We* have it in our collective power to be the first theatre community in the world to attain and sustain full gender equality. Imagine what that would be like.

All inequality is an outrage. Rage out against it in determination without despair until there is nothing to be outraged about. In this chaotic global moment, let's open up – ignite *all* our stages with big complex messy conversations, using *all* our talent, *all* our genders, *all* our diversity. Make our theatre a beacon for equity, not a bystander to a burning world. International Women's Day 2021 beckons us. *Let's get it done.*

PART THREE

FIFTEEN

After the End: Legacy and Impact

There is power in shaping a story, not only on the page or stage, but in the world. Through our combined efforts we made extraordinary advances in just a year. #WakingTheFeminists had a profound effect on Irish theatre, and it still reverberates within Irish society. It was not only inspirational and influential: it was highly effective.

After the year-long campaign ended, we stepped away and let the theatre organisations step in, in their own way, and at their own pace, but with a five-year deadline to keep up some level of urgency. That level of campaigning is not only exhausting, it's unsustainable; if we had maintained it, the core #WakingTheFeminists group would have burned out, and fallen away. We were prepared to play a part in fixing the problem, but not the only part. It was not solely or even mainly up to us as women to fix this. All too often there is an onus within activism for the marginalised group to have to do all the heavy lifting. This is an additional burden of labour, often unpaid, to 'help' the dominant power structure understand and alter itself and which in most cases leads to burn out and 'protest fatigue'. This dynamic abdicates the dominant group's responsibility to think deeply and take action. Those in power can continue blithely as usual, and while there may be a veneer of change, the systemic work necessary to achieve enduring change is not actually being done.

Our key successes can be summarised as: grassroots ownership and involvement; widespread visibility of the campaign[1]; setting firm objectives including a five year deadline to gender equality; broad recognition that gender bias was indeed a problem everyone is susceptible to; responsibility and accountability placed at the top of organisations; completing baseline research from which to measure progress; negotiating buy-in from all key organisations and funders; and a sea change in relation to gender in Irish society. There are so many impacts and ripple effects of the campaign that we are aware of, and undoubtedly many we are not; a few key ones are outlined below.

Gender Equality Policy Working Group

The commitment, collaboration, and actions of the Gender Equality Policy Working Group, set up as a result of the sectoral meeting we held following the final public event in the Abbey 14 November 2016, continued the work begun by #WakingTheFeminists. The working group, which was spearheaded by Loughlin Deegan as Director of the Lir Academy and Julie Kelleher, Director of the Everyman Theatre, also included representatives from the Abbey Theatre, Druid, Dublin Theatre Festival, Fishamble: The New Play Company, Gate Theatre, Rough Magic, and Corn Exchange, with Lian Bell as a post-#WakingTheFeminists representative.

It was the first and only time that these major theatre organisations worked collaboratively in this way. Regular meetings over the course of the following year necessitated people to talk honestly through the real life implications and responsibilities of making change in their organisations. They learnt from each other, were mutually supportive, and accountable to each other; a powerful demonstration of the network effect of collective action. Had the Abbey just worked alone, there would not have been the equivalent transformative impact on the Irish theatre ecosystem. In some ways, this was the legacy from what we learned of the ethos of Tonic Theatre's Advance programme.

This work culminated in the launch of gender policies by ten major Irish theatre organisations on 9 July 2018 at The Lir Academy by Josepha Madigan TD, Minister for Tourism, Culture, Arts, Gaeltacht, Sport and Media.

The press release accompanying the launch read:

> *Gender Equality in Practice in Irish Theatre* began after #WakingTheFeminists drew international attention to the gender inequality that then existed within Irish theatre. This cultural phenomenon encouraged the participating theatre organisations to consider their own record in programming and supporting women within the sector and identify processes that would ensure gender parity and dignity at work in the future.
>
> Each gender policy statement has been ratified by the boards of the

organisations and each organisation has undertaken to measure their progress against their published targets on an annual basis using the #WakingTheFeminists *Gender Counts* guidelines.

Included in the list of measures are the following:

1. Gender blind readings for plays

2. Unconscious bias training for all staff

3. Achieve equality of gender of board members

4. 50% of new play commissions to be allocated to women writers

5. Gender blind casting

6. Addition of Dignity at Work clauses to employees charter

7. Re-examination of the female canon

8. Work with third level institutions to encourage gender parity in areas that do not reflect equality of gender.

9. To achieve gender balance in programming within a 5 year period.

Keeping Track of the Changing Numbers

Five years on from the start of the campaign, the #WakingTheFeminists research group voluntarily worked on follow-up quantitative research. The overall picture showed that Irish theatre was coming very close to gender equality for women in nearly five years.

In late 2020, the researchers published their follow-up report counting the years from 2017–2019 inclusive to check progress since *Gender Counts*, their study of 2006–2015[2]:

> There is evidence to support the strong correlation between executive and/or board support within an organisation and best practice in gender counting, tracking, and reporting. Supportive governance structures correspond to how complete the data set is and how regularly it is reviewed and reported – in line with the recommendation from #WakingTheFeminists to have sustainable policies and processes with measurable results.
>
> The percentage of work being written/created by women has increased across all organisations included in the original research, who also submitted figures for the period since.
>
> Since Season 1 of 2017, the Gate Theatre has increased female representation overall, notably with directors at 68% (up from 8%), and creators/writers at 26% (up from 6%). This is an overall increase

across categories measured by #WakingTheFeminists by an average increase of 23%.

The Abbey Theatre has seen an improvement in its female representation across every category, with directors up to 46% (from 20%) over the past three years, and creators/writers at 35% (up from 17%). This is an average increase of 16% across seven categories.

Achieving gender equality in some roles in some organisations can be a case of reducing rather than increasing representation – for example, Rough Magic Theatre Company has come closer to gender equality in the role of director, at 62% (down from 80%).

One of the figures that hasn't shifted significantly, across all companies, is the percentage of female representation in the category of Cast. This continues to average below 50%, with the exception of The Ark and Rough Magic Theatre Company, although The Lir Academy figures show acting students for the period 2016–2020 were 57% female – raising questions about the parts being written, by both men and women.

In addition to the recommendations from the original report, which are still valid, we recommend:

1. the implementation of a standardised template across the sector for counting, recording, and publishing gender statistics.

2. that theatre organisations ensure that they track gender figures across creative roles. Some organisations have only provided statistics for selected roles, and we recommend that all roles be tracked.

3. that the gender pay gap be tracked alongside gender representation statistics in order to give a fuller view of gender equality.

4. that gender representation should continue to be a key consideration for the planning of future and proposed productions.

The opportunities for, and careers of, many women in theatre have improved greatly as a result of the campaign.[3] Many plays have been commissioned and programmed that would most likely not have seen the light of day had #WakingTheFeminists not happened, including (to name but a few from the first years after the campaign): *The Remains of Maisie Duggan* by Carmel Winters at the Abbey in 2016; a remount of *Katie Roche* by Teresa Deevy at the Abbey in 2017; *Rathmines Road* by Deirdre Kinahan produced by Fishamble at the Civic Theatre Tallaght as part of Dublin Theatre Festival in 2018; *The Patient Gloria* by Gina Moxley produced by the Abbey Theatre and Gina Moxley in association with Pan Pan as part of the Dublin Theatre Festival 2018; *Asking*

For It adapted by Meadhbh McHugh in collaboration with Annabelle Comyn from the book by Louise O'Neill, produced by Landmark Productions and The Everyman in association with the Abbey Theatre and Cork Midsummer Festival in 2018; *This Beautiful Village* by Lisa Tierney Keogh at the Abbey in 2019; and *The Beacon* by Nancy Harris, co-produced by Druid and Gate Theatre, 2019.

Influence on National Policy

In November 2016 a #WakingTheFeminists delegation of Anne Clarke, Caroline Williams, Lian Bell and Loughlin Deegan met with Minister for Arts, Heather Humphreys TD, and presented her with a framed photograph of the first public meeting. They suggested some key actions that she and her department could take to improve gender equality.

In 2017, Minister Humphreys instructed all national cultural institutions and funding bodies to have gender equality and diversity policies in place by the end of 2018, to coincide with the celebration of 100 years of women's right to vote. To begin this process, a workshop with leaders of all these organisations was held at the National Museum, Collins Barracks. Lian and Sarah addressed the group. As a direct result of #WakingTheFeminists' action and advocacy, all national cultural institutions now have policies in place.

> **Heather Humphreys**
> @HHumphreysFG
>
> Great to get an update from @lianbell y'day eve on #WakingTheFeminists one year on: a lot of progress made & I hope to help deliver more

Lian Bell and Minister Heather Humphreys

In 2019, the Arts Council published a comprehensive Equality Human Rights and Diversity (EHRD) Policy and strategy[4] that stated:

> The Arts Council, in everything it does, strives to respect, support, and ensure the inclusion of all voices and cultures that make up Ireland today, from all sections of society, from existing and new communities, and from all social backgrounds, ethnicities and traditions.
>
> ...
>
> Harnessing diversity provides unparalleled opportunity for creative collaboration, innovation, and learning. We also believe that through promoting equality, human rights, and diversity in the arts in Ireland,

we can benefit from rich artistic outcomes and contemporary practice that is challenging, relevant and more accurately reflective of our society today.

Through this EHRD Policy, and in the context of its civic and statutory role, the Arts Council:

- States its absolute commitment to the Public Sector Duty (and equality legislation), which outlaws discrimination and requires all publicly-funded organisations to take positive policy measures to promote equality of opportunity, access and outcomes for all those living in Ireland regardless of their gender, sexual orientation, civil or family status, religion, age, disability, race or membership of the Traveller community. Furthermore, the Arts Council notes the ground of socio-economic background as a further basis for which equality of opportunity, access and outcomes must be guaranteed.

- Asserts its belief that a diverse organisation is a more dynamic and effective organisation and undertakes as a State Agency to become more representative of the population in Ireland today.

- Is invested in the creative case for diversity, recognising that increased diversity and equality in the arts supports richer creativity in Ireland and impacts positively on arts development, as well as wider social, cultural, and economic development.

- Sets out its understanding of the need for the arts sector to be reflective of Ireland in all its diversity, ensuring equality of opportunity; equality of access, participation and outcomes; and equality of representation.

- Undertakes to review and adjust its awards and funding programmes, towards ensuring their recipients and beneficiaries better reflect the population profile of contemporary Ireland, inclusive of the most disadvantaged groups.

In September 2020 #WakingTheFeminists was asked to present to the Citizens' Assembly on Gender Equality. The Citizens' Assembly is a forum of 99 citizens and a chairperson that makes recommendations to the Oireachtas (Irish parliament) on key constitutional issues. #WakingTheFeminists and Amplify Women drew up a submission with input from Dr Brenda Donohue and Sarah Durcan.[5] The submission and its five key recommendations were presented to the Assembly by Lian Bell; online due to Covid-19 pandemic restrictions. The key recommendations were summarised:

1. Build-in accountability at the top: at government, board, and executive levels.
   Unless there is ownership at the top, the issues won't be taken seriously enough, and sufficient progress in inclusive, equitable practices won't happen.

2. Focus on policies, processes, practices, and personal beliefs.
   Too often policies aren't implemented. It is simple day-to-day actions that need to change, which is why processes and practices are equally important in changing systemic gender inequality.

3. Make sure there is equitable pay and conditions.
   Understanding that a gender-equal society is better for everyone, that gender equality will be much better for boys and men and their wellbeing too, and will also significantly boost our economy.

4. Keep counting so the changes are measurable.
   See it, say it, count it, change it. Experience shows that short-term gains can slip backwards. Counting and publishing the results keeps us honest about how progress is really going. Ambitious targets and/or quotas need to be set.

Lian Bell wearing a Repeal jumper, a badge from the Artists' Campaign to Repeal the Eighth Amendment, and the #WakingTheFeminists necklace designed by Love and Robots on her way to the March for Choice, 24 September 2016. Photo: Lian Bell

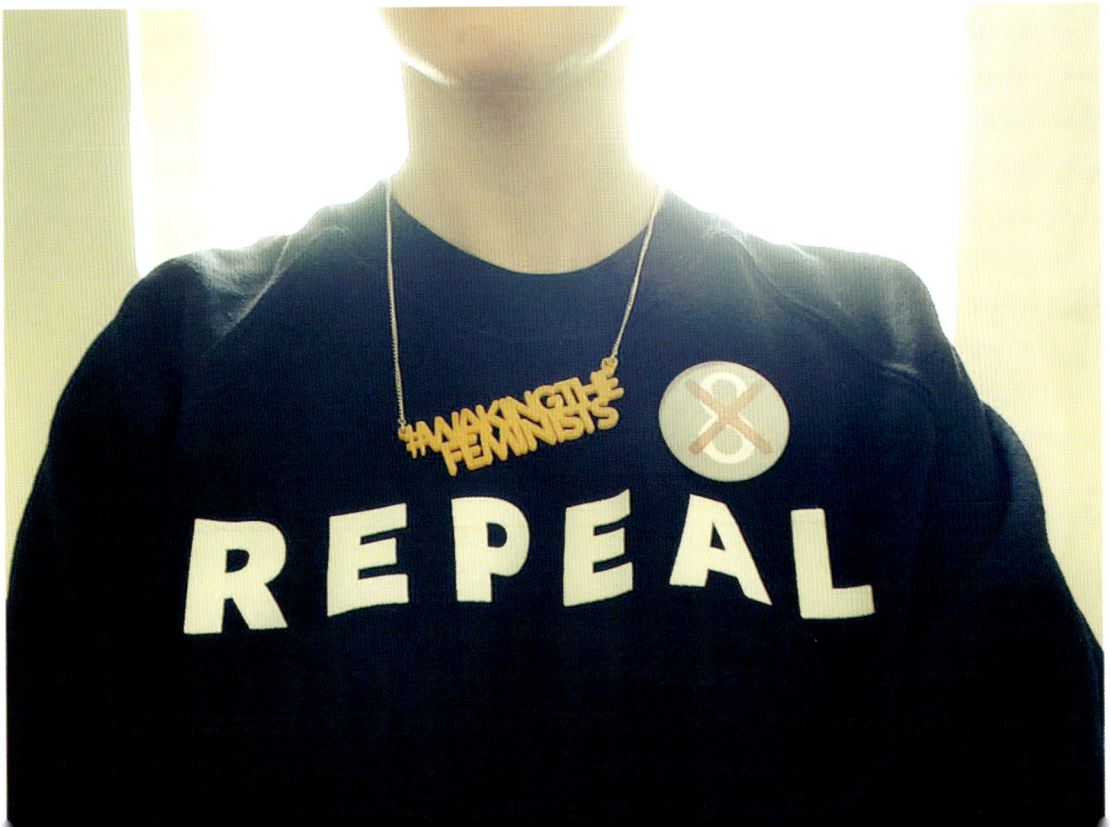

5. De-gender schools, and address gender inequity in its earliest development.

Gender differences, and abilities traditionally ascribed to different genders, are set by society at a very early age. It is limiting to boys and girls and their sense of what is possible in their lives.

Inspiring Other Action Groups

While the groups Women on Air and Women in Film and Television pre-existed #WakingTheFeminists, other groups were inspired to form by the campaign. These included: #WakingTheFeminists NI in Northern Ireland; Sounding the Feminists for women composers, musicians, and sound designers; FairPlé for women in traditional music; and Mothers Artists Makers (MAMs). Many of these groups continue to advocate for equality in their respective sectors.

Several groups came together to form Amplify Women in early 2017 to prepare a submission for the National Women's Strategy consultation and another submission on the gender pay gap to the Department of Justice and Equality later that year. Amplify Women was an umbrella group of organisations who represent, or carry out research on, women working in the cultural and media industries including Women in Film & Television, Irish Equity, Women in Animation, members of #WakingTheFeminists, Writers' Guild of Ireland, Broadly Speaking, Screen Producers Ireland, and Screen Directors Guild of Ireland.

Waking The Feminists NI

While #WakingTheFeminists focused on changing policy and outcome for women in theatre in the Republic of Ireland, an active group sprung up to seek to achieve similar aims in Northern Ireland, which operated under different funding mechanisms and governing structures.

On and offline conversations were gathering pace, and a get together on 3 May 2016 at The Sunflower Pub in Belfast was instigated by artist Amanda Coogan (who had interpreted the first public meeting at the Abbey in Irish Sign Language), which Lian attended. This was followed by another gathering on 28 May in the Lyric Theatre, which Caroline Williams attended. In June 2016 theatre practitioners Jo Egan and Fionnuala Kennedy:

> hosted a meeting at The Barracks performance space and out of this Waking The Feminists NI (WTFNI) was born. From its formation, two distinct strands of activism began to emerge; the first was to address

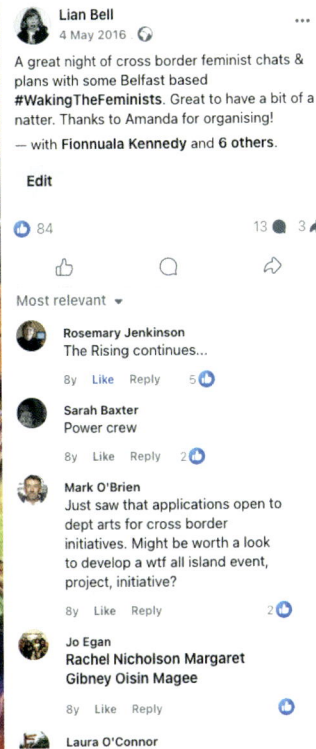

#WakingTheFeminists gathering in Belfast 3 May 2016, with Amanda Coogan, Fionnuala Kennedy, Margaret Gibney, Jo Egan, Oisin Magee, Rachel Nicholson, Rosemary Jenkinson, Lian Bell, and Melanie Clarke Pullen.

the issue of sexual abuse, bullying and harassment in Northern Ireland's Performing Arts industry, through the creation of a 'safe space'. The second remit was the collection of data in relation to gender representation from a number of publicly funded theatre companies.

... it is important to note that the creation of a 'safe space' allowed people to come forward and to talk in confidence about their experiences of abuse, bullying and harassment. This made a significant contribution to the Department of the Economy's decision to close down a theatrical agency in Belfast and to ban the agent running it, for ten years.[6]

On 29 November 2021, Waking The Feminists NI and Cultural Policy Observatory Ireland published a report, *The Headcount: A survey on the gender breakdown of eight Arts Council of Northern Ireland core-funded theatre companies 2014-2019*,[7] written by Maggie Cronin, which was based on the *Gender Counts* methodology with some modifications. Strikingly, this report also found that the more public funding a theatre in Northern Ireland receives, the fewer women artists it programmes. For example, the Lyric Theatre in Belfast receives over 54 per cent of the public funding of the companies surveyed, yet its overall gender breakdown across creative roles for the period 2014–2019 was 37 per cent female to 62 per cent male. The Lyric's figures for directors for the same period was 29.7 per cent female to 70.2 per cent male; and for writers only 12.5 per cent female to 87.5 per cent male.[8] This is particularly shocking given at least four of the years covered in the WTFNI survey were post-#WakingTheFeminists. Clearly there is a lot more work for those in power to do in Northern Ireland to achieve equality, and no time to waste.

#MeToo and Irish Theatre

In late 2017 the #MeToo movement reignited in the United States. Within a few weeks Dublin-based theatre director Grace Dyas published a blogpost of her experience of alleged bullying behaviour from Michael Colgan while he was Director of the Gate Theatre. Grace's actions essentially kickstarted #MeToo in Ireland, and she has said that her experience of #WakingTheFeminists was a contributing factor to her being able to speak out.

On 4 November 2017 an article was published in the *Irish Times* where seven young women, all former Gate employees, alleged abuse and harassment by Michael Colgan,[9] who had retired after 33 years as the Director of the Gate by this stage. Michael published an apology in the *Sunday Independent* on 12 November 2017 where he said he was sorry for causing distress to some of those with whom he worked, insisted his behaviour should not be equated with sexual crimes, and that it was wrong that he had been the subject of insinuations that he was guilty of more than misjudged behaviour.[10] An Arts Council statement said they did not doubt its *bona fides* and sincerity and noted that the issue was no longer about him but about the women who had come forward.

The board of the Gate instigated an independent review into his behaviour conducted by workplace relations expert Gaye Cunningham, the report of which was eventually made public in March 2018. Testimonies from some of the 65 interviewees included in the report stated that he 'managed by fury and threats and fear', 'regularly told people "you won't work in this industry again"', and 'held absolute power and control' while 'the Board comprised many of his closest friends'. It also included testimonies of inappropriate behaviour and sexual harassment. The investigation found that there was 'a case to answer': that 'behaviours of Michael Colgan described by individuals could reasonably be regarded as undermining the individual's right to dignity at work', and that there was a case to answer 'in relation to abuse of power' and 'in accordance with the definition of sexual harassment'.[11] Michael Colgan was given a right of reply in the independent report, and said,

> There being no degree in Artistic Direction, you need to have a big personality. He stated that he is a tactile person, he would be often seen throwing his arms around actors and writers. This was not confined to women. He denied shouting at staff or using profane language. He stated that he was a demanding boss, but thought that everyone liked him ... He stated that he now realizes that he should have had a code of ethics, proper hierarchies and rules of conduct in place. He stated that he had high standards and that he was exacting. He stated that there was an element of all powerfulness which was a result of one Artistic Director rather than having a separate General Manager. He stated that he was not politically correct. He stated that the type of work in theatre is personality driven. Actors are full of ego and when you don't give them a job, they take it personally ... The Board should have played a stronger role in having processes and procedures of dealing with complaints and putting investigations in place. He denies being a bully but regrets not putting a process in place for dealing with any complaints. He rejected outright allegations of sexual harassment.[12]

A case to answer; however, by this point it wasn't clear who he could be answerable to, as he had already retired. Soon after the report was released, the Board of the Gate apologised unreservedly 'to those who experienced the behaviours reported to Ms. Cunningham'.[13]

After Grace spoke out, many other women felt empowered to share their experiences publicly of bullying and harassment, including sexual harassment, while working in Irish theatre. In November 2017, Amplify Women quickly published a *Harassment Toolkit*[14] to advise people in theatre, especially freelancers, of their rights and resources in cases of harassment. This prepared the ground for a significant piece of work carried out by Irish Theatre Institute (ITI) at the behest of the Minister for the Arts. Originally titled Speak Up & Call It Out, it initially comprised a public meeting on bullying and harassment at Liberty Hall on 21 March 2018, survey, and research study. Within a few years ITI developed a comprehensive policy, code of behaviour, and action plan with training sessions rolled out across the island, north and south, now under the umbrella of Safe to Create,[15] funded by the Department of Tourism, Culture, Arts, Gaeltacht, Sport and Media.

While #MeToo was happening in Ireland, journalist Una Mullally hosted Waking The Media, a meeting at Project Arts Centre in November 2017, to discuss women's experiences working in media. This was an unprecedented gathering of women working across multiple media organisations, coming together in solidarity despite working in a notoriously competitive industry. Both Lian Bell and Grace Dyas were asked to speak, along with Simone George (human rights lawyer and activist), and Sarah Kieran (media lawyer) on behalf of Amplify Women.

Women in Technical Theatre Roadshow

Following her inspiring speech at the second #WakingTheFeminists public meeting, Kate Ferris, producer and lecturer at The Lir Academy, spearheaded the Women in Technical Theatre Roadshow in 2017 alongside the Abbey Theatre's Education department. This important initiative continues to introduce young women to careers in technical theatre, lighting, sound, and stage management by engaging female pupils from secondary-level schools throughout Ireland in workshops geared towards increasing awareness of the importance that these departments play in the professional creation of live performance. The workshops are designed and overseen by industry professionals who lead technical departments at The Lir Academy. This has led to a significant increase in the number of women graduating in technical roles and working in the industry. In 2023, 20 venues around Ireland hosted a roadshow event, for a total of 320 participants.[16]

The video of Kate's speech has been used for many years by a professor at Queensland University of Technology in Australia to teach students of technical theatre.

Preserved in our National Collections

Following the campaign, Lian chased the National Library and National Museum to see if they could preserve #WakingTheFeminists in their collections, including in all its digital aspects. The National Museum took some of the key ephemera from the year including the iconic banner, Lian's #WakingTheFeminists necklace, campaign badges, bags, awards, programmes, and documents.[17] After some considerable discussion with the #WakingTheFeminist group and individual permissions from organisers, contributors, and photographers, a digital collection of emails, photographs, meeting minutes, speech transcripts, articles, and our Slack channel was handed over to the National Library.

In 2021, during a Covid-19 lockdown, there was an online ceremony to commemorate the handing over of the collection to the National Library. Lian's speech from that event was subsequently included in Sonja Tiernan's

Irish Women's Speeches Volume II. This archive is one of three in their 'digital pilots' project alongside the Yes Equality archive, and the archive of author Marian Keyes.

All too often, women's movements and activism have been written out of the official narrative of our country. Placing the records of #WakingTheFeminists into two national collections will help ensure that anyone who wants to can access this story for research and historical purposes long into the future.

Leadership Changes

The gender of who is in charge is less important than what they do with their power and the systems they oversee. More women in positions of power at our most well-funded theatres doesn't automatically translate to better outcomes and more representation for women in general. As we learned from Lucy Kerbel in Tonic Theatre, it's about having more feminists in positions of power.

However, while there has been much more movement in the theatre community than we can chart here, some key roles are worth highlighting. Since #WakingTheFeminists, the Gate has now had two female artistic directors: Selina Cartmell (2016–2022) and Róisín McBrinn since 2022. Caitríona McLaughlin has been Artistic Director of the Abbey Theatre since 2021, the first woman since Garry Hynes in 1994. Róise Goan was appointed in 2024 as the first female Director of Dublin Theatre Festival in its 67 years. Sophie Motley was appointed Artistic Director of Project Arts Centre in 2024, after her tenure as Artistic Director of The Everyman in Cork 2017–2023. Oonagh Murphy was appointed as CEO/Artistic Director of Dublin Municipal Theatre[18] in 2025.

What We Have Done Since

The campaign also had a profound impact on all of us who worked on it, both personally and professionally. We gained a stronger sense of our power and influence, as well as an increased confidence in recognising and calling out what was amiss not only in our industry but in wider Irish society. While we can't capture all the exceptional work that has been done over the last decade, this is a brief overview of what core and affiliated #WakingTheFeminists activists have been up to:

Aisling O'Brien has worked with some of Ireland's leading artists, organisations and festivals. She continues to develop artist support and engagement initiatives and takes an authentic, intuitive, and kind approach in every element of her work practice. She recently completed the Advanced Diploma in Personal, Leadership and Executive Coaching & Mentorship with Kingstown College, and Relational Dynamic Coaching with Relational Dynamics 1st Ltd. She is currently the Assistant Arts Officer with Meath Arts Office.

Anne Clarke and her company Landmark Productions celebrated 20 years in 2024. She has produced many award-winning, sell-out, star-studded productions – including in the West End and on Broadway. She has served on the boards of Theatre Forum and Cork Midsummer Festival, and currently sits on the board of The Lir Academy.

Aoife Spillane-Hinks is an opera and theatre director and dramaturg based in Dublin. She is the Artistic Director of Then This Theatre, and is the lead artist and founder of the Literary Department at Axis Ballymun. Aoife most recently directed *Lady Gregory in America*, an opera in one act by Alberto Caruso, with libretto by Colm Tóibín, at Wexford Festival Opera. She was a recipient of a 2022 Markievicz Award from the Arts Council.

Dr Brenda Donohue is a Research Fellow at the Educational Research Centre, and Board Member of the Riverbank Arts Centre.

Caroline Williams is now Venue Director at Riverbank Arts Centre Newbridge, County Kildare.

Christine Monk has been Director of Communications and Marketing at the Abbey Theatre since 2021. She was Head of Public Relations for the Gate Theatre (2017–2021).

Cian O'Brien is now Director of COBA: Cian O'Brien Arts. He was Director of Project Arts Centre (2011–2024). He is Chairperson of Dead Centre Theatre and former Chairperson of Baboró International Arts Festival for Children, and was a committee member of National Campaign for the Arts (2016–2022). He is a member of the Strategy Committee, and Chair of the Programme Committee of the Centre Culturel Irlandais, Paris.

Dr Ciara L. Murphy is Vice President of the Irish Society for Theatre Research (ISTR) and a Lecturer in Drama at TU Dublin. Her recent monograph *Performing Social Change on the Island of Ireland: From Republic to Pandemic* was published by Routledge in 2023. Ciara is currently the Lead Researcher on the national Safe to Create project, which aims to change the culture and practices of the arts and creative sectors in Ireland.

Dr Ciara O'Dowd is Head of Research and Operations at Science Gallery International since 2022. Ciara was a theatre assessor and advisor to the Arts

Council of Ireland for ten years. Her book *Wild-Looking but Fine: Abbey Theatre Actresses of the 1930s* was published by UCD Press in 2024.

Dairne O'Sullivan is Marketing Manager with Screen Ireland (since 2024). Prior to that she was Arts Marketing and Press Services for Creative Ireland (2021–2024), the government agency that promotes well-being through creativity.

Gavin Kostick is a playwright and dramaturg. He is Literary Manager of Fishamble: The New Play Company, and tutor at both The Lir Academy and Trinity College Dublin.

Gina Moxley was elected to Aosdána in 2020, a group which honours artists whose work has made an outstanding contribution to the arts in Ireland. In 2018, her play *The Patient Gloria* was staged at the Abbey Theatre, won Fringe First and Herald Angel awards at the 2019 Edinburgh Festival Fringe, and played at St. Ann's Warehouse, New York in 2022. Her play *I Fall Down* premiered in 2023 at Cork Midsummer Festival and will be presented at Dublin Theatre Festival 2025. She performed in *Endgame* at the Gate Theatre in 2022 and *The Quare Fellow* at the Abbey Theatre in 2023.

Grace Dyas is an artist, activist, writer, director, filmmaker, producer, performer, actor, and experienced public speaker, living and working between inner-city Dublin, Limerick City, and Inis Oírr, Aran Islands. She directed *Waiting Day* by Lynn Ruane, which won the Best Short Film Award at London Irish Film Festival 2023 and was nominated for Best Short Live Action Short Film at the Irish Film and Television Awards.

Irma McLoughlin is Director of Performing Arts Forum Ireland since 2024, prior to which she was their Producer and General Manager. She is currently completing a micro-credential in Climate Leadership at Trinity College Dublin.

Jane Daly is a consultant and facilitator with Jane Daly Arts Management. She was Co-Director of Irish Theatre Institute 2000–2022. Jane was awarded a Special Achievement Award with her ITI co-Director Siobhán Bourke at the Irish Times Irish Theatre Awards 2017. She also co-led ITI's Speak Up & Call It Out initiative, a starting point to establish a code of behaviour for Irish theatre. She was a member of the ministerially appointed Arts & Culture Covid Recovery Taskforce 2020.

Jen Coppinger joined the Abbey Theatre as Head of Producing in 2018 after many years as Producer for HotForTheatre and The Emergency Room, as well as producing work of other artists. She served as Chairperson of Youth Theatre Ireland (2017–2020) and of United Fall (2017–2024).

Jo Mangan is Creative Director and CEO of The Performance Corporation (Ireland) and Performance XR (UK). She also works as a director and curator in theatre, opera, and extended reality, and leads the SPACE Programme, a technology and arts residency in Paris. She is a Board Member of the Gate Theatre since 2022 and has recently been appointed to the board of IETM International Network for Contemporary Performing Arts. Jo was Chairperson of National Campaign for the Arts 2015–2018. She also worked as Director/ CEO of Carlow Arts Festival (2016–2021).

Kate Ferris was curator of *Young Radicals* with Dublin Fringe Festival, and from 2018–2022 she led on Women In Technical Theatre, a nationwide workshop series partnership between The Lir Academy and the Abbey Theatre encouraging young teen women to consider a career in technical theatre. Since 2022 Kate is Head of Producing at the Gate Theatre, Dublin.

Kate Harris is Founder and Director of 4Elements Theatre Company. Kate devised, directed, and toured *Daughters of the Revolution*, a musical reflecting women's experience with maternity services in Ireland. The documentation of this project became the chapter 'Performing the Revolution' in the 2018 book *Untangling the Maternity Crisis*.

Kathleen Cawley is a freelance producer and dramaturg. She is Communication and Events Officer with Volunteer Ireland. She is completing a PhD in contemporary Irish drama.

Lian Bell re-focused on her artistic work, developing a practice that empowers artists, strengthens community, creates space for attention, and challenges how arts organisations habitually operate. She continued to speak publicly about #WakingTheFeminists nationally and internationally for a number of years, trained as a coach, was a board member of Rua Red (2018–2024), and has been a member of the National Library of Ireland's Readers Advisory Committee since 2022.

Lisa Tierney Keogh moved home to Dublin from New York in 2018. Her play, *This Beautiful Village*, was performed at the Abbey Theatre in 2019 to sold-out crowds, was critically acclaimed, and was awarded Best New Play at the Irish Times Irish Theatre Awards. Lisa has written extensively for theatre and media, advocates for women's health, and coaches girls' basketball.

Loughlin Deegan was appointed to the Arts Council, and served for five years from 2016–2021. He was Director of The Lir Academy until 2023, and is currently Interim Executive Director at Wexford Festival Opera.

Lynne Parker is Artistic Director of Rough Magic Theatre Company, founded in 1984. Recent work for Rough Magic includes *Children of the Sun* by Hilary Fannin after Gorky in co-production with the Abbey Theatre 2024, *Freefalling* by Georgina Miller with Lime Tree | Belltable for Cork Midsummer Festival 2023, *Solar Bones* by Mike McCormack with Kilkenny Arts Festival in 2020, and *Hecuba* by Marina Carr with the Dublin Theatre Festival 2019.

Olwen Fouéré is an actor, creator, and director whose recent stage work includes *The President* (Sydney Theatre Company and Gate Theatre, Dublin, 2024), *iGirl* by Marina Carr (Abbey Theatre 2021), and the role of Winter in *The Last Season* by Force Majeure (Sydney Arts Festival 2021). Recent directing credits include *Unspeakable Conversations* by Christian O'Reilly, which she co-directed with Kellie Hughes (Galway International Arts Festival 2024). Recent writing credits include a duet for the international Not Beckett festival 2024–2025. Recent TV includes *The Tourist S2*, *The Crown*, *Halo*, and *Derry Girls*. Recent film work includes *The Watchers* and *The Actor*. Olwen was conferred with an Honorary Doctorate in Philosophy from Dublin City University in April 2016.

Oonagh Murphy went on to contribute to the Repeal the 8th and End Direct Provision campaigns, receiving the Jo Cox Award for Young Female Campaigner in 2018. Alongside her work as a theatre director, she has led projects at the intersection of art and social change, including the launch of the London Ticket Bank, a cultural variation on a foodbank, and a range of participatory co-design projects with communities who have been historically excluded from the arts. In 2025, Oonagh became CEO/Artistic Director of the newly established Dublin Municipal Theatre.

Maria Fleming is CEO of the First Fortnight Festival since 2021, and Chairperson of the National Campaign for the Arts since 2022. She was General Manager at Dublin Theatre Festival 2018–2021. Maria is a Board Member of the Irish Cancer Society since 2022.

Niamh Ní Chonchubhair is a cultural producer. She is Head of Producing for An Taibhdhearc, Amharclann Náisiúnta na Gaeilge. She was Programme Manager, then Director of Axis Ballymun from 2008–2024 and served as Chairperson of Arts and Disability Ireland from 2017–2022.

Noelia Ruiz is a freelance communications consultant/manager and producer, and an occasional lecturer in UCD's School of English, Drama & Film.

Róise Goan has been Director of Dublin Theatre Festival since February 2025. Róise served on the Arts Council 2022–2024. She was Artistic Co-ordinator at the Kunstencentrum VIERNULVIER in Belgium 2023–2025, Director of Artsadmin in London 2019–2023, and was a member of the board of The Lir Academy 2016–2019.

Sarah Durcan was appointed to the board of the Abbey in July 2016 and served until January 2020, when she stepped down from the board to run for election to the Dáil, (the parliament) in Dublin Bay South with the Social Democrats. She is now Executive Director of Science Gallery International.

Siobhán Bourke is Producer with and Co-Founder of Saffron Pictures. She was Founder and Co-Director of Irish Theatre Institute 2000–2022. Siobhán was awarded a Special Achievement Award with her ITI co-Director Jane Daly at the Irish Times Irish Theatre Awards 2017. She also co-led ITI's Speak Up & Call It Out initiative, a starting point to establish a code of behaviour for Irish theatre.

Dr Tanya Dean is a Lecturer and Programme Coordinator of the B.A. (Hons) in Drama (Performance) at Technological University Dublin, and is Script Associate in the Literary & New Work Department at the Abbey Theatre.

Tríona Ní Dhuibhir is a singer/songwriter and arts consultant. She founded The Secret Singers in 2023 to support women from diverse backgrounds who are already on a musical journey but who are not yet widely recognised. She was appointed as CEO of Cruit Éireann|Harp Ireland in 2025.

SIXTEEN

What Now? Looking to the Future

#WakingTheFeminists was such a watershed there are now no excuses whatsoever to continue to ignore glaring inequalities in our theatre or in any area of the arts and public life. However, the end is never the end; in dismantling patriarchy or any imbalanced power system, the struggle is always ongoing. And we can't fully dismantle patriarchy without also attending to class, sexuality, race, ability/disability, colonialism, and inequitable economic and political systems. However, we can celebrate the successes of #WakingTheFeminists and its transformational effect on Irish theatre and impact on Irish society *and* also acknowledge the incompleteness of the struggle and the need for ongoing work.

We must keep pressing on to make our cultural systems more representative of the whole breadth of society. More than that, we must continue to press for equality, equity, and inclusion in all aspects of Irish society. We need new, inclusive frameworks, designed with those who are still marginalised for change to be effective. Inequality is not an accident – it's inherent in the systems' design. Let's continue to question everything we do, how we do it, and who gets to be involved.

We must remain vigilant. Any progress made can be easily undone, as we are seeing in 2025 particularly in the USA, with the horrifying rollback of rights and dismantling of access, equality diversity and inclusion principles and initiatives (variously known as DEI or EDI), against women (particularly reproductive rights), people of colour, immigrants, and LGBTQI+ (especially trans people). There is always a backlash against progress when the power system feels threatened. We need to guard ferociously and expand the grounds we've gained. Patriarchal forces have always twisted language in order to undermine and roll-back progress; this 'anti-woke' backlash is just the latest variation. We need to continue to stand up for each other.

While we have seen a marked increase in women in positions of power in theatre in Ireland, it could be argued that there has been a price for this increased representation. A joint letter from Irish Theatre Institute and Performing Arts Forum and co-signed by 778 artists sent to the Arts Council on 27 November 2024,[1] outlined concerns about the falling proportion of theatre funding in comparison to overall arts funding:

> Since 2008, the Arts Council's budget has increased by 64.2 per cent (from €81.62 million to €134 million). In that time, theatre funding has increased by just 5.8 per cent. As a result, theatre's share of the overall budget has dropped significantly, from 25 per cent to 15 per cent. Theatre funding in 2024 was €20.4m. If it had kept pace with the Council's own increase, theatre funding would be €32 million in 2024.

The letter also stated that '[d]espite the Council's rising budget, funding for theatre has stagnated and, in some cases, been critically reduced, limiting the sector's diversity, impact, and future viability.' Correlation is not causation, and there are likely a number of contributing reasons for this apparent deprioritisation of theatre; gender should however be factored into a fuller analysis.

Alongside this stagnation in funding there has been fragmentation within the community. With the changes in social media platforms in the last years, we lost a space for debate and discussion between ourselves, one that was vital to how #WakingTheFeminists played out. The experience of lockdowns on live theatre due to the Covid pandemic shook the community to the core, and fundamentally disrupted a chain of legacy knowledge passed between older and younger generations of artists; short-term freelance work has a short memory. We have not recovered yet. There has also been a sharp falling away of specialised professional criticism and reviews of theatre productions in our national press, particularly of any work presented outside of the capital. It is over ten years since *Irish Theatre Magazine* ceased operations after the Arts Council decided to not offer further funding.[2] Cutting off avenues for writing about theatre leaves it less visible to its potential public. Alongside that, the *Irish Times* Irish Theatre Awards met its demise in 2023.[3] All of these issues impact the whole theatre community, but critically hamper the forward movement towards intersectional gender equality. An improvement of the status of women and a move towards equality and inclusivity for all is undermined if theatre's presence and power in our society is diminished, defunded, fragmented, and made less visible.

The theatre community (not to mention society in general) still has a lot of work to do. The view of ourselves as good people can keep us from properly interrogating our biases and our role in upholding and perpetuating this unequal system. Without deep and radical reflection, our norms and un-questioned practices will continue to harbour bias. We need to be especially alert to phrases like 'common sense' or 'that's just how it's done'. We need to question our habitual work, cultural, social and political patterning, and always assume that bias is in there. It always is. Our routines, moulded over generations, inherently favour those already in power. For us to break this pattern, we first need to recognise that we're part of it and get comfortable with our own discomfort in confronting our inadequacies. If we only stick to what's familiar, and therefore what 'feels normal' we can't expect a change. We need to reassess our perception of being a liberal, inclusive community. It is on us to stop reinforcing inequality, whether it's ableist, sexist, classist, homophobic, or racist.

We pride ourselves in theatre on our ability to hold a mirror to society and critique power structures. Our job is to also signpost and imaginatively explore alternative futures. We must be honest enough to know that we, by our constant actions and repetitions of processes, uphold these systems, and therefore have the agency to begin to change them. And we must be humble enough to recognise we can't outrun our own biases.

The work this requires can be exhausting, unrelenting, and make us deeply uncomfortable, as it takes us to unfamiliar places. We are primed to remain comfortable at all costs. We blame the marginalised for their own exclusion. Even mild questioning of the status quo becomes problematic and must be undermined, shut down, silenced, and sidelined. Meritocracy is a myth created to make individuals believe that their success or failure is on them alone. An actual meritocracy is impossible without equal opportunity and equitable access. Diversity and inclusion *increase* the likelihood of people being appointed and promoted on actual merit.

Therefore the theatre community must build better structures and frameworks and processes that are co-designed with marginalised groups to counteract our habitual biases. This requires us slowing down so we can really interrogate our ways of working.

Tracking the numbers remains essential to keep check on representation. However, numbers alone are a limited metric of progress – they cannot inform us about the quality of that representation.[4] We recommend that more significant qualitative research into the deeper roots of inequality is carried out, to help develop new processes and practices.

Some have expressed that the 'pendulum has swung too far', and believe women are now over represented. It's ridiculous to say we've gone 'too far' when equality hasn't even been reached. That's just the patriarchy talking itself up again. The work of #WakingTheFeminists was not about replacing the dominance of male voices and stories with the dominance of women's voices and stories. It is about achieving a diverse multiplicity and balance of stories and perspectives in rich dialogue with each other, so we all can see ourselves on our stages and in our wider power structures.

If we don't all do the difficult and ongoing work to ensure that the systems and practices are in place to ensure marginalised people feel comfortable and included, then we are not actually doing transformative work, and it's no wonder we're perpetually surprised when surface level and temporary efforts don't work in the long term, or don't fundamentally change the culture we produce and consume, our governing structures, or the society we live in. Stay awake, keep questioning, and gather your people. Inequality benefits the few, equality benefits everyone.

Waking Patriarchy

Moynagh Sullivan

Moynagh Sullivan is a Professor of English at Maynooth University, where she was also Faculty of Arts Associate Dean for Equality, Diversity and Inclusion. Her research is intersectional, and she has published extensively on motherhoods, gender, class, race and neurodiversity in Irish culture. Recent publications include, '"That old shame trick": Mothering, trauma and neurodiversity', in Emilie Pine's Ruth & Pen', in Irish Shame: A Literary Reckoning, *eds. Seán Kennedy and Joseph Valente (Edinburgh, 2025), and 'Rematriating mid-century modernism: Carla Lanyon Lanyon', in* The Cambridge History of Irish Women Poets, *ed. Ailbhe D'Arcy and David Wheatley (Cambridge, 2021). A former Fulbright Fellow at the University of California, Berkeley, she was Visiting Professor of Irish Studies at Boston College, MA, and a Visiting Fellow at the Moore Institute/Irish Centre for Irish Studies at UG. She is currently working on* Maternal Imaginaries in Contemporary Irish Culture, *a monograph about the recent amplification of motherhoods and grandmothers in Irish cultural practices.*

In her now famous and landmark Facebook post on 28 October 2015, set designer and arts manager Lian Bell had simply pointed out the gender balance in the Abbey Theatre's announcement of its 2016 Decade of Centenary Waking the Nation programme. Lian's tally revealed that the programme included only one female writer to nine male, and two female directors to seven males.[1] In expressing her stunned disbelief at such a disparity, Lian unknowingly started the #WakingtheFeminists movement, which was to become an historic event in Irish theatre, an arena that Christopher Murray once described as a 'long, energetic dispute with a changing audience over the same basic issues: where we from, where we are now, and where we are headed'.[2] This 'energetic dispute' was further revitalised[3] by Lian's shocked response to a programme that further platformed men in a culture where masculine authority was already naturalised by the iterative sight and sound of men on multiple stages – in pulpits, on punditry panels, and podiums. By aligning with the historical socio–political and cultural de–platforming of women in Ireland, the programme sent strong and unwelcome signals about a woman's place, with Lian's post sounding alarm bells inside and outside the theatre world. If Irish national theatre – represented by the Abbey – is indeed this key space for testing definitions of identities against the shape of the nation, due in part, as Emer O'Toole noted, to its 'central role in the cultural nationalist movement that informed the Easter Rising',[4] then #WakingtheFeminists inadvertently reframed 'cultural nationalism' as 'intersectional cultural internationalism', becoming what Ciara L. Murphy described as the 'most important event of 2015 for Irish theatre',[5] both extending the national stage to include non–hegemonic and hybrid virtual spaces, and changing audiences and representational landscapes.

Feminist scholars had long been documenting how women's writing and creative work has been periodically 'lost'. In 2007, Melissa Sihra noted in the introduction to *Women in Irish Drama: A Century of Authorship and Representation*, how 'striking' it was that so many essays in the collection were 'about the early success of plays written by Irish women, plays that later go missing on the stage and in the canon.'[6] In a review essay of Volumes IV and V of the *Field Day Anthology of Irish Women's Writing*, Margaret Kelleher observed that a 'historical perspective shows how swiftly women's writings may disappear from view', and she showed how waves of 'recovery' of lost women's writings and art have been followed by periods of 'forgetting'.[7] Volumes IV and V had been commissioned as a corrective to the bewildering and extensive underrepresentation of women writers in the first three volumes, the publication of which, in 1991, prompted the same perplexing shock, hurt, and outrage from women, queer and feminist writers, and scholars that was expressed by #WakingTheFeminists activists over 25 years later. #WakingTheFeminists' shock was swiftly mirrored and followed by the dismay of yet another generation of women writers and scholars in what Claire Bracken describes as the 'severe underrepresentation of both women poets and academic contributors'[8] in Gerard Dawe's 2017 book, *The Cambridge Companion to Irish Poets*, and in Nicholas Greene's and Chris Morash's 2016 book, *The Oxford Handbook of Modern Irish Theatre*, 'which included 41 essays on Irish theatre, of which only two chapters were on Irish women and the theatre, and there were no chapters on the many women playwrights but there were specific chapters on Wilde, Yeats, Shaw and others'.[9] Poethead founder Christine Murray,[10] described the *Companion* as 'part of a larger process by which the significance of works by women is attenuated as they become inaccessible or obscured, simply by virtue of their absence from canonical text books',[11] an attrition she, along with other writers, countered with *Fired! Irish Women Poets and the Canon*,[12] a movement modelled on some of the #WakingTheFeminists actions; while Ailbhe D'Arcy's and David Wheatley's edited collection, *A History of Irish Women's Poetry*,[13] *The Golden Thread: Irish Women Playwrights, 1716–2016*, co-edited by David Clare, Fiona McDonagh and Justine Nakase, and *The Irish Women Playwrights and Theatremakers* Conference in 2017, all also provided much needed correctives.[14]

Waking the Nation and parallel omissions were all the more egregious given that by 2015 it was already old news that Irish culture was impoverished by lack of diversity of all kinds, and most especially by the paucity of diverse women's/assigned female at birth (AFAB)'s outlooks and outputs. Intersectional feminist Irish scholarship was embedded in a growing global awareness that not only did the noxious concept of race emerge from racism and not the other way around, but also that the gender binary emerged from, and was an organ of, patriarchy. In 2007, Melissa Sihra had written about 'the persistent institutional and critical gatekeeping that prevents women playwrights and practitioners from making the impact they should, even when their work appears on stage',[15] while earlier in 2003, Kelleher took up Gerardine Meaney's 2002 editorial invitation in *Field Day* IV and V to 'put existing maps into question',[16] arguing that 'a crucial factor' in remapping literary traditions by integrating women's writing was to ensure 'institutional support and recognition'.[17] Yet just over ten years later, Waking the Nation displayed a blatant 'lack of institutional support and recognition' in its significant exclusion of women writers and directors during the most consequential time of national cultural reflection in the Abbey Theatre in over a hundred years.[18] A flagship, half a million euro, Government of Ireland-backed and publicly-funded programme, described by O'Toole as 'in many ways anti-hegemonic',[19] and purporting to symbolise and represent the public that was funding it, had 'forgotten' most of the women writers and directors who worked alongside the men writers and directors remembered by the programme – as had the contemporaneous canonical handbooks and companions in theatre and poetry. Arguably, women were acknowledged in The Theatre Of Change, the conference substrate of the Abbey programme, which was in O'Toole's words, 'unmistakably and confrontationally pro-choice'[20]; this however, appears more in keeping with what Anne Fogarty identified in 2002, when she argued that instead of women 'simply being silenced', their being 'invoked in latterday [sic] Irish literary histories as an absent presence … sanctions cultural debates which still remain inveterately male–centred'.[21] How was it then, despite the years of feminist scholarship and research in the arts, that women were still being avowed to be disavowed?

Psychoanalytically inflected feminist scholarship such as Fogarty's identifies a strong subconscious current at play in these ongoing acts of invoking and forgetting. Bracken's *Irish Feminist Futures*,[22] Meaney's *Race, Sex and Nation*, and Patricia Coughlan's extensive body of work, beginning with the milestone essay 'Bog Queens: The Representation of Women in the poetry of John Montague and Seamus Heaney', all identify the oedipal underpinnings of Irish literary traditions. Harold Bloom, a highly influential scholar in anglophone literatures, used Sophocles' play *Oedipus Rex* as a foundational text for theorising the struggle for primacy or a place in the canon between younger and older male writers, which he called an 'agon', and considered a symbolic conflict between literary sons and fathers. Bloom argued this was essential to the formation of literary traditions and his theories have shaped the understanding of such traditions across the anglophone world. I have argued elsewhere that this model, while obviously privileging masculinist concerns and perspectives structurally restricts women to what philosopher and psychoanalyst Luce Irigaray calls the 'place of the mother',[23] which supports intergenerational legacy between men, but forbids it between women.[24] Playing by patriarchal rules, women can therefore only appear as the 'exception', the one or two 'exceptional' women who appear in the canon, or on the programme, and not as the rule (or ruler) and historical continuity and lineage between generations of women is structurally prohibited. Gerardine Meaney made the case for decentring oedipal structures in a 2011 essay, the title of which foreshadowed #WakingTheFeminists. In 'Waking the Dead: Antigone, Ismene and Anne Enright's Narrators in Mourning', Meaney's analysis of Anne Enright shifts her sights away from oedipal modes of reading to bring sisters, daughters, mothers, and others into focus to produce a model of ongoing cultural continuity and community between women.[25] But the oedipal dynamics shifted by Meaney in scholarship were to prove much more difficult to move in actuality given its entrenchment in all aspects of cultural life.

It was no small irony that the Waking the Nation programme literally adapted and dramatised the Oedipal dynamics underwriting Irish culture for a new century by staging an adaptation of *Oedipus* as part of its 2016 suite. Moreover, the programme was itself explicitly agonistic, with commissioned plays from a new generation of male playwrights staged 'in a conversation' with 'familiar classics from the Abbey's repertoire',[26] all of which were written by men; this was framed as a conflict with legacy and history expressed in the announcement that the programme would 'interrogate and question the legacy of the Easter Rising rather than celebrate the centenary.'[27] Molly Mullin has shown how in Ireland, 'much of the power of the prevailing hegemonic order rests on control over authoritative representations of history, both public historical spectacles as well as the more quotidian structuring of time, including notions of what is temporal and what is not; what is ordered into the 'past', 'present', and 'future'.[28] Thus, women writers and directors were categorically placed, in Eavan Boland's words, not only 'Outside History',[29] but also 'outside' the 'present' and 'future' too. Artistic value depends on proof of provenance, and, in literary terms, this is established by a work's citation of, links to, and dialogue with literary precedents that lend it authority and build it a lineage; the 2016 Waking the Nation programme staged no historical work by women playwrights to 'interrogate' or 'celebrate', thus contemporary work by women was structurally precluded – unless patriarchally identified via the 'place of the mother', like Ali White's *Me, Mollser*, a monologue for children, or critique, such as was the case with Marina Carr's *On Raftery's Hill*, and the belated addition of Carmel Winters' *The Remains of Maisie Duggan*.[30] Without the possibility of 'citation' we lose what Sarah Browne describes as a 'feminist practice' of 'a successful reproductive technology'.[31]

The cultural reproduction of this patriarchal structure carries a high cost for women/AFABs and other minoritised and feminised people, not only in the arts but across all aspects of intimate, social, and political life. Clara Fischer meditates on 'wave' as a metaphor to evoke 'the peaks and troughs' of the feminist movement across time, or rather, as she also suggests its tidal 'ebb and flow'.[32] Crucially, this 'ebb and flow' is not 'natural', but conditioned by patriarchal pressures that resist feminist change through a complex set of intersections that make up what Patricia Hill Collins calls the 'Matrix of Domination'.[33] Writing in the context of North American black feminist activism and intellectual traditions, she describes how this 'matrix of domination' is 'structured along certain axes – race, gender, class, sexuality, and nation' and notes how 'it operates through interconnected domains of power – structural, interpersonal, disciplinary, and hegemonic' showing how the 'dialectical relationship linking oppression and activism is far more complex than simple models of oppressors and oppressed would suggest'.[34] As Kelleher shows, intentional feminist actions support women's creative work and research, and are crucial to protecting against the periodical deletion of women from historical narratives; removing women's work from view may not be intentional on the part of individuals, but it is not accidental; it is systemically produced by a backlash that has followed every period of increased equality and visibility for women. For instance after the gains of second wave feminism, women were put 'back in their place' by the proliferation of 'punishment porn', involving silencing through occupying women's mouths and increased levels of degradation, creating a seemingly naturalised confluence between sex and violence that is still intensifying today.[35] This silencing and shaming also takes other forms, such as excluding, excising, exiling, and incarcerating, specifically creating in Ireland, as Miriam Haughton has argued, 'a culture of silence and sexual oppression' that was 'facilitated and intensified by the power of ideology, not only promoted by major hegemonic institutions, but reproduced in daily life by communities, families, and individual men and women.'[36]

Delegitimising the concept of 'feminism' is also part of how it operates through forms of violence and coercion to invalidate women's claims to our own authority, self-narration and right to shape the shared public imaginary.[37] The work of #WakingtheFeminists insisted on a comprehensive gender awareness, yet Lian Bell, who became Campaign Director during this historic shift in Irish Theatre, could not have defined feminism when she first posted about stark and shocking gender asymmetries. Musing on the word 'feminist' she recounted that,

> other people say to me that they don't feel comfortable with the use of the word Feminist. Late 2015 hasn't yet seen the full-blown reclamation of that word, and it still has a mildly embarrassing hectoring fustiness about it. I feel it myself but pretend not to.

In this, Lian highlights the importance of words, and how vulnerable we are all to the embarrassment of being mislabelled, misunderstood, and misrepresented by the words we use, or that are used about us. Small wonder that in 2015, after over a century of trivialising and pathologising feminists who revealed and resisted repressive misogynist state policies towards women,[38] as well as over two decades of the use of the term 'feminazi' in some parts of the Irish media, there were women reluctant to identify as feminist, a term that had been untied from its roots in equality and retethered to negative stereotypes of ugly, unlovable, and humourless man-haters. The widespread normalisation of feminist bashing and the use of the term feminazi is but one representation of a 'history of resistance to feminist theory [that] testifies to the impact of ideological power' of patriarchy, as described by Nancy Folbre in *The Rise and Decline of Patriarchal Systems: An Intersectional Political Economy*. Folbre goes on to note that feminist 'efforts to analyse patriarchal institutions have often been and are sometimes still derided by those in positions of authority.'[39] Such derision amounts to what Gayatri Chakravorty Spivak calls 'epistemic violence',[40] which is the delegitimating of the expertise – also identified as a 'subjugated knowledge' – belonging to a group that is opposed to that of the dominant culture. Epistemological violence was enacted by the lack of opportunity for women to add their 'subjugated knowledges', expertise and experience to the 2016 Waking the Nation programme, as well as to the controversial companions and handbooks; to contribute perspectives, narratives and portrayals with potential to reshape national stories of belonging and human value, and generate cultural capital for those who historically had little or none. The exclusion also enacted an ontological violence that stripped the stage, back and front, of women's self-narrated and directed embodied presence.

The allegations of inappropriate behaviour in Irish theatre, courageously led by Grace Dyas and detailed in Workplace Relations expert, Gaye Cunningham's report,[41] as well as in numerous personal accounts on social media, shows how gatekeeping the authority of patriarchal platforms is supported by deeper issues. Further evidence was shown in the need for Speak Up & Call It Out and Irish Theatre Institute's report,[42] Amplify Women's Harassment Toolkit,[43] the establishment of FairPlé and #MiseFosta,[44] and the eventual creation of Safe To Create Dignity at Work programme managed by Irish Theatre Institute, in partnership with the Arts Council, Screen Ireland, and Minding Creative Minds, on behalf of the Department of Tourism, Culture, Arts, Gaeltacht, Sport and Media.[45] For freelancers, which includes most workers in the arts, the lack of an overseeing organisation meant that before #WakingTheFeminists there were few procedures or official pathways that were easily accessible, available or effective to direct complaints about assault, harassment, and abuse linked to exclusion and discrimination. The establishment of these bodies has been crucial for freelancers, who are especially vulnerable given the precarity of creative industries and the cult of male genius and personality that still pervades arts spaces. Cultural epistemic and ontological violence towards women's self-representation is tethered to sexual and gender violence in ecclesiastical, juridical, military, health, political, educational, cultural, public, virtual, and intimate spaces.[46] Gender violence and rape is not, as it is often portrayed, an anomaly in patriarchy, merely the work of a few rogue men, but is fundamental to patriarchy as a system, as Rana M. Jaleel, demonstrates in *The Work of Rape.*[47] Let me very clearly state that this essay in no way suggests that any individuals involved in the exclusion of women from arts programmes have been involved in gender and sexual violence; instead this analysis highlights how systemic gender violence biopolitically underwrites, conditions, and polices women/AFAB's enunciation and embodiment on the social, political and cultural stages of patriarchal systems.[48] This is evidenced by the ongoing pattern of abuse revelations across multiple institutions and organisations: organised religion (regardless of denomination), the police service, the military, education, sport, health, creative industries, government, the paramilitary, organised crime, the media and cultural industries, and various carceral spaces have all perpetuated and covered up systemic gender and sexuality abuses against women, children, feminised, non-conforming, and otherwise vulnerable populations. Investigations, tribunals, and reports treat each scandal as culturally unique, siloed, and specific to the dynamics of each organisation; commissioned investigations have yet to link an individual body to the larger pattern that a meta-analysis would show – that each has patriarchal structures in common.

Structurally, patriarchal systems are not designed to support, value, and credit women's narration of events. This is not a coincidence but a baked-in feature of how patriarchy works, and invalidation of women's voices happens across multiple representational stages. Research emphatically demonstrates how many rape victims are unwilling to be epistemically violated again in court.[49] For the small number of victims who ever get to court, even with the best legal representation, women consistently report being misrepresented, misread, having their words twisted, not being given the time and space to tell it their own way, and liken the experience to being violated again. Susan McKay's description of how feminists were treated as they sought to address widespread rapist tolerance and to support victims of rapists in the Ireland of the 1970s and 1980s is strikingly similar to that of #WakingTheFeminists activists seeking equality of opportunity and fair play. In a 2007 essay, McKay quotes politician Gemma Hussey's recollection of raising the subject of rape in Ireland at the end of the 1970s: '[y]ou were up against a strange hostility that gave you a shock each time you encountered it … Rape was just not spoken about.'[50] Writing about researching her 2005 book, *Without Fear: 25 Years of the Dublin Rape Crisis Centre*, McKay notes that those seeking to support rape victims had to 'struggle for recognition and they had to struggle for every penny of the funds they needed'. On top of this, they 'were accused of propaganda and lying'.[51] McKay's observations about hostility, forbidden subjects, struggle for recognition and funding, as well as the distortion of evidence and research, maps onto the experiences of the #WakingTheFeminists activists nearly 40 years later, for whom feminist politics and even the word feminist had been polluted.

Lucy Caldwell's short story, 'Words for Things',[52] explores how feminist sensibility and language was voided for young women coming of age in the backlash culture of the notoriously laddish and rapey media landscape of the 1990s and 2000s. In the story, the speakers reflect on how their younger selves lacked 'words' to name the wrongs being done to women (such as Monica Lewinsky, Tonya Harding, Amy Winehouse, Shannen Doherty, Jade Goody, and Britney Spears) who were victims of highly public misogynist abuse and stalking by the press. Caldwell demonstrates how the speakers, young women navigating a world in which feminism had become a dirty word, instead had their psyches and values structured by the sexist words that had been normalised; chauvinist idioms with which the protagonists reproduced the same judgements against the women being slut-shamed and publicly maltreated. 'Words for Things', shows not only how women are horizontally pitted against each other – for the favours that patriarchy bestows on the well-behaved women (such as a good marriage or selection as the 'exceptional' woman whose work might get published or staged), it also demonstrates the vertical or intergenerational loss of words that otherwise could have transported feminist consciousness across time. Second wave feminists documented clearly how rapist culture[53] functioned as a weapon of patriarchal dominance, and Caldwell tells the story of the loss of this knowledge and language, and the attendant loss of empowerment.[54]

Self-consciousness about how these operations of language support the architectural arc of national culture is crucial to resisting the epistemological power they wield. Caldwell highlights how her characters' fascination with celebrity scandal disguises how intently they study celebrities in order to avoid the same fate as the young women being 'made a spectacle of' by those who violated them reputationally, photographically, and physically (upskirting). By joining in the slut-shaming, the narrator distanced herself and her friends from the possibility of the same happening to them; victim-blaming by women is a well-documented dissociative fear response intended to create an illusory sense of control in a world in which women and girls live with a pervasive threat of gender violence. 'Words for Things', shows how the speakers' younger complicity with patriarchy was as much an act of survival as it was an act of (self) abuse, also compassionately revealing the personal cost to women and girls of rapist culture, as they learn to blame themselves while seeking to safeguard themselves and resist being victims in a system stacked against their freedom in speech or in public space.[55] Sarah Durcan's and Lian Bell's description of the deep personal cost of internalisation of self-reproach had on the many women who travailed against invisible odds in the world of theatre is strikingly resonant of Caldwell's descriptions; it also recalls the effect books such as *The Feminine Mystique* and *The Women's Room*, *This Bridge that is My Back*, *Sister Outsider*, *Borderlands/La Frontera: The New Mestiza*, *Against our Will*, and *In Search of Our Mothers' Gardens* had on women pivoting from self-condemnation to systemic accountability via exposure to such in the 1960s, 1970s, and 1980s. #WakingTheFeminists activists recount the dawning realisation that the burden of failure and self-condemnation carried by individual women in the theatre was not of their own making, but was instead generated by a flawed and distorted system that was designed to produce feelings of privatised shame and inadequacy in women and other minoritised peoples across the sector. They write:

> For many years, women in Irish theatre had known that opportunities for them were scarcer than for men. If this was acknowledged or

spoken about at all, it was in whispered private conversations, not on public stages or media platforms. In these conversations women would talk about how they were racked with personal doubts, inadequacies and imposter syndrome; it is clear now that this was internalised misogyny and the result of millennia of systemic inequality and of bias that has profoundly warped our own sense of our abilities. This forced many talented and ambitious women out of theatre. They eventually chose not to compete in this skewed system or left the country to find flourishing careers elsewhere. The theatre industry masqueraded as meritocratic, while privileging men over women season after season, year after year. If you didn't 'make it', it was a personal fault.

Folbre tells us that '[s]ocial structures are not easy to picture or explain', but the #WakingTheFeminists testimony above pictures how, 'their components can be distinguished, their buttresses revealed'.[56] The 'whisper networks', in which women in many institutions have shared information crucial for survival and safety is gendered and trivialised as 'gossip', another form of shaming and quieting women's tongues. When men's voices resonate on public stages and platforms, their discussions are classed as 'debate', 'analysis', 'news', 'politics', 'history', 'objectivity', and 'visionary'. Men's speech acts are not widely depicted as 'underhanded', 'forked-tongued', 'duplicitous', 'stroppy', 'forward', 'emotional', 'irrational', 'subjective', or 'personalised', nor are their voices tone-policed as 'sharp', 'grating', 'shrill', 'whining', 'harsh', 'nagging', 'hectoring', 'bitchy', 'bossy', 'abrasive', or 'strident'.[57] The backstage, offstage spaces into which patriarchy forces women are bound up with the ways in which women's voices are pathologised with judgments about *how* women speak, invalidating *what* we say, with devastating effects for women and children and feminised populations in multiple spheres.[58]

Sara Ahmed underscores this in *Complaint!* when she shows how 'if it takes time to make a complaint, it takes time to reach a complaint'.[59] *Complaint!*, Ahmed's archive of 'subjected knowledge' of sexual harassment in third level education, represents the transformation from backstage fear and intimidation to centre stage analysis of how patriarchy is actively invested in invalidating women's testimony and resisting equality actions. *Complaint!* reveals how the system works 'by stopping those who are trying to transform the system'.[60] The self-blame that #WakingTheFeminists activists recount maps onto similar accounts Ahmed has archived; below Ahmed recounts the internal monologue of a student who tried to talk herself out of her own experience of being sexually harassed by her male supervisor:

She tells herself off, even; she gives herself a talking to; she tells herself to stop being paranoid, to stop being a feminazi, to stop being a feminist, perhaps. It is striking how in questioning herself, she also exercised familiar stereotypes of feminists as feminazis, with the implication that gender is a judgment that is imposed upon a situation from the outside. External judgments can be given voice as internal doubt.[61]

Ahmed cites many such examples of how women and other minoritised people are atomised via internalisation of self-doubt and blame across multiple intersectional registers, to give, as Folbre observes, 'mature heterosexual men power over others'.[62] Such power is maintained, as Hill Collins described, not only through hegemonic, structural, and disciplinary actions, but also through interconnection with the interpersonal, and #WakingTheFeminists activists recount their fear of betraying the Irish theatre community, which has historically welcomed diverse and/or marginalised or minoritised people, challenged neoliberalism and the instrumentalisation of the arts, and is strongly bonded by its collective belief in speaking, staging, and dramatising 'truth to power'. But, as became all too clear with Waking the Nation, without intersectional awareness, 'unity' premised on the priorities of the larger group and often 'uncritical rallying around misogynist politics and patriarchal values',[63] results in women and AFABs being further marginalised in their originary group. Kimberlé Crenshaw's pioneering work in intersectionality demonstrates how black women remain marginalised in discourses of anti-racism that do not also take gender into account:

> Although collective opposition to racist practice has been and continues to be crucially important in protecting black interests, an empowered Black feminist sensibility would require that the terms of unity no longer reflect priorities premised upon the continued marginalization of Black women.[64]

Women workers in Irish theatre learned this lesson far too cruelly, along with the shock of absorbing how the financial scales were weighted against them for the benefits of those for whom reproducing masculinist narratives paid. Folbre reminds us that while power 'is multidimensional … its impact on policies (including laws), ideologies (including norms), and the ownership and control of resources (including people) can be assessed by a direct question: "who benefits?"'[65] The 2015 reveal of the Abbey programme mirrored Irish society in microcosm in which the ongoing reproduction of masculinist perspectives benefitted women little, even though their labour, support, trust, and goodwill was presumed, thus replicating the pattern that used but didn't credit the women political activists before and during the Easter Rising.[66] Published in the same month that Waking the Nation was announced, Fearghal McGarry's *The Abbey Rebels of 1916: A Lost Revolution*, which extensively drew on the Abbey archives, provided a detailed study of Abbey Theatre employees, usher Ellen Bushell, leading actress and Abbey founder Máire Nic Shiubhlaigh, and actress Helena Molony, who were also active in fighting during Easter week, but whose lives were not commemorated by the 1916 programme.[67] The accounts of #WakingTheFeminists activists during the campaign show how frightening and dangerous it felt to speak up and out, and how it risked not only retaliative pushback in the form of loss of future work in an already precarious sector, but speaking out also crucially jeopardised cherished and important personal and professional relationships; while many feminist men became stalwart allies for #WakingTheFeminists and equality and diversity in Irish creative sectors, some previously close working relationships more broadly for women in Irish Theatre and the culture sector remain strained to this day; this a common pattern replicated in other fields when steps are taken to achieve parity of access for women and other minoritised people.

Resistance involves empowerment through reclamation of language, information sharing, and rebuilding bonds that are deliberately divided by patriarchy; Hill Collins reminds us that just 'as oppression is complex, so must resistance aimed at fostering empowerment demonstrate a similar complexity'.[68] An ideological focus on atomised individualism and independence in neurocapitalism,[69] as the metric for participation in the social body or workplace, health, or well-being, also negatively impacts women whose social roles are constructed interdependently via parenting and care that is unsupported in policy or practice, with especially negative effects for women in the creative industries, as the MAMs group highlighted as part of the #WakingTheFeminists actions.[70] Folbre describes how an ongoing 'lack of structural supports for interdependence and care in patriarchal economies' means that 'women's creative lives and outputs' cannot be 'supported across a lifetime'.[71] Further, reproductive and care work is either unpaid or underpaid, constituting an invisible workforce upon which, as Silvia Federici shows, patriarchal capitalism depends to reproduce its current asymmetries.[72] Research has shown that in the creative industries, which depend largely on a 'grace and favour' model of funding, and are linked to informal reputational networks, the 'maternal wall' is a serious obstacle to women's participation.[73] Structural lack of supports – such as funding bodies not including childcare as a legitimate budgetary cost – contribute, along with presumptions that women upon motherhood will no longer be available for gigs, to what Joanne Cusack refers to as the 'disappearing act' in the careers of women in traditional music and dance. This tracks with what Folbre describes as the 'three somewhat overlapping categories' of 'patriarchal political institutions':

> property rights over women and children; explicit restrictions on the individual rights of women, children, and sexually nonconforming individuals (often including limits on access to productive physical assets such as land or financial wealth); and rules of remuneration for time, effort, and resources devoted to the care of others, especially dependents.[74]

Enacting care was central to the #WakingTheFeminists group as they faced into the enormity of the task they had set themselves and it became ever more crucial as they fast learned about institutions work from the 'wear and tear of coming up against them'.[75] Awareness of interdependence and the importance of sustainability informed the prescient wisdom that propelled #WakingTheFeminists to set a deadline of a year to achieve their outcomes. Complaint work is, as Ahmed reminds us, above all, 'embodied work'[76]; and bodies cannot continue to push themselves against an apparatus that works 'by stopping those who are trying to transform the system',[77] without incurring significant physical or mental health costs, that may take the form of serious and even life-threatening disease and illness, or that can also potentially translate into wearied fractures among otherwise like-minded and supportive campaigners. Equality actions that address gender and other intersectional oppressions are exhausting – both by virtue of the David and Goliath struggle involved in challenging the matrix of dominations already outlined – and because of the process which is designed to be attritional and deplete people out of the juridical and complaint system as Ahmed observes: 'we can be worn down as well as worn out by what we have to do when we go through a complaints process'.[78] #WakingTheFeminists built in measures to counter the debilitating 'wear and tear' of taking on powerful interlocking systems; Sarah Durcan and Lian Bell recount with warmth and wit how #WakingTheFeminists' core group responded with differing degrees of engagement, ambivalence, and scepticism to practices of 'self-care'. For all the self-consciousness and playfulness of narrating this aspect of their activist work, it seems clear that insisting on care as a core value played a central and crucial part in the extraordinary efficacy and success of #WakingTheFeminists as a movement.

#WakingTheFeminists' collective wisdom in defining a year's worth of highly focussed activist work, along with key strategic goals linked to limits on the investment of individual time in order to respect health and other commitments distinguished #WakingTheFeminists from other social media moments, as Claire Keogh has observed: '[w]ith origins on social media, #WakingTheFeminists could have been another flash of online outrage, but what unfolded in late 2015 and throughout 2016 was a strategic campaign for gender equality that has had an impressive impact on Irish culture.'[79] In a manner similar to how the word 'feminism' has been voided for many women, 'self-care' is yet another phrase that has removed from the lexicon of realistic resistance, because it has to resist both the patriarchally defined narrative of self-sacrifice as a measure of feminine worth, as well as a neoliberal mediatised distortion of feminism into an easily trivialised form of 'I'm worth it' individualism.[80] #WakingTheFeminists bypassed this to connect via an ethics of care for each other and those to whom they felt responsible to a much deeper history of feminist resistance and an aspect of care-economies that has feminist anti-racist and anti-capitalist potential. For the concept of 'self-care' had its roots in the collective and community actions of North American black women activists seeking to heal the ongoing 'wear and tear' of racism, sexism and the trauma and epigenetic legacy of the Middle Passage, chattel slavery, and Jim Crow and Jane Crow.[81] Audre Lorde in her 1988 collection of essays, *A Burst of Light*,[82] outlined how her body was working not only to counter intersectional oppressions but also to survive breast cancer; taking her own energetic regulation as a model for healthy engagement with social justice work, Lorde recognised how minding her body-mind was not a luxury but represented a baseline model for wider community healing work.[83] Lorde identifies 'self-care' as self-preservation, a political act, and crucially, yet anti-intuitively, fundamentally a collective practice, linking with Folbre's analysis about how 'collective empowerment and mobilization' have 'played a particularly large part in global efforts to combat violence against women'.[84] #WakingTheFeminists' collective work resulting in its data-led policy changes and legacy, evidence-based dissemination, and awareness-raising through multiple media (including this book) represents urgent historiographical acts; #WakingTheFeminists' documentation of the campaign colours in some of the missing 'half of the picture' of humanity, to borrow the phrase Guerrilla Girls used to describe the incompleteness of culture because of the loss of women's arts.[85] Equally, connectivity has been what enabled #WakingTheFeminists to cope with the pushback and the benign agreement couched in assurances and sympathy linked with inaction, tracking with what Ahmed called 'non-performativity,' which describes 'institutional speech acts that do not bring into effect what they name'.[86]

Much of their frustration at this form of attritional organisational stonewalling was processed privately within the group. A related issue was how to negotiate actions that have a double effect due to extent structures that protect existing gender asymmetries. #WakingTheFeminists intentionally strategised for sustainable solutions by respecting privacy and creating diplomatic and safe spaces in which to manage the difficult conversations that would promote positive change; however, by virtue of how patriarchal power operates through epistemological shut down, vouchsafing privacy, although crucial as well as psychologically wise, necessarily also aligns with how patriarchy manages disruptive feminist discourse through recourse to privacy laws and NDAs,[87] demonstrating Elizabeth M. Schneider's argument that the concept of privacy can be weaponised to protect patriarchal interests because, 'the rationale of privacy legitimates and supports violence against women; woman–abuse reveals the violence of privacy'.[88] From multiple key angles the work of #WakingTheFeminists found 'the methodical in the unofficial' and in doing so 'reveal[ed] something about institutions'[89]; showing the obduracy of patriarchy's multiple informal resistances to the sharing of resources and power. Further, it asks us to rethink what knowledge is, how it is built, and where it resides by highlighting the deep organisational and operational expertise developed by #WakingTheFeminists activists during the campaign; Ahmed notes that 'thinking about complaint as institutional mechanics (and the complainer as an institutional mechanic) is a way to show what those who make complaints come to know about how institutions are working'.[90] This book dramatises the mechanics of patriarchy at work in the creative industries, and through narrating #WakingTheFeminists' experience of pushback, and #WakingTheFeminists' expertise in navigating barriers and obstacles it sends a clear invitation to men and male–identified folk to become more active participants in dismantling patriarchy and resisting its active distortions, prohibitions, and punishments for women, non–binary, trans, and queer folk, as well as other minoritised populations.[91] #WakingTheFeminists woke many folk, revitalised yet others already woke and weary, and made unprecedented inroads in equality during an intense and focused year, creating a roadmap for other equality activists.[92] As #WakingTheFeminists describes in this account, although already saturated with cyberbullying, revenge porn, and gender violence threats, the internet in 2015 was not yet the increasingly punitive place it has since become.[93] As what Laura Bates and Debbie Ging have identified as the 'manosphere', has pervaded the internet making both virtual and physical spaces even more toxic and unsafe for girls, women, trans, and queer folk, the urgency of male–identified allies becomes ever more apparent to ensure equality actions continue. Feminists have been doing equality heavy lifting for long enough – seeking change that has benefits for all across multiple social justice registers. What #WakingTheFeminists found out during the campaign was that women were not the problem nor in need of 'fixing' – instead the problematic system needed fixing. As #WakingTheFeminists is showing us, the feminists are already woke in all of the most positive registers of this term; deep systemic changes means waking everyone *up to* the patriarchy so it can finally be laid to rest.

Afterword

Catriona Crowe

Catriona Crowe is former Head of Special Projects at the National Archives of Ireland. She regularly reviews for the Irish Times *and presented the RTÉ documentaries* Ireland before the Rising *and* Life After the Rising. *She is an Honorary President of the Irish Labour History Society, and a former President of the Women's History Association of Ireland. She is in receipt of four honorary doctorates, from the University of Limerick, Maynooth University, Trinity College Dublin, and University College Dublin. She is a member of the Royal Irish Academy.*

When I was involved in feminist activism in the late 70s and 80s, it was a different world. Mobile phones didn't exist. Social media didn't exist. Meetings took place in the upstairs rooms of pubs. Communication of our messages about contraception, abortion and divorce took place through difficult-to-access radio and TV, through print media (then mercifully blessed with a cohort of brilliant feminist journalists), and through leaflets and pamphlets, which had to be distributed through individual letterboxes.

Canvassing for the two referendums of 1983 (abortion) and 1986 (divorce) meant encountering a majority of people often vehemently opposed to our views and aspirations. We were spat at, cursed, had doors slammed in our faces, dogs set on us, and were generally treated as pariahs. A lot of the people doing this were women. Anyone who thinks 'the women of Ireland' is a united cohort of progressive feminists is living in a fool's paradise.

My moment of negative apotheosis was encountering two women in their 50s on Gardiner Street one day in 1983. They stopped me to discuss my large anti-Amendment badge, and to caution me about the murderous nature of abortion. I politely disagreed with them, mentioned choice, and tried to move on. They detained me to let me know they would pray for me. For some reason that offer was utterly infuriating, and I became profane in my insistence that they not bother storming heaven on my account. I still remember the smug grins on their faces. They had me!

One of the major differences between the 1980s and the 2010s is that back then, we were fighting a major backlash against the feminist achievements of the 1970s, and particularly Roe v. Wade,[1] which Irish Catholic conservatives saw as a harbinger of future reproductive rights for Irish women. The brutal refusal of the electorate to allow 50 per cent of the population reproductive rights, and 100 per cent of the population a second chance if marriages broke down (2/3 to 1/3 voted for the 8th amendment; the same proportion voted against divorce) made many of us feel we were not wanted in our own country.

For me and others involved at the time, that feeling didn't end until 2018, when the 8th amendment was finally voted out. Back in the day, Nell McCafferty referred to 'the pig-ignorant slurry of woman-hating that did us temporarily down'.[2] It was a great relief to know that at least 2/3 of voters were now in favour of our right to choose. Of course, that doesn't mean woman hatred has ceased: high profile rape trials like the Belfast rape trial, and the sink of vicious misogyny that social media now is, remind us that Margaret Atwood was right when she said that rights granted to women could easily be taken away. Just look at what has happened to Roe v. Wade.

WTF HAPPENED reminds us that the struggle continues. For a while, the term 'feminist' became unfashionable, something that made those of us who so designated ourselves both furious and sad. Lian Bell, that exemplary modern feminist, refers to this in this book. The reclamation of the term, by such a vibrant and effective group of people, was a source of joy to many older women and men. The story told in this book is an important addition to the canon of Irish feminist literature, and along with the #WakingTheFeminists archive, safely deposited in the National Library and National Museum, will be a primary source for the study of a particular and unique phase of the movement.

WTF HAPPENED itself is a kind of archive, using as it does social media posts as primary source documents and reproducing the many speeches made at #WakingTheFeminists events, thus magnifying the number of voices presented and adding real-time freshness to the narrative. From the first post by Lian Bell, commenting on the lamentable absence of women in the Abbey Theatre's 2016 programme, ending with the resounding 'But, like, *really*?', to Sonya Kelly's wickedly funny speech to the second public meeting on International Women's Day 2016, which brilliantly caricatures the casual sexism encountered by women in theatre, the book reads like the rollercoaster the campaign actually was.

One of the points made by the authors is the expertise of the group which coalesced around #WakingTheFeminists in putting on a good show. This is obvious when you think about it – they all work in theatre after all – but it was an invaluable resource when it came to quickly organising a huge public meeting at very short notice. The outward face of theatre encompasses actors and directors; most people rarely think about all of the other experts who go to make up a production: lighting designers, set designers, set builders, costume and hair specialists, writers, stage managers, technical crew, PR people, voice coaches, producers, and many more.

Kate Ferris's now iconic speech on International Women's Day 2016 highlighted these less visible but essential people by focusing on Emma and Jane, both up a ladder rigging the lighting system for the meeting, and afraid to join #WakingTheFeminists publicly for fear of adverse consequences to their careers. Kate recounts several instances of sexism encountered by them, and reflects on the precarious nature of freelance employment and its particular adverse effects on women wishing to have children. She ends with these words:

> I do not want this to be the only ladder that Emma and Jane reach the top of. I want to see them advance to senior positions in technical theatre. I want to see highly competent, organised and excellent female technicians and stage managers progressing to be production managers and technical managers where their skills are so obviously transferable. I want our industry to enable them to achieve every opportunity on the career ladder.[3]

To have achieved what #WakingTheFeminists did in a year – commitment to positive, measurable changes in gender policy and practice in most Irish theatre companies – and to be able to see tangible progress in them all after a few years, is astounding. Our sclerotic, expensive public service has a lot to learn from this extraordinary campaign run by people with very little experience in campaigning, media, organisation, management, finance, and research who created, implemented, and concluded a set of far-reaching changes in Irish theatre in the space of a year, for tiny sums of money.

The spirit of those public meetings reminded me of the famous Mansion House meeting organised by the Irish Women's Liberation Movement in April 1971, attended by over 1,000 women, bursting to tell their stories of discrimination, sexism and suffering. It was the first time a woman publicly announced herself as an unmarried mother.[4] So much depends on testimonies, and the empowerment that comes with recounting personal experience. The same instincts of profound dissatisfaction, desire for change and emphasis on personal accounts animated these gatherings 50 years apart.

#WakingTheFeminists also neatly preceded and fed into the #MeToo movement, started here by theatre maker Grace Dyas and leading to serious reckonings with harassment and bullying in the theatre community, long tolerated but now no longer endured. And it is probably no coincidence that now the directors of almost all our major theatres and companies, as well as the heads of our cultural institutions, are all women.

Reading WTF HAPPENED is a joyful experience for an old feminist like me. The anger, enthusiasm, efficiency, eloquence, and organisational brilliance of the movement and its leaders are a wonderful reminder that the most important philosophical and social movement of the last 200 years is still thriving in Ireland. The ghosts of Mary Wollstonecraft, Isabella Tod, Anna Haslam, Hanna Sheehy Skeffington, Hilda Tweedy, June Levine, Nell McCafferty, Nuala O'Faolain, and many more would be proud to see their long struggle for women's rights continue in such a vibrant way.

Sarah Durcan's closing words to the final #WakingTheFeminists meeting in November 2016 are a clarion call:

> All inequality is an outrage. Rage out against it in determination without despair until there is nothing to be outraged about. In this chaotic global moment, let's open up – ignite *all* our stages with big complex messy conversations, using *all* our talent, *all* our genders, *all* our diversity. Make our theatre a beacon for equity, not a bystander to a burning world. International Women's Day 2021 beckons us. *Let's get it done.*

#WakingTheFeminists made me realise that men who seem to be motivated by art or idealism can actually be motivated by the need for something high, important – possibly self important – and that 'high' to them, is axiomatically, male. I realised the connection between this high yearning and the kind of unease, fear, dismissal, and disgust around women that I have experienced, in Ireland, all my life. In 2016 I knew, for the first time, that this sense of aspiration runs so deep in the history of Irish national idealism that the bias involved could only be exposed and uprooted by force. There was no point asking any more, because the people who thought they were listening, really were not listening. And besides, what is that posture? The one where you ask, and are accepted or turned down? I realised we had to come at it from outside the system because the system was incapable of regulating or fixing itself. In 2016 I learned the power of counting, because numbers are factual, and the facts don't lie, or feel sorry for themselves, or quote Yeats back at you, or wish you were more like their mother, or less like their mother. In 2016 I realised that men find it hard to change when it is not in their interests to change so, sadly, sometimes you have to run them over with a truck. Or with a crowd. In 2016 I did something I find difficult, as an individual artist, to do: I joined a benevolent and righteous crowd. I have not looked back.

Anne Enright, writer and Laureate for Irish Fiction, reflection written in 2020, five years after the start of #WakingTheFeminists

Notes

Foreword

1. The Expert Advisory Group on Centenary Commemorations. https://www.decadeofcentenaries.com/expert-advisory-group/ accessed11/11/2021.

2. Ibid.

3. Maeve Casserly and Ciaran O'Neill 'Public History, Invisibility, and Women in the Republic of Ireland' in *The Public Historian*, May 2017, 39:2, p. 25.

4. Meetings to introduce Hackett's story to the public were held in Liberty Hall, addressed by activists, historians, and members of the Hackett/Gray family. The online campaign included 'Reasons for Rosie', while the online petition was signed by 2,221 supporters.

5. Laura McAtackney 'Public Memory, Conflict and Women; Commemoration in Contemporary Ireland' in Paul Astoon, Tanya Evans and Paula Hamilton (ed.) *Making Histories* (Berlin, 2010) p. 104.

6. Ibid., p. 104.

7. Mary Moynihan 'How Waking the Feminists set an equality agenda for Irish theatre' in RTÉ. https://www.rte.ie/brainstorm/2018/1122/1012586-how-waking-the-feminists-set-an-equality-agenda-for-irish-theatre/.

8. Ibid.

How This Book Was Written

1. Speakers pre-submitted written speeches before each event, and these are documented in the archive in the National Library. However, in reviewing footage from the events, some speakers delivered slightly different or updated versions. The speeches included in this book are as they were spoken on the day.

2. From Equality Now's Theory of Change.

3. Equality Now, the international network of lawyers and activists working to create a more just world for women and girls, states: 'Using defamation lawsuits to silence survivors from speaking up and raising awareness of their experiences or to retaliate against them, is a form of gender-based violence and in violation of international human rights law.'

[I]n her 2021 report to the UN General Assembly, the Special Rapporteur on the promotion and protection of the right to freedom of opinion and expression, Irene Khan, raised the alarm bell on 'gendered censorship' and highlighted the 'perverse twist in the #MeToo age' of 'women who publicly denounce alleged perpetrators of sexual violence online' finding themselves 'increasingly subject to ... criminal libel or the false reporting of crimes.' She concludes strongly that 'weaponizing the justice system to silence women feeds impunity while also undermining free speech (United Nations General Assembly, 2021).' Tejal Jesrani, Daimiris Garcia, 'Gendered SLAPPs: Addressing criminal prosecutions against exposers of sexual and gender-based violence under international human rights law', International Journal of Law, Crime and Justice, 80, 2025, https://doi.org/10.1016/j.ijlcj.2025.100729. (https://www.sciencedirect.com/science/article/pii/S1756061625000059)

At the time of publication, The Defamation (Amendment) Bill 2024 is proceeding through the Oireachtas, to 'give effect to Directive (EU) 2024/1069 of the European Parliament and of the Council of 11 April 2024 on protecting persons who engage in public participation from manifestly unfounded claims or abusive court proceedings ('Strategic lawsuits against public participation') in so far as it relates to defamation proceedings.'

Who's Who

* No notes.

Timeline of the Year

* No notes.

Introduction

1. Rebecca Solnit writes in *The Mother of All Questions*: 'For a century, the human response to stress and danger has been defined as "fight or flight". A 2000 UCLA study by several psychologists noted that this research was based largely on studies of male rats and male human beings. But studying women led them to a third, often deployed option: gather for solidarity, support, advice. They noted that "behaviorally, females" responses are more marked by a pattern of "tend-and-befriend." Tending involves nurturant activities designed to protect the self and offspring that promote safety and reduce distress; befriending is the creation and maintenance of social networks that may aid in this process." Much of this is done through speech, through telling of one's plight, through being heard, through hearing compassion and understanding in the response of the people you tend to, whom you befriend.' (London, 2018), pp 18–19.

2. Laura Bates, *Men Who Hate Women: From Incels to Pickup Artists, The Truth About Extreme Misogyny and How It Affects Us All* (London, 2020).

3. Ronan McCreevy, ed., *CENTENARY, Ireland Remembers 1916* (Dublin, 2017). It referred to #WakingTheFeminists as: 'One of the most significant events of the commemoration period' and noted it 'was entirely unscheduled'.

4. Tarana J. Burke started this movement in 2006. In 2017, the #MeToo hashtag went viral.

5. 'In 2013, three radical Black organizers – Alicia Garza, Patrisse Cullors, and Opal Tometi – created a Black-centered political-movement-building project called

#BlackLivesMatter in response to the acquittal of Trayvon Martin's murderer, George Zimmerman'. https://blacklivesmatter.com/our-history/.

6. #LoveWins was coined by the Human Rights Campaign, the US organisation that 'fights to make equality, equity and liberation a reality for all LGBTQ+ people'. https://shortyawards.com/8th/hrcs-lovewins-hashtag-goes-viral-celebrates-marriage-equality-victory.

7. A joint campaign by GLEN, Marriage Equality, and the ICCL was launched in March 2015.

8. A joint campaign by the Abortion Rights Campaign, the Coalition to Repeal the 8th Amendment, and the National Women's Council of Ireland, was launched in March 2018.

9. Gráinne Healy, Brian Sheehan and Noel Whelan, *Ireland Says Yes: The Inside Story of How the Vote for Marriage Equality Was Won* (Dublin, 2015).

10. Hereinafter referred to as 'the Abbey', as theatre folks colloquially refer to it.

11. Abbey Theatre Archive and https://artsandculture.google.com/story/gQURwAt kljMoJw.

12. https://microsites.museum.ie/rollofhonour1916/roleofwomen.aspx.

13. Gerardine Meaney, *Gender, Ireland and Cultural Change: Race, Sex and Nation* (New York, 2011).

14. Margaret Ward, *Unmanageable Revolutionaries: Women and Irish Nationalism* (New York, 1983).

Nell Regan, 'Helena Molony (1883–1967)', Mary Cullen and Maria Luddy, ed., *Female Activists: Irish Women and Change 1900–1960* (New York, 2001).

15. Sara Keating, 'Beyond the Abbey: the trouble for women in theatre', *Irish Times*, 6 November 2015.

https://www.irishtimes.com/culture/stage/beyond-the-abbey-the-trouble-for-women-in-theatre-1.2419983.

16. 'The understanding of multivalent Irishness in the final lines of Inventing Ireland is enabled by the trope of Ireland as woman on which it can be draped ... The locus for negotiations of Irishness is here figured as a woman. The subject of Irish studies, as it is presently defined, is assured for as long as Cathleen Ni Houlihan remains in place and extrinsic and intrinsic to the connected patch-work. Ni Houlihan simply supports this diversity; she is not a part of it. Woman functions as an object through which Irish studies can mediate its relationship to itself' Moynagh Sullivan, 'Feminism, Postmodernism, and the Subject of Irish and Women's Studies', in PJ Mathews, ed., *New Voices in Irish Criticism*, 2000, pp 243–51.

17. Irish culture has long been a key component of the 'soft power' of the Irish State, and used to promote Ireland around the world.

18. Kirsty Blake Knox, 'Abbey hopes 1916 programme will Wake nation' *Irish Independent*, 29 Oct 2015. https://www.independent.ie/entertainment/theatre-arts/abbey-hopes-1916-programme-will-wake-nation-34151255.html.

19. Government of Ireland equality policies are in turn frameworked by EU and UN equality strategy and goals.

20. 'Analysis of Arts Council Funding 2002–2012', Theatre Forum Ireland (now Performing Arts Forum Ireland), 2012.

21. Building-based institutions are theatre or multidisciplinary arts organisations that operate in and from a public venue, such as the Abbey, the Gate, Project Arts Centre,

and arts centres around Ireland. Independent theatre companies mostly operate from small offices and present their work at venues that they do not run.

22. Kimberlé W. Crenshaw, *On Intersectionality: Essential Writings* (New York, 2014).

PART ONE
Chapter 1: Social Media Storm

1. https://www.rte.ie/entertainment/2015/1028/737979-abbey-theatre-gets-set-to-wake-the-nation-in-2016/.

2. Fiach Mac Conghail went on to become CEO of the Digital Hub Development Agency, where he instigated DEI policies and action plans.

3. Abbey Theatre celebrates 1916 centenary with only one woman playwright, Una Mullally, *Irish Times*, 2 November 2015. https://www.irishtimes.com/opinion/una-mullally-abbey-theatre-celebrates-1916-centenary-with-only-one-woman-playwright-1.2413277.

4. Erica Murray, *Irish Times*, Letters, 2 November 2015.

5. Brenda Donohue, *Irish Times*, Letters, 4 November 2015.

6. Jimmy Murphy, *Irish Times*, Letters, 4 November 2015.

7. John Delaney, *Irish Times*, Letters, 5 November 2015.

8. Garry Hynes, *Irish Times*, Letters, 5 November 2015.

9. Aoife Kelly, 'Debra Messing voices support for #WakingTheFeminists and female playwrights in Ireland', *Irish Independent*, 9 November 2015.

10. Eleanor Tiernan, 'A stage of one's own', *The Times*, Saturday, 7 November 2015.

11. https://www.irishtimes.com/opinion/una-mullally-abbey-theatre-celebrates-1916-centenary-with-only-one-woman-playwright-1.2413277.

12. Michael West's full post: https://mrwestfoulpapers.wordpress.com/2015/11/12/waking-the-feminists-going-clear/.

Chapter 2: Gathering and Planning

1. Sara Keating, 'Abbey director 'regrets exclusions' in programme', *Irish Times*, 06 November 2015.

2. Now known as Performing Arts Forum.

3. The petition went live on Monday, 9 November 2015.

4. Justine McCarthy, 'The Abbey is waking the nation to how women's voices are being ignored', *Sunday Times*, 8 November 2015.

5. https://www.irishtimes.com/life-and-style/people/i-think-the-main-thing-the-abbey-can-do-right-now-is-listen-the-women-s-podcast-1.2422734.

6. Helen Meany, 'Irish theatre abounds with brilliant women – unlike the Abbey's programme', *The Guardian*, 9 November 2015.

7. The original three volumes of the *Field Day Anthology of Irish Writing*, all edited by men, had omitted all but a handful of women writers. A public outcry and apology ensued and 12 years later volumes IV and V were published, filled with writing by women.

Chapter 3: Public Meeting at the Abbey Theatre

1. Annie Horniman (1860–1937) bought the property on Abbey Street and had it converted into a theatre. She supported the Abbey financially from 1904–1910. Portrait by John Butler Yeats, commissioned by Annie Horniman for the opening of the Abbey in December 1904.

2. The Abbey's first leading lady. Portrait by John B Yeats, 1904. Also a Cumann na mBan officer, she took part in the Easter Rising of 1916 serving at Jacob's Biscuit Factory.

3. Paula Geraghty contacted Lian out of the blue to offer her services in documenting the event. Paula, aka Trade Union TV, is a photojournalist who has been documenting socially progressive movements, often workers and community protests since 2009, as a way of supporting these groups to tell their stories.

4. Annie Horniman funded the Abbey in its early days, Lady Augusta Gregory was a co-founder with W.B. Yeats, and warrior Queen Medhb (Maeve) was featured on the logo with her Irish Wolfhound.

5. Incidentally the same hotel where Cumann na mBan was founded in 1914 (see Mary McAuliffe's foreword.)

Chapter 4: Speeches from the Public Meeting

1. The noble call is an Irish tradition where someone is invited to sing a song or say a poem. In February 2014, drag queen and gay rights activist Panti Bliss/Rory O'Neill was invited by the Abbey to make a noble call after a performance of *Strumpet City*. Rory had previously stated that two prominent journalists were homophobic while being interviewed on RTÉ. RTÉ swiftly apologised to the journalists and paid them a settlement, which caused a public uproar. At the Abbey Panti gave a speech about internalised homophobia, and having to 'check myself' in public. The speech was filmed (coincidently by Lian Bell's brother, Conor Horgan), went viral around the world, and had a significant impact in the run up to the referendum on Marriage Equality.

2. Reference to Fiach's tweet to Belinda during the first public Twitter exchange, 'Write your play.'

3. Travellers were finally formally recognised as an ethnic group by the Irish State on 1 March 2017 after many decades of campaigning by the Irish Traveller Movement and other Traveller activists and organisations.

4. This text has been slightly amended by Rosaleen.

5. Lanigan's pub in Dublin at that time had a small theatre venue for new work upstairs, set up in 2012 by Karl Shiels and Laura Honan.

6. The Lir National Academy of Dramatic Art at Trinity College Dublin.

7. Until 2018, abortion was illegal in the Republic of Ireland, therefore many women had to travel abroad, often to the UK, to access abortion care.

8. Rough Magic's musical *The Train*, by Bill Whelan and Arthur Riordan and directed by Lynne Parker, had a sellout run at the 2015 Dublin Theatre Festival. It was revived in 2017, was performed on the Abbey stage and at the MAC in Belfast, and incorporated the actual #WakingTheFeminists banner into the set, when it was flown in for the final song.

9. Ian Maleney, 'Marina Carr: How wonderful to burn down the whole world', *Irish Times,* 22 August 2015.

10. Ali White's play, *Me, Mollser*, was described in the Abbey launch promotional material as 'a monologue for children'. It was the only play written by a woman announced in the programme.

11. The Lyric is the principle producing theatre in Northern Ireland.

12. Eleanor coined this as a portmanteau of Easter Rising and Estrogen.

13. The actor Mick Lally was the third of the three founding members of Druid Theatre Company in Galway in 1975.

14. Thank you.

15. Thank you.

16. Justin Trudeau was elected Canada's prime minister in October 2015.

Jessica Murphy, 'Trudeau gives Canada first cabinet with equal number of men and women', *The Guardian*, 4 November 2015.

17. Annie Horiman funded the Abbey in its early days, Lady Augusta Gregory was a co-founder with W. B. Yeats, and warrior Queen Medhb/Maeve with her Irish Wolfhound was the Abbey logo.

PART TWO
Chapter 5: Preparing for a Year of Campaigning

1. This is pure sarcasm. It referred to the inclusion of Michael Colgan, Director of the Gate Theatre, on the panel of the Marian Finucane Show on RTÉ Radio One, and his being asked to explain this feminist movement to the nation days after the public meeting.

2. In thinking about structuring the #WakingTheFeminists website we looked at what other campaigns were doing, particularly Black Lives Matter.

3. This further demonstrates the need for the work of Women On Air, founded in 2010 by journalist and entrepreneur Margaret E. Ward. All these spheres of silencing and marginalising women in the public sphere work together to reinforce the patriarchy.

4. Justine McCarthy, journalist with the *Sunday Independent*, discussed the #WakingTheFeminists event with Marian and Michael. None of them had attended. Justine commented:

> I think it was a very important day, and I think it might be a turning point. I felt very sorry for him [Fiach Mac Conghail], actually, from the start, because he suffered from something I think most of us suffer from, and this is that unconscious bias that we have. I think he was mortified, and very disappointed in himself when he realised it. I thought it was admirable that he didn't spend long trying to defend it, and he did become contrite and he used that extraordinary expression that he failed to check his privilege, which I think will enter the jargon or the conversation of the nation. As a woman, I do fail to check my prejudice sometimes. I think we are so conditioned by this, that we don't even see it.

Michael Colgan griped about not having reserved a ticket to the public meeting reserved for him, saying: 'I would have thought if they do want to influence people who do make decisions, they might have found a spot for me, but they didn't in any event. But Fiach, because it was his building, you know he's the landlord, he got his own seat, and that was great. Maybe he might have preferred to give it to me.' He went on to say:

> But the fact is there is an injustice, and it goes into other things. It's not just confined to this. I'm absolutely convinced I would have subliminal prejudice. Now what I would never do, and what Fiach would never do, and what nobody

would never do, we would never turn down a great play because it was written by a woman, but we're not talking about that. And I do think that Nadine O'Regan's article in the *Sunday Business Post* goes over the top, because she talks about that meeting, and I'll quote, which put a horror into me: 'even women who have worked for the Abbey Theatre, a vulnerable few with a lot to lose, stood up and were counted.' Now, that is absolutely preposterous, as if somebody would penalise somebody. She goes on to say that one of the writers, people said, Gina Moxley said 'Women with opinions or ambition, are regarded as trouble. Awkward c-words, crazy bitches and are sidelined or blacklisted.' This is now going far too far and that doesn't happen. I've been working for thirty two years, and you know, there's seven of us in the administration hub – six women and myself – there's a great deal in the Fringe, there's an awful lot of great women – Grace Dyas and people like that who are working, and we mustn't lose sight of the real fact – is there should be more women playwrights and there has to be a reason why they aren't, and we have to get to that reason and work out why it is.

The Marian Finucane Show, *RTÉ Radio One*, 15 November 2015. https://www.rte.ie/radio/radio1/marian-finucane/2015/1115/742060-marian-finucane-sunday-15-november-2015/.

5. A ground-breaking programme to tackle gender inequality in UK theatre, initiated in 2013 by Lucy Kerbel. http://www.tonictheatre-advance.co.uk/about/.

6. http://www.americantheatre.org/2015/06/09/7-steps-for-achieving-gender-parity-in-the-theatre/.

7. https://playwrightsguild.ca/wp-content/uploads/2024/12/FINAL-EIT-Report_4-22-15.pdf.

8. Several months later, Lian and Sarah attended two days of intensive media training organised by Women on Air. By that stage there wasn't the intensity of media interest and a lot of learning had already been done on the hoof. Nonetheless, the training was very useful.

9. https://www.irishtheatreinstitute.ie/news/bust-of-christine-longford-unveiled-at-gate-theatre/.

10. The core committee started as: Anne Clarke (with press and marketing sign off), Caroline Williams, Cian O'Brien, Dairne O'Sullivan (press officer), Lian Bell, Loughlin Deegan, Lynne Parker, Maria Fleming, Niamh Ní Chonchubhair (social media connector), Sarah Durcan, and Tanya Dean (research connector). The research group was led by Brenda Donohue, and liaised with the Irish Theatre Institute. The social media and website group were Oonagh Murphy and Noelia Ruiz. Lisa Tierney Keogh was the international organisation link-up and formed the New York chapter of #WakingTheFeminists. Kate Ferris was the liaison with the technical theatre sector.

11. The reasons why are further explored in the following chapters.

12. Irish Theatre Institute is a resource organisation that nurtures, promotes and drives the ambition of Irish theatre makers and Irish theatre.

13. Deputy Prime Minister.

14. Emer O'Kelly, 'Theatre: GBS strikes the right note of humour', *Irish Independent*, 14 December 2015.

15. https://womenandhollywood.com/guest-post-waking-the-feminists-starts-a-revolution-in-ireland-6001d361561c/.

16. This is borne out in Arts Council research in their 'Arts Insights Report 2024'.

17. Susan Coughlan. https://artofchange.ie/

18. Community Foundation Ireland is a philanthropic hub for Ireland which is a source of knowledge, expertise and information to ensure effective and strategic giving, with a mission of equality for all in thriving communities. https://www.communityfoundation.ie/

Chapter 6: Seeking Advice and Meeting the Arts Council and Government Ministers

1. The National Women's Council is the leading national representative organisation for women and women's groups in Ireland, founded in 1973.

2. The Abortion Rights Campaign (ARC) is a grassroots all-volunteer group dedicated to achieving free, safe and legal abortion care everywhere on the island of Ireland.

3. The Artists' Campaign to Repeal the Eighth Amendment was set up in 2015 by Cecily Brennan, Alice Maher, Eithne Jordan, and Paula Meehan.

4. Tanya Dean met with Michelle O'Donnell Keating from Women for Election at the National Gallery café on 26 November 2015.

5. Women in Film and Television Ireland (WFT) is a voluntary body promoting greater representation of women on screen and behind the camera. Lian Bell and Róise Goan met Rachel Lysaght of WFT on 12 July 2016 in the Filmbase café in Temple Bar.

6. 'The League of Professional Theatre Women is a not-for-profit organization that seeks to promote visibility and increase opportunities for women in the Professional Theatre. We do this through numerous programs and events.' http://theatrewomen.org/.

7. The Lillys, established in 2010 to promote gender and racial parity in American theatre, are discussed more in chapter nine.

8. 'The Kilroys are a gang of playwrights and producers in LA who are done talking about gender parity and are taking action. We mobilize others in our field and leverage our own power to support one another.' http://thekilroys.org/about/.

9. On 19 March 2016, Lian Bell met with Polly Kemp of Equal Representation for Actresses (ERA) in the Young Vic Theatre in London. ERA was set up in 2015 by actresses Lizzie Berrington and Polly Kemp.

10. https://www.aist.ie/team.

11. The BOI lounge was central, quiet, and free to book for any BOI business customer. We used it frequently throughout the year as it was also a neutral space for all parties.

12. Good advice that Lian completely forgot in 2018 when agreeing to take part in an event about contemporary feminism organised by a student society in Trinity College Dublin, as one of a panel of five white women. Students, including Shubhangi Karmakar of the Graduate Students Union, rightly protested its lack of diversity and the event was cancelled.

13. State Boards is part of publicjobs.ie, the centralised provider of recruitment, assessment and selection services in Ireland for the Civil Service, Local Authorities, the Health Service Executive, An Garda Síochána, and public bodies.

14. Represented by Anne Clarke, Lisa Tierney Keogh, Maria Fleming, Róise Goan, and Sarah Durcan.

15. Archbishop Desmond Tutu was Archbishop Emeritus of Cape Town and Nobel Peace Laureate; a veteran anti-apartheid activist and peace campaigner widely regarded as 'South Africa's moral conscience'. The Elders was founded by Nelson Mandela in 2007 as an independent group of global leaders working for peace, justice, human rights, and a sustainable planet.

16. Silicon Republic's international event which brought creative minds in science, technology and the arts together for fresh perspectives on leadership, innovation, and diversity.

17. Our aspirational version of Advance was soon to be referred to as *Ardú*, meaning raise or uplift in Irish, and is described in more detail in the next chapter.

18. https://www.tonictheatre.co.uk/advance/.

19. To support our call for research, we talked through figures that already existed according to an analysis of Irish Theatre Institute's Irish Playography, which holds information on all new plays produced in Ireland. According to the statistics gathered from the Playography, only 29 per cent of new plays staged in Ireland's main theatres from 2000–2014 were written by women, and 17 per cent of those performed at the Abbey Theatre. Similarly only 36 per cent of all new plays in the same period were directed by women, 13 per cent at the Abbey. We also highlighted statistics from Theatre Forum's 2015 Payscales Survey. The majority of people working in theatre were earning less than €35,000 a year. There were considerably more women than men working in theatre overall, but as the pay scale rises, women dropped off a steep cliff. At the top of the scale, just a few men were earning the biggest salaries.

20. Represented by Cian O'Brian, Caroline Williams, and Jen Coppinger.

21. Olwen Dawe is a leading Policy Analyst and Consultant who specialises in developing and implementing equality, diversity and inclusion projects. Olwen was instrumental in the years after #WakingTheFeminists in developing EDI strategies for the Arts Council and several other national cultural institutions.

22. The Strategy's overarching aim was an Ireland where all women enjoy equality with men and can achieve their full potential, while enjoying a safe and fulfilling life. It contained 20 key objectives and over 200 planned actions to achieve this vision, grouped under three key themes: equalising socio–economic opportunity for women; ensuring the well–being of women; and engaging women as equal and active citizens.

Chapter 7: Meetings with Theatre Companies, and the Advance Programme (*Ardú*)

1. Lian Bell, '#WakingTheFeminists still waiting for the Abbey', *Irish Times,* 16 December 2016.

2. Fintan O'Toole, 'Three arts questions that need answers', *Irish Times*, 13 November 2015.

3. The fourth member of the committee, Mark Ryan, was not available to attend this meeting.

4. Full list of Advance participants in 2014 and 2016 can be found at https://www.tonictheatre.co.uk/advance/#participants.

5. https://www.tonictheatre.co.uk/advance/.

6. Attendees included Loretta Dignam and Deirdre Kinahan, Abbey board members and members of its gender equality subcommittee; Teerth Chungh, the Gate's Head of Production; Willie White, Director of Dublin Theatre Festival; Bride Rosney, board member for Druid with Sarah Lynch, Executive Director; Kris Nelson, Director of Dublin Fringe Festival; Cian O'Brien, Director of Project Arts Centre; Andrew Parkes, board member of Fishamble with Gavin Kostick, Literary Manager of Fishamble; and Caroline Williams, Producer of Rough Magic.

7. See page XXX

Chapter 8: Other Events and Power Plays

1. Nollaig na mBan (Women's Christmas) is traditionally a day when women, having done all the work to prepare for Christmas (not to mention year-round), were given a 'day off' to socialise with their relatives and friends, while the men took on domestic duties.

2. Garry Hynes on *The Marian Finucane Show*, *RTÉ Radio One*, 16 January 2016.

Chapter 9: Winning Awards

1. Lian was also given a number of other awards in 2016 for her work, including the Praeses Elit Award (Trinity College Dublin's Law Society), the Bram Stoker Award (Trinity College Dublin's Philosophical Society), and an Outstanding Young Person Award from the Dublin branch of Junior Chamber International. She was made an Honorary Patron of DU Players, Trinity College Dublin's drama society, in 2018.

2. The Lillys started as an awards ceremony in New York in 2010, established by Julia Jordan, Theresa Rebeck, and Marsha Norman. Named after the writer Lillian Hellman, the group describe their purpose as 'celebrating, funding and fighting for women by promoting gender and racial parity in the American theatre.' Since 2015, in collaboration with the Dramatists Guild (USA), they have conducted a national survey called The Count. In early 2016, through Lisa Tierney Keogh, Julia and Marsha contacted Lian. They all met in April in New York while Lian was on tour as designer with Corn Exchange's *A Girl is a Half-Formed Thing*. There was much mutual solidarity and they agreed to share resources and help amplify each other's work. Julia and Marsha told Lian that they wanted to present #WakingTheFeminists with the first International Lilly Award. As Sarah was going to Washington for work in May, she extended her trip to include attending the awards with Lisa Tierney Keogh.

3. See chapter one.

4. HowlRound Theatre Commons YouTube video of the 2016 Lilly Awards can be found here: https://www.youtube.com/watch?v=sP2OvTve90k.

5. See Ciara O'Dowd's *Wild-Looking But Fine: Abbey Actresses of the 1930s* (Dublin, 2024) for more on the long relationship between the Irish and New York theatre scenes.

6. Shari Lifland, 'The 2016 Lilly Awards Honor Achievements of Women in the Theater', *Huffpost*, 25 May 2016.

7. https://www.irishtimes.com/culture/stage/waking-the-feminists-wins-special-us-award-1.2659404.

8. https://www.tonictheatre.co.uk/tonic-awards-2018/.

9. Rebecca Solnit, *Hope in the Dark: Untold Histories, Wild Possibilities* (Edinburgh, 2016).

Chapter 10: *Spring Forward*: International Women's Day Public Meeting and Speeches

1. Róise Goan sourced the speakers and Oonagh Murphy shaped the material and directed. Maria Fleming and Kate Ferris liaised with Liberty Hall, Molly O'Cathain worked on stage dressing, Zia Holly on lights, and Aisling O'Brien and Jen Coppinger worked on box office. Niamh Ní Chonchubhair was on social media, and Noelia Ruiz updated our website and ran a live stream so people could view remotely.

2. Despite conducting a series of interviews, the documentary was unfortunately not completed. An overview of the project can be found here: https://themsthebreaksfilm.tumblr.com/.

3. Diva Voces is an all-female choir based in Dublin.

4. Elaine Burke, 'Accenture International Women's Day event celebrates spectrum of success', *Silicon Republic*, 8 March 2016.

5. Paige Reynolds, 'At Law Soc, Awe-Inspiring Panel of Eight Women Discuss New-Wave Feminism', *University Times*, 9 March 2016.

6. Garry Hynes was working in the US.

7. This is how stage managers call lighting cues.

Chapter 11: The Things We May Not Say In Case We Get in Trouble

* No notes

Chapter 12: Research, Statistics, and Data Analysis

1. On 10 November 2016, #WakingTheFeminists received a letter of support signed by 38 members of the Feminist Research group of the International Federation of Theatre Research, representing feminist scholars, critics, and artists from Sweden, India, Pakistan, Britain, Sri Lanka, China, Japan, South Korea, Finland, Chile, Spain, Germany, Ireland, Canada, Australia, Greece, Brazil, Slovenia, and the United States.

2. https://www.irishtimes.com/opinion/letters/women-and-the-abbey-theatre-1.2415780

3. PLAYOGRAPHYIreland comprises two comprehensive online searchable databases: Irish Playography (all new professionally produced Irish plays written in English since the formation of the Abbey in 1904) and Playography na Gaeilge (all new plays written and produced in the Irish language since 1901).

4. https://implicit.harvard.edu/implicit/takeatest.html.

5. Emily Glassberg Sands, *Opening the Curtain on Playwright Gender: An Integrated Economic Analysis of Discrimination in American Theater* (Princeton, 2009).

6. 'Survey of Payscales 2016', Theatre Forum, February 2016.

7. http://www.wakingthefeminists.org/2015/11/10/triona-ni-dhuibhir/.

8. Research from *Gender Counts* by Dr Brenda Donohue et al.

9. Pan Pan's Co-Artistic Director, Gavin Quinn, directs the company's shows.

10. Further research can be found at http://www.wakingthefeminists.org/research/.

Chapter 13: *One Thing More*: Final Public Event

1. She changed her name to V in 2019 to free her identity from that of the father who abused her.

2. The Safe Ireland Summit, 14–15 November 2015, was designed with the aim of making a safer world for women and children, and challenging the culture that facilitates domestic violence.

3. Later in December, as a final wrap up gift to the companies participating in the research, we gave them a copy of her book.

4. Eltahawy's first book, *Headscarves and Hymens: Why the Middle East Needs a Sexual Revolution*, was published in the United States in 2015, by Farrar, Straus and Giroux. In 2020, she founded the newsletter *Feminist Giant*.

5. V's *The Vagina Monologues*, has been published in over 48 languages, performed in over 140 countries, and heralded by *The New York Times* as one of the 'best American plays' of the past 25 years and that 'no recent hour of theater has had a greater impact worldwide.'

6. https://mamsireland.wordpress.com/

7. It's not feminism's fault. It's experience of long-term structural disempowerment that can lead to this 'in-fighting' among women.

8. https://camilleosullivan.com/.

9. We did celebrate a little that same evening in the Black Sheep on Capel Street. Sarah Durcan left the gathering early to go to TV3 studios to speak about #WakingTheFeminists on *Tonight with Vincent Browne*.

10. Rebecca Moynihan, Deputy Lord Mayor, had offered to arrange this after she attended the *One Thing More* event.

Chapter 14: Speeches from *One Thing More*

1. National University of Ireland Galway, now University of Galway.

2. Isabella Tod (1836–96) established the North of Ireland Women's Suffrage Association *c*.1871.

3. Anna Haslam (1829–1922) was secretary, then president of the newly founded Dublin Women's Suffrage Association (DWSA).

4. Hilda Tweedy (1911–2005) co-founded the Irish Housewives Association, and was first Chairperson of The Council for the Status of Women (later the National Women's Council).

5. Andrée Sheehy Skeffington (1910–98). Her daughter, Micheline Sheehy Skeffington, spoke at *One Thing More*.

6. Selina Cartmell was appointed in 2016. She served a five year term, and was followed by co-CEOs Róisín McBrinn (Artistic Director) and Colm O'Callaghan (Executive Director).

7. Selina had been announced as the incoming Director of the Gate, but had not yet taken up the position.

8. Col Maureen O'Brien became the first female Major General in the Irish Defence Forces in 2021 (the second highest rank), and was appointed as a UN military advisor on peacekeeping operations.

9. Hanna Sheehy Skeffington (1877–1946), political activist and journalist. When Hanna married Frank Skeffington (1878–1916) in 1903, they took each other's surnames as a symbol of the equality of their relationship. The couple were committed to many causes, particularly feminism, pacifism, socialism, and nationalism. Francis Sheehy Skeffington was shot dead while being detained by the British during the 1916 Rising. He was wearing a *Votes for Women* pin at the time, which is now part of the collection of the National Museum of Ireland. Hanna edited the Irish suffrage paper The Irish Citizen from 1916–20.

10. National University of Ireland, Galway, now University of Galway.

11. The High Court case was settled by NUIG in 2018. 'Sheehy Skeffington donated her compensation to help the female lecturers – Dr Margaret Hodgins, Dr Sylvie Lannegrand, Dr Adrienne Gorman and Dr Róisín Healy – with their case.'

12. See https://michelinesthreeconditions.wordpress.com for details of the case and campaign.

13. The Globe Theatre in London, a reconstructed Shakespearean venue. Emma Rice assumed the role of Artistic Director in April 2016, but by November 2016, just at the end of her first season, announced she was stepping down.

14. Eve Ensler changed her name to V in 2019 to free her identity from that of the father who abused her.

15. Reference to Danai Gurira's speech at the 2016 Lilly Awards.

16. Referring to the result of the 2016 election in the USA.

PART THREE
Chapter 15: After the End: Legacy and Impact

1. Over 90 media outlets in Ireland and internationally covered the campaign during the year, many featuring it multiple times.

2. Ciara L. Murphy et al., '5 Years On: Gender in Irish Theatre, #WakingThe Feminists', 2020. http://www.wakingthefeminists.org/wp-content/uploads/2020/11/5-Years-On_-Gender-in-Irish-Theatre-FINAL.pdf.

3. Mary Moynihan, 'How Waking The Feminists set an equality agenda for Irish theatre', *RTÉ*, 22 November 2018.

4. https://artscouncil.ie/developing-the-arts/developmental-policies/equality-diversity-and-inclusion-policy-and-implementation-plan/.

5. https://citizensassembly.ie/wp-content/uploads/2023/03/lian-bell-waking-the-feminists.pdf.

6. Maggie Cronin, '"The Headcount": A survey on the gender breakdown of eight Arts Council of Northern Ireland core-funded theatre companies 2014-2019' (Belfast, 2021), pp 6-7.

7. https://culturalpolicyireland.org/2021/11/29/waking-the-feminists-the-headcount-report/ research team: Maggie Cronin, Vittoria Caffola, Caoileann Curry-Thompson, Liz Cullinane, and Louise Parker.

8. Ibid.

9. Conor Gallagher and Laurence Mackin, 'Seven women allege abuse and harassment by Michael Colgan', *Irish Times*, 4 November 2017.

10. Michael Colgan, 'I have been responsible for causing distress and I am truly sorry', *Sunday Independent*, 12 November 2017.

11. Gate Theatre Confidential Independent Review Report, Gaye Cunningham, 1 March 2018. https://gatetheatre.ie/wp-content/uploads/2018/03/Independent-Review-Report-into-Gate-Theatre-by-Gaye-Cunningham.pdf.

12. Ibid.

13. 'The Board Of The Gate Theatre Issues Apology', 9 February 2018. The full statement can be found at https://gatetheatre.ie/the-board-of-the-gate-theatre-issues-apology/.

14. While #WakingTheFeminists was wound-up at this point, Sarah Durcan thought a multi-disciplinary approach would be helpful as so many in the theatre are not aware of their rights. Sarah contacted Olwen Dawe, Dr Brenda Donohue, and legal expert Sarah Kieran and others to suggest this practical intervention. The toolkit was compiled by Olwen and Brenda, with expert insight from: Ivana Bacik, Katie Cadden, Sarah Kieran, and Orlaith Mannion. Designed by Siobhan Griffin of Alphabet Soup, and published 13 November 2017. (And yes, we should have called it the 'Anti-Harassment Toolkit', as Bride Rosney pointed out to us at the Speak Up & Call It Out event in Liberty Hall on 21 March 2018.)

15. Safe to Create is a collaborative programme of supports looking to transform workplace culture and practices, and to provide safe and respectful working conditions for those working in the arts and creative sectors. It is managed by Irish Theatre Institute, in partnership with the Arts Council, Screen Ireland and Minding Creative Minds, on behalf of the Department of Tourism, Culture, Arts, Gaeltacht, Sport and Media.

16. Abbey Theatre Annual Review 2023, p. 81.

17. It also includes a portrait of Lian printed on a bathmat in a charity shop gilt frame; a joke by friends in tribute to the iconic tapestry portrait of Mary Robinson that sat in the window of a Turkish rug shop on Dame Street, Dublin through the early 2000s.

18. Formerly Smock Alley Theatre, Temple Bar, Dublin.

Chapter 16: What Now? Looking to the Future

1. Lynne Parker, 'The Abbey does so much. But Ireland needs a national theatre for the 21st century', *Irish Times*, 24 February 2025.

2. http://itmarchive.ie/web/News/Current/Irish-Theatre-Magazine-Press-Release. aspx.html.

3. Mary Carolan, 'Irish Theatre Awards judging for 2023 paused while review of process takes place', *Irish Times*, 20 February 2023.

The awards were 'paused' after the Abbey Theatre made a statement about the 2022 nominations: 'Although the cast of *An Octoroon* was made up of a majority of people of colour (8/10), a decision was made to only recognise the two white actors for nominations among all the individuals in the cast and creative team. We believe this is unacceptable. It is worth noting that all 16 acting nominations are white.'

Mark Hilliard, 'Theatre group finds awards nominations "unacceptable"', *Irish Times*, 11 February 2023.

4. Additional research along the model of Emily Glassberg Sands' research could be carried out, tracking box-office income, venue capacity and duration of run against the gender of the main creative artists. Emily Glassberg Sands, *Opening the Curtain on Playwright Gender: An Integrated Economic Analysis of Discrimination in American Theater* (Princeton, 2009).

Waking to Patriarchy

1. As Emer O'Toole put it, 'ninety percent of the plays were written by men' and 'eighty percent of the plays were directed by men'. Emer O'Toole, 'Waking the Feminists: Re-imagining the Space of the National Theatre in the Era of the Celtic Phoenix' in *LIT: Literature Interpretation Theory*, 28:2 (2017), p. 2.

2. Christopher Murray, *Twentieth-Century Irish Drama: Mirror Up to Nation* (Manchester, 1997), p. 1.

3. Clare Wallace and Ondřej Pilný argued had already intensified during the 21st century via a 'critical interest in Irish theatre' that was 'spurred on in part by the Abbey Theatre centenary in 2004 and reassessments of its history', as well as 'by the emergence of a vibrant new generation of playwrights and the international success of a handful of Irish directors and dramatists'.

Wallace, Clare, and Ondřej Pilný. 'Home Places: Irish Drama since 1990', Scott Brewster and Michael Parker, eds., in *Irish Literature Since 1990: Diverse Voices* (Manchester, 2009), p. 43.

4. Emer O'Toole, 'Waking the Feminists: Re-imagining the Space of the National Theatre in the Era of the Celtic Phoenix' in *LIT: Literature Interpretation Theory*, 28:2 (2017), p. 1.

5. Murphy, Ciara L., 'Reflecting Irishness, Mirroring Histories: Performing Commemoration in Irish Theatre in 2015' in *New Hibernia Review / Iris Éireannach Nua*, 20:3, (2016), pp 123–4.

6. Melissa Sihra, 'Introduction' in *Women in Irish Drama: A Century of Authorship and Representation* (New York, 2007), p. 1.

7. Margaret Kelleher, 'The Field Day Anthology and Irish Women's Literary Studies', in *The Irish Review*, 30 (2003), p. 92.

8. Claire Bracken, 'Gender and Irish Studies since 2008' in Renée Fox, Mike Cronin and Brian Ó Conchubhair, eds., *Routledge Handbook of Irish Studies* (Oxfordshire, 2021), p. 239.

9. Ibid., p. 241.

10. Poethead is 'a woman-friendly publishing platform that prioritised women poets, their translators, and their editors' run by poet Chris Murray, https://poethead.wordpress.com/c-murray-the-poethead-site/.

11. https://poethead.wordpress.com/2017/12/16/fired-irish-women-poets-and-the-canon-preamble-to-the-pledge/.

12. 'Fired! Women Poets and the Canon has been a collaborative effort occurring over some months of discussion and debate. We would like to acknowledge the help and support of Eavan Boland, Rita Ann Higgins, Dr. Lucy Collins, Emma Penney, Ailbhe Darcy, Mary O'Donnell, Chris Allen, Jaclyn Allen, Kate Dempsey, Kimberly Campanello, Laura Loftus, Maria McManus, Moyra Donaldson, Melony Bethala, Kate O'Shea, Alex Pryce, Katie Donovan, Doireann Ní Ghríofa, Nessa O'Mahony, Sarah Clancy, Elaine Feeny, Elaine Cosgrove, Fióna Bolger, Victoria Kennefick, Dr. Anne Mulhall, Barbara Smith, Gillian Hamill, Anne Tannam, Maureen Boyle, Stephanie Conn, Alice Kinsella, Paul Casey, Lia Mills, Katie Donovan, Colin Dardis (Lagan Online), Mark Andresen, and Selina Guinness. Thank you for writing, editing, suggesting and supporting this project in whatever way that you could over these months. Thank you to our northern Irish poet friends who hosted the first Fired! (Maria McManus, you did trojan work, thanks). Thanks to Bernadette Dignam who provided our site and events artwork.' https://thepledgearchived.home.blog/responses-to-fired/fired-acknowledgements/.

13. Ailbhe D'Arcy and David Wheatley, eds, *A History of Irish Women's Poetry* (Cambridge, 2021).

14. David Clare, Fiona McDonagh, Justine Nakase, eds, *The Golden Thread: Irish Women Playwrights, 1716 – 2016* (Limerick, 2017).

15. Melissa Sihra, 'Introduction' in Melissa Sihra, ed., *Women in Irish Drama: A Century of Authorship and Representation* (New York, 2007), p. 3.

16. Gerardine Meaney, *The Field Day Anthology of Irish Writing Volumes 4 and 5: Irish Women's Writing and Traditions*, 4 (Cork; New York, 2002), p. 771.

17. Margaret Kelleher, 'The Field Day Anthology and Irish Women's Literary Studies', in *The Irish Review*, 30 (2003), p. 92.

18. An important part of keeping women's work in view is represented by *The Golden Thread: Irish Women Playwrights, 1716–2016,* David Clare, Fiona McDonagh, Justine Nakase, eds., (Limerick, 2017).

19. Emer O'Toole, 'Waking the Feminists: Re-imagining the Space of the National Theatre in the Era of the Celtic Phoenix', in *LIT: Literature Interpretation Theory*, 28:2, (2017), p. 16.

20. Ibid., p. 3. This also featured O'Toole's own breath-taking dramatisation with Susan Cahill in which O'Toole personified the patriarchy in dialogue with Cahill, who recounted her own experience of an unplanned pregnancy.

21. See Fogarty, Anne. 'Deliberately personal?: The politics of identity in contemporary Irish women's writing', in *Nordic Irish Studies*, 1 (2002), p. 1.

22. Claire Bracken, *Irish Feminist Futures* (Oxfordshire, 2016).

23. Luce Irigaray, *This Sex which is Not One*, translated by Catherine Porter with Carolyn Burke (Ithaca, 1985).

24. See Fogarty, Anne, '"The influence of absences": Eavan Boland and the silenced history of Irish women's poetry,' in *Colby Quarterly*, 35: 4 (2019), pp 256–74.

25. Gerardine Meaney, 'Waking the Dead: Antigone, Ismene and Anne Enright's narrators in mourning', in Claire Bracken and Susan Cahill, eds, *Irish Writers in their Time: Anne Enright* (Dublin, 2011), pp 99–113.

26. Sean O'Casey's *The Plough and the Stars*, Frank McGuinness's *Observe the Sons of Ulster Marching Towards the Somme* and Tom Murphy's *The Wake*.

27. https://www.irishtimes.com/culture/stage/abbey-theatre-to-interrogate-rather-than-celebrate-easter-rising-1.2408870.

28. Molly Mullin, 'Representations of history, Irish feminism, and the politics of difference', in *Feminist Studies*, 17:1 (1991), p. 34.

29. Eavan Boland, *Outside History: Selected Poems 1980–1990* (Manchester, 1990).

30. O'Toole points out that, '[t]hough the quality of White's work is not in question here, it is telling that women tend to be afforded more recognition in the Irish arts when the work is aimed at children'. Emer O'Toole, 'Waking the Feminists: Re-imagining the space of the National Theatre in the era of the Celtic Phoenix', in *LIT: Literature Interpretation Theory*, 28:2 (2017), p. 4.

31. Sarah Browne, 'Feminism, survival and the arts in Ireland', in *L'Internationale Online* (May 2018) https://www.internationaleonline.org/contributions/feminism-survival-and-the-arts-in-ireland/ (2018). Browne cites Sara Ahmed: 'Citation is feminist memory. It is how we leave a trail of where we have been and who helped us along the way.'

32. Clara Fischer, 'Gender, Nation, and the Politics of Shame: Magdalen Laundries and the institutionalization of feminine transgression in Modern Ireland' in *Signs*, 41:4 (2016), pp 821–43.

33. Susan McKay, 'Ireland and rape crises', in *The Irish Review*, 35 (2007), p. 93.

34. Patricia Hill Collins, *Black Feminist Thought: Knowledge, Consciousness, And the Politics of Empowerment,* (Oxfordshire, 2009) pp 287–88.

35. For a discussion of the intensification of the overlap between sex and violence physical and digital spaces, as well as the significant rise in the amount of young women reporting being strangled without consent in sex, see Debbie Ging and Eugenia Siapera, eds., *Gender Hate Online: Understanding the New Anti-feminism* (London, 2019); Debbie Ging, 'Digital culture, online misogyny and gender-based violence' in Margaret Gallagher and Aimee Vega Montiel, eds, *Handbook on Gender, Communication and Women's Human Rights* (Hoboken, 2023), pp 213–27; Debbie Ging, 'Tactics of Hate: toxic 'creativity' in anti-feminist men's rights politics', in Alan Boyle and Susan Berridge, eds, *The Routledge Companion to Gender, Media and Violence* (Oxfordshire, 2024), pp 348–58.

36. Miriam Haughton, 'From Laundries to Labour Camps: Staging Ireland's 'Rule of Silence' in Anu Productions' *Laundry*' in *Modern Drama*, 57:1 (2014), p. 70.

37. Ibid.

38. See Nell McCafferty, *Goodnight Sisters: Selected Writings* (Cork, 1990).

39. Nancy Folbre, *The Rise and Decline of Patriarchal Systems: An Intersectional Political Economy* (New York, 2021), p. 23.

40. Gayatri Chakravorty Spivak, 'Can the subaltern speak?', in Rosalind C. Morris, ed., *Can the Subaltern Speak?: Reflections on the History of an Idea*, (New York, 2010), pp 21–78.

41. https://gatetheatre.ie/wp-content/uploads/2018/03/Independent-Review-Report-into-Gate-Theatre-by-Gaye-Cunningham-1.pdf.

42. https://www.irishtheatreinstitute.ie/wp-content/uploads/2021/10/ITI-Speak-Up-A-Call-for-Change-Report-Oct2021_Final_WEB.pdf.

43. https://wft.ie/wp-content/uploads/2017/11/WTF_Harassment_Toolkit_AmplifyWomen-1.pdf.

44. https://www.fairple.com/report.

45. https://www.safetocreate.ie.

46. Physical assault – whether in intimate or public space – goes hand in glove with verbal and psychological assault in intimate, public or virtual spaces as the 'manosphere' has become increasingly unsafe for women. Women's Aid 2025 Audit reported there 'were increased reports of all forms of abuse against women: physical (+22 per cent), Sexual (+30 per cent), Emotional (+15 per cent) and Economic abuse (+5 per cent), and previously that 'more than one in three [Irish women] have now experienced psychological, physical and/or sexual abuse from an intimate partner'. More information can be found at https://www.womensaid.ie/get-informed/news-events/media-releases/record-number-of-contacts-with-and-disclosures-of-domestic-abuse-to-womens-aid-in-2024/.

Patriarchal structures are very clearly evident in a system that expects a woman and her children to uproot their lives and leave the family home and community, being displaced and facing precarity and possible homelessness, rather than removing the abuser and assuring continuity and familiarity for the family. In public spaces, '60% of women in Ireland have been harassed when running, with 6% having feared for their lives'; 'female members of the Oireachtas were significantly more likely to experience harassment online and be targeted by gendered abuse, such as slurs, threats of sexual violence, sexual harassment, and comments on their physical appearance, and 47% of abuse directed at all politicians is related to Women's Rights'; Violence Against Women in Politics 'is highly racialised, with black and minority ethnic women disproportionately targeted for abuse, particularly in online spaces. Younger women and LGBTQ+ women in politics are also at a greater risk'; and 'social media has become the number one place in which psychological violence – particularly in the form of sexist and misogynistic remarks, humiliating images, mobbing, intimidation and threats – is perpetrated against women parliamentarians.' Claire McGing and Valesca Lima, 'Online abuse of women in politics: The response of political parties in demonstrating leadership in promoting civil discourse in public life', 'Submission to the Oireachtas Task Force on Safe Participation in Political Life', https://data.oireachtas.ie/ie/oireachtas/parliamentaryBusiness/other/2024-05-15__submission-dr-claire-mcging-institute-of-art-design-and-technology-iadt_en.pdf.

47. Rana M. Jaleel, *The Work of Rape* (Durham, 2021).

48. See Nancy Folbre, *The Rise and Decline of Patriarchal Systems: An Intersectional Political Economy* (New York, 2021).

49. It is notable that in terms of the breaking scandals regarding sexual abuse and institutions, action accelerates when male victims speak out, they are – and rightly – embraced, believed and supported; while there are other factors that negatively impact male victims of patriarchal gender and sexual violence, male victims have rarely subjected to the same discrediting and speculation female victims have undergone in the media.

50. Susan McKay, 'Ireland and rape crises', in *The Irish Review,* 35 (2007) p. 92.

51. Ibid.

52. Lucy Caldwell, *Intimacies* (London, 2021).

53. 'Rapist culture', describes the actions of the perpetrator, while 'rape culture', describes a culture without any one with responsibility for intentional action, much as the description 'a woman was raped', only visualises the victim, while the phrase 'a man raped a woman/girl/boy', brings the perpetrator into the picture, with a clearer description of the intentional actions and behaviour needed to commit this crime.

54. Susan Brownmiller, *Against Our Will: Men, Women, and Rape* (New York, 1975). See also The Combahee River Collective, *The Combahee River Collective Statement*, 1977, http://circuitous.org/scraps/combahee.html; Johanna Fateman and Amy Scholder, eds., *Andrea Dworkin, Last Days at Hot Slit: The Radical Feminism of Andrea Dworkin* (Cambridge, 2019); Gloria Anzaldúa, *Borderlands/La Frontera: The New Mestiza,* (San Francisco, 1987); Barbara Christian, *Black Feminist Criticism: Perspectives on Black Women Writers* (Oxford, 1985).

55. Susan McKay, 'Ireland and rape crises', p. 93.

56. Nancy Folbre, *The Rise and Decline of Patriarchal Systems: An Intersectional Political Economy* (New York, 2021), p.23.

57. Patricia Hill Collins, *Black Feminist Thought: Knowledge, Consciousness, and the Politics of Empowerment,* (Oxfordshire, 2009), p. 288.

58. See Jennifer Redmond and Mary McAuliffe, eds, *The Politics of Gender and Sexuality in Modern Ireland: A Reader* (Dublin, 2024).

59. Sara Ahmed, *Complaint!* (Durham, 2021), p. 104.

60. Ibid.

61. Ibid.

62. Nancy Folbre, *The Rise and Decline of Patriarchal Systems: An Intersectional Political Economy* (New York, 2021), p. 22.

63. Kimberlé Williams Crenshaw, 'Mapping the margins: Intersectionality, identity politics, and violence against women of color', in *Stanford Law Review*, 43:6 (1991), p. 1,296.

64. Ibid.

65. Nancy Folbre, *The Rise and Decline of Patriarchal Systems: An Intersectional Political Economy* (New York, 2021), p. 22.

66. Emer O'Toole, 'Waking the Feminists: re-imagining the space of the national theatre in the era of the Celtic Phoenix' in *LIT: Literature, Interpretation, Theory*, 28: 2 (2017), p. 2: 'If little interrogation of masculine domination in Ireland was present in the Abbey's centenary reflections, there was little distortion either. At the time the program was announced, 84% of Dáil Eireann consisted of men; 72% of voices on current affairs radio programmes were male voices (Walsh, Suiter and O'Connor 35); over 90% of board members of Irish private companies 50 were men (Barry 11); men comprised 79% of broadsheet byline writers (Deane and O'Mahony); 82% of those at professorial level at University were men (and there has yet to be a female president of any Irish university) (O'Connor 24–25); 87% of produced screenplay writers in the Irish film industry were by men (Liddy 903); and men, of course, comprised 100% of 55 bishops in the Catholic church, an organization that continues to have immense influence over Ireland's education and health sectors'.

67. Fearghal McGarry, *The Abbey Rebels of 1916: A Lost Revolution* (Dublin, 2015).

68. Patricia Hill Collins, *Black Feminist Thought*: *Knowledge, Consciousness, and the Politics of Empowerment* (Oxfordshire, 2009), p. 288

69. See Robert Chapman, *Empire of Normality: Neurodiversity and Capitalism* (London, 2023).

70. For an extensive analysis of the role of MAMs in #WakingTheFeminists, see Brenda O'Connell, 'Waking The Feminists: Gender "Counts"' in Oona Frawley, ed., *Women and the Decade Of Commemorations* (Bloomington, 2021), pp 242–66.

71. The Care Collective, Andreas Chatzidakis, Jamie Hakim, Jo Littler, Catherine Rottenberg, and Lynne Segal, *The Care Manifesto*: *The Politics of Interdependence* (New York, 2020).

72. Silvia Federici, *Caliban and the Witch: Women, Capitalism and Primitive Accumulation* (New York, 2005).

73. See Anne O'Brien and Sarah Arnold, 'Creative Industries New Entrants as Equality, Diversity and Inclusion Change Agents?' in *Cultural Trends*, 33:2 (2022), pp 174–88; Anne O'Brien, *Women, Inequality and Media Work* (Oxfordshire, 2019), and Anne O'Brien, Paraic Kerrigan, and Susan Liddy, 'Conceptualising change in equality, diversity and inclusion: A case study of the Irish film and television sector', in *European Journal of Cultural Studies*, 26:3 (2022), pp 336–53.

74. Nancy Folbre, *The Rise and Decline of Patriarchal Systems: An Intersectional Political Economy* (New York, 2021), p. 88.

75. Sara Ahmed, *Complaint!* (Durham, 2021), p. 28.

76. Ibid.

77. Ibid.

78. Ibid.

79. Clare Keogh, '#WakingTheFeminists and the Data-Driven Revolution in Irish Theatre' in Elaine Aston and Melissa Sihra, eds, *Elements in Women Theatre Makers Series* (Cambridge, 2025), pp 1–65.

80. See: The Care Collective: Andreas Chatzidakis, Jamie Hakim, Jo Littler, Catherine Rottenberg, and Lynne Segal, *The Care Manifesto*: *The Politics of Interdependence* (New York, 2020); also, Ai-jen Poo, *The Age of Dignity: Preparing for the Elder Boom in a Changing America* (New York, 2016).

81. The pioneering lawyer, civil and women's rights activist Pauli (Anna Pauline) Murray, 'coined the term "Jane Crow" to describe that intersection [of being a Black woman in America], alluding to the Jim Crow laws across the South that enforced racial segregation'. Josie Cox, *Women Money Power: The Rise and Fall of Economic Equality* (New York, 2024), p. 86; Murray's landmark article, 'Jane Crow and the Law: Sex Discrimination and Title VII', in *The George Washington Law Review*, following the passage of the 1964 Civil Rights Act, explained how certain legal statutes meant to protect the civil rights of African Americans continued to limit the scope of liberties afforded to women.

82. 'I had to examine, in my dreams as well as in my immune–function tests, the devastating effects of overextension. Overextending myself is not stretching myself. I had to accept how difficult it is to monitor the difference. Necessary for me as cutting down on sugar. Crucial. Physically. Psychically. Caring for myself is not self–indulgence, it is self–preservation, and that is an act of political warfare'. Audre Lorde, *A Burst of Light* (Ithaca, 1988), p. 125.

83. Ibid.

84. Nancy Folbre, *The Rise and Decline of Patriarchal Systems: An Intersectional Political Economy* (New York, 2021), p. 11

85. https://www.tate.org.uk/art/artworks/guerrilla–girls–youre–seeing–less–than–half–the–picture–p78790.

86. Sara Ahmed, *Complaint!* (Durham, 2021), p. 30.

87. Ibid. See for more about the use of NDAs to prevent knowledge sharing and transfer about abuses of power.

88. Elizabeth M. Schneider, 'The violence of privacy', in *Brooklyn Law School: Brooklyn Works*, 1991, p. 998. She also points out that for women who have historically been considered either public or private property, the right to privacy and safety is crucial and that many feminists have argued for its reconceptualising as 'liberty', p. 997.

89. Sara Ahmed, *Complaint!* (Durham, 2021).

90. Ibid.

91. Even the most fleeting of glances at how language is weaponised against women entering any pubic discursive space demonstrate the power of this at work; current linguistic violence in digital space on the internet is an iteration of the same pubic is enough to. See Laura Bates, *Men Who Hate Women: From Incels to Pickup Artists, the Truth About Extreme Misogyny and How It Affects Us All* (New York, 2020).

92. 'Woke' was another term that originated in black activism, see Ishena Robinson, 'How Woke Went From "Black" to "Bad"', https://www.naacpldf.org/woke–black–bad/.

93. To the extent that by 2017 a 'Reclaim the Internet movement, modelled on the second wave feminist Reclaim the Night movement, was founded to address retaliative gender–violent responses to women, girls and non–conforming people taking up virtual public space'. See https://www.fawcettsociety.org.uk/reclaim–the–internet and https://www.fawcettsociety.org.uk/reclaim–the–internet.

Afterword

1. Roe v. Wade was a landmark 1973 US Supreme Court decision that established the constitutional right to abortion and legalised abortion nationwide.

2. Reference to a 1983 article written by Irish journalist, playwright, civil rights campaigner, and feminist Nell McCafferty about the Abortion Referendum. https://thedublinreview.com/article/testimony-to-a-flowering/

3. See Kate Ferris's speech in chapter ten.

4. The Irish Women's Liberation Movement demanded equal pay, equality before the law, equal education, contraception, and justice for deserted wives, unmarried mothers and widows. https://www.mna100.ie/exhibitions/1970-79/

Acknowledgements

The authors would like to thank:

The core organisers of the campaign, including (but definitely not limited to) Anne Clarke, Caroline Williams, Ciara O'Dowd, Tanya Dean, Loughlin Deegan, Brenda Donohue, Dairne O'Sullivan, Kate Ferris, and Maria Fleming; all of the speakers and photographers who let us include their work in the publication; Dr Mary McAuliffe, Professor Moynagh Sullivan, and Catriona Crowe for their chapters; Niamh O'Donnell, Jane Daly, Siobhán Bourke, and all at Irish Theatre Institute; Noelle Moran, Caitlin O'Neill, and all at UCD Press for their support and expertise; Shane Gough and Fiachra McCarthy for their design work; thank you to the readers for the helpful feedback on the text; and Audrey Whitty and Della Keating and all at the National Library of Ireland for their ongoing work with the #WakingTheFeminists digital archive.

Sarah would particularly like to thank her wife Amanda Verlaque; all the interviewees; Sinéad Macdonald, Anne-Marie Carey, Olwen Dawe, Mary Carty, and Tania Banotti; Anne Tannam and Orla Tinsley for encouraging the writing of this book in its early stages; and all the staff at the Tyrone Guthrie Centre at Annaghmakerrig. To her nieces and nephews, Amelia, Matthew, Ava, Lucas, and Cameron, who inspire her to keep pushing so they may grow up in a more equal and inclusive world.

Lian would like to particularly thank Sara Horgan, Allan Bell, Kate Horgan, Conor Horgan, and Rory Pierce for their support and encouragement throughout the campaign (and beyond). And Jen Coppinger, Michelle Browne, and Nicola Morris for the bathmat portrait.

Most importantly, we acknowledge the countless artists and arts workers who put their shoulders to the wheel to get #WakingTheFeminists going, who did what they could to make it a success, and were part of changing Irish theatre for the better. You are, and always will be, #WakingTheFeminists.

Dublin, August 2025

Sarah Durcan and Lian Bell

Select Bibliography and Further Reading

Ahmed, Sarah, *Living a Feminist Life* (Durham, 2017).

———. *Complaint!* (Durham, 2021).

———. *The Feminist Killjoy Handbook* (London, 2024).

Bates, Laura, *Everyday Sexism* (London, 2015).

———. *Men Who Hate Women: From Incels to Pickup Artists: The Truth About Extreme Misogyny and How It Affects Us All* (London, 2020).

Barukh Milstein, Cindy, *Constellations of Care: Anarcha-Feminism in Practice* (London, 2024).

Battilana, Julie, and Tiziana Casciaro, *Power, for All: How It Really Works and Why It's Everyone's Business* (New York, 2021).

Beard, Mary, *Women & Power: A Manifesto* (London, 2017).

Bohnet, Iris, *What Works: Gender Equality By Design* (Boston, 2016).

Brook, Orian, Dave O'Brien and Mark Taylor, *Culture is Bad for You: Inequality in the Cultural and Creative Industries* (Manchester, 2020).

Butler, Judith, *Who's Afraid of Gender?* (New York, 2024).

Chatzidakis, Andreas, Jamie Hakim, Jo Littler, Catherine Rottenberg, and Lynne Segal, *The Care Manifesto: The Politics of Interdependence* (London, 2020).

Conlon, Evelyn, and Rebecca Pelan, *After the Train: Irishwomen United and a Network of Change* (Dublin, 2025).

Coogan Byrne, Linda, *Why Not Her? A Manifesto for Cultural Change* (London, 2025).

Cox, Josie, *Women Money Power: The Rise and Fall of Economic Inequality* (New York, 2024).

Crenshaw, Kimberlé W., *On Intersectionality: Essential Writings* (New York, 2014).

Criado Perez, Caroline, *Invisible Women: Exposing Data Bias in a World Designed for Men* (London, 2019).

Cullen, Mary, and Maria Luddy, ed., *Female Activists: Irish Women and Change 1900–1960* (Dublin, 2000).

Davis, Angela Y., *Women, Race and Class* (New York, 1981).

Diehl, Amy, and Leanne M Dzubinski, *Glass Walls: Shattering the Six Gender Bias Barriers Still Holding Women Back at Work* (Lanham, 2023).

Eagly, Alice H. and Linda L. Carli, *Through the Labyrinth: The Truth About How Women Become Leaders* (Boston, 2007).

Eltahawy, Mona, *The Seven Necessary Sins for Women and Girls* (Dublin, 2021).

Fearon, Kate, *Women's Work: The Story of the Northern Ireland Women's Coalition* (Belfast, 1999).

Fine, Cordelia, *Delusions of Gender: The Real Science Behind Sex Differences* (London, 2010).

——–. *Testosterone Rex: Unmasking the Myths of Our Gendered Minds* (London, 2017).

Folbre, Nancy, *The Rise and Decline of Patriarchal Systems: An Intersectional Political Economy* (London, 2021).

Frawley, Oona, ed., *Women and the Decade of Commemorations* (Bloomington, 2021).

Gay, Roxane, *Bad Feminist* (New York, 2014).

Gotby, Alva, *They Call It Love: The Politics of Emotional Life* (London, 2023).

Hamad, Ruby, *White Tears, Brown Scars: How White Feminism Betrays Women of Colour* (London, 2020).

Haughton, Miriam, and Mária Kurdi, *Radical contemporary theatre practices by women in Ireland* (Dublin, 2015).

Healy, Gráinne, Brian Sheehan and Noel Whelan, *Ireland Says Yes: The Inside Story of How the Vote for Marriage Equality Was Won* (Dublin, 2015).

Hill Collins, Patricia, *Black Feminist Thought: Knowledge, Consciousness, and the Politics of Empowerment* (Oxfordshire, 2009).

Kahane, Adam, *Collaborating with the Enemy: How to Work with People You Don't Agree with or Like or Trust* (New York, 2017).

Kahneman, Daniel, *Thinking, Fast and Slow* (New York, 2011)

Keltner, Dacher. *The Power Paradox: How We Gain and Lose Influence* (London, 2016).

Keogh, Claire, *#WakingTheFeminists and the Data-Driven Revolution in Irish Theatre* (Cambridge, 2025).

Kerbel, Lucy, *All Change Please: A Practical Guide to Achieving Gender Equality in Theatre* (London, 2017).

——–. *100 Great Plays for Women* (London, 2013).

King, Michelle, *The Fix: Overcoming the Barriers That Hold Women Back at Work* (London, 2020).

Leeney, Cathy, *Irish Women Playwrights, 1900-1939: Gender and Violence on Stage* (New York, 2010).

Licata, Nick, *Becoming A Citizen Activist: Stories, Strategies and Advice for Changing Our World* (Seattle, 2016).

Liu, Eric, *You're More Powerful Than You Think: A Citizen's Guide to Making Change Happen* (New York, 2017).

Lorde, Audre, *The Master's Tools Will Never Dismantle The Master's House* (London, 2018).

Mayer, Catherine, *Attack of the 50ft. Women: How Gender Equality Can Save The World* (London, 2017).

McAuliffe, Mary, *We Were There; 77 Women of the Easter Rising* (Dublin, 2016).

McCreevy, Ronan, ed., *Centenary, Ireland Remembers 1916* (Dublin, 2017).

Meaney, Gerardine, *Gender, Ireland and Cultural Change: Race, Sex and Nation* (Oxfordshire, 2011).

Ngozi Adichie, Chimamanda, *We Should All Be Feminists* (London, 2014).

O'Dowd, Ciara, *Wild-Looking but Fine: Abbey Actresses of the 1930s* (Dublin, 2024).

Olufemi, Lola, *Feminism Interrupted: Disrupting Power* (London, 2020).

O'Toole, Emer, *Contemporary Irish Theatre and Social Change: Activist Aesthetics* (London; New York, 2023).

Parker, Priya, *The Art of Gathering: How We Meet and Why It Matters* (London, 2018).

Redmond, Jennifer, and Mary McAuliffe, eds, *The Politics of Gender and Sexuality in Modern Ireland: A Reader* (Dublin, 2024).

Saini, Angela, *Inferior: The True Power of Women and the Science that Shows It* (London, 2017).

Sihra, Melissa, *Women in Irish Drama: A Century of Authorship and Representation* (London, 2007).

Sieghart, Mary Ann, *The Authority Gap: Why Women are Still Taken Less Seriously Than Men, and What We Can Do About It* (New York, 2021).

Simon, Nina, *The Art of Relevance* (Santa Cruz, 2016).

Sinclair, Amanda, *Leadership for the Disillusioned* (Melbourne, 2007).

Slaughter, Anne Marie, *Unfinished Business: Women, Men, Work, Family* (London, 2015).

Solnit, Rebecca, *Hope in the Dark: Untold Histories, Wild Possibilities* (Edinburgh, 2005).

———. *Men Explain Things to Me: And Other Essays* (London, 2014).

———. *The Mother of All Questions: Further Feminisms* (London, 2017).

Sullivan, Moynagh, 'Feminism, Postmodernism, and the Subject of Irish and Women's Studies', in PJ Mathews, ed., *New Voices in Irish Criticism* (London, 2000).

Tiernan, Sonja, *Irish Women's Speeches, Volume II* (Dublin, 2022).

Ward, Margaret, *Unmanageable Revolutionaries: Women and Irish Nationalism* (New York, 1983).

Watkins, Sarah-Beth, *Ireland's Suffragettes: the women who fought for the vote* (Dublin, 2014).

Papers, Policies and Reports

Amplify Women and #WakingTheFeminists Submission to the Citizen's Assembly on Gender Equality, 2020. https://citizensassembly.ie/wp-content/uploads/2023/03/lian-bell-waking-the-feminists.pdf.

Arts In Ireland: Arts Insights Report 2024, The Arts Council. https://www.artscouncil.ie/uploadedFiles/wwwartscouncilie/Content/Arts_in_Ireland/Strategic_Development/Arts%20Insight%202024.pdf.

Cronin, M. et al 'The Headcount: A survey on the gender breakdown of eight Arts Council of Northern Ireland core-funded theatre companies 2014-2019', Waking The Feminists NI and Cultural Policy Observatory Ireland (Belfast, 2021). https://culturalpolicyireland.org/2021/11/29/waking-the-feminists-the-headcount-report/.

Dawe, O. (2020). Converting Advocacy to Action: #WakingTheFeminists Legacy. *Irish Journal of Arts Management and Cultural Policy*, 7 (2019–20), pp 28–42.

Donohue, B., O'Dowd, C., Dean, T., Murphy, C., Cawley, K., & Harris, K. (2017). *Gender Counts: An analysis of gender in Irish theatre 2006-2015* (Dublin, 2017).

Equality Human Rights and Diversity Policy, Arts Council 2019. https://artscouncil.ie/developing-the-arts/developmental-policies/equality-diversity-and-inclusion-policy-and-implementation-plan/

Glassberg Sands, E. *Opening the Curtain on Playwright Gender: An Integrated Economic Analysis of Discrimination in American Theater* (New Jersey, 2009).

MacArthur, Michelle, 'Achieving Equity in Canadian Theatre: A Report with Best Practice Recommendations' Equity In Theatre, Playwrights Guild of Canada, April 2015. https://playwrightsguild.ca/wp-content/uploads/2024/12/FINAL-EIT-Report_4-22-15.pdf.

McAuliffe, Mary. 'From Inghinidhe na hÉireann to the Irish Citizen Army: Women, radical politics and the 1916 Rising', 1 June 2016, *Saothar*, p 41.

McGarry, F. (2015). 'Helena Molony: Rebel and Activist' in M. McAuliffe, ed., *Rosie. Essays in Honour of Rosanna 'Rosie' Hackett (1893-1976): Revolutionary and Trade Unionist* (Dublin, 2016), pp 99–107.

Murphy, C., O'Dowd, C., Donohue, B. Durcan, S., (2020) *5 Years On: Gender in Irish Theatre* (Dublin, 2020), http://www.wakingthefeminists.org/wp-content/uploads/2020/11/5-Years-On_-Gender-in-Irish-Theatre-FINAL.pdf.

Murphy, Ciara L., 'Reflecting Irishness, Mirroring Histories: Performing Commemoration in Irish Theatre in 2015', in *New Hibernia Review / Iris* Éireannach *Nua*, 20:3, 2016.

O'Connell, Brenda. 'Waking The Feminists: Gender "Counts"'. *Women And The Decade Of Commemorations*, edited by Oona Frawley (Bloomington, 2021).

O'Toole, Emer 'Waking the Feminists: Re-imagining the Space of the National Theatre in the Era of the Celtic Phoenix', in *Lit: Literature Interpretation Theory*, 2017, 28:2, pp 1–19. https://doi.org/10.1080/10436928.2017.1315549.

'7 Steps for Achieving Gender Parity in the Theatre' American Theatre, 2015. http://www.americantheatre.org/2015/06/09/7-steps-for-achieving-gender-parity-in-the-theatre/.

Websites

Amplify Women [Anti-]Harassment Toolkit: https://wft.ie/wp-content/uploads/2017/11/WTF_Harassment_Toolkit_AmplifyWomen-1.pdf

Equality Now: https://equalitynow.org/

FairPlé: https://www.fairple.com/

Geena Davis Institute on Gender in Media: https://geenadavisinstitute.org/

MAMs Ireland: https://mamsireland.wordpress.com/

Olwen Dawe: https://www.olwendawe.com/

Performing Arts Forum: https://performingartsforum.ie/

Project Implicit: https://www.projectimplicit.net/

PLAYOGRAPHYIreland: https://irishplayography.com/

Irish Society for Theatre Research: https://istr.ie/

Irish Theatre Institute: https://www.irishtheatreinstitute.ie

Safe to Create: https://www.safetocreate.ie/

Susan Coughlan: https://artofchange.ie/

Tonic Theatre: http://www.tonictheatre-advance.co.uk/

The Lillys: https://the-lillys.org/

#WakingTheFeminists: http://www.wakingthefeminists.org/

#WakingTheFeminists YouTube: https://www.youtube.com/@wakingthefeminists761

Why Not Her: https://whynother.eu/

Women For Election: https://www.womenforelection.ie/
Women in Film and Television Ireland: https://wft.ie/
Women On Air: https://womenonair.ie/

Index

#BlackLivesMatter xxii

#fairplayforwomen 104

#IStandWithYouWomenInIrishTheatre 16, 123

#LoveWins xxii

#MeToo xxii, xxiv–xxv, 324–6, 356

#MiseFosta 344

#RepealThe8th xii

Abbey Theatre xxii, xxviii, 82, 124, 147–51, 157–8, 181, 189, 191, 228, 236–7, 258, 261, 291, 316, 318–19, 327, 339
  archive 102
  Education department 326
  Fairer Sex programme 5, 24, 229
  Gender Equality Committee 291
  Guiding Principles for Gender Equality 154–6, 258, 261, 291, 310
  New Playwrights programme 98
  Peacock stage 228
  Theatre of Change symposium 165–72, 340
  Waking the Nation programme xi, xxv–xxvi, xxx, 3–6, 28, 44–7, 109, 124, 338, 340–3, 348–9

Abortion Rights Campaign 61, 137

Accenture 138

Advance (UK) *see* Tonic Theatre

advertising industry 285

Ahmed, Sara 347–8, 350, 352

Akram, Yasmine 267

Amplify Women 322, 326

Harassment Toolkit 325, 344

Anderson, Anne 177

Anderson, Ioanna 200

Angelou, Maya 307

ANU Productions xxix, 33

Ardú/Advance (Ireland) 144, 154, 156–9, 189–90, 243

Ark, The 236, 318

Arquette, Patricia 168

Artists' Campaign to Repeal the Eighth Amendment 137, *321*

Arts Council xi, xxviii, 31–2, 82, 122, 124–5, 137–145, 150, 172, 197, 243, 259, 324
  EHRD (equality, human rights and diversity) policy 319–20
  funding xxviii, 31–2, 130, 134–5, 142, 146, 157–9, 188, 232, 236–7, 259, 334, 344
  meeting with 140–3

Arts Council of Northern Ireland 167, 323

Association of Irish Stage Technicians 138

Atwood, Margaret 354

awards 173–9

Bacik, Ivana 64, 69–70, 116

badges *50*, 61

Banotti, Tania 148, 285

Baranksi, Christine 16, *52*, 53

Barnstorm Theatre Company 236

Barr, Sarah 182

Barrett, Clare *183*

Barry, Olga 242

Bates, Laura 352

Baxter, Sarah 34

Beamish, Áine 38

Belarus Free Theatre Company 16

Bell, Lian xvi, xxx, 40–4, 46–9, 55, 67,
  68, 123, 125, 127, 129–31, 139–40,
  147, 154, 165, 177, *178*, 178, *179*,
  238, 241–4, 246, 316, 319, *321*, 323,
  326, 330, 338, 343, 346, 350, 354
  campaign director 135
  opinion piece 148–9
  social media posts 3–11, 23–4, 29,
    49, 121–2, 162–3
  speeches 62–3, 71, 170–1, 174, 182,
    187–90, 258–60, 320

Belltable Theatre 268

Belton, Cathy *63*

bias, implicit 231
  Harvard Implicit Association Test
    230, 301

bias, unconscious xxiii, 85, 91, 94, 141,
  169, 199, 231, 244, 293
  training 11, 142–3, 152, 157–8,
    243–4, 284, 317

Black women 77, 90, 342, 348, 351

Blinder Films 182, 209

Bliss, Panti *see* O'Neill, Rory

Bloom, Harold 341

Bohnet, Iris 240

Boland, Eavan 342

Boss, Owen 218

Bourke, Siobhán xvi, 9, 41, *55*, 122,
  331–2

Bowler, Laura 95

Boyd, Pom *62*, 200

Bracken, Claire 339, 341

Broadcasting Authority of Ireland (BAI)
  210

Broadly Speaking 322

Brown, Noelle 92

Browne, Sarah 342

bullying xxv, 129–30, 139, 141–2, 188,
  245, 323–5, 356

Burke, Sinéad 295

Burton, Joan xxvi, 130, 143, 195

Bushell, Ellen xxv, 349

Business to Arts 135

Butler, Octavia 279

Byrne, Gabriel 16, *19*, 123

Byrne, Rose 16, *17*

Caldwell, Lucy 345–6

Callow, Simon 16, *19*
  campaign director role 134–5, 343

campaign objectives 71, 121–4, 139, 181,
  315

campaigning advice 138–40

Carr, Marina 16, 85, 342

Cartmell, Selina 281, 327

Cawley, Kathleen xvii, 229, 330

Celtic Revival xxv

Chakravorty Spivak, Gayatri 343

Charabanc Theatre Company 166

Cherish 256

childcare 45, 48–9, 56, 80, 104, 138,
  240, 245, 264

Chungh, Teerth 154, 242

Citizens' Assembly on Gender Equality
  320–2

Civic Theatre, Tallaght 318

Clare, David 340

Clarke, Anne xv, 8, 16, 30, 41–2, 51, *55*,
  60, 122, 131, 134, 138, 140, 143, 145,
  147, 154, 158–9, 173, 182, *184*, *238*,
  241–2, 252, 328

Clarke Pullen, Melanie *323*

Clarkin, Sarah 140

Clinton, Hillary 241, 283, 298, 301

Colgan, Michael 124, 126, 130, 154,
  171–2, 182, *186*, 197–8, 324–5

Colley, Dan 164

Commission on the Status of Women
  256

Community Foundation of Ireland 135,
  259

Company SJ xxviii

Comyn, Annabelle 253, 319

Condon, Kerry *20*

Conlon, Evelyn 107

Conroy, Amy xxviii, 63, 72, 88, 131
Contraceptive Train xii, 83, 256
Conway, Kerryann 47
Coogan, Amanda 64, 111, 322, 323
Coppinger, Jen xvi, 9, 55, 56, 61, 88, 177, 178, 238, 329
Corcoran, Monica 142
Corcoran, Sarah 182
core group 127–36, 175, 182, 213, 233, 242, 350
Cork Midsummer Festival 319
Corn Exchange xxviii, 316
Corscadden, Margarita 54, 56
Cosgrove, Aedín xxix
Coughlan, Patricia 341
Coughlan, Susan 133–4, 242
Covid-19 pandemic 320, 326, 334
Crawley, Joanna 234, 270
Crenshaw, Kimberlé 348
Cronin, Maggie 323
Crotty, Derbhle 63, 78, 253
Crowe, Catriona 246, 255–7, 353
Crowley, Sinéad 56, 67
Culleton, Jim 148, 268–9
cultural nationalism xi
Cultural Policy Observatory Ireland 323
Cumann na mBan ix–xi
Cummins, Jo 96
Cunningham, Gaye 324, 344
Curran, Ali xxviii
Cusack, Joanne 349–50

Daly, Jane xvi, 9, 41, 55, 242, 296, 329
Daly, Peter 148
D'Arcy, Ailbhe 340
Dawe, Gerard 339
Dawe, Olwen 143
Dean, Tanya xvi, xvii, 8, 25–6, 55, 57, 104, 122, 229, 235, 235, 238, 332
Deasy, Jane 282
Decade of Centenaries ix, xi–xii
Deegan, Loughlin xvi, 8–9, 41, 61, 111, 122, 128, 130, 159, 165–6, 168–72, 242–3, 316, 330

Deevy, Teresa 318
Delaney, John 13
Delany, Dana 16, 21
Dell EMC 293
Dent, Donna 166
Department of the Arts, Heritage and the Gaeltacht 82, 124
Department of Justice and Equality 322
Department of Tourism, Culture, Arts, Gaeltacht, Sport and Media 325, 344
Derrington, Tara 248, 288
Devlin, Anne 54, 55, 61, 202
Dignam, Loretta 147, 154, 191, 249, 291
disability 25, 64, 77, 140, 193, 287, 320, 333
Diva Voces 182
diversity xxiii, 26, 34, 65, 77, 117, 131, 134, 140, 154, 170–1, 188, 197, 200, 212, 277, 287, 293, 311, 333–5, 340, 349, 356
    policies 142, 150, 152, 172, 245, 319–20
Dobson, Bryan 67
Donmar Warehouse 16, 20
Donoghue, Emma 16, 19, 203, 272
Donohue, Brenda xv, xvii, 12–13, 47, 107, 123, 130–1, 142, 186, 228–35, 235, 238, 328
Doolan, Lelia xxviii
Downes, Eugene 148
Druid Theatre xxviii, 147–8, 158, 181, 189, 192, 236, 300, 316, 319
Dublin Fringe Festival xxviii, 148, 153–4, 157, 181, 189, 193–4, 236, 268, 287
Dublin Municipal Theatre 327
Dublin Theatre Festival xxviii, 148, 153, 157–8, 181, 189, 195–6, 236, 284, 316, 318, 327
    Next Stage programme 3
Duffin, Aoife 84
Duffin, Mary 57, 90
Dunbar, Karen 20
Dunne, Clare 299
Dunne, Shaun 220–1

Durcan, Sarah xvi, 38, 41–2, 48–9, 51–2, 53–4, *55*, 60–1, 64–7, 131, 134, 139–40, 143, 147, 154, 158, 170, 174–5, *176*, 177, *238*, 242, 331, 346, 350, 356
social media posts 8, 11
speeches 117–18, 175, 309–11
Dwan, Lisa 271
Dyas, Grace xvi, xxix, 10, 122, 130, 324–6, 329, 344, 356

Easter Rising 339, 348–9
centenary of xi, xxv, 302
Egan, Jo 322, *323*
Eltahawy, Mona 240, *246*, 278–9
Enright, Anne 16, 246, 254, 341, 357
Ensler, Eve *see* V
Equal Representation for Actresses (ERA) (UK) 138, 188
Equity in Theatre (Canada) 188
ethnic minorities 77, 80, 212, 287, 293, 319
European Social Fund, PEIL (Programme for Employability, Inclusion and Learning) 2014–2020 144
Everyman Theatre 316, 319, 327

Facebook xxi, xxx, 3–39 *passim*, 51, 138, 175
Fairer Sex, The *see* Abbey Theatre
FairPlé 322
Fanning, Hillary 200
Farrell, Collette 148, 284
Fay, Hilda xxvi
Fay, Jimmy 9, 33–4
Featherstone, Vicky 35
Federici, Silvia 349
Feldman, Susan *20*, 303
Feminist Initiative (Sweden) 264
Ferris, Kate xvi, 41, 43, 46, 48, *55*, 56, *57*, 60, 131, 134, 181, *185*, 214–17, 326, 330, 355
Field Day Anthology of Irish Women's Writing 339
Field Day Anthology of Irish Writing 8, 48, 340

Field Day Theatre Company 167
Fiennes, Sophie 253
Finan, Mary 154
financial crash (2008–2009) xxix, 143
Finucane, Marian 124, 164
Fischer, Clara 342
Fishamble: The New Play Company 147–8, 158, 268–9, 316, 318
New Writing Award 268
Fitzgibbon, Sarah 4, 31
Flaherty, Craig 242
Flanagan, Fionnula 16
Fleming, Maria xvi, 41, 54, *55*, 60, 122, 132–3, 139, 147, 150, 182, *238*, 330
Flynn, Tara 274
Fogarty, Anne 148, 200–1, 340–1
Folbre, Nancy 343, 347, 349
Fordham University 187
Fouéré, Olwen xvi, 16, 25, 84, 88, *164*, 177, 331
freelancers 41, 142, 215–16, 244–5, 325, 334, 344, 355
Friedan, Betty 256
funding/fundraising 134–5, 137, 141–4, 157, 159, 182, 190, 243
Furey, Rob 56
Furlong, Tara 35–6, 56

Galway Film Fleadh 209
Gate Theatre xxviii, 128, 154, 157, 172, 181, 189, 197–8, 236–7, 281, 316–19, 324–5, 327
independent report 324–5
gender balance xxviii, 110, 142, 147, 151, 154–5, 169, 189, 195, 200, 213, 237, 253, 259, 268–9, 277, 284
policies 152, 188, 244, 316–17, 321
Gender Counts report 229–38
follow-up 317–19
gender equality xii, xxii, xxiv, 10, 12, 25, 31, 34, 47, 70–1, 109–14, 129, 151, 154, 158, 168–9, 175, 188–9, 191, 196, 239–42, 267, 292, 296, 311, 315, 317–21
policies 124, 126, 140–2, 144, 152, 172, 181, 198, 210, 243, 280, 284 *see also* Abbey Theatre

(Guiding Principles for Gender Equality); *One Thing More* (The List)

Gender Equality Policy Working Group 243, 316–17

gender inequality xxvii, xxix–xxx, 69, 148–50, 192, 202, 230, 235–8, 338

George, Simone 239, 326

Geraghty, Paula 56, 182

Gibney, Margaret *323*

Gilmore, Kate 83

Ging, Debbie 352

Glassberg Sands, Emily 230–1

Glasshouse Productions 203, 272

Glennon, Louise 140

Goan, Cathal 147

Goan, Róise xvi, xxviii, 9, *55*, 102, *103*, 122, 134, 139, 239, 327, 331

Gonne, Maud x

Gough, Denise 16, *22*, 276

Gray, Eileen 253

Greene, Nicholas 339

Gregory, Lady Augusta xxv, 102, 302

Gunning, John 52

Gurira, Danai 175–7, 310

Hackett, Rosie 302 *see also* Rosie Hackett Bridge

Haile, Yordanos *17*

harassment 207–8 *see also* bullying; sexual harassment

Harley, Eithne 148

Harris, Kate xvii, 229, *238*, 330

Harris, Nancy 93, 178, *179*, 319

Haslam, Anna 255, 356

Haughton, Miriam 343

Heffernan, Kate 50, 182

Henry IV cast (Donmar Warehouse) *20*

Hetherington, Andrew 135

Higgins, Alice Mary 140

Hill Collins, Patricia 342, 348–9

Holahan, Breffni *183*

Holly, Katie 182, 209–11, 253

Holly, Zia 91, 214, 253

Hoover, Sarah 268

Horgan, Kate 54, 56, 182

Horgan, Sara 243

Horniman, Annie, 56

HotForTheatre xxviii

Howard, Aideen 229, 242

Hughes, Kellie 88

Human Rights and Equality Commission Act 2014 310–11

Humphreys, Heather xxvi, 124, 319, *319*

Hussey, Gemma 345

Huston, Jenny 38

Hyland, Aisling 139

Hynes, Garry xxviii, 13, 101, 148, 164–5

Inghinidhe na hÉireann x–xi

Ingle, Róisín 47, *184*

Inspirefest 139–40

International Women's Day event 129, 135, 139 *see also Spring Forward*

Ireland 2016 Centenary Programme 135, 259

Irigaray, Luce 341

Irish Art Center, New York 187

Irish Constitution xii, xxiii, xxv, 12, 73, 256

    Eighth Amendment xii, 256, 306, 354

Irish Defence Forces 286

Irish Equity 138–9, 188, 322

Irish Film Board 123, 210–11

Irish Theatre Institute (ITI) 229, 268, 325, 334, 325, 334, 344

Irish Theatre Magazine 334

Irish Times Irish Theatre Awards 173–4, 334

Irish Times Women's Podcast 47, 182

Irish Women's Franchise League (IWFL) 255

Irish Women's Liberation Movement (IWLM) xii, 83, 256, 355

Irishwomen United xii

Jackson, Glenda 298

Jaleel, Rana M. 344

Jenkinson, Rosemary 200, *323*

Jennings, Jenny, 38

Jones, Cherry 16, *21*
Jordan, Emma 89
Jordan, Julia 177, 239
Jubilee Project, US 110

Kaminska, Liadain 52
Kavanagh, Úna 219
Keane, Raymond 31
Kearney, Oonagh 35, 61
Kearns, Maree 253
Keating, Sara xxvi
Kelleher, Julie 242, 275, 316
Kelleher, Margaret 339–40, 342
Keller, Fiona *55*, 56
Kelliher, Alma 214
Kelly, Sean 242
Kelly, Sonya 40, 173–4, *185*, 204–6, 354
Kennedy, Fionnuala 322, *323*
Keogh, Claire 350
Kerbel, Lucy 111, *111*, 112–15, 189, 241, 327
Kerslake, Seána 262–3
Keyes, Marian *184*, 327
Kidman, Nicole 16, 123
Kieran, Sarah 326
Kilroys, The (USA) 137
Kinahan, Deirdre 67, 147, 154, 291, 318
Kirby, Simone 16
Kostick, Gavin xv, 4–5, 41, 148, 329
Kuti, Elizabeth 200

Labour Party 130
LaChapelle, David 304
Lagasse, Terhas *17*
Lally, Mick 101
Landmark Productions 41, 143, 319, 328
Larragy, Marian 35
Lawlor, Áine 54, 182
League of Professional Theatre Women (US) 137
Leeney, Cathy 229
Levine, June 356
LGBTQI+ xxvii, 64, 131, 304, 333
Liddy, Susan 210

Lillys, The (USA) 137
Lilly Awards 174–7, 188
Lir Academy 97, 170–2, 214, 318, 326
Lloyd, Phyllida *20*
Lonergan, Patrick 229
Longford, Earl of (Edward Packenham) 128
Longford, Christine 128
Lorde, Audre 350
Louise White Performance xxviii
Lowe, Andrew 148
Lowe, Louise xxix, 218–19
Lunny, Niamh 147, 154, 291
Lynch, Sarah 148
Lyric Theatre, Belfast 324

McAleevey, Bernadette 35
McAtackney, Laura xi
McAuliffe, Mary ix
McBride, Orlaith 140, 302
McBrinn, Róisín 178, *179*, 327
McCafferty, Nell 354, 356
Mac Conghail, Fiach xxvi, 5–6, 44–7, 51, 54, 64, *108*, 108–10, 126, 130, 149, 151, 165, 229
McCurry, Charlotte 36
McDonagh, Fiona 340
McDonagh, Rosaleen 60–1, 77
MacEvilly, Nichola 131
McGarry, Fearghal 349
McGowan, Ruth 242
McHugh, Meadhbh 319
McKay, Susan 345
McKenna, Sinéad 253
McKeon, Belinda 5–6, 16, 27–8, 47, 76
McLaren, Graham 46, 242, 261
McLaughlin, Caitríona 28, *74*, 75, 327
McLoughlin, Irma xvi, *55*, 142, 329
McMahon, Bryan 147–8, 150
McNulty, Lisa *17*
Madigan, Josepha 316
Magee, Oisin *323*
Majekodunmi, Jess *18*
Mangan, Jo xvi, xxviii, 41, *127*, 329–30

Martin, Emma 88

May, Lorraine 242

Me, Mollser see White, Ali

Meaney, Gerardine 340–1

Meaney, Liz 140, 142

Meehan, Paula 200

Men Advocating Real Change (MARC) 293

merchandise xiii, 50, 134–5, *183*, 326

Messing, Debra 16

Metcalfe, Amelie 250, 297

Methven, Eleanor 96, 165–7

Minding Creative Minds 344

misogyny xxvii, 27, 42, 77, 208, 213, 266, 270–1, 275, 290, 303, 306, 343, 345, 347–8, 354

Moloney, Mary 148

Moloney, Orla 242

Molony, Helena xxvi, 349

Monaghan, Aaron 36–7

Monk, Christine xv, 16, *55*, 56, *57*, 122, *127*, 328

Moonfish Theatre xxviii, 96, 99

Moran, Janet 57, 60, 105, *106*

Morash, Chris 339

Morgan, Fiona 54, 60

Morning Ireland (RTÉ) 53–4

motherhood 39, 288, 349

Mothers Artists Makers (MAMs) 240–1, 288, 322, 349

Motley, Sophie xxviii–xxix, 239, 327

Moxley, Gina xv, *55*, 82, 88, 122, *127*, 130, 200, 318, 329

Mullally, Una 11–12, 31, 48, 182, 207–8, 241, 325–6

Mullen, Marie 101

Mullin, Molly 341–2

Murphy, Barney, xxv–xxvi

Murphy, Bridie xxvi

Murphy, Catherine 182

Murphy, Ciara L. xvii, 229, 233, 235, *235*, 328, 339

Murphy, Jimmy 13

Murphy, Oonagh xvi, 29–30, 51, *55*, 80–1, *81*, 122, 140, 162, 327, 330

Murray, Christine 339–40

Murray, Christopher 338

Murray, Erica 12, 97

Murray, Neil 46, 242, 261

Murray, Rachel 38

Najimy, Kathy 174, *176*

Nakase, Justine 340

National Concert Hall, Composing the Island 282

national cultural institutions (NCIs) xxviii, 282, 319

National Library of Ireland xxii, 233, 326–7, 354

National Museum of Ireland xxii, 326, 354

National Strategy for Women and Girls (2017–2020) 322

National Women's Council of Ireland 137, 140, 188

National Women's Strategy (2007–2016) 143–4

Nelson, Kris 9–10, 148, 193–4

Ngozi Adiche, Chimamanda 90

Ní Chonchubhair, Niamh xvi, *55*, *238*, 331

Ní Chróinín, Ionia xxviii, 99–100

Ní Chróinín, Máiréad xxviii

Ní Dhuibhir, Tríona xvi, 31–2, 41, *55*, 122, 231, 332

Ní Shuilleabháin, Aoibhinn 182

nic Shiubhlaigh, Máire xxv, 56, 349

Nicholson, Rachel *323*

Nikolaisen, Donna 212

Nollaig na mBan (Women's Christmas) events 129, *160*, 162–4, 187–8

Norman, Marsha 239

Nugent, Liz *19*, 148

O'Brien, Aisling xv, *55*, 56, 61, 327–8

O'Brien, Cian xv, 9–10, *55*, 61, 128, 140, 148, 153, 199, 242, 277, 328

O'Brien, Kathy Rose 61

O'Brien, Mark 9

O'Brien, Col. Maureen *247*, 286

O'Byrne, Brían F. 4–5, 16, 37, 289

O'Byrne, Rachel
O'Cathain, Molly 52, *183*, 280
O'Clery, Joan 94, 258
Ó Conchúir, Fearghus
O'Connor, Orla 140
O'Dea, Anne 139
O'Donnell, Niamh 287
O'Dowd, Ciara xvii, 229, 235, *235*, *238*, 328
O'Faolain, Nuala 356
O'Gorman, Colm 306
O'Grady, Emma 24
O'Halloran, John 148
O'Hanlon, Amy *55*, 243
O'Kane, Emma 219
O'Kelly, Donal 37
O'Kelly, Emer 130–1
O'Leary, Caroline 64
O'Loughlin, Karan 139, 264–5
O'Melia, Ciaran 34
One City, One Book 254
One Thing More 239–50, *251–311*
    The List 244–5
O'Neill, Claire *55*
O'Neill, Louise 319
O'Neill, Rory (Panti Bliss) 27, 116, 301
O'Reilly, Shane 173–4
O'Reilly, Yvonne *55*
Ó Ríordán, Aodhán xxvi, 143
O'Rourke, Terence 148
O'Sullivan, Aisling 253, 283
O'Sullivan, Camille 241, *308*
O'Sullivan, Dairne xv, 41–3, 53, *55*, 56, 57, 61, 67, 122, 329
O'Toole, Emer 339–40
O'Toole, Fintan 47, 149–50, 203
O'Toole, Kate *57*

Packenham, Edward, Earl of Longford 128
Pan Pan Theatre xxix, 236–7, 318
Pankhurst, Alula 16, *22*
Parker, Lynne xvi, xxviii, 8–9, 33, 41, 46–7, *55*, 122, 147–8, 213, *238*, 330

Parkes, Andrew 148
Parnell, David 140
patriarchy xxiii, xxv–xxvi, xxix–xxx, 25, 169, 256, 270, 279, 282, 304, 333–4, 336, 340–52
Paulus, Diane 175, 239
Performance Corporation xxviii
Performing Arts Forum 334 *see also* Theatre Forum
Perry, Caitríona 174
petitions, online
    Rosie Hackett Bridge x
    #WakingTheFeminists x, 46, 49, 71, 121–2
Pierce, Sarah 148
Playography Ireland 102, 229
Plimpton, Martha 16, *18*, 174
Polish theatre 270
Pollak, Gráinne 284
Pratschke, Sheila 140
Prime Cut 89
Proclamation of the Republic xxv
Project Arts Centre 61, 148, 153–4, 157–8, 181, 189, 199, 233, 236, 277, 327
Project Implicit 230
public meeting at Abbey Theatre 53–118, 121, 123–4, 165

Quinn, Marian 210

race 158, 193, 202, 212, 261, 287, 295, 320, 333, 340, 342
racism 25, 64, 295, 304, 335, 340, 348, 351
Rape Crisis Centre 256
Regan, Morna 200
referendums 353
    marriage equality xxiii–xxiv
    repeal the 8th Amendment xxiii, 256, 354
Rice, Emma 294
Richmond Barracks xi
Robinson, Mary 295
Rodriguez, Elizabeth 16, *19*
Roe v. Wade 354

Ronan, Saoirse 16, *21*, 123
Rosie Hackett Bridge x
Rosney, Bride 139, 147, 241, 300
Rough Magic Theatre Company xxviii,
    41, 43, 148, 151–3, 158, 181, 189,
    200–1, 213, 236, 316, 318
    SEEDS programme 200–1, 280
Rourke, Josie 216
Royal Commission on Labour, 1894
Royal Court Theatre, London 202
Roycroft, Dee 39
RTÉ 210
Ruiz, Noelia xvi, *55*, 64, 122, 162, 331
Ryan, Amy 16, *21*
Ryan, Annie xxviii, 26
Ryan, Avril 242
Ryan, Lucy 38, 242
Ryan, Mark 147, 291

Safe to Create 325, 328, 344
Safe Ireland Summit 239–40
Sarma, Ursula Rani 24, 79, 178, *179*
Scaife, Sarah Jane xxviii, 63, 73
Scales, Linda 134
Scanlon, Eva 148, 242
Schneider, Elizabeth M. 352
Schyman, Gudrun 264
Science Gallery International 42
Screen Directors Guild of Ireland 211,
    322
Screen Ireland 344
Screen Producers Ireland 322
Screen Training Ireland 210
Serner, Anna 210
sexism 7, 25, 35, 77, 92, 170, 204, 215,
    244, 290, 295, 345, 351, 354–5
Sexton, Laoisa *52*
sexual harassment xxv, 129, 139, 152,
    207, 245, 323–5, 347
Sheehy-Skeffington, Andrée 256
Sheehy-Skeffington, Hanna 255, 356
Sheehy Skeffington, Micheline 292
Sheridan, Kathy 47
Shiels, Sarah Jane xxix

Show In A Bag 268
Sihra, Melissa 229, 339–40
Silicon Republic 140
Singleton, Brian 32
SIPTU (Services, Industrial, Professional
    and Technical Union) 138–9
Six One News 67
Smyth, Gerard 148
social media x, xxi–xxiii, 123–4, 127 *see
    also* Facebook; Twitter
Sophocles 341
Sounding the Feminists 322
Spallen, Abbie 24–25
Speak Up & Call It Out 344
Spillane-Hinks, Aoife xv, 328
Spittle, Alison 290
Spring Forward 181–221
Spring Forward meeting 154
Stack, Róisín 192
Stafford-Clark, Max 202
Stanley Brennan, Kate xxvi
Stanton, David 143
Statera Foundation (US) 188
Steinem, Gloria 174, *176*
Stokes, Sara 135
Stone, Maeve 6, 57, 85, 164
Streep, Meryl xi, *52*, 53, 123
suffrage, women's ix, xii, 12, 255
Sullivan, Moynagh 338

Tanner, Jamie 56
technical theatre 181, 214–17, 326, 355
TG4 210
Theatre of Change Symposium *see*
    Abbey Theatre
theatre companies, meetings with
    146–59
    agenda 151–3
theatre criticism 130–1, 270, 334
Theatre Forum (Performing Arts
    Forum) xxviii, 46, 138, 142–3, 188,
    231
THEATREclub xxix
Them's The Breaks documentary 182
Thompson, William 255

Thornton, Colin 262
Thornton, Darren 262
Tiernan, Sonja 326–7
Tierney, Marie 266
Tierney Keogh, Lisa xvi, 13–16, *52*, *53*,
    98, 131, 174–5, *176*, 187, 239, *248*,
    307–8, 319, 330
Tiger Dublin Fringe 268
Tighe, Dylan 25
Tod, Isabella 255, 356
Together for Yes xxiii
Tóibín, Colm 148
Tonic Theatre (UK) 110–14, 135, 152,
    156–8, 178, 327
    Advance programme 111, 125, 135,
        140–2, 146, 156–7, 189, 316
    Tonic Awards 178
Townsend, Niamh 293
Transgender Equality Network Ireland
    (TENI) 229
Travellers 33, 64, 77, 193, 320
Trump, Donald 283, 304, 306
Tutu, Desmond 139
Tweedy, Hilda 256, 356
Twitter xxi–xxii, xxx, 3–39 *passim*, 51,
    66, 138, 175

V (Eve Ensler) 239–40, 304–5
Varadkar, Leo, 53–4
Vaughan Lawlor, Tom, 273
Veprek, Charlie 16, 174

Waking The Feminists NI 322–4, *323*
Waking The Media 325
Waking the Nation *see* Abbey Theatre
WakingTheFeminists company 134–5
Walsh, Anna *55*, 122, 142, 242
Walsh, Enda 16, *19*
Walter, Harriet 16, 298–9
Ward, Margaret E. (Mags) 138–9, 241
Waters, Kilian 174
Well Woman Clinics 256
Wenders, Wim 16, *21*

West, Kerry 38
West, Michael 37–8
West, Rachel 242
Wheatley, David 340
Wheeler, Anna 255
White, Ali 31, *86*, 87
    Me, Mollser 4, 87, 109, 342
White, Aoife *55*, *178*, 242
White, Louise xxviii
White, Willie 9, 34, 148, 195–6, 243
WillFredd xxix
Williams, Caroline xv, 8–9, 40–3, 47–8,
    55, 122, *127*, 131–2, 134, 139–40,
    147–8, 153–4, 203, *234*, 239,
    241–2, 272, 328
Winters, Carmel 318, 342
Wodajo, Alemtsehay 16, *18*
Wollstonecraft, Mary 356
Women on Air 138, 188, 322
Women Aloud Northern Ireland 188
Women in Animation 322
Women for Election 104, 137–8, 188
Women in Film and Television 137, 188,
    211, 322
Women in Technical Theatre Roadshow
    326
Women in Theatre and Screen
    (Australia) *17*, 188
Women's Aid 256
Women's History Association of Ireland
    (WHAI) xi
Women's Project Theatre Lab, New
    York *18*
Women's Voices Festival, New York 79
Writers' Guild of Ireland 211, 322

Yeats, W. B. xxv, 192
Yergainharsian, Nyree xxvi
Yer Only mBan 164
Yes Equality campaign xxiii–xxiv
YouTube 182

Zola, Émile 281